DICTIONARY OF MANAGEMENT AND BUSINESS ADMINISTRATION

DICTIONARY OF MANAGEMENT AND BUSINESS ADMINISTRATION

Edited by

Dr. Niraj Kumar

Shri Sanjay Medhavi

Dr. Shiba Charan Panda

GYAN PUBLISHING HOUSE

New Delhi-110002

DICTIONARY OF MANAGEMENT AND BUSINESS ADMINISTRATION
[*Management and Business*]

ISBN: 81-212-0566-2

First Edition: 1998

Published in 1998 in India by
Gyan Publishing House
5, Ansari Road
New Delhi 110 002

Laser Typeset at Akshar, Delhi
Printed at Mehra Offset Press, New Delhi.

Preface

Management and Business Administration are both Art and Science that play a pivotal role in the development of national economy. As business has become more complicated, management as a subject has kept pace with it, oiling the wheels of economic progress.

This dictionary is intended to be a guide to the jargons and concepts, which a management student is most likely to come across in his everyday study and practice. This compilation work covers all the branches of management — finance, accounting, personnel, marketing, production, industrial relations, business laws and what not.

This dictionary will serve as a handy guide not only to professional managers, administrators and graduate and post graduate students of management but also prove to be asset as a reference guide to persons who have some professional interest in the subject.

My thanks are due to my sub-editors for their significant contributions. I am deeply grateful to the authors and publishers of the various works from which consciously and unconsciously material has been drawn to prepare the present compilation. Errors and omissions in this dictionary should naturally appear as debit on my own account.

25.12.1997

Dr. Niraj Kumar

A

Abandoned Option: Means a share option not exercised because the price is against the buyer (or taker) on declaration day, i.e., the situation is unprofitable.

ABC Analysis: It is a technique of effective material control. The inventories of certain concerns consist of a small number of items representing a major portion of the inventory value and a large number of items representing only a minor portion of the inventory value. In case of such concerns a selective approach to stores control is necessary. The items may be divided into three categories—A, B and C. Category 'A' may include more costly items, while category B may consist of less costly items and category C of the least costly items. Such an analysis of inventories is known as ABC Analysis System of stores control. (Some accountants prefer to call it as "Always Better Control" stores technique).

Activity-based Costing (ABC): Traditionally, accounting identified costs according to the category of expense (for example, salaries, fixed assets, etc.) ABC, on the other hand, determines costs according to what is paid for the different tasks employees perform. ABC provides decision makers a much more accurate breakdown of the cost data.

ABC Method: Attention, Benefit, Close sales method, where the customer's attention is attracted by the sales person who shows the benefits of the product to the satisfaction of the customer to the customer, and finally close the deal.

Ability To Pay Tax: The most common principle on which the tax burden is based. Income, property, or consumption can be used as a basis for measuring ability to pay. Theoretically ability to pay is measured by sacrifice (loss of utility).

Above Par: A Stock Exchange term which means shares are said to be above par when their price is above the share's nominal value.

Above The Line: An expression relating to the profit and loss account or income statement. The line in question is the net profit, or the profit on ordinary activities after taxation, of such statements. Below-the-line amounts are appropriations such as dividends. Thus above-the-line amounts are expenses or revenues of the business. Earnings per share figures are calculated excluding below-the-line amounts or for that part of a company's marketing budget that is spent on advertising in the media as opposed to other activities like sales promotion and direct marketing, which are (emotively and much to the disgust of their practitioners) described as below-the-line. The origin of the "line" probably lies in accounting terminology. Marketeers increasingly talk of "crossing the line" when referring to their attempts to create integrated communications.

Absence: Not being at work or at a meeting; **in absence of:** when someone is not here.

Absentee: Person who is absent; worker who stays away from work for no good reason

Absenteeism: Failure of workers to report for work on schedule owing to unwillingness rather than incapacity. Voluntary absence is usually considered to be avoidable and without reasonable cause; in effect the employee chooses to be absent. A high absenteeism rate is a sign of organizational ill health in a work organization. It is also likely that much of the absenteeism through sickness is job related, either physically in the form of industrial diseases or emotionally in the form of psychosomatic disorders.

Absolute Monopoly: Means the control of the entire output of a commodity or service, for which there exists no substitute, by a single producer or supplier.

Absorption Accounting: An accounting system in which all costs (fixed or variable, direct or indirect) are "absorbed" by the goods or services produced within the accounting period.

Absorption Costing: Refers to a method of costing in which both variable and fixed overhead have been treated as product costs and, to the extent that goods manufactured during the period remain unsold, carried forward as part of the cost of stocks (inventories) or the allocation of all fixed costs and variable costs in the calculation of the cost of goods or services produced.

Accelerator Principle: The theory which states that the level of aggregate net investment has been found to depend on the expected change in output.

Accelerated Depreciation: Depreciation at a faster rate than usual. In recent years used to refer to tax amortization certificates which upon government consent allow writing off an asset in five years for income tax purposes regardless of its life.

Acceleration Clause: A selection of a contract that makes an entire debt become immediately due because of failure to pay on time because of some other failure.

Accept: to agree formally to receive something or to be responsible for something:**to accept a bill-**to sign a bill of exchange to indicate that it will be paid: **accepted bill—** bill of exchange which has been signed, and therefore accepted by the buyer: **to accept delivery of a shipment:** to take goods into the warehouse officially when they are delivered to take something which is being offered or to say "yes" or to agree to something.

Acceptance (a)**:** Signing a bill of exchange to show that you agree to pay it; **to present a bill for acceptance:** to send a bill for payment by the person who has accepted it. (b) **acceptance of an offer:** agreeing to an offer; **to give an offer a conditional acceptance:** to accept provided that certain things happen or that certain terms apply; **we have his letter of acceptance:** we have received a letter from him accepting the offer; **clean acceptance:** unconditional acceptance and acceptance which cannot be withdrawn; **acceptance against documents:** transaction where the seller takes charge of the shipping documents for a consignment of goods when a buyer accepts a bill of exchange; **acceptance sampling:** testing a small part of a batch to see if the whole batch is good enough. (c) **Agreement:** an offer and binding to the terms of a contract. (d) The agreement of a party to a contract or other arrangement submitted to him for consideration. (e) When a contract is made there must be both offer and acceptance. unless it is a contract by deed. If one person offers to do something for another, the contract is not complete until the offer is accepted. Acceptance must be in the same terms as the offer and must be communicated to the offeror.

Acceptance Credit: Also termed as a 'letter of acceptance'. It is a method of payment which is widely used in inland and international trade. If the credit of a foreign import merchant is regarded satisfactory an accepting house may open an exporter may then be financed by means of a bill of exchange drawn on the accepting house. The exporter can then obtain his money quickly as the bill can be easily discounted in the bank.

Acceptance House or Accepting House: A financial enterprise whose principal function lies in facilitating the negotiation of bills of exchange either by accepting them or guaranteeing them. The signature of an established accepting house on a bill of exchange is a sign of the reliability of that bill and will enable the holder to discount it at the most favourable rates. In their modern role of merchant banks they also add speed to international trade by lending money to an exporter on a trade bill, thus bridging the gap between the release of goods and payment by the foreign buyer. Such a loan is sometimes referred to as an acceptance credit.

Acceptor: The person drawing a bill of exchange is the drawer and the person on whom the bill is drawn is the drawee, when the drawee has accepted the bill, i.e., has accepted liability, he is known as the acceptor. The normal form of acceptance is by signature on the face of the bill. He cannot deny the existence and capacity of the drawer or payee or the signature of the drawer—he can, however question an Endorsement (he would not be obliged to pay on a forged endorsement). Delivery is necessary for complete acceptance: this means the acceptor willingly parts with possession or gives notice of acceptance. If the bill is in the hands of a holder in due course, delivery is presumed. It is possible for a bill to be negotiated before acceptance. It is then up to the holder of the bill to present it for acceptance before or at the time of payment. Presentation for acceptance is not obligatory except where the bill so stipulates or where is payable after sight, or payable elsewhere than at the residence or place of business of the drawee.

Access: (a) To have **access to something:** to be able to obtain or reach something: **he has access to large amounts of venture capital: access to the market:** (i) legal right to sell in a particular market; (ii) ability to reach a market by promotion and distribution: **access time:** time taken by a computer to find data stored in it: (b) to call up (data) which is stored in a computer.

Accident: An unexpected, unplanned event that may result in injury is an accident. Mishaps that take place at work and may be caused by carelessness, by inadequate safety precautions, or by chance.

Accident Prevention: The policy or procedures followed in a workplace to prevent accidents to employees, or at least to reduce the occurrence of accidents. It includes physical aspects—proper maintenance of machinery or the provision of protective shields, and managerial aspects such as effective supervision and training.

Accommodation: Lodgings or a place to live.

Accommodation Bill: A bill of exchange signed by one person to accommodate another. The person signing is a guarantor and receives no consideration. Once value has been given for the bill, he is liable if the acceptor fail to pay at the proper time.

Accord and Satisfaction: When one party has completed his/her obligations in a contract he/she may agree to release the other party from that party's obligations. This may be by a document under seal or by receiving some new consideration. Release in return for new consideration is known as accord and satisfaction.

Account: (a) record of money paid or owed: **please send me your account**; or **a detailed**; or **an itemized account; expense account:** money which a businessperson is allowed by his/her company to spend on travelling and entertaining clients in connection with his/her business; **he charged his hotel bill to his expense account**; (b) (in a shop) arrangement whereby a customer pays for the goods he or she buys at a later date (usually the end of the month); **to have an account**; or **a credit account with bank; put it on my account;** or **charge it to my account;** (of a customer) **to open my account;** to start or to supply goods which will be paid for at a later date; (of a shop) **to open an account** or **to close an account: to start or to stop supplying a customer on credit;** to settle an account; **to pay all the money owed on an account;** to stop an account: **to stop supplying a customer until he or she has paid what is owing;** on account: **as part of a total bill;** to pay money on account= **to pay money in settlement of part of a bill;** advance on account: **money paid as** a part payment; (c) arrangement which a company has with an advertising agency, where the agency deals with all: **promotion for the company;** (d): **customer who does a large amount of business with a firm and has an account with it:** he is one of our largest accounts twice a month; call on their best accounts twice a month; **frings accounts:** accounts that are not very profitable for the supplier; **national account:** customer with branches or offices all over the country; (d) **the accounts of a business:** or **a company's accounts:** detailed record of a company's accounts or detailed record of a company's financial affairs: **to keep the accounts:** to write each sum of money in the account book: **the accountant's job is to enter all the money received in the accounts; annual accounts:** accounts prepared at the end of a financial year; **management accounts:** financial information (sales, expenditure, credit, and profitability) prepared for a manager so that he or she can take decisions; **profit and loss account:** accounts for a company with expenditure and income balanced to show a final profit or loss; **accounts department:** department in a company which deals with money paid, received, borrowed and owed; **accounts manager:** a manager of an accounts department who is responsible to check the entries entered by an accountant in books, he also deals with clients, employees and directors of his company and tries to settle the financial matter; **accounts payable:** money owed by a company; **accounts receivable:** money owed to a company; (e) **bank account:** arrangement to keep money in a bank; **budget account:** bank account where you plan income and expenditure to allow for periods when expenditure is high; **current account** or **cheque account** or account which pays no interest but from which the customer can withdraw money at any by writing cheques; **deposit account:** account which pays interest but from which the customer can withdrawn only after notice has been given; **external account:** account with a bank held by someone who is living in another country; **frozen account:** account where the money cannot be used or transfered because of a court order; **joint account:** account for two people; **overdrawn account:** account where you have taken out more money than you have put in (i.e. where the bank is lending your money); **saving account:** account where you regularly put money and which pays interest; **to close an account:** to take all money out of a bank account and stop the account; (f) (Stock Exchange) period of credit (usually fourteen days) at the end of which you must pay for shares you have **bought account; account day:** day on which **shares:** which have been bought must be paid for; **share prices rose at the account and:** or **the end of the account;** (g) notice; **to take account inflation:** or **to take inflation into account:** to assume that there will be a certain percentage inflation when making calculations; **to account for:** to explain and record a money deal; **to account for a loss or a discrepancy; the representatives have to account for all their expenses to the sales manager**.

Account Policies: The detailed methods of valuation, measurement and recognition which a particular company has chosen from those generally accepted by law, Accounting Standards or commercial practice.

Account, Credit: A term normally reserved for credit arrangements made by a purchaser with a particular trader. The purchaser is permitted to buy goods up to a certain value without paying for them on acquisition—the value is set as a maximum for a specific time period, often one month. He receives a summary of his transactions at agreed intervals and pays on a basis specified when the account is opened.

Account, Current: This refers to the cheque account opened by an individual or an organization with a bank or building society. It is an account into which monies are paid or from which sums are withdrawn either in cash or by cheque in the course of everyday affairs. Most individuals keep a current account on which to draw cheques in settlement of debts.

Accountability: Being answerable to others for some actions, e.g., to a supervisor for completing a task or to a board of directors for company performance. Having responsibility and authority for seeing that something is carried out as expected, e.g., that sales targets are met or that a budget has been properly spent.

Accountable: Liable to be required by a specified person or group of people to report on and justify actions in relation to specified matters.

Accountancy: The terms accountancy and accounting are used interchangeably by many people. However, they might say 'the Accountancy Profession' but 'Management Accounting'; the former tends to be associated with the profession and the latter with the subject matter, particularly in the context of education or theory. Accounting includes mechanical aspects such as Double Entry bookkeeping, which might be said to be part of Financial Accounting. The latter also involves the preparation, presentation and interpretation of financial statements. Management accounting is more concerned with the use of accounting data for decision-making and control by managers.

Accountant: Person trained in keeping or drawing up accounts or arranging systems of accounts; person who keeps a company's accounts or person who advises a company on its finances or person who examines accounts; certified accountant; accountant who has passed the professional examinations and is a member of the Association of Certified Accountants; Chartered Accountant: a person who has passed the professional examinations and is a member of the Institute of Chartered Accountants; cost accountant: accountant who gives managers information about their business costs; management accountant: accountant who prepares financial information for managers so that they can take decisions.

Accounting Concept: An expression commonly used for the fundamental conceptual rules of accounting (see Accounting Principles).

Accounting Convention: Another expression commonly used for the fundamental conceptual rules of accounting. Accounting conventions are certain fundamental accounting principles that include those customs and traditions which guide the accountants while preparing the financial statements. For example, the convention of conservatism makes the accountant feel the need for making a provision for expected loss but, at the same time, to ignore expected profits.

Accounting Costs: Costs regarded as recorded costs only; economic costs might be larger or smaller when alternative costs or opportunity costs and external effects have been taken into account.

Accounting Cycle: The repetitive processing of financial transactions during an accounting 'cycle'—typically one month. The basic steps in the accounting cycle are: (1) entering transactions in one or more journals, (2) balancing the journals, (3) posting information from the journals to the general ledger, (4) posting information from the journals to the subsidiary ledger accounts, (5) reconciling and balancing the ledger accounts, (6) preparing financial statements, and (7) using the resulting information to improve operations.

Accounting Data: It is the data used for preparation of accounts, cost and price considerations and allied requirements of management. It includes the ability to use the accounting data developed for tax or financial purposes to identify those elements of income, expense, or investment that really change with the alternatives considered. The accounting department, in preparing statement for the income tax authorities, must follow certain conventions. On the other hand, the finance department, in submitting reports to stockholders, creditors, and various governmental agencies, may be required to follow different conventions. When projected in financial terms, it is entirely possible for the same group of alternatives to look quite different depending on the set of conventions used. As decision-makers we should be aware of how decision will look to a tax collector, a stockholder, or a regulatory agency of the Government. But it is probably more important to know how it will look in terms of the real impact on the elements of profit that the firm can control.

Accounting Equation: A mathematical representation of the basic relationships between parts of a financial statement. For example, the accounting equation for the relationship among assets, liabilities, and fund balances (on a balance sheet) is: A = L + FB Assets = Liabilities + Fund Balances. An algebraic representation of a summary of what happens in the Double Entry system. The Balance-Sheet might be expressed as A0 = L0 + C0 (that is, total Assets at time zero equal total figure Liabilities and Capital at time zero). The capital figure grows from time zero to time one by the earning of profit for the period; that is, C0 + P1 = C1 (Equation 2). The profit (P1) is made up of the total Revenues less the total Expenses of the period: that is, P1 = R1 - E1 (Equation 3). It is, of course, also the case that A1 = L1 + C1 (Equation 4). So inserting Equation 3 in Equation 2 gives: C1 = C0 + R1 – E1 Inserting this in Equation 4 gives: A1 = L1 + C0 + R1 – E1 Rearranging this gives: A1 + E1 = L1 + C0 + R1. That is, the items on the left (assets and expenses) are all the debits, which are seen to equal the items on the right (liabilities, capital and revenues) which are all the credits. This is a basic principle of double entry.

Accounting for Inflation: In times of inflation accounts do not give an accurate picture of real profits or the real present value of capital employed. In order to give both the public and the investor a proper appreciation of business results it is thought desirable to eliminate, as far as possible variations that result from, and changes in the value of money, e.g., if the price level has doubled over five years, or, which is to state the same point, the value of money has halved over that period.

Accounting Period: Refers to the period between two successive balance sheets and that for which profit and loss accounts (income statements) and funds statements are prepared.

Accounting Principles: The word 'principles' poses a slight problem in accounting. In the USA it tends to mean conventions of practice, whereas in the UK it means something more fundamental and theoretical. Thus the US Generally Accepted Accounting Principles encompass a wide range of broad and detailed accounting rules of practice. In the UK the detailed rules are often called practices, policies or bases; and broader matters such as Accruals or Prudence were traditionally referred to as concepts or conventions. However, perhaps because lawyers (and those in Brussels at that) were involved in the drafting of the EC's Fourth Directive which led to the 1981 Companies Act in the UK, British usage is now broad 'principles' of accounting: Going concern. Consistency, prudence, accruals and individual valuation. The first four were all to be found in the UK's SSAP 2, described as 'concepts'. The problem with these broad principles in any country is the possibility of conflict. For example, in a going concern, the matching concept suggests that development costs ought to be carried forward and matched against the future revenue that they are designed to create (see Research and Development). However, prudence suggests that, because it is possible that no benefits will arise, all R & D costs should be immediately charged as expenses. This would also lead to greater expenditure. In the USA Conservatism and consistency win in the shape of SFAS 2, which does not allow the capitalization of R & D costs. In the UK the initial exposure draft (ED 14) followed that precedent, but and the subsequent SSAP 13 allowed capitalization of development expenditure under prudent conditions. Under SSAP 2 prudence is required to override other conventions when there is conflict. Under UK Company Law no such provision exists. It is fortunate, then, that these broken in (disclosed) special circumstances or in order to allow a True and Fair View. There are many other accounting conventions such as Materiality and Money Measurement.

Accounting Rate of Return: Refers to a method of Capital Investment

Appraisal which measures the average net profit of a project as a percentage of the average book value.

Accounting Standards: In view of the diversity of available principles which at one time could be legally applied in the preparation of the published accounts of limited companies and by extension to accounts generally certain professional accounting bodies have attempted to define standards which should be adopted by their members when preparing such accounts.

Accounting System: Refers to a set of records and procedure which are designed so as to handle in routine fashion the Transactions (especially those concerning cash, sales and purchases) and other events affecting an enterprise's operations, performance and financial position. **Accounting:** The establishment, maintenance, collection and analysis of financial records. It is used to provide data on the financial position of an organization and any changes that have occurred, or may occur over time. This is one aspect of the profession (or art) of accountancy.

Accounts and Audit Control: Accounts of the public corporations are kept in the forms to be settled in consultation with the Government or the Auditor General and the audit of their accounts is either done by the Auditor-General of India or by auditors appointed by the Government.

Accounts Payable: Amounts which are owing by an enterprise, distinguished from Accrued Expenses and other Current Liabilities not arising out of trading transactions.

Accounts Receivable: Amounts which are owing to an enterprise, distinguished from prepaid Expenses and other Current Assets not arising out of trading transactions.

Accounts: Records of all the bookkeeping entries relating to a particular item. For example, the wages account would record all the payments of wages. An account in the Double Entry system has a debit side (left) and a credit side (right). Often accounts are referred to as T-accounts, because of the rulings on the pages that divide that left from the right and underline the title. A business may have thousands of accounts, including one for each debtor and creditor. In the early days of accounting there were only personal accounts (for people who owed and were owed money). Later there were 'real' accounts for property of various sorts; and 'nominal' accounts for impersonal, unreal items such as wages and electricity. Accounts may be collected together in groups in Ledgers or Books of Account. In the UK accounts may also mean financial statements, such as the Balance Sheet and Profit and Loss Accounts.

Accounts, Consolidated: Some companies have subsidiary companies. The holding company must, in addition to the normal requirements of the Companies Act, file group accounts. These can take various forms but essentially they are intended to show the results for the relevant financial period, and the state of affairs at the end of that period, of the group as a whole.

Accrual Accounting: Refers to an accounting system which, unlike Cash Flow Accounting, recognized revenues and expenses as they are earned or incurred, not as cash is received or paid.

Accruals Concept: An expression used to describe the standard practice whereby Expenses or Revenues are included in the Accounts of the period to which they relate rather than of the period in which cash is paid or received. It is also known as the Matching Principle, particularly in North America.

Accrued Charges: An accrued charge is the measure of an expense incurred for which no charge has yet been made by the creditor.

Accrued Expenses: Those Expenses which relate to a year but will not be paid until the following year. They result from the need regularly to draw up financial statements at a fixed time (for example, at the end of a company's financial year). During a year electricity will be used or properties will be rented, yet at the year end the related bills may not have been paid. These accrued expenses are charged against income by accountants even though cash has not been paid nor perhaps the bills received. The Double Entry for these is the creations of Current Liabilities on the Balance Sheet, which are the Credit corresponding to the Debit accrued expenses. This practice may apply also to wages and salaries, taxes, and so on. An allocation of amounts to 'this year' and 'next year' may be necessary where a supplier's accounts straddles two accounting years. The practice is an example of the use of the matching concept.

Accumulated Depreciation: That part of an asset's costs that have been depreciated (that is, for accounting purposes considered to have been consumed or used up). Under this method the depreciation provided for every year gets accumulated separately called accumulated depreciation A/c and the value of asset is shown at its Original Cost.

Accurate: Correct; **Accurate Description:** Honest and true description of a product or service in an advertisement of catalogue; as the advertisement was clearly not an accurate description of the product, the company had to pay a fine; it is not an accurate description of the product to state that it gives out more light than the sun.

Accrued Expenses: Refers to the expenses (e.g. wages) which have been incurred but not yet paid at balance-sheet date.

Acid Test Ratio: See Quick Ratio.

Acquire: To buy; **to acquire a company**.

Acquisition: Thing bought: act of getting or buying something: **Acquisition: Data Acquisition:** or **Acquisition of Data:** Obtaining and classifying data.

Acquisitions and Mergers: Large stockholders in a closely held company want to convert their assets into marketable securities or cash, frequently in anticipation of high inheritance taxes. Poor health or old age makes them willing to merge at an attractive price. Mergers involve more than identifying a major economic advantage and negotiating a deal. The two enterprises have to be fitted together into a new composite institution. Unless this true amalgamation is done effectively, many of the anticipated benefits may not materialize.

Acting: Working in place of someone for a short time.

Action: (a) Thing which is done; process of doing something; to take action: to do something (b) direct action: strike or go slow by the workforce; to take industrial action: to do something (usually to go on strike) to show that you are not happy with conditions at work (c) case in a law court where a person or company sues another person or company; civil action: case brought by a person or company against someone who has done them wrong; criminal action: case brought by the state against someone who is charged with a crime.

Action Plan: A blow-by-blow description of the tactics devised to achieve a particular strategy. An action plan includes schedules of what has to be done when, how and by whom. In marketing an action plan should typically include: Times and places of specific promotions of the product (for example, special sample offers, point-of-sale displays, or coupons); trade shows to be attended; Advertising campaigns to be launched; and publicity release to be distributed. It should also included a budget for each type of promotion.

Activating Mode: Why sound decisions developed and implemented by a good organization fail to achieve desired results even though the decisions are understood and acted on with commitment? Why even the best control systems occasionally fail to spot problems on time or help in pinpointing the causes? May be in this unpredictable and frequently competitive world imperfect planners, organizers and controllers guess wrong or are beaten by competitors. However, just as we seek to improve the quality of management functions, so too we must focus on achieving optimum performance through what is called activating.

Activity Ratio: A financial ratio that indicates how much use a firm makes of its assets, usually the ratio of total sales revenue over a period to the average value of a particular class of assets (such as stocks of finished goods, cash, fixed assets) during the period. (Also known as 'efficiency ratio').

Actual Cost: Refers to a cost which is determined on the basis of historical costs incurred as distinct from budgeted or standard costs.

Actuary: A person technically trained in statistics, accounting, and mathematics, who proposes policy and calculated premium rates, reserves, and dividends. The actuary also recommends what assumptions should be made with respect to each of the insurance risk factors involved in given situations. Risk factors include the frequency of occurrence of some specific peril, the average benefit that will be payable, the rate of investment earnings, expenses, and persistency rates or facetiously described as someone who finds accounting too exciting. Actuaries contemplate (then calculate) the probability of death occurring to others within prescribed periods of time. This enables Insurance companies and the like to determine what premium they should charge to those taking out life-assurance policies.

Acuity: Term used to describe someone's ability to discriminate fine detail in using one of the senses.

Ad Referendum: When applied to a contract, this term means that although the contract has been signed, certain matters have been left over for consideration when they actually arise.

Ad Valorem (ad val): According to value. Especially a tax that is proportional to the value of the goods or transaction, on which it is levied.

Ad Valorem Tax: A duty which has been imposed on commodities in proportion to their value, i.e., a duty which expressed as a percentage and not a flat amount. It has been commonly used in respect of import tariffs.

Added Value: A concept that has become of particular importance since the introduction of value added tax: it refers to the value of the improvement made to goods or services at any particular and separate stage in their production, i.e., it is the difference between the price of a product or service taken in as the basis for improvement and the price at which the improved or finished product or service is sold either to the next operative in line or to the consumer. The term is synonymous with value added.

Adjourn: To stop a meeting for a period.

Adjournment: Act of adjourning.

Adjudicate: To give a judgment between two parties in law; to decide a legal problem.

Adjudication: Act of giving a judgment or of deciding a legal problem; adjudication tribunal: group which adjudicates in industrial disputes.

Adjudication Provisions: While the upward spiralling of wages and process is not looked upon with favour by the government, it is agreed that increased wages should be granted in order to remove anomalies and to restore the level of real wages in cases where the levels were abnormally low. While awarding considerable increases in pay, the industrial courts have contributed to the thinking regarding standardization of wages within industries. They have made use of the family budget enquiries in the areas, the standard per capita requirements of food, clothing, fuel, etc., as recommended by various authorities the size of the average family, etc., in deciding the actual quantum of minimum wages.

Adjudicator: Person who gives a decision on a problem.

Administer: To organize or to manage or to direct the whole of an organization or part of one.

Administration: Direction or control or management of a whole organization or part of one; **administration expenses:** costs of management, not including production, marketing or distribution costs. **letters of administration:** letter given by a court to allow someone to deal with the estate of a person who has died.

Administration and Management: The terms Administration and Management have been used by different management authorities in a manner that sometimes they seem to be one and the same while at some other time, they diverge. According to most of the modern writers like Fayol, Koontz, Allen and Perry, there is no real distinction between these two terms. Fayol, for instance, stated: "All undertakings require planning, organization, command, coordination and control and in order to function properly, all must observe to some general principles. We are no longer confronted with several administrative science but with one which can be applied equally well to public and private affairs". Broadly, however, Management refers to the day to day function of an organisation whereas administration concerns itself to policy framework of the organisation.

Administrator: Person who manages or directs an organization or part of one.

Adoption: Decision to buy or use a particular product; line on a graph showing how many consumers adopt or buy a new product at various time periods after the launch date.

Advance: (a) Money paid as a loan or as a part of a payment to be made later; (b) in advance: early or before something happens.

Adverse: Unfavourable; **adverse action:** personnel decision which has unfavourable consequences for employees.

Advertise: To arrange and pay for publicity designed to help the sale of products or services or to find new employees; to announce that something is for sale or that a job is vacant or that a service is offered.

Advertisement: Notice which shows that something is for or that a service is offered or that someone wants something or that a job is vacant, etc.; short film on television, short announcement on the radio, or an eye catching description of the product in newspaper, magazine or in pamphlet, which tries to persuade people to use a certain product or services; advertisement listed in a newspaper under special headings (such as 'property for sale' or 'jobs wanted'); **display advertisement:** advertisement which is set apart from other advertisements by having its own typeface, borders, illustrations, etc.

Advertiser: Person or company which advertises.

Advertising: A key part of Marketing, but far from being (as is often assumed) the sum total of it. Advertising is the use of media to inform consumers about something and/or to persuade them to do something. In other words we can say advertising is the art of making your products known to the world in such a manner that a desire for buying that product is created in the hearts of people. Advertising brings products and consumers together, and then modulates the relationship between them. Communications is a central part of the advertising business, but the industry has not been very successful at communicating its own value. It is widely criticised for creating illusory desires in consumers to the sole benefit of industrial corporations. There is a contradiction in the general public's attitude to advertising. On the one hand it is seen as manipulative and cunning (as in); on the other hand it is seen as unfocused and crude. It can, of course, be both; but not at the same time. Most professional advertising is not haphazard. Different approaches and different messages are required for different stages of the relationship between consumer and product. These stages are categorised in the Hierarchy of Effects: awareness; knowledge; linking; preference; conviction and purchase. They are also commonly remembered by the mnemonic AIDA (attention, interest, desire, action). Advertising is not solely concerned with commercial products. In most countries producers of goods and services account for about half is spent by marketing intermediaries (such as retailers and banks), by governments in all their guises, by service organizations (such as charities), and by individuals (in a Classified Advertisement, for example).

Advertising Agency: A firm that handles the advertising needs of a number of clients. The agency is an intermediary between the producer of goods or services and the media that will communicate the producer's message to the consumer. A typical modern agency will have a number of different departments. **Research**. To provide Market Research relevant to the agency's clients. Data on market behaviour will be gathered either from secondary sources of from specially commissioned surveys carried out of on behalf of the client. Some agencies are part of a group within which there is also a market research firm to keep such survey work within the corporate 'family'. **Planning**. To give specialist marketing advice to the 'generalist' Account Directors. In some agencies the planning department is merged with the research department. **Creative**. The place where bright new advertising ideas are supposed to be fermented. **Media**. Responsible for planning advertising schedules and for buying space in the media. **Production**. Concerned with the marking of all material for television, film or radio, and for the production of ready-to-print press advertising material. Smaller agencies subcontract much of their production outside the firm, but most bigger agencies have their own fully fledged production departments. **Traffic**. This is sometimes called the control department, and is responsible for seeing that each stage of the production process is completed on schedule. The deadlines that the department works on are created by publication dates or by broadcast transmission times. **Accounts**. Similar to accounts departments in most commercial firms. It is responsible for billing the clients, for buying media space, and for paying freelance artists, photographers or writers. One agency's advice on how best to use an agency is as follows. Provided it with a clear and practical brief. Establish a clear and workable budget. Provide a realistic timetable. Carefully check the agency's copy, artwork, and so on.

Advertising and Salesmanship: Relationship between Advertising and Salesmanship are not mutually exclusive but they are complementary to each other. These are not substitute for each other, that is why it is said that advertising is a printed salesmanship. Advertising prepares basic ground and salesmanship realises it. Advertising will attract a large number of potential customers, but the ultimate result will be obtained by salesmanship making actual sales. Due to this type of relationship between them both should be equally effective.

Advertising Campaign: A coordinated series of advertisements appearing over a defined period of time and in different media. An advertising campaign aims to obtain the maximum influence on a Target Market for a given amount of money. It is used most effectively for launching a new product or relaunching an old one.

Advertising Copy: Advertising copy is the name given to the published advertisements issued by a company. The advertising copy should give the message in the briefest, most interesting and forceful manner. The copy must be addressed to the type of people who are exposed to the advertising medium.

Advertising Manager: An employee of a firm who supervises the production of the firm's advertisements and decides which media will carry them.

Advertising Messages: Advertising includes the following forms of messages: the messages carried in newspapers and magazines; on outdoor boards, on street cars and posters, on radio and T.V. broadcasts, and in circulars of all kinds, whether distributed by mail, by person through tradesmen, or by insertions in packages; dealer help materials, window display and counter-display materials and efforts; neon signs; house organs when directed to dealers and consumers; motion pictures used for advertising; and novelties bearing advertising messages of signature of the advertiser. Labels, tags and other literature accompanying merchandise are deemed advertising because they reasonably may be said to fall within the definition of advertising media given above.

Advertising Standard Authority (ASA): Independent body which oversees the system of self-regulation in the British advertising industry.

Advertising, Informative: This refers to that branch of advertising which aims to advise producers or consumers of new products, changes in old ones, recent inventions or innovations, etc. of which they might otherwise be ignorant, in such a way that although primarily for the reader's benefit it is also to the advantage of advertisers themselves.

Advertising, Subliminal: A particularly insidious form of advertising aimed at the consumer's subconscious. A message or blurb is flashed across a visual screen at such a speed that it does not register in the conscious mind. The idea which has been proved effective, it that the massage is registered subconsciously and will influence the recipient to buy the goods promoted.

Advertising-Benefits to Society: Advertising brings to the greatest number of people actual knowledge concerning useful thing, it is essentially a form of education and the progress of civilization depends on education. (i) Provides

Employment (ii) Supports Press (iii) Improves Standard of Living (iv) Motivates Hard Work.

Advertising, Competitive: Designed to sell one's own products at the expense of those of others.

Advertising, Persuasive: This form of advertising comes into the 'no holds barred' category. The aim is to sell the product or service without reference to the need of the consumer or the economic or public good, artificial markets by promoting a product in such a way that consumers are encouraged to satisfy needs which have arisen solely from the insinuation of advertisers. Advertisers succeed when they can sell something of no intrinsic value to consumers who neither want nor need it, consumers may rush out to buy a product which they cannot afford, just to fulfil a desire created in them by the manufacturer and advertiser.

Advice: Opinion given about what action to take or how to behave or express or direction for a particular mode of action.

Advice Note: A document sent by a supplier to the customer prior to the invoice. Sometimes it precedes the goods and sometimes accompanies them: it states the mature and quantity of the goods but not their price. Essentially just an indication that the goods are no the way, it is sometimes confused with a delivery note.

Adviser: Person who suggests what should be done.

Affidavit: A declaration in writing made on oath before a person entitled to administer oaths - a commissioner for oaths, normally a solicitor. It is a criminal offence deliberately to make a false statement in an affidavit. After-sales service. A continuing service of maintenance, repair, supply of information on possible uses, and so on, provided to buyers of a product by the seller (or sometimes the manufacturer if the sale was made by a retailer).

Affirmation of Contract: A person induced to enter a contract by a misrepresentation may be bound by the contract and lose his right to rescission and/or damages, if he expressly or implicitly affirms the contract with full knowledge of the facts. This he may do by verbal affirmation or simply by failing to take action within a reasonable time.

After-Hours: After-hours buying or selling or dealing: buying or selling or dealing in shares after the Stock Exchange has officially closed for the day.

After-Sales Service: A continuing service of maintenance, repair, supply of information on possible uses, and so on, provided to buyers of a product by the seller (or sometimes the manufacturer if the sale was made by a retailer) or a service provided by a manufacturer to a consumer after the consumer has bought the manufacturer's product. After-sales service has been particularly significant in the marketing of consumer durables like washing machines, heating systems and personal computers. It includes things like regular checks, repairs, supplying spare parts, and so on. Such a service may be provided under the terms of a specific maintenance agreement (separate from the purchase) for which the consumer pays a regular fee.

After-Tax Profit: Profit after tax has been deducted.

Agency: (a) Office or job of representing another company in an area; sole agency: agreement to be the only person to represent a company or to sell a product in a certain area; (b) office: business which arranges things for other companies; advertising agency = office which plans or designs and manages advertising for companies.

Agency, Creation of: An agency is contractual arrangement, either express or implied written or verbal, whereby one person may act on behalf of another and bind that other as if he or she had acted personally.

Agenda: Details of business to be transacted at a meeting, made out by the person calling the meeting or the secretary appointed to do so. The agenda is sent out to those invited to attend. It is generally accompanied by an invitation to appoint a proxy if a member cannot attend personally.

Agent: (a) A person with express or implied authority to act for another person (the principal) the object being to establish a contractual relationship between the principal and third parties, (b) Someone who transacts business on behalf of others. In law, a person who has the power and authority to put another person (who is called the 'principal' of the agent) into binding legal relationships.

Ageing Schedule: A related aspect of the average collection period in the Ageing Schedule. While the former is concerned with the liquidity of debtors/receivables as a whole, the latter analyses them in a disaggregative manner by dividing the outstanding debtors on the basis of the duration during which they have been outstanding. The usefulness of the ageing schedule lies in the fact that it enables the analyst to identify the slow-paying debtors in respect of whom the firm may have to encounter a serious collection problem.

Agreement: Contract between two parties which explains how they will act; **blank agreement:** agreement which covers many different items; **exclusive agreement:** agreement whereby a company is appointed sole agent for a product in a market; **gentleman's agreement:** verbal agreement between two parties who trust each other.

Agro-Industries: An area of management where managers can set up, expand agro-industries including processing industry, which has a natural advantage due to the lower wage of the population and lower cost of production of all vegetables and food, etc. Large unit must encourage the setting up of ancillaries and small unit to meet these objectives.

AIDA: Attention, Interest, Desire, Action model showing stages in the effects of advertising on consumers.

Aim: Something which you try to do; the company has done all the things it had hoped to do.

Air Cargo: Goods sent by air.

Air Freight: Method of shipping goods in an aircraft; **to send a shipment by air freight; air freight charges:** or **rates**.

Allocation: Reservation of something (e.g. stock of materials or an amount of money) for a particular purpose of person. Also the quantity reserved. Also, identification of the process, product or cost centre that has accrued or benefited from a particular expenditure or the process of dividing resources or costs between different sections or functions of an organization; the amount of resources in a given budget.

Allotment of Shares: When a company receives an application for shares issued by means of a prospectus, it proceeds to allot the shares on a predetermined basis (which is set out in the prospectus.) Where applications exceed the shares available, allotment is made proportionately, though often application for shares up to a stated number are accepted in full. The allotment of shares is made by means of a letter of allotment. This entitles the recipient to a certificate for the number of shares stated in the letter. His title may, however, depend on his paying the sum previously stated as due on allotment.

Allotment: The acquisition, by one or more persons, of newly issued securities; commonly as a result of an administrative decision by which securities are allocated among applicants.

Amalgamation: (a) A merge by agreement of two or more concerns with or into a major organization. (b) Refers to the absorption by one company of the business and net assets of another company, the latter company being dissolved or both companies being dissolved and a new company formed to take over both business. (c) Within the world of companies an amalgamation refers to the coming together by arrangement of two or more individually registered companies for the purpose of mutual benefit of the companies concerned.

Ambush Marketing: Linking a promotion campaign to an event (such as a sporting contest which is sponsored by another manufacturers) without paying a fee.

Amend: To change and make more correct or acceptable.

Amendment: Change to a document.

Amenities: Services provided by an organization for the people who work in it.

American Depositary Receipt (ADR): American depositary receipts are securities, in the name of nominees, issued by United States banking housed in exchange for shares in companies deposited with them. This makes trading in the shares of these companies possible on the New York and other US stock exchanges, whether or not the shares are actually listed on those exchanges.

American Express: A credit card company which operates on an international basis.

Amortisation: A word used, particularly in North America, to refer to certain types of depreciations, mainly that owing to the passing of time. In commercial parlance this has particular reference to the writing off of assets the lives of which are determined not by deterioration or obsolescence but by the expiry of the tenure of ownership. The principal instance would be a leasehold property or it is the writing off of assets- the lives of which are determined not be deterioration or obsolescence but the expiry of the tenure of ownership. The principal instance would be a leasehold property. A business with a fixed lease of an asset, particularly a building or land, would wish to provide for the renewal of the lease or its replacement with another type of tenure by writing off the cost of the asset over its fixed life and, in addition, probably putting an equal amount each year into a sinking fund which would be invested to provide monies for the eventual replacement or renewal. This manner of writing off an asset is called amortization. It is distinguished from depreciation in that there is generally no deterioration in the performance of the asset during its or in financial management it basically refers to the redemption of a loan by means of payments into a Sinking Fund.

Amount: (a) quantity of money; (b) to amount to: to make a total of.

Analyse: or **analyze:** to examine someone or something in detail by separating it into parts; to analyse a statement of accounts; to analyse the market potential.

Analysis: Close study of someone or something by separating its parts and establishing their relationship.

Analysis of Variance: (Also known as ANOVA) Refers to the breakdown of the total variation in a dependent variable (with total variation defined as the sum of squared deviations from its mean) into the proportions which have been accounted for by variation in individual, or groups of explanatory variables, and the unexplained or residual variation.

Analyst: An expert person who studies the progress of companies and of industries in order to make judgments and recommendations about the value of different stocks and shares, or about the value of different DEBT instruments. Such analysts normally work for financial firms like stockbrokers and Insurance companies, for example. The word analyst is also used to refer to those people who analyse markets from inside manufacturing companies.

Ancillaries-To-Trade: Services which support trade, such as banking and advertising.

Annual Accounts: Financial statements showing the state of affairs of a business or other organization at a particular date and the results or operations during the period, usually one year, which ends on that date. The nature of these accounts will vary according to the entity to which they apply and with the various regulations and provisions, legal or otherwise, relating thereto.

Annual General Meeting (AGM): (a) The annual general meeting of an organization and in particular a meeting of the members (i.e. the shareholders) of a company held at intervals of not more than fifteen months. (b) A meeting of members of an association held once a year to review the association's activities, elect officers and discuss future policy. Usually an association's rules require the holding of an AGM. Specifically, a meeting of the members of a registered company, described as an annual general meeting in the notice convening it and held in accordance with the provisions of Companies Act, 1948.

Annual Report: A document sent to shareholders after a company's year end. It must contain a report by the directors, the financial statement and notes, and the report of the auditors. Most large companies also include a less formal report in the form of a chairman's statement.

Annualized: Shown on an annual basis.

Annuity: Money paid each year to a retired person, usually in return for a lump-sum payment; life annuity: annual payments made to someone as long as he is alive; reversionary annuity: annuity paid to someonc on the death of another person originally an investment that bought a fixed annual payment for the investor (called the annuitant) until his or her death. A number of complications have been added on to that basic format. For example, the payment of the benefits is nowadays more likely to be quarterly or semi-annual than annual. There is also a wide range of specialised annuities. **Deferred Annuity**. The regular payments do not begin until after a certain specified period. **Joint Annuity**. The benefit is paid throughout the lifetime of two people (usually husband and wife) and continues with until both are dead. **Perpetual Annuity**. The payments go on for ever (to survivors that is). **Tontine Annuity**. A joint annuity where the payment increases as the number of annuitants decreases (that is, when the husband dies the wife regularly gets a bigger payment).

Annul: To cancel or to stop something being legal.

Anticipation: Doing something before it is due to be done.

Appeal: 1 (a) Being attractive; customer appeal: being attractive to customers; sales appeal: quality which makes customers want to buy (b) asking a court or a government department to change its decision; 2 (a) to attract; (b) to ask a government department or a law court to alter its decision.

Apperception: See Thematic.

Applicant: Person who applies for something.

Application: Asking for something, usually in writing.

Application Money: Refers to the amount per share or unit of stock payable on application for a new issue of shares or debentures.

Apply: (a) To ask for something, usually in writing (b) to affect or to touch.

Appoint: To choose someone for a particular job or position of responsibility.

Appointee: Person who is appointed to a job or position.

Appointment: (a) Arrangement to meet, (b) being appointed to a job;

Appraisal: Calculation of the value of someone or something

Appreciation: In general commercial usage this is an accounting term relating to the increase in value of an asset, particularly a fixed asset. In this sense it is the reverse of depreciation, which measures the fall in value of fixed assets over their normal lifetime.

Apprentice: One who signs a contract or indenture, agreeing to serve for a definite period with one employer or master. The apprentice's intention is to learn a trade, and although he may receive only a nominal wage; he expects to gain valuable experience. The master agrees to teach his trade to the apprentice.

Apprenticeship: The period of time spent, mostly at the workplace and usually on low wages, in learning the basic skills of a craft, trade or profession.

Appropriation Account: (a) An account which is prepared at the end of the financial year of the spending by central government departments of monies voted by Parliament (b) an accounting term referring to that part of the annual accounts of a business wherein the net profit, having been determined, is allocated to various claimants as the directors so determine. It will disclose, inter alia, amounts declared as dividends and amounts transferred to named reserves.

Appropriation: Act of putting money aside for a special purpose; **advertising appropriation:** money set aside by an organization for its advertising.

Appropriation of Payments: When a creditor receives money from a debtor he can, in the absence of instruction to the contrary by the debtor, appropriate the payment to any debt outstanding on that debtor's account.

Aptitude: Ability (to do task).

Arbitrage: One who signs a contract or indenture, agreeing to serve for a definite period with one employer or master. The apprentice's intention is to learn a trade and although he may receive only a nominal wage, he expects to gain valuable experience. The master agrees to teach his trade to the apprentice.

Arbitrate: To be chosen by both sides to try to settle an industrial dispute.

Arbitration: (a) The reference for settlement of a dispute normally arising out of contract to one or more independent persons rather than to a court of law. The arbitration must be agreed initially, it cannot be imposed afterwards. Some advantages are: simplicity, speed, economy and the avoidance of publicity. There is, of course, no guarantee of justice or impartiality on the part of the arbitrator. (b) person not concerned with a dispute who is chosen by both sides to try to settle it. Advisory arbitration: arbitration which recommends a solution to a dispute, but is not binding on either party; arbitration board or arbitration tribunal: group which arbitrates; industrial arbitration tribunal: court which decides in industrial disputes.

Area: (a) Measurement of the space taken up by something calculated by multiplying the length by the width (b) region of the world; free trade area: group of countries practicing free trade.

Area Manager: Manager who is responsible for a part of the country.

Arithmetic Mean: Average or a statistical term used for the figure obtained by totalling a series of values and dividing that total by the number of items in that series.

Arithmetic Progression: A mathematical term often connected with statistics. It refers to a numerical series within which the difference between consecutive items is constant.

Armchair Research: looking information that has already been compiled and published in reference books such as directories.

Arrears: Money which is owed, but which has not been paid at the right time; in arrears: owing money which should have been paid earlier.

Arrears of Dividends: Where dividends are in arrears and are payable.

Article: (a) Product or thing for sale, (b) section of a legal agreement;

US articles of incorporation: document which regulates that way in which a company's affairs are managed; articles of partnership: document which sets up the legal conditions of a partnership (d) articles: time when a clerk is working in a solicitor's office learning the law; articles of indenture: contract by which a trainee craftsman works for a master for some years to learn a trade; to serve articles: to work in a solicitor's office to learn the law.

Articled Clerk: A sophisticated name for an apprentice, usually applied to a person apprenticed in a professional firm e.g. of accountants or solicitors.

Articles of Association: A document drawn up at the foundation of a company, setting out the rights and duties of the share-holders and directors, and the relationship between one class of shareholder and another. These are the internal regulations on the running of a company. They are registered when the company is formed. They bind the company to the members as if each member had signed them, but do not bind the company or the members to outside persons. The articles are subject to the memorandum of association and must not contain anything illegal or ultra vires. **Alteration of Articles of Association:** The articles may be altered by a special resolution at a general meeting. The alteration must be within the powers given by the memorandum of association. It must concern legal acts and must not be a fraud on a minority of shareholders: that is it must be for the good of the company and must not be an attempt by the majority to take advantage of their position.

ASA: Advertising Standards Authority.

Assembly Line: A means of mass production, based on the ideas of Gilbreth and Taylor, which was invented by Henry Ford in 1913 for his model-T car factory. It quickly became the leading method of producing standardized goods in large volumes. The method requires each worker to carry out his particular task on the product as it passes in front of him along a conveyor belt, each worker adding something to the product along the way.

Assessment: The process or activity or an act of determining an amount of tax to be paid, also the amount of tax so determined. Synonym for appraisal.

Asset: Anything owned, whether in possession or by right to take possession, by a person or group of persons acting together, e.g., a company, the value of which can be expressed in monetary terms.

Asset Management: The art of getting the best return possible from the (financial) assets that an institution owns or manages. This involves finding the ideal balance between the yield from the assets on the one hand, and their risk, maturity and liquidity on the other. Financial institutions used to devote much attention to asset management. When there was little competition for saver's deposits, their liabilities took care of themselves. But with the rapid deregulation of financial markets in the 1980s competition for deposits and savings grew rapidly. With it grew the amount of attention paid to the different game of liabilities management.

Asset Stripping: The term used for identifying and selling off the easily separable assets of a company that has been the object of a successful takeover bid.

Asset Turnover: The ratio of net sales to average assets for a defined fiscal period. The ratio expresses financial activity in an analysis of return on investment.

Asset Valuation: The traditional method of valuation in accounting is Historical Cost Accounting, whereby Assets are valued at purchase price or production cost, less depreciation (that is, at Net Historical Cost). There are good reasons for this, such as conservatism and a desire for objectivity. However, particularly when prices have risen, the historical cost of an asset may be misleading, given that many non-accountants assume that assets are recorded at a market price. In some countries, including are sometimes revalued to reflect the increase in what they could be sold for. The problem is that there are few rules: some companies revalue annually, some every five years, some never; fixed assets other than land and buildings tend to be more uniformly shown at net historical cost, but an exact measurement, current assets are valued at the lower of cost and net realisable value, although in North America replacement cost is used where it is even lower, debtors are valued at what the lender prudently expects to receive, and cash is valued at its face value.

Asset Value: The asset value of shares, or, more correctly, the net asset value, is obtained by estimating the realizable value of the company's assets, deducting known liabilities and dividing the result among the equity shares.

Assets: An asset is expressed in the following equation: Assets = Liabilities + Owner's equity. The equation may also be represented as: Assets – Liabilities = Owner's equity Or Assets = Creditor's equities + Owner's equities Or Assets = Liabilities + Capital. The book value of items owned by an enterprise or jurisdiction, as reflected on a balance-sheet, also, all of the property of a person, association, corporation or estate that may be applied to or subjected to payment of obligatory debts. Current assets consist of cash and those highly liquid items that are easily convertible into a known amount of cash, usually within a year (e.g. accounts receivable, securities, inventory, and amounts due from other funds). Fixed assets are those items that are normally not convertible into cash within a year (such as buildings, equipment and machinery). In more general terms, Assets are valuable resources owned by a business and acquired at a measurable money cost. A resource is valuable it is cash or convertible into cash or expected to benefit the future operation of the business. Assets include (a) physical resources like land, machinery, inventory; (b) non-physical resources like cash (currency notes), securities, accounts receivable, (c) intangible resources such as goodwill, trade-mark and (d) future benefits like insurance premium paid in advance for protection against future misfortunes. Sometimes, even nebulous benefits like incorporation cost of a company, discount on issue of debentures, etc., are treated as assets, called fictitious assets.

Assets, Liquid: An accounting term referring to those assets of a business concern which are represented by cash or near cash (e.g. money at call and at short notice) trade debtors short term bills, etc.

Assign: To transfer an instrument by endorsement.

Assignee: A person or party or parties to whom an assignment is made. An assignee may also be one to whom a title, interest or right of some kind has been transferred. The person from whom the transfer is received is the assignor.

Assignment: The transfer of rights and/ or obligations by one person to another particularly with reference to a contract, so that under certain strictly defined conditions the second person takes over those rights and obligations and can enforce them, or have them enforced against him.

Associated Company: Often a company has a substantial interest in another to the extent that they might be de facto, if not de jure, partners in some venture, whilst the holding of the former company is not such as to render the latter a subsidiary company as legally defined the relationship needs to be drawn attention to and the latter is referred to, as an associated company.

Association: A group of people or organizations sharing the same interest who wish to be affiliated with each other. This affiliation may be formal or informal; highly organized or loosely structured; worldwide in scope or restricted to a single building.

Assurance: Distinguished from insurance in that assurance does not depend upon a possibility. It is a payment of premium at regular intervals in return for a fixed sum which will become payable at a stated time. The obvious examples are life and endowment assurance. With life assurance, payment becomes due on the death of the life assured. With endowment assurance, payment becomes due at a stated date. It is common to combine both in a life and endowment policy.

At a Premium: At a price which is higher than par value, or higher than normal, because of special circumstances.

At Par: Par value or face value.

Atomistic Test: The separate testing on individual elements of the Design of a new advertisement for Level's jeans the Jingle might be tried out on an audience separately from the look of the male model wearing the jeans, or of the female model looking at the male model who is looking at the jeans, and so on. A 'holistic test' of all these elements together.

Attachment: Prevention of a debtor from disposing of specific money or goods in the hands of third parties, until the debt has been settled.

Attendance: Being present at a meeting or at work; attendance money: payment made to workers who turn up even when there is no work for them to do; attendance time: hours spent at work that are paid for.

Attendant: lower-level employee who is given a measure of responsibility.

Attention: (a) Careful consideration and treatment; (b) receiving the message conveyed by an advertisement a retaining it in the mind (see also AIDA [Advertisement]).

Attitude: Way in which a person views someone or something; **attitude measurement:** or **attitude testing:** ascertaining the way in which a person views something by assigning scores to various factors; **attitude research:** carrying out surveys to discover people's attitudes to products, advertisements or the companies producing them; **attitude scale:** device which measures of tests attitudes by analysing a subject's responses.

Attorney: A person practicing at the Bar. It may also mean someone who holds a power of attorney.

Auction: When goods are offered for sale in public by an auctioneer, the result is auction. Normally goods are sold to the highest bidder. The auctioneer acts as agent for the seller. Sale of goods at an auction may be subject to a reserve price stated by the seller (this should be known to those persons attending the auction, though the price need not be stated). If the hammer is clocked down before the price is reached, the sale can be avoided. It is illegal for a dealer to offer a person a reward not to bid at the sale; penalties can be levied on both parties. A dealer is a person who buys for resale it. An audit may also be said to be such examination of books, accounts and vouchers of a business, as will enable the auditor to report, whether he is satisfied that the balance-sheet is properly drawn up so as to give a true and fair view of the state of affairs of the business and that the profit or loss for the financial period, according to the best of the information and explanations given to him and as shown by the books; and if not, to report in what respect he is not satisfied.

Audience Research: The process of measuring and analysing radio and television audiences. The size and composition of such audiences are basic bread-and-butter information for the marketing manager and Advertising Agency, as are the circulation figures of newspapers and magazines (see Audit Bureau of Circulation). In the USA national television audience measurement is undertaken by A.C. Nielsen, a company that prepares the definitive Nielsen Television Index (NTI) and the Nielsen Audience Compositions (NAC). Surveys of local television audiences are done by American Research Bureau (ARB). It also provides data on radio audiences. Any attempt to measure TV audiences is dogged to point out. Audience research can measure the number of television sets that are actually switched on and the channel that they are switched on to. It cannot take account of the fact that many television sets are switched on but unwatched. Many so-called 'viewers' are asleep, in another room, or arguing with their spouses.

Audit: In general, this term refers to the mechanism within the process of accountability whereby the performance of those in control of the resources of an organization is checked or monitored by or on behalf of interested parties. 1 (a) examination of the books and accounts of a company; independent audit: audit carried out by an independent auditor; internal audit: audit carried out by a department inside the company, (b) detailed examination of something in order to assess it, (c) to examine the books and accounts of a company, (d) a survey of the sales of a product, at different retail outlets, by price, size, and so on. Such surveys are carried out by a number of research companies.

Audit and Accountancy: It is not the duty of the auditor to prepare the accounts. He is mainly concerned with the detail and critical examination of the books and accounts already prepared by accountant (or a group of accountants) who are employees of their organization. Accountancy is the work of an accountant and is confined chiefly to the checking of arithmetical accuracy of the books of accounts, extracting the trial balance, preparing the Profit and Loss Account and Balance Sheet in such a way that one can clearly know the state of affairs of the business. Auditing involves a detailed and critical examination and verification of such accounts and statements by an independent expert for the purpose of ascertaining the true and fair position of a business. Thus, an audit does not entail the preparation of accounts but denotes something much wider in concept-verification of the facts recorded.

Audit Evidence: Information which is obtained by an auditor in arriving at the conclusion on which he bases his opinion on financial statements.

Audit Opinion: Refers to the opinion which is expressed by an auditor upon financial statements.

Audit Report: A report made by an auditor upon financial statements.

Audit Trial: Refers to the impact of a transaction through all the relevant stages of an accounting system.

Auditing: Action of examining the books and accounts. The basic aim of a modern audit is to give an opinion on whether the financial statements drawn up by the directors of a company give a Fair Presentation (in the USA) or a True and Fair View (in the UK). In order to do this the auditors need to check the physical existence and valuation of important assets and to examine the systems of Internal Control to ensure that transactions are likely to have been recorded correctly. If internal control is poor they will ask for it to be improved and increase the amount of checking done on sample transactions. If the control systems look good, relatively small samples of various types of transactions may be checked. The auditors would generally be expected to circularise a sample of some of the debtors to confirm that they exist. They would normally attend the annual stock. They would try to spot and to question unusual items in the books of account or financial statements. The rules for auditing vary from firm to firm, but are to some extent found in Auditing Standards. The directors and auditors will be hoping that the Audit Report can be 'unqualified' as a result of the relevant laws and standards being followed, and the overall impression of a fair view being given. In order to achieve this the auditors will try to persuade the directors to make any necessary changes to the published accounts. Auditing is a very ancient activity. It means 'hearing' (audit is derived from the Latin for 'he hears'). Auditing was thus originally the process whereby the owner heard the account given by his steward of the use of the owner's resources for a period (see Stewardship). By the 19th century the owners of a large company would appointment one of their number to be a specific auditor of the financial statements prepared by the directors whom they had appointed to manage the company. This was partly because the process of auditing had become more complicated as business itself became more complicated. Auditing has become so complex that high standards of training are necessary. Both entry standards and examinations are now of high quality. In Anglo-Saxon countries auditing is carried out by individual or by firms which vary greatly in size. Some firms have hundreds of partners and thousands of staff. However, the audit is always the ultimate responsibility of a member of one of the appropriate professional bodies. (See also Internal Audit.)

Auditing Standards: Refers to the standards to give credibility to the independence, objectivity and technical skill of auditors.

Authorised Share Capital: The maximum amount of a particular type of share in a particular company that may be issued. The amount is laid down in the Company's Memorandum of Association.

Authoritarian Management: A type of management which emphasizes the discipline and control of people and sees little value in consulting them about the job-what you would expect from an authoritarian personality. It is usually contrasted with democratic management.

Authority: The right, inherent in a job or function to use power in the fulfilment of one's responsibilities. Power and authority do not always go together of course. People in position of authority may be ineffective in using power because they do not command the respect or loyalty of their subordinates and people with no official authority may exert a powerful effect on an organization by virtue of their personal qualities, their long experience or the fact that they married the boss's daughter; the term is also used of a public body with statutory power and responsibilities such as a Local Authority.

Authorized Capital: The amount of capital stated in the memorandum of association of a company. A company cannot issue more unless the amount is first increased by the methods prescribed in the Companies Act.

Authorized Share Capital: The maximum amount of Share Capital which a Company Limited by Shares has authority to issue.

Autocratic Leadership Style: It is closely associated with the classical approach to management. This type of leader usually supervises closely and motivates through incentives and fear following carrot and stick policy. To the autocrat, formal authority is the basis for legitimate leadership. The autocratic leader is task-oriented and places little value on showing consideration to subordinates as a leadership technique.

Automate: To arrange a job so that part or all of the decision making and control previously performed by humans is performed by machines.

Automatic Merchandising: The selling of goods through an automat, a method in which only one human hand (the consumer's) is involved. Automatic merchandising is particularly appropriate in locations where there is a heavy round-the-clock stream of human traffic like railway stations, airports, or the lobbies of big office blocks. It is also suited for particular products: cigarettes and soft drinks account for about 70% of all automatic merchandising.

Automation: A term used to describe the employment of machines that reduce or dispense entirely with human communication, computation or control in relation to a job. It is particularly important in information processing and intelligent knowledge-based systems. (a) Typical objectives of automation are increased human productivity, an expanded physical and mental capacity for workers, increased precision or accuracy, and reduced costs. (b) Use of machines to do work with very little supervision by people.

Average: A single number taken to be typical of a series of numbers or, alternatively, that central number in a series around which others revolve or on which they tend to converge, there are various kinds of average. The most common is the arithmetic mean.

Average Collection Period: Refers to the speed at which a company collects its debts. It can be calculated as average, debtors × 365 days Credit sales.

Average Cost: In the context of valuation of stocks (Inventories), average cost (AVCO) is a method of determining the historical cost of any unit of stock or material used is deemed to be the average of the unit costs at which the stock was bought. The average can be worked out at set intervals or each time there is a further purchase. The average cost of producing goods, also referred to as the unit cost. It is customary, in the accounting world, to distinguish average fixed cost from average variable cost. There is also an important difference between the short-term average and the long-term average. The average cost of producing a single batch of goods or of one month's production, may be very different from the average taken over a long period. This distinction is important in price fixing especially under free competition, for although a company cannot fix prices below the long-term average on a permanent basis, it can bring them down to the short-term average and below if any competitive advantage is to be gained. **Average Total Unit Cost:** The total costs divided by the number of units produced at the point under consideration.

Average Cost Pricing: A pricing rule according to which firms add a mark-up into average variable costs (AVC) so as to cover its average total costs. hence price (P) may be put as follows: P = AVC + GPM = AC where GPM denotes the gross profit margin make up and is comprised of an overhead element and a fixed net profit margin thought 'normal' or 'fair' for industry.

Average Fixed Cost: The total of those costs of a business that do not vary with the amount of business done, divided by the number of units produced at the point under consideration.

Average Rate of Tax: (also known as **effective rate of tax**.) Usually taken to mean total income tax payments as a proportion of income. The definition to income normally means the gross income, i.e., before allowances, also refers to the amount which is paid in tax as a percentage of income received during a given period.

Average Revenue (per unit): The total revenue from the sale of given quantity of the same good divided by the number of units sold. Thus average revenue per unit is equal to price per unit. As total revenue will consist of price x quantity (P.X) then we have AR = A.X, X = P.

Average Variable Cost: The total of those costs of a business that vary with the amount of business done, divided by the number of units produced at the point under consideration.

Award: (a) Money which an industrial tribunal decides should be paid by an employer to an employee in settling a dispute (such as a dismissal); basic award: award based on the employee's age, length of service and current salary; compensatory award: award based on what the tribunal considers is just compensation for the employee's loss (b) to decide the amount of money to be given to someone.

Awareness: Being conscious of an advertisement's message or of a brand's existence and qualities.

B

Back duty: Tax which should have been paid in the past by an individual who failed to provide adequate information at the time for a correct assessment to be made of tax payable.

Back Out: To stop being part of a deal or an agreement.

Back-to-Back: (1) A reference to offsetting loans, generally made in one currency in one country against a loan in another currency in another country; it is involving two parties: matching assets and liabilities in opposite directions. (2) Collateral provided by importers to back credit extended to them by exports. In the case of importers in developing countries who are buying from developed countries where they are not known, such collateral could be something like a band deposit held abroad by the importer.

Back-to-Credit: A term used in finance. It is credit given by a finance house acting as go-between for a foreign buyer and a foreign seller. The foreign seller delivers the relevant documents to the finance house, the finance house then issues its own documents in place of them, and the seller's name is not mentioned.

Backdate: To put an earlier date on a cheque or an invoice.

Backload: To make sure that most of the costs of a promotional campaign come in the later stages, so that they can be received (the campaign can then be cut back if the response rate is inadequate this is opposed to frontloading, where most of the costs are incurred in the early stages).

Backup: Supporting or helping; **backup ad:** advertisement designed to accompany editorial material in a publication; **backup copy:** copy of a computer disk to be kept in case the original disk is damaged.

Bad Debts: Amount of Debtors (Accounts Receivable) that have become or are expected to become uncollectable. There are various levels of bad debt. Normally a person or company would hope and expect that a great majority of debts would eventually be paid. However, conservatism requires that all reasonable likely losses be anticipated. Thus, debts which are almost certainly irrecoverable are deducted from the total; debts which are reasonably likely to be uncollectable have a specific provision (in the UK) or allowance (in the USA) made against the remaining debts on previous experience with unexpected bad debts. In each of the three cases there will be an expense charged against income, and a reduction in the figure for debtors or accounts receivable shown on the Balance Sheet.

Bait: Article which is sold at a loss to attract customers.

Balance: 1 (a) amount in an account which makes the total debits and credits equal; credit balance: balance in an account showing that more money has been received than is owed; debit balance: balance in an account showing that more money is owed than has been received; balance in hand; cash held to pay small debts; balance brought down: amount entered in an account at the end of a period to balance income and expenditure; balance forward or balance carried forward: amount entered in an account at the end of a period to balance the expenditure and income which is then taken forward start the new period (b) rest of an amount owed; balance due to us: amount owed to us which is due to be paid.

Balance of Payments: Refers to the relation between the payments of all kinds made from one country to the rest of the world and its receipts from all other countries, over a period.

Balance of Trade: Refers to the relationship between the values of a country's imports and exports, i.e. the 'visible' balance. **Adverse Balance of trade:** Situation where a country imports more than its exports.

Balance Sheet: A snapshot of the accounting records of Assets, Liabilities and Capital of a business at a particular moment, most obviously the accounting year end. The balance sheet is the longest-established of the main financial statements produced by a business. As its name suggests, it is a sheet of the balances from the Double Entry System at a particular time. It is important to note that it is probably not an indication of what the business's items of value are recognised by accountants as assets, and because the Asset Valuation methods used are normally based on past costs rather than on present market values. Initially the balance sheet was not designed as a statement of worth at all; it was merely a mechanical by-product of the periodical closing of books in the double entry system; it is balances because the double-entry system creates equal totals of debits and credits. The worth of a business was more sensible calculated by taking a quite separate inventory of all the assets and liabilities at a particular date. Annual balance sheets are compulsory requirements of Company Law and the Securities and Exchange Commission. Before the 1981 Companies Act in the UK (and still in some other English-speaking countries) formats and terminology varied substantially. In the USA many balance sheets use an 'account format' with assets on the left and capital and liabilities on the right. The Current Assets are shown above the Fixed Assets. Even the title of the balance sheet may be expressed differently; for example, 'statement of financial position'. In the UK, account form balance sheets were the norm until the second half of the 20th century and are still used by partnerships and sole traders. Unlike US and continental European balance sheets, the assets were on the right and the capital and liabilities on the left. However, long before the 1981 Companies Act, large companies in the UK had taken to using a statement (or vertical) format. This allows the presentation of Net Current Assets (or working capital), and avoids the confusion that undistributed profit might appear to be a liability. UK Company Law (now the 1985 Companies Act) sets out two balance sheet formats and allows companies to choose, although they must be consistent, between them. The other format has very similar heading but is in account form, with the assets on the left, starting with fixed assets. The heading further level of subheadings which must either be shown on the balance sheet or, where clearer, in the notes to the balance sheet. The notes will also include other compulsory disclosures connected amounts of Depreciation (See also Capital Commitments and Contingent Liabilities).

Banded Pack: A sales promotion device similar to a quantity discount. Two or more items of the same product are bound together as a single pack; they are then offered for sale at a price that is less than the combined price of the items sold singly. Banded packs include familiar offers like "Three for the price of two", or "Buy two and get a third free". They are frequently used for selling items such as bars of soap or toothpaste. But even airlines occasionally sell banded packs: 'fly first-class to Miami and bring a friend for free'.

Banding: A way of organizing a salary structure where a series of different levels are first established into which jobs are then classified by level, or band rather then fixing a different rate of pay for each job individually.

Bank: An institution that deals in money and (most significantly) creates money by making loans that do not have to be rapid until some future date. Because of this function, governments have always kept a close eye on their banks. There are many types of bank and the main differences among them is the amount of emphasis that they place on various fundamental banking services. These include the following: (a) Collecting deposits from savers and paying interest on those deposits (the cost of having the use of the money over time). (b) Granting loans to borrowers who seem likely to make good use of them. This is what banks do in order to earn enough interest to pay their depositors. (c) Money transmission. A service which enables customers of one bank to transfer funds directly from their account to the account of somebody else at another bank. This service is provided by means of things like a Cheque, Standing Order and Direct Debit. (d) Advisory services. In particular, advising companies on how and where to raise new Capital, and then arranging for the capital to be raised. (e) Lending their good name to help customers that they trust. This is fundamental to trade finance. An exporter gives Credit to an importer because the importer's bank gives it word to the exporter's bank that payment will be forthcoming. The two banks trust each other; if the importer and exporter did too they would not need the banks. Providing services to other banks in order, for example, for them to clear funds among themselves. This is a principal function of central banks. The first three of these services are fundamental to the business of commercial banks; the fourth and fifth are fee-earning services that are at the heart of the business of merchant banks.

Bank Account: Account which a customer has with a bank, where the customer can deposit and withdraw money.

Bank Advance: An amount lent by a bank to its customer either as a bank loan or an overdraft.

Bank Balance: State of a bank account at any particular time.

Bank Bill: A bill of exchange issued or accepted by a bank.

Bank Book: Book, given by a bank, which shows money which you deposit or withdraw from our savings account.

Bank Charges: These are the charges made by a bank to the customer who maintains a current accounts at that bank.

Bank Credit: A written promise by a bank that an organization or person may borrow up to a specified amount.

Bank Deposits: The funds deposited in bank accounts. In reality they have been simply records of indebtedness of a bank to the depositor, and they arise from the character of banks as financial intermediaries.

Bank Draft: This has the same relation to a cheque as a bank bill has to a trade bill. Bank drafts are basically cheques drawn on a particular bank and obtained from that bank by a debtor for the payment of a debt where the creditor will not accept the debtor's personal cheques or the debtor does not have a bank account.

Bank Holiday: A particular weekday when banks are closed.

Bank Loan: Any advance by a bank, but there is a distinction in bank lending between overdraft terms and loan term. A bank advance specifically in the form of a loan gets credited in full to the borrower's account at the outset and the interest liability might be a fixed sum calculated on the initial loan, and its duration. In some cases, e.g. personal and term loans, there occurs provision for repayment by regular instalments.

Bank Note: Refers to a form of currency issued by a bank, and in essence a 'negotiable' evidence of the bank's indebtedness to the value of the note.

Bank Overdraft: Short term facilities to withdraw more money out of a bank account which contains less than the amount of withdrawal. This enables customers to overdraw within agreed limits and at any time. The bank will charge interest on excess drawings but it will be charged on a day-to-day basis and will not, as with a bank loan be a fixed sum for a stated period. Bank overdraft is granted when the customer has a current account in the bank. Under an overdraft arrangement, a depositor is allowed to draw by a cheque more than the deposited amount to his credit, but up to a specified limit. Interest is charged on the exact amount overdrawn by the customer. The rate of interest on it is always higher than that charged on the loans. This facility is given by banks on the security of some assets or on the personal security of the customer.

Bank Reconciliation: As at any particular time cheques, etc. issued or received, may not be banked, the balance shown on a bank statement at a particular date will not necessarily agree with the balance shown at that date in the cash book. It is therefore necessary, in order to prove that the records have been properly kept, to prepare a bank reconciliation. This begins with the balance in the cash book and then details the cheques issued but not banked, and the monies received but not banked. The former will be added and the latter deducted after any other necessary adjustment for direct bank debits or credits the resultant balance should be the same as that on the bank statement.

Bank Statement: It is extract of the customer's account from the point of view of the bank and in principle should disclose a balance equal and opposite to that shown in the customer's cash at bank account in his own ledger at the date stated.

Banker: Person who is in an **important:** position in a bank; **banker's bill:** or **bank bill:** order by one bank telling another bank (usually in another country) to pay money to someone; **banker's order:** order written by a customer asking a bank to make a regular payment.

Banker's Cheque: A cheque drawn by one bank on another either for clearing purposes or for transferring customers money.

Banker's Draft: An order from a buyer or importer to its bank instructing it to make a payment to the seller or exporter's bank. The draft is sent to the seller, which present it to its bank for payment. The seller's bank in turn presents it to the buyer's bank for reimbursement.

Banking Finance: Banks give financial help to the industries in the following ways: (a) advancing against tangible marketable securities, lodged or pledged with the bank, (b) advances against the personal credit of the borrower only.

Banking System: Refers to a network of commercial banks coordinated, influenced and controlled by statutory regulation and a central bank.

Bankruptcy: Bankruptcy is a situation in which debtors are not only insolvent (i.e., unable to pay debts as and when they become due) but have made it clear that they are unable to do so and do not expect to pay their debts in full. They will then, either by their own petition or by that of a third party, be adjudged legally bankrupt by the court. A bankrupt's property passes into the hands of a trustee in bankruptcy who is authorised to divide it among the creditors.

Bar Chart: Chart where values or quantities are shown as thick columns of different heights set on a base line, the different lengths expressing the quantity of the item or unit.

Bargain: (a) Agreement on the price of something; **to drive a hard bargain:** to sell only at terms which are favourable to yourself; **strike a hard bargain:** to agree a deal which is favourable to you; **its a bad bargain:** it's not worth the price (b): thing which is cheaper than usual; **bargain hunter:** person who looks for cheap deals (c): sale of one lot of shares on the number of deals made on the Stock Exchange during a day.

Bargaining: A term used in industrial relations to describe negotiations between two parties, usually employers and employees or their representatives, to achieve a settlement regarding wages and conditions of employment: the kind of behaviour studied in various areas of social psychology, especially game theory, where people with different interests try to influence each other in order to improve their transacting business on the stock exchange. **(free) collective bargaining:** negotiations between employers and employee's representatives over wage increases and conditions; **bargaining power:** strength of one person or group when discussing prices or wage settlements; **bargaining position:** statement of position by one group during negotiations.

Barriers to Communication: There are many obstacles in communication that must be overcome and the conditions that must be met before the communication problems find a more general solution. An initial barrier to effective communication in organizations is the plain fact that many organizations really do not expect substantial two-way communication.

Barter: (1) Paying for goods with other goods or services. Batter is at least as old as the Asian silk routes, and often just as devious. It enjoyed a renaissance with the opening up of the former Soviet Union and eastern Europe, regions with a huge demand for imports (particularly of capital goods) but with little foreign currency to pay for them. Financial institutions are not too keen on barter since it threatens greatly to reduce the need for their services. Some financial institutions, however, have decided that if you cannot beat 'em, join 'em. They have set up specialist barter departments to organize and service the complicated deals that are increasingly being put together. (2) The direct exchange of commodities or services by way of trade, without the use of an intermediate and neutral currency such as coin, promissory notes, or bills or exchange. Barter is the most primitive manner of trading, but, in certain circumstances, the most satisfactory.

Base-pay technique: It provides for minimum compensation for a particular job and is a type of continuous reinforcement schedule. Pay by the hour for workers and the base salary for many are examples.

Base Rate: The minimum rate of interest that a bank will demand on money loaned, rather than the actual rate, which will be fixed according to normal market pressures and the element of risk involved.

Basic (a): normal; **basic discount:** normal discount without extra percentage; **settlement; basic price:** or **basic rate:** price of a product or service that does not include any extras; (b): most important; **basic commodities:** ordinary farm produces, corn, rice, sugar, etc.; (c): simple or from which everything starts.

Basic Rate: The minimum wage rate for a job excluding any allowances such as overtime premium or bonus. Used as a nominal rate from which other rates (e.g., overtime rates) are calculated. Also called 'base rate' or 'basic wage rate'. It is also the minimum wage rate for a job agreed in a national agreement but subject to local increase.

Batch Costing: Process or activity of allocating costs to a batch or identical production, treated as a single unit.

Batch Processing: The grouping and (manual and/or computer) processing of similar data in a single operational sequence.

Batch Production: Productive activity, of which the output over a period of time, consists of numerous small batches of different products and in which any production facility is involved, at different times, in work connected with various products.

Bayesian Decision Theory: Segmentation or division of the market according to customers' buying habits and usage of a product.

Bearer Securities (Bearer Bonds): Documents of title, to stocks, shares, debentures, etc. transferable by hand being made out to bearer and not to a named person.

Bearer Security: A bond or share certificate that is not registered in the name of its owner. Whoever holds the certificate (or bears it) can collect the interest or dividend due, usually by detaching a coupon. A bearer security can be bought or sold without being endorsed; it is as liquid as cash, and equally vulnerable to theft. A eurobond is a bearer bond. Bearer bonds have the great advantage of being more easily kept out of the tax authorities' eye than normal registered securities.

Beggar-my-Neighbour Policies: The economic measures which are taken by a country to improve its domestic, economic conditions, normally to reduce unemployment, and which have adverse effects on other economics.

Below-the-Line: (a) Any promotional activity other than advertising in the media used to be described as below-the-line. But with the popularity of integrated communication the distinction between what is 'above' and what is 'below' is becoming increasingly blurred. (See Above-the-Line). (b) Refers to that part of the profit and loss account (income statement) below the measure of earnings on which Earnings Per Share (EPS) is based. The line in question is that showing the Net Profit after tax in a Profit and Loss Account (in the UK) or the Net Income in an Income Statement (in the USA). (See Above-the-Line).

Below-the-Line Advertising: This is a form of sale promotion which use outlets such as direct mail, special discounts and point-of-sail offers as opposed to the mass media used in above-the-line advertising.

Benchmark: Point or-level which is important, and can be used as a reference when making evaluations or assessments.

Benchmarking: The process of comparing work and service methods against the best practices and outcomes for the purpose of identifying changes that will result in higher-quality output.

Benefit: Profit or gain in terms of monetary/non-monetary advantage. **Benefit Segmentation:** Division of a market into segments according to the types of benefit obtained by the customer from a product (such as case of availability, light weights, etc.); **fringe benefits:** Extra items given by a company to workers in addition to their salaries (such as company cars, private health insurance, etc.).

Benefit-in-Kind: Benefits other than money received by employees by reason of their employers cannot force employees to take wages in kind. May be given in addition to wages and used as incentives.

Beta: Refers to a measure of the Systematic Risk of a company's shares, i.e., the sensitivity of the share price of movements in the market. A share having a beta of 1.0 (a 'neutral' share) will on average move in line with the market. A share with a beta greater than 1.0 (an 'aggressive' share) will on average go up faster in a Bull market and down faster in Bear market. A share having a beta of less than 1.0 (a 'defensive' share) will on average fluctuate less than the market as a whole Betas change over time but most are reasonably stationary.

Bias: Prejudice or subjective feeling on the part of a researcher that distorts the results of a survey or test.

Bid (a) Offer to buy something at a certain price; **to make a bid for something:** to offer to buy something; **to make a cash bid:** to offer to pay cash for something; **to put in a bid for something:** or **to enter a bid for something:** to offer (usually in writing) to buy something; (at an auction) **opening bid:** first bid; **closing bid:** last bid at an auction or the bid which is successful (b) offer to do stated work at a certain price; US offer to sell something at a stated price; (c): **takeover bid:** offer to buy all or a majority of the shares in a company so as to control it; **the company rejected the takeover bid:** the directors recommended that the shareholders should not accept it; **to bid for something:** to offer to buy something.

Bid Price: A term associated with unit trusts. Units are quoted at two prices: the bid price, which is the sum that the management company will pay for units held by third parties; and the offer price, which is the figure at which they will sell. The offer price is higher than the bid price so that when people buy units they must, if they are not to lose on the investment, retain them until they have risen to a point above the bid price. For this reason unit trusts are seen as a long-term rather than a short-term investment.

Big Bang: What occurs on the day when a significant financial market removes a plethora of old-fashioned rules and regulations. The most famous Big Bang occurred at the London Stock Exchange (renamed the International Stock Exchange) on October 27th 1986. From that date: Stockbrokers were obliged to abandon their long-standing fixed scale of commission; for the first time foreigners were allowed to own a majority stake in a UK broker; and dual capacity was introduced, allowing brokers to be market makers and vice versa. The biggest bang on the day, however, came from the stock exchange's newly computerised dealing and quotations system which collapsed under the strain. The US equivalent was called May-day and took place on May 1st 1975, the day on which minimum commissions were abolished on the New York Stock Exchange.

Bilateral Trade: Trade between two countries, strictly interpreted the value of the goods and services exported by country A to country B must be exactly matched by the value of the exports from country B to country A.

Bill: A short-term debt instrument which is in the form of a document ordering the drawee (i.e. the debtor) to pay the drawer (the creditor) a stated sum at a specified date, or 'at sight' which means on demand. As used in commerce and finance, a generic term identifying a variety of documents having to do with currency, the shipment of goods and the collection of debts. The term is used as an abbreviation of a bill of exchange or as synonymous with a draft often in association with one of a number of qualifying or descriptive objectives. Thus acceptance bill is a bill of exchange adopted for eventual payment: **advance bill**, one drawn in advance of a shipment: **bankable bill**, one easily discounted: **banker's bill**, one drawn on a bank: **blank bill**, one with the name of the creditor omitted: **clear bill**, one with no documents attached: **credit bill**, one drawn against credit already established by the debtor: **demand bill**, one payable at sight: **documentary bill**, one having documents attached: **domestic bill**, one drawn and payable in the same country: **finance bill**, one drawn by a bank in one country on a bank in another country usually against securities held by the latter bank, and good for a relatively long period of time: **foreign bill**, one drawn in one country and payable in another: **inland bill**, one drawn in one country and payable in the same country: **investment bill**, one purchased at discount for the interest it will yield at maturity: **payment bill**, one presented for payment rather than for acceptance: **prime bill**, one which is an excellent credit risk: **sight bill**, same as demand bill: **time bill**, one payable at a future date. 1 (a): written list of charges to be paid; **to foot the bill:** to pay the costs (b): list of charges in a restaurant; (c): written paper promising to pay money; **bill of exchange:** document which tells a bank to pay a person (usually used in payments in foreign currency); **accommodation bill:** bill of exchange which the person signs in order to help someone raise a loan; **bank bill:** bill of exchange endorsed by a bank; **demand bill:** bill of exchange which must be paid when payment is asked for; **to accept a bill:** to sign a bill of exchange to show that you promise to pay it; **to discount a bill:** to buy at a lower price than that written; **bills payable:** bills which a debtor will have to pay; **bills receivable:** bills held by a creditor awaiting payment (d) **bill of entry:** written details of goods to go through customs (e) **bill of sale:** document which the seller gives to the buyer to show that the sale has taken place (f): draft of a new.

Bill Discounting: The practice of obtaining money on the security of book debts, i.e., money to be received. A company which finds that it has too much working capital tied up in book debts may sell these debts to a finance company. This is known as bill discounting.

Bill of Exchange: This is defined officially as an unconditional order in writing, addressed by one person to another, signed by the person giving it, requiring the person to whom it is addressed to pay on demand, or at a fixed or determinable future time, a sum certain in money to or to the order of, a specified person, or to the bearer; Bills of exchange involve the payment of money only.

Bill of Lading: A document used in foreign trade similar in some respects to a delivery note. It sets out the name and address of the customer, the nature of the goods, etc. In carriage by sea there are three copies: one retained by the seller, one given to the master of the ship, one forwarded to the buyer or is agent. The buyer obtains the goods by presenting his copy to the master of the ship. The bill is usually accompanied by a bill of exchange drawn upon the purchaser.

Billing: A measure of the size of an advertising agency. Generally, advertising agencies are paid a percentage to the amount that is costs to put their clients' advertisements in the media. This cost is called the advertiser's 'billing' and gives a rough guide to the amount of business that an agency is doing.

Bills Payable: An accounting term for bill of exchange due for payment at sometime in the future. They will be included with current liabilities.

Bills Receivable: An accounting term for bills of exchange held and due to be paid to the holder at sometime in the future. They will be included with current assets.

Bin Card: A card kept in a storehouse recording the actual quantity of material in a bin or other receptacle. The card is marked each time items are purchased or requisitioned.

Biodegradable: The ability of a product to be broken down 'naturally', that is by the forces of nature. Leave a biodegradable product in the ground for sometime and it will not in any recognisable form. Paper, bananas and cats are all biodegradable. In today's environmentally conscious marketing, biodegradable is a valuable attribute of a brand. Consumers feel good about buying biodegradable packaging. But some products sold as biodegradable have been found to cause considerable harm to the environment (as they rot).

Biofeedback: The feedback of information to individuals about their biological functions. Using biofeedback it is possible for people to gain a certain amount of control of such functions as heart rate, blood pressure and brain waves through a form of conditioning process.

Biotechnology: The use of biologically-based processes in existing manufacturing and service industries.

Black: be in the black: have money in one's bank account, in black and white: in writing or in print, blackmail: demanding money from someone by threatening to reveal information which could harm him, blackguard: dishonourable person.

Black Economy: Unofficial economic activity which, although technically contributing to the gross national product, is not contained within national statistics. It is for the most part conducted on a cash or barter basis and, although generating a substantial portion of the unofficial national income the fact that it is not formally recorded in any accounting records takes it out of the tax net. It is the very fact that income earned within the black economy escapes taxation that renders it attractive to those working within.

Black Market: An illegal trade in goods or services the demand for which has outstripped the officially available supply. It is caused by the imposition of official measures designed to cope with the shortfall, like rationing or price controls.

Blackleg: A derogatory term (origin unknown) used to describe someone who does not support the industrial action of his fellow workers and continues to work during a strike or replaces a striking worker.

Blacklist: A list of people of organization against whom some kind of discrimination will be practiced, usually for political reason.

Blank Cheque: A cheque where no sum of money is stated. The holder can fill in the amount himself. Blank cheques are often used in transactions where the price of the goods to be purchases is not known. The buyer may send a blank cheque but writes, Not to exceed Rs. ...... on it. The bank will usually respect this instruction.

Blank Transfer: A blank transfer of shares. Shares are transferred by completion of a transfer form. Where the name of the transferee is left blank, this is known as a blank transfer.

Blanket Agreement: agreement which covers many items; **blanket branding:** giving a whole group or line of products the same brand name; **blanket coverage:** advertising to the general public with no particular target audience in mind; **blanket insurance:** insurance which covers various items (such as a house and its contents); **blanket refusal:** refusal to accept anything although many different items have been suggested.

Blanket Policy: An insurance term for a policy which covers many different types of risk. For instance property may be insured against fire, theft, etc.

Blind Test: A market-research technique in which two unidentified products are sampled by consumers who indicate their preference. Blind testing is often used in new product research to test the product against an established brand. Because brand names and packing heavily influence consumer's perception of products, blind testing is the only way to measure factors such as taste, smell and texture on a comparative basis. For example, in some blind tests unlabelled Australian wines have been preferred to unlabelled French wines by people who in general consider French wines to be superior than Australian. Blind testing is a familiar feature of television commercials, in which it has by law to be genuine. Pepsi-Cola ran a series of commercials called the Pepsi Challenge, in which it was claimed that a majority of people preferred Pepsi to Coca-Cola. These tests helped Pepsi to raise its profile in markets where Coke is synonymous with Cola. But the fact of the matter is that neither Cola nor anything else is sold under blind-test conditions.

Blister Pack: A form of packaging in which products are wrapped in clear plastic (or with a clear transparent 'window') so that consumers can properly see what they are buying before they buy it.

Blocked Account: A bank account from which monies cannot be drawn except in defined circumstances.

Blue Chip: A listed company which because of its large size, long history of profitable trading and good management, commands a high level of confidence among stock market investors. Also an ordinary share of such a company. (High value chips of gambling-e.g. in poker are coloured blue.) The stock of a first-rate industrial company, which is one with a long record of continuous and steadily rising profit, and of uninterrupted dividend payments.

Blue Chip Investment: An investment which, though not gilt-edged, is considered to be safe, so that there is little likelihood of losing capital or income. It can be generally in the form of well-known companies.

Blue Collar: Of relating to, or performing manual work with no (or very few) supervisory responsibilities. (Form the traditional blue colour of overalls with white collar.)

Blurb: The short piece of copy that appears on the jacket or inside cover of a book. Hence any short piece of copy that praises something extravagantly.

Board: (a) official group of people; board interview: interview in which a candidate is asked questions by several representatives of an organization (b) official body; arbitration board or arbitration tribunal: group which arbitrates in industrial disputes; (c) group of people who run a trust or a society; (d) GB board of directors: group of directors elected by the shareholders to run a company.

Board Meetings: Meetings of directors.

Board of Directors: The effective management committee of a company limited by shares. In theory the members of the board represent the interests of the shareholders and are appointed by them for that purpose.

Body Language: Communication by people using gestures or movements of the body also known as kinesics.

Bonafide: Literal meaning of the phrase 'In good faith'. It is used in the law of contract, e.g., 'a bonafide purchaser of value'.

Bond: A term widely used to describe fixed-interest securities issued by the state or by local authorities. Bonds may fall into various categories named for convenience 'long', 'medium' or 'short', reflecting the date on which they are redeemable. It is also a deed by which one person (called the 'obligor') promises ('binds' himself) to do or not to do some act in order to benefit a second person (called 'obligee'). A security that has a nominal value and which entitles its holder to payment of interest (calculated as a percentage of the nominal value) by the issuer at regular intervals (typically, twice a year) until the issuer redeems the bond. At redemption the issuer pays the nominal value of the bond to its holder (occasionally more than the nominal value is paid either as a call premium or as a redemption premium) or an Interest bearing instrument issued by governments, corporations and some other organizations, and sold to investors in order to raise capital. Bonds may be bought and sold many times over in the Secondary Market before they are finally redeemed. They are sold at a Discount (or Premium) to their face value, such discount (or premium) reflecting the difference between the (fixed) interest rate. (See also Bearer Security and Junk Bond)

Bond Note: A term used in shipping with reference to export of goods.

Dutiable goods must be put in bond. A bond note is issued indicating that the necessary formalities have been observed. The note acts as authority for recovering the goods from the warehouse and exporting them.

Bonus Issue: An issue of shares to existing shareholders without further payment on their part. Also termed as a scrip issue or a capitalization issue.

Bonus Share: Shares of a company that are wholly or partly paid up by capitalization of realized or unrealized profits or by a transfer from capital redemption reserve to share capital account.

Bonus Shares: Shares issued to existing shareholders of a company in proportion to their shareholdings. Such shares are free, as their name suggests; no cash changes hands. The purpose is usually to lower the share price, perhaps for the psychological reason that it seems high in relation to other shares or has gone into two digits. If a one-for-one issue is made the result would be a doubling of shares. Since nothing else about the company has changed, the share price ought to halve; but sometimes it falls less, perhaps because favourable attention is drawn to the company. Accounting for the issue is straightforward; reserves of various kinds can be relabelled 'share capital' to the total value of the par value of the shares. Bonus issues are sometimes called scrip issues or capitalization issue (because reserves are being capitalized).

Book Keeping: The collecting, compiling, and retaining an organization's financial information in an organized fashion. Book keeping precedes the preparation of financial statements. It is a component of accounting.

Book Value: The value of a company's assets as expressed in its balance sheet. This can be less than the assets' market value since accounting convention may dictate that the assets be included in the accounts at their purchase price, inflation alone may well have ensured that this is less than the assets' current market value.

Books of Account: Those books in which the transactions of a business are recorded. The term is often prefaced by the word 'proper', proper books of account are those that the law demands shall be kept by certain categories of businesses.

Boom: The point in the trade cycle where the upward movement is complete, prices and employment being at their maximum.

Boost: (a) Help to increase; (b) to make something increase.

Borrow: To take money from someone for a time, possibly paying interest for it, and repaying it at the end of the period; **borrower:** person who borrows.

Borrowing: (a) action of borrowing money; borrowing power: amount of money which a company can borrow (b) borrowings: money borrowed.

Boss: Informal employer or person in charge of a company or an office.

Bottleneck: Position when business activity is slowed down because of section of the operation cannot cops with the amount of work.

Bounded rationality: It imposes limits on a decision, such as that it should be economical or logistically practical. These limits serve as a screening device, eliminating some of the alternatives. The manager must choose from the options that have filtered through the restrictions. The decision maker simply selects the best alternative, given various specifications that must be met.

Boycott: (a) refusal to duty or to deal in certain products; (b) to refuse to buy or to deal in a certain product.

Brainstorming: Intensive discussion in small groups as a way of producing new ideas of solutions to problems, from the spontaneous exchanges between people taking part.

Brand: According to Philip Kotler, author of Marketing Management, the world's standard marketing textbook, a brand is: A name, term, symbol or design (or a combination of them) which is intended to signify the goods or services of one seller or group of sellers and to differentiate them from those of competitors. When marketed successfully a brand becomes a powerful force in the market place; Hoover, Mars, Kleenex, Levi, for example, instantly identify products familiar to everyone. In markets where famous brands exist, competitors are always at a disadvantage. Brands may be used in different ways. Family brands are product names which all contain the name of the company: Heinz Tomato Ketchup, Heinz Baked Beans, and so on; Cadbury's Fruit and Nut, Cadbury's Smash, and so on. Individual brands stand alone. Procter & Gamble's products all carry individual brand names, for instance, Ariel, Flash, Pampers. Some companies use a different brand name for a different Product Line; Sears, Roebuck, for example, sells appliances under the brand name Kenmore and tools under the brand name Craftsman. Sometimes the brand name is attached to a company or divisional name. This is known as an umbrella brand, and is used to endorse the product while at the same time allowing it to develop its own brand personality. Brands can be people as well as things. The word 'brand' has been around for a long time. It is derived from an old Norse word *brandr* which means to burn; hence the 'branding' of livestock or make of product, which can be recognized by a name or by a design; **brand awareness:** consciousness by the public of a brand's existence and qualities; **brand image:** ideas which the public associate with a particular brand; **brand leader:** brand with the largest market share; **brand loyalty:** inclination of the customer to keep on buying the same brand; **brand manager:** manager or executive responsible for the marketing of a particular brand; **brand name:** name of a brand; **brand positioning:** acquiring a position for a brand in a market, so that it is recognizable to the public; **brand recognition:** being able to recognize or identify a brand on sight; **brand switching:** changing from buying one brand to another, showing little brand loyalty; **brand X:** the anonymous brand which is used on TV commercials as a comparison to the named brand being advertised; **own brand:** products which are specially packed for a store and carry its name on the label.

Brand Image: The aura behind a particular Brand. In his books World Class Brands Chris Macrae developed a typology of brands. In it there are six main categories: (a) **The ritual brand**. Associated with special occasions, such as champagne for a wedding cranberry sauce for a Thanks giving dinner. (b) **The symbol brand:** For example, the famous Lacoste alligator or Louis Vuitton's LV monogram. The symbol is the value; what it is attached to is almost irrelevant. (c) **The 'heritage of good' brand**. This is usually the first brand to establish itself as providing specific benefits: Kellogg's for a 'bright start to the day'; The Body Shop for 'how to have an environmentally clean conscience, painless feet and no wrinkles'. (d) **The aloof snob brand**. Ferraris, American Express, Platinum Cards, and so on. For the rich who, despite what Scott Fitzgerald said, still feel the need to emphasise that they are different. (e) **Belonging brands:** These gives the consumer a feeling of belonging to a group. For example, Marlboro (although when Marlboro was first launched they were all smart city women); or wearers of Benetton clothes, who are all members of a multiracial, multicoloured global village. (f) **The legend**. For example, the Levi 501 jean (the first ever made by the company) or the Porsche Carrera, in an early model of which James Dean, the moody-young-man 'brand' of the 1950s, crashed and died.

Brand Loyalty: The aim of all 'brand managers' to secure the sustained loyalty of consumers to their particular product. Brand loyalty comes about through consumers' continuing satisfaction with the product, and through effective and often heavy promotion. Strong brand loyalty reduces the impact of advertising by competitive brands, and discourages brand switching.

Brand Management: Also known as product management. A management system developed in the 1930s by Procter & Gamble, it has grown into a widely accepted method of managing individual brands in multiproduct companies. A brand manager is given responsibility for a single brand, and becomes that product's champion and enthusiast within the company. He or she sets the brand's marketing objectives (such as target market identification, advertising, sales promotion, packaging, and so on), schedules and coordinates all the marketing activities, and reports to the product group management. Most companies using this P&G system of brand management treat the brand manager's domain as a profit centre. Brand management is an ideal training ground for future marketing directors, and jobs as assistant brand managers are usually in great demand.

Brand Values: A variety of intangible asset which has become of increasing relevance to company balance sheets in recent years. Businesses which develop products bearing a brand name which has become synonymous with the product itself are apt to attribute substantial monetary value to the brand name on the grounds that when the business is sold the value of the brand name is a significant component of any purchase price.

Branded Goods: Goods marketed as proprietary brands, pre-packed by manufacturers, with the name of the product displayed.

Breach: Failure to carry out the terms of an agreement; breach of contract: failing to do something which is in a contract; breach of trust: legal terms of the failure of an employee to carry out duties properly and honestly; breach of warranty: supplying goods which do not meet the standards of the warranty applied to them.

Breach of Warranty of Authority: Where an agent acts outside his actual and apparent authority, the principal is not liable and third party can sue the agent for breach of warranty of authority.

Break: 1 (a) short space of time when you can rest (b) break point: dividing point between one job or element and the next, or between one level established on a job evaluation and the next.

Break Down: (a) to stop working because of mechanical failure; (b) to stop (c) to show all the items in a total list of costs or expenditure.

Break Even: To balance costs and receipts, but not make a profit; **break even analysis:** analysis of fixed and a variable costs and sales to determine at what level of production the break even point will be reached; **break even point:** point at which sales cover costs, but do not show a profit. It is a no profit no loss point.

Break Even Analysis: The costs of

producing a good have been splitted into two main parts. Fixed costs have been those that remain the same for the firm however many goods are produced, i.e., rates, rent, etc. Variable costs vary with the number of items produced, i.e., raw materials for the goods, labour to produce them, etc. From the cost accountant's point of view, the break even sales volume may be defined as that which ensures that all fixed and variable costs are covered, given a particular selling price.

Break Up Value: An alternative to selling a business as a going concern is to sell it piecemeal, each asset separately. The value put on a business or a group of related assets sold in this manner is referred to as the break-up value and, in most instances, this will be the maximum amount realizable on disposal of those assets.

Break-Even Chart: A chart used to give information about the viability of an enterprise and effective in warning of approaching disaster. In its simplest form the figures charted are those of total costs and total revenue. When these totals are equal, a 'break even' point has been reached, i.e., the business is neither making money nor losing it.

Break-Even Point: Refers to the point at which total revenue equals total cost. It can be expressed either in monetary units or in units or product sold.

Break-Even Level of Income: The point at which consumption expenditures have been just equal to income, below this point consumption has been greater than income, that is dis-saving occurs, above this point consumption has been less than income that is saving occurs.

Bribe: A bribe is a payment by which the payer obtains some right, benefit or preference to which he has no legal entitlement and which he would not have obtained but for the payment of the money. It is a criminal offence to accept a bribe.

Bridging Loan: A temporary loan made to 'bridge' the gap between receipt of funds from the buyer and handing them over to the seller. It is particularly common in house or property purchase, where a bank may lend, in the short term. The monies needed by the purchaser to complete the transaction before the main source of funds arrives.

Broad Sheet: Large size of newspaper page (as opposed to tabloid).

Brochure: Publicity booklet.

Broker(a): dealer; **foreign exchange broker:** person who buys and sells foreign currency on behalf of other people; **insurance broker:** person who sells insurance to clients; **media broker:** business which offers companies a media buying service; **ship broker:** person who sells shipping or transport of goods to clients (b) **stock broker:** person who buys or sells shares for clients. An agent who, in the nature of his business, makes contracts in regard to shares, goods or property. He need not carry the goods or documents of ownership. There are also specialized brokers, e.g., in stock exchange, commodity markets, and even insurance or in services. A mercantile agent who, in the nature of his business, makes contracts to goods or property, where he has neither the goods nor the documents of title but brings together buyer and seller for a commission. There are specialized brokers, e.g., insurance brokers and stock brokers, dealing in services rather than goods.

Brokerage: A fixed cost or percentage which is charged by the broker for each act of investment or encashment of bonds and other financial assets.

Brown Goods: Consumer durables that used to be encased in brown veneer, such as old-fashioned radios, televisions in cabinets, and gramophones. brown goods were usually contrasted with white goods. Nowadays white goods are still by and large encased in white, but brown goods are more often wrapped in black, or in shades of grey. Hence the expression 'brown goods' has fallen into disuse.

Buddy System: US on the job training system, where a trainee works with an experienced employee.

Budget 1(a)**:** plan of expected spending and income (usually for one year);**advertising budget:** money planned for spending on advertising; **cash budget:** plan of cash income and expenditure;**overhead budget:** (see overhead) plan of probable overhead costs; **publicity budget:** plan of probable sales (b) **the Budget:** the annual plan of taxes and government spending proposed by a finance minister; **to balance the budget:** to plan income and expenditure so that they balance; (c) **budget department:** cheaper department; **budget prices:** low prices **2:** to plan probable income and expenditure.

Budget Account: An account designed to help individuals make bulky bothersome payments (like telephone or electricity bills) more smoothly. Regular payments into the account allow the account-holder to borrow several times the value of each payment. Sometimes it is overdrawn. The plan, however, is that it should have the same balance at the end of a year as it has at the beginning. (b) An account is the period of two weeks (occasionally three weeks) on the London stock market prior to the settlement date. No security that has been bought within the duration of the preceding account. After deducting holidays, there are 24 accounts within each calendar year. The free credit period represented by the account gives gamblers a chance to dream about making serious gains without putting any investment up-front. They buy shares right at the beginning of an account, hoping to sell at a profit before the day of reckoning, that is, settlement day.

Budget Controller: The head of the committee responsible for budgetary control in an organization.

Budgetary Control: A system of controlling expenditure and income used by the management of a business. Each department in the business forecasts its probable expenditure or income for the coming financial period. These forecasts or budgets are scrutinized and approved at top management level, so that a provisional profit and loss account for the coming year can be drawn up and, if necessary, expenses pruned or sales policies revised.

Budgetary: Referring to a budget; **budgetary policy:** policy of planning income and expenditure.

Budgetary Control: Keeping a check on spending; **budgetary requirement:** spending or income required to meet the budget forecasts.

Buffer Stock: In common parlance this is a stock, usually of raw materials, created and kept in reserve against hard times or unexpected hold-up in normal supplies.

Built-In: Forming part of the system or of a machine; **built-in obsolescence:** method of ensuring continuing sales of a product by making it in such a way that it will soon become obsolete.

Bulk Cargo: A shipping term meaning cargo which can fill the whole space by one commodity.

Bull: On the Stock Exchange the obverse of the bear. Bull speculators buy shares, commodities currencies, etc., forward, i.e., they contract to buy at a price fixed in advance at a future date in the anticipation that when the contract matures the price in the market will have risen. In a period of rising prices they will, therefore, have the advantage of buying at a price lower than that prevailing at the time the contract falls due for completion and will profit accordingly.

Bullet: A loan on which all the principal is repaid in one go at the end of the period of the loan. During the life of the loan borrower pays interest only.

Bullion: Gold and silver of a recognized degree of purity, it may be in various forms, normally gold or silver bars.

Bumping: US (i) lay-off procedure that allows an employee with greater seniority to displace a more junior employee; (ii) situation where a senior employee takes the place of a junior (in a restaurant).

Bunny Bond: A bond where the investor has the option to receive interest in cash or in the form of more of the same bond.

Burnout: It is characterised by emotional exhaustion, depersonalization and diminished personal accomplishment. It is sometimes interchangeably used with 'stress'. (see stress)

Bureaucracy: System of administration where an individual person's responsibilities and powers are strictly defined and processes are strictly followed.

Business (a): work in buying or selling; **business call:** visit to talk to someone on business; **business centre:** part of a town where the main banks, shops and offices are located; **business class:** type of airline travel which is less expensive than first class and more comfortable than tourist class; **business correspondent:** journalist who writes articles on business news for newspapers; **business cycle:** movement of trade from a point of high activity and upwards again in the form of a regular cycle; **business efficiency exhibition:** exhibition which shows products (computers, word processors, etc.) intended to help a business to be more efficient; **business environment:** elements or factors outside a business organization which directly affect it, such as supply of raw materials and product demand; **business games:** games, often run on computers, in which individuals or teams compete to do business in a hypothetical market; **business letter:** letter about commercial matters; **business lunch:** lunch to discuss business matters; **business portfolio analysis:** method of categorizing a firm's products according to their relative competitive position and business growth rate in order to lay the foundations for sound strategic planning; **business publications:** magazines or newspapers which are only concerned with business matters (such as trade journals); **business trip:** trip to discuss business matters with clients; **to be in business:** to be engaged in commercial activities; **to go into business:** to start a commercial firm; **to go out of business:** to stop trading; **on business:** for commercial purposes or as part of one's job; (b): commercial company; **business address:** details of number, street and town where a company is located; **business card:** card showing a businessman's name and the name and address of the company he works for; **business correspondence:** letters concerned with a business; **business equipment:** machines used in an office; **business expansion scheme:** system in Britain where money invested for some years in a new company is free from tax; **business expenses:** money spent on running a business, not on stock or assets; **business hours:** hours during which a shop, factory or office is open for work; **big business:** very large commercial firms **(c):** affairs discussed; **any other business:** item at the end of an agenda, where any matter can be raised.

Business Objectives of: (i) Earning profits (ii) Growth and expansion (iii) Creating markets (iv) Innovations (v) consumer satisfaction and (vi) employees satisfaction.

Business Risk: The risk that firm's profits will decrease because there is a decline in the demand for its product or an increase in the cost of its materials.

Business Schools: These are colleges of higher education that offer graduate and post graduate courses in the various skills and strategies pertinent to effective business management in the contemporary world. In addition to research facilities, these schools offer in depth study of a wide range of business orientated disciplines. These include resource management, corporate financial strategy, performance evaluation and the effective use of all available technological and electronic management-orientated equipment. The extensive range of courses available is geared to current industrial and commercial requirements and leads to a variety of qualifications up to and including Master of Business Administration (MBA). These business schools cater not only for full-time students of business management, but also for senior managers already in positions of responsibility within both the private and public sector.

Business Sector of: Consists of both public sector and private sector undertakings carrying activities in relation to business, 1. Public sector Owned and managed by the state, and Public sector has the objectives: **Social:** (i) Employment (ii) Better Quality (iii) Economic Price (iv) Better standard of living (v) Reducing concentration of wealth and disparities of income. **Human:** (i) Good working conditions (ii) Fair wages (iii) Work with honour (iv) Encouraging creativity and initiative (v) job satisfaction (vi) Growth opportunities. 2. **Private sector:** Business undertakings owned by private individuals are known as 'private sector' or 'private enterprise' as opposed to public sector, where state is the owner. From the point of view of ownership, there are five main forms in which private, commercial or industrial activities may be organized (i) Sole Proprietorship (ii) Joint Hindu Family Business (iii) Partnership (iv) Joint Stock Company (v) Co-operative Societies. 3. **Joint sector:** It is an extension of the concept of mixed economy. Government, private entrepreneur and the public jointly share the ownership, management and control.

Business-to-Business Advertising: Sometimes called industrial advertising. The majority of advertising is directed at individual consumers, but businesses for businesses: manufactures of machine tools or construction equipment do not market their products to individuals; they market them to other companies. Specialist trade journals and trade fairs are very important media for these companies, and for business-to-business advertising in general. (In the USA there are almost three times as many specialist trade journals as consumer magazines.)

Businessman Or Businesswoman: Man or woman engaged in business; **a small businessman:** man who owns a small business.

Buyer (a) Person who buys; **there were no buyers:** no one wanted to buy; **buyer's risk:** risk taken by a buyer when accepting goods or services with no guarantee;**buyer's surplus:** (also called consumer's surplus) difference between what a buyer would be willing to pay for something and what he or she does pay for it in the end;**impulse buyer:** person who buys something when he see it, not because he was planning to buy it; **media buyer:** person in an advertising agency who places advertisements in the media on behalf of clients; **space buyer:** person who buys advertising space in magazines and newspapers;**time buyer:** person who buys advertising time on radio or TV, (b) person who buys a certain type of goods wholesale for a large store to stock and sell; **head buyer:** most important buyer in a store;

Buyer's Market: Always contrasted with seller's market. Any market in which supply exceed demand. Such a market can arise either because the supply of a product has been increased by a number of new entrants into the market; or because the demand for the product has declined as recession or changing consumer tastes have hit the market. Either way, buyers will force down prices in such a market until supply is cut by a reduction in the number of suppliers.

By-Product: A product made by a manufacturer or processor on a much smaller scale than another product of his but using the same materials and initially at least, with the same operations or processes.

C

Call: A demand made by a company on a shareholder for payment for shares that have been issued as partly paid.

Call In: (a) to visit (b) to telephone to make contact (c) to ask for debt to be paid.

Call Money: Money at call and at short notice.

Call Option: A contract to buy a certain number of shares at a stated price (the strike price) within a specified period of time. A call option will be exercised when the spot price goes above the strike price. If it is not exercised, the option expires at the end of the specified period of time.

Call-Back Pay: Compensation given to a worker who has been called back to work after completing a normal working shift.

Called-Up Share Capital: Refers to the amount of the Issued Share Capital which has been called up, i.e., the amounts the shareholders have been asked to pay to date.

Called-Up Capital: That proportion of the issued share capital of a company that has actually been called up.

Calls: A term used in company law for demands made by a company that members should pay certain sums due on the shares they hold.

Camel: An acronym for the five things that Bank supervisors look for most keenly when examining a bank.(a) Capital adequacy.(b)Asset quality. (c) Management quality. (d) Earnings. (e) Liquidity.

Campaign: Series of coordinated activities to reach an objective; **sales campaign:** co-ordinated activities to achieve higher sales; **publicity campaign** or **advertising:** coordinated publicity or advertising drive to sell a product.

Cancel: (a) to stop something which has been agreed or planned.

Cancellation: Stopping something which has been agreed or planned; cancellation clause: clause in a contract which states the terms on which the contract may be cancelled.

Candidate: Person who applies or is considered suitable for a job or for training course.

Cannibalization: When increased sales of one brand result in decreased sales of another within the same product line. Cannibalization is a danger when products or brands in a company's brand managers becomes too intense (see branded management). There is always a risk of cannibalization when a company extends a product line. For example, when powder-based detergents were first marketed in liquid form there was a danger that the extension brand (the liquid detergent) would reduce sales of the original powdered brand to such an extent that the combined sales (of powder and liquid) were less than the sales of the original powder on its own.

Capable: Able or clever enough to do something.

Capacity: (a) Amount which can be produce or amount of work which can be done (b) amount of apace.

Capital : A word used somewhat loosely in the business world, in general, and even by accountants. It may mean the total of a company's finance, including all share capital, past profits, long-term loans and current liabilities. Such an aggregation might be called total capital. It would, of course, equal total assets. However, capital might also be used to mean the long-term finance; that is, the above total less current liabilities. Yet another meaning might be all the elements of capital belonging to shareholders (Shareholders' Equity); or even just the amount of money contributed in the past by the shareholders. Unfortunately the reader will have to determine the exact meaning by the context. At least you have been warned. The expression 'capital employed' is also seen on balance sheets and in profitability ratios. It tends to mean the total long-term capital, although such an aggregate might be called 'net capital employed' because it does not include current liabilities. (a): money, property and assets used in a business; **a company with 10,000 capital:** or: **with a capital of 10,000; authorized capital:** maximum capital which is permitted by a company's articles of association; **capital account:** account of dealings (money invested in the company, or taken out of the company) by the owners of a company; **capital bonus:** bonus payment by an insurance company which is produced by capital gain; **capital equipment:** equipment which a factory or office uses to work; **capital expenditure:** or **investment:** or **outlay:** money spent on fixed assets (property, machines, furniture); **capital levy:** tax of the value of a person's property and possessions; **capital structure of a company:** way in which a company's capital is set up; **capital transfer tax:** tax on gifts or bequests of money or property; **circulating capital:** capital in the form of raw materials, finished products and work in progress required for a company to carry on its business; **equity capital:** amount of a company's capital which is owned by the shareholders; **fixed capital:** capital in the form of buildings and machinery; **issued capital:** amount of capital issued as shares to the shareholders; **paid-up capital:** amount of money paid for the issued capital shares; **reserved capital:** part of share capital which can be used only when a company is woundup; **risk capital:** or **venture capital:** capital for investment which may easily be lost in risky projects; **share capital:** the sum total of the nominal value of shares of a company is called its share capital; **working capital:** capital in cash and stocks needed for a company to be able to work when refers to gross working capital, it means total of Current Assets (See Current Asset) and when it relates to net working capital it means the excess of current assets over current liabilities (see Current Liabilities) (b) money for investment;**flight of capital:** rapid movement of capital out of one country because of lack of confidence in that country's economic future.

Capital Allowances: Refer to the deductions from gross business profits for the purpose of covering the depreciation of assets which are allowed by the tax authorities when calculating taxable income.

Capital Asset Pricing Model (CAPM): Refers to a model of the securities market which is based on portfolio analysis. According to the CAPM the expected return in equilibrium on any risky asset in a perfect capital market is given by: $R_j = i + (R_m - i) \beta_j$ Where R_j refers to the expected rate of return for security J. R_m is the expected rate of return for the market portfolio, i refers to the risk free rate of return and β_j (beta) is a measure of the Systematic Risk of security j.

Capital Asset: The term used for an asset, which is not bought or sold as part of the everyday running of a business. Examples include property, land, or shares in another company.

Capital Authorised, Nominal or Registered: Synonymous terms for capital fixed by the Memorandum of Association of a company, i.e., maximum amount a company can raise as its capital.

Capital Budgeting: The process of allocating investible funds to capital projects. Many techniques are used for this purpose. There are traditional accountants' methods like payback period and rate of return on capital employed.

Capital Cost of: The cost of obtaining the total capital employed by a business, expressed as a rate of interest.

Capital Employed: The aggregate finance used by a business. Sometimes the expression is used to refer to the total of all liabilities and capital; sometimes it excludes current liabilities (see Capital). The capital in use in a business. There is no universally agreed definition of what this includes, but it is usually taken to mean net assets (that is, current assets plus fixed assets less current liabilities) plus bank loans and overdrafts.

Capital forms of: Every business house needs two types of capital: (a) fixed capital and (b) working capital. Fixed capital is required for permanent investments. Working capital is required to meet day-today needs of the business and to finance floating assets. Amount spent in purchasing land, constructing building, fixing machinery, etc., constitutes fixed capital while assets such as stock and raw material which are continuously changing and are purchased to be converted at an augmented price are known as working capital. Capacity for service of the items constituting fixed capital is not exhausted by single used in production. They do not call for frequent replacement. But the items comprising working capital are used up in the individual processes of production they are employed and thus, necessitate continuous replacements or renewals. Working capital is mostly kept in circulation by ploughing it back after selling the products and reinvesting it in further production. It is because of this regular cycle that the working capital requirements are usually for shorter periods.

Capital Gain: Refers to the difference between the purchase price of an asset and its resale price at some later date where that difference has been positive.

Capital Gains Tax: As the name suggests this is a tax on profits or gains made in the course of capital transactions, i.e., on the buying and selling of assets other than in the normal course of a taxable business.

Capital Goods: Goods which are made for the purpose of producing consumer goods and other capital goods, e.g., machinery of all kinds. This term is synonymous with 'producer goods'.

Capital Intensity: The ratio of capital to labour employed in production.

Capital Intensive Industry: Refers to industry in which the ratio of capital input to labor input has been higher than the average ratio for industry as a whole. In other words, a huge amount of capital provides a very small number of employment. The capital input could be found out by the depreciation costs of plant and equipment.

Capital Loss: The opposite of capital profit but calculated for most purposes in the same manner.

Capital Market: A market comprising institutions which are involved in the purchase and sale of securities, e.g., the new issuc market and the stock exchange.

Capital Market Instruments: Financial instruments like company shares and bonds, long-term government bonds, and local government bonds.

Capital Market Line: Refers to a line which expresses graphically all the available combinations of the Market Portfolio with riskless borrowing and lending.

Capital Movements: Refer to international flows of funds which may be undertaken by either private individuals or governments. An important element in the balance of payments.

Capital of a Company Sources of: A joint stock enterprise may raise funds to meet its requirements of fixed and working capital in either of the following ways: (a) By issuing shares. (b) By issuing debentures. (c) By accepting public deposits. (d) By borrowing money from the banks. (e) By seeking financial assistance from different financial institutions set up by the Central and the State Government.

Capital Profit: A profit or surplus arising from the transfer (for cash or kind) of an asset other than the one normally bought for resale in the course of business. A capital profit is also called capital gain when a personal asset (e.g., a house or some land or a car) is sold for a price exceeding that at which it was purchased. With limited companies the term has an additional significance. Capital profits made by companies are quite different from ordinary revenue or trading profits and are treated separately in the company's accounts.

Capital Ratio: Closely related to solvency ratio, the Capital Gearing Ratio is mainly used to analyse the capital structure of a company. The term 'capital gearing,' or leverage normally refers to the proportion between the fixed interest or dividend bearing funds and non-fixed interest or dividend bearing funds. Capital Gearing Ratio: Equity Share Capital/Fixed Interest Bearing Funds.

Capital Rationing: A situation where there has been a budgetary constraint on the amount of funds available for investment in projects over and above the normal market constraints determined by the relationship between cost of capital and expected returns.

Capital Recovery: Refers to the process by which the original investment in a physical asset has been recovered over its economic life. In the absence of inflation, capital recovery has been achieved through depreciation allowances.

Capital Redemption Reserve: The term used for an undistributable reserve arising from the redemption of preference shares, debenture or the purchase by a company of its own debenture.

Capital Return On: The relating of profit to the estimate of average capital employed to yield a ratio, commonly called the primary ratio, as follows: Profit. Capital.

Capital-Intensive: An adjective used to describe those industries where the amount of fixed capital used in production is high, both absolutely and as an amount per person employed. Capital intensive industries are those which depend more on the machines involved in production than on the people employed to tend them.

Capitalism: An economic system characterized by the private ownership of a society's resources; by competition in the pursuit of financial gain; and by support for the ideal of a free market in goods and services.

Capitalization: It can refer to the composition of a company's long term sources of funds, i.e., its Capital Structure, or to the total market value of its issued shares (Market Capitalization). The term can refer to the process of obtaining a Net Present Value by applying on annuity or perpetuity formula to future earnings or cash flows.

Capitalize: To exchange (actually) or conceptually a stream of future receipts for a lumpsum. Specifically, to compute the present value of future receipts. To decide that a certain sum of money will in future be treated as capital. Specifically, to decide that retained earnings or share premium will be treated as share capital. To turn to one's advantage.

Caption: Short description at the bottom of an illustration or photograph.

Captive Audience: People who cannot avoid being exposed to an advertisement.

Captive Market: A group of consumers that has no choice. This may be either because products (or services) are provided by a monopoly supplier (like telecoms services in most countries), or because the consumers are in a particular situation which does not allow them choice. For example, travellers by train or plane can only have the food and drink that decides to make available to them. Therefore it is the term used for a market in which the supplier of a good or service has been in a monopolistic position, the consumer being unable to get suitable substitutes or to do without.

Career: Job which you are trained for, and which you expect to do all your life.

Cargo: Load of goods which are sent in a ship or plane, etc.; **The ship was taking on cargo:** was being loaded with goods; **to load cargo:** to put cargo on a ship; **air cargo:** goods sent by air; **berth cargo:** cargo carried at specially low rate; **deck cargo:** cargo carried on the open deck of a ship, rather than in the hold; **cargo liner:** cargo ship with a regular schedule, **Lisbon; cargo ship:** or **cargo plane:** ship or plane which carries only cargo and not passengers.

Carnet: International document which allows dutiable goods to cross several European countries by road without paying duty until the goods reach their final destination.

Carousel Training: Training which involves moving from job to job or from department to department in an organization.

Carriage: Transporting goods from one place to another; cost or transport of goods; **carriage free:** deal where the customer does not pay for the shipping; **carriage**

forward: deal where the customer will pay for the shipping when the goods arrive.

Carrot and Stick Approach: Traditionally, management has resorted to be autocratic. This form of motivation in industry emphasises authority and economic rewards. This approach consists of forcing people to work by threatening to punish or dismiss them or to cut their rewards if they do not work. 'Carrot' as per this concept refers to reward whereas 'Stick' refers to punishment.

Carry Over (a) **to carry over a balance:** to take a balance from the end of one page or period to the beginning of the next (b) **to carry over stock:** to hold stock from the end of one stocktaking period to the beginning of the next.

Carrying: Transporting from one place to another.

Carrying Cost: Expenses incurred in maintaining inventories. Carrying cost include rent, utilities, spoilage, taxes and insurance.

Cartel: A term implying bonding together of business houses producing similar type of goods with a view associate to secure a monopoly of the market. A cartel is a voluntary agreement of capitalistic enterprises of the same branch for a regulation of the sales market with a view of improving the profitability of its members' business by agreeing to limit competition among themselves.

Cash (1)(a)**:** money in coins or notes; **cash in hand:** money and notes in the till, kept to pay small debts; **hard cash:** money in notes and coins, as opposed to cheques or credit cards; **petty cash:** small amounts of money kept in an office for making small payments; **ready cash:** money which is immediately available for payment; **cash account:** account which records the money which is received and spent; **cash advance:** loan in cash against a future payment; **cash balance:** balance in cash, as opposed to amounts owed; **cash book:** book in which cash transactions are entered; **cash box:** metal box for keeping cash; **cash budget:** plan of cash income and expenditure; **cash card:** card used to obtain money from a cash dispenser; **cash cow:** in the Boston matrix, a product that consistently generate good profits and maintains its market share, but will not provide growth; **cash desk:** place in a store where you pay for the goods you have bought; **cash dispenser:** machine which gives out money when a special card is inserted and instructions given; **cash float:** cash put into the cash box at the beginning of the day or week to allow business to start; **cash offer:** offer to pay in cash; **cash payment:** payment in cash; **cash purchases:** purchases made in cash; **cash register:** or **cash till:** machine which shows and adds the prices of items bought, and which has a drawer for keeping the cash received; **cash reserves:** a company's reserves in cash, deposits or bills, kept in case of urgent need (b): using money in coins or notes; **to pay cash down:** to pay in cash immediately; **cash against documents:** system whereby a buyer receives documents for the goods on payment of a bill of exchange;**cash discount:** or**discount for cash:** discount given for payment is cash; **cash price:** or **cash terms:** (i) price of goods when cash is used for payment; (ii) lower price or terms which apply if the customer pays cash; **cash sale:** or **cash transaction:** transaction paid for in cash; **cash settlement:** or **settlement in cash:** paying a bill in cash;**terms cash with order:** terms of sale showing that payment has to be made in cash when the order is placed; cash when goods are delivered; **to cash a cheque:** to exchange a cheque for cash.

Cash and Carry: An epithet applied to a manufacturer's or whole seller's collection of goods for sale to the general public; cash and carry is a kind of retailer's supermarket. The retailer or customer gets a minimal service. There is no sales force, no delivery service, no credit, no reordering assistance; in short, no frills. The retailer or customer goes to the ware house, pays for the goods, and takes them away. It means lower costs to the wholesaler and lower prices to the retailer. The success of the cash-and-carry concept owed much to changing patterns of consumer shopping. As shoppers turned more and more to smaller independent retailers (like corner groceries or village stores) could compete was by cutting costs to the bone, that included buying from the cash-and-carry chains. Small hotels and restaurants also rely heavily on cash-and-carry outlets.

Cash Discount: A discount which is receivable or allowable on payment of an invoice within an agreed period.

Cash Dispenser: A customer can obtain cash from his account without needing to go into the bank (e.g. after hours). The normal method is to supply a customer with a coded plastic card which when inserted into the particular machine outside the bank will as the result of the customer punching certain digits, cause specific sums in notes to be delivered and, at the same time, retain a record that will automatically result in the customer's account being charged with the amount.

Cash Flow: Refers to the sum of retained earnings and depreciation provision made by firms. As such it has been the source of internally generated long term funds available to the company cash which comes into a company from sales less the money which goes out in purchase or overhead expenditure; **cash flow forecast:** forecast or when cash will be received or paid out; **cash flow statement:** report which shows cash sales and purchases; **discounted cash flow:** calculating the forecast return on capital investment in current terms, with reductions for current interest rates; **net cash flow:** difference between the money coming in and the money going where more money is going out of a company than is coming in; **positive cash flow:** situation where more money is going out of a company than is coming in; **the company is suffering from cash flow problems:** cash income is not coming in fast enough to cover expenditure.

Cash Flow Statement: A statement of a firm's actual of projected cash inflows and cash outflows measured at suitable intervals over a period.

Cash Management: Refers to the management of the cash balances of an enterprise in such a fashion as to maximize the availability of cash and of investment income on cash not invested in fixed assets or inventories and also so as to avoid the risk of insolvency.

Cash Market: The term used for a market for the immediate delivery of, and payment for commodities.

Cash Price: The price at which a vendor is prepared to part with goods: that is, the money to be tendered at the time when they are bought. This is opposed to the hire purchase price, which includes interest depending on the period of payment.

Cash Settlement: Refers to a procedure for settlement of contracts by automatic close-out at a cash price which is designated by the clearing house in future markets which make no provision for delivery.

Cashier: Generally this term is applied to a person who has the responsibility of accounting for cash transaction and keeping a record thereof. In a narrower sense it denotes a particular job at a bank normally that of handling cash transactions with the public at the bank counter.

Cashless Society: Refers to a society either so primitive that exchanges through barter alone, or so controlled that goods and services are provided on vouchers only, or sophisticated through the use of credit cards and instant debiting that bank notes and cash become redundant.

Casting Vote: Vote given (especially by a chairperson) to decide an issue when votes on each side are equal.

Casualty. In which there is no certainty that the thing insured against will occur. Common forms of casualty insurance are against accidents (in cars or boats or planes), against damage to buildings, and against sickness.

Catalogue: 1. publication which lists items for sale, usually showing their prices; **an office equipment catalogue: classified catalogue:** catalogue where the items are listed in categories; **mail order catalogue:** catalogue from which a customer orders items to be sent by mail; **catalogue price:** price as marked in a catalogue 2: to put an item into a catalogue.

Catering (a): supplying food and drink for a party, etc.; **the catering trade:** food trade, especially the sector which supplies food ready to eat (b) **catering for:** which provides for.

Ceiling: High point; upper limit placed on wages or prices or output.

Census: Official count of a country's population, including such data as the age, sex, and occupation of individuals.

Centralization: This can be referred to an organization that has all its operations under one roof or in one geographic or territorial region.

Central Processing Unit (CPU): The principal data-processing devices within a computer; consisting of an arithmetic unit, a control unit and a store. The store in the CPU is normally an immediate access store.

Certificate of Incorporation: The document issued by the Registrar of Companies to a new company once it is registered as per the Companies Act. It gives the recipient the legal status of 'company' which affords the right to contract in the company name as legal persona. It is still necessary for other conditions to be met, however, before a public company can be given permission to commence business.

Chain Store: A shop, or store, one of many in common ownership, each in a different location, not to be confused with a department store or supermarket though either of these might be a member of chain store group. Chain stores may be defined as retail selling organization with a number of branches which are centrally owned and controlled.

Chairman: (a) person who is in charge of a meeting (b) person who presides over the board meeting of company.

Chairman of Company: Normally the senior person in a company, and often merely a figurehead who takes no active part but presides as chairman at meetings of directors. An active chairman is often both chairman and managing director or chief executive.

Chairman's Report: A report, generally made annually on the activities of a company, and signed by the chairman, it is normally given at the annual general meeting and included in the annual report.

Chairmanship: Being a chairman.

Chairperson: The presiding officer of an organization, committee, task force, or meeting. 'Chairperson' (or 'chair') generally has replaced the term 'chairman'.

Chairwoman: Woman who is in charge of a meeting.

Challenger: Company which challenges other companies which are already established in the market place; **market challenger strategy:** strategy adopted by a company which is challenging the market leaders by pricing aggressive advertising or product design.

Channel (a): means by which information or goods pass from one place to another; **to go through the official channels:** to deal with government officials (especially when making a request); **to open up new channels of communication:** to find new ways of communicating with someone; **distribution channels:** or **channels of distribution:** means by which goods pass from the manufacturer to the consumer, via wholesalers and retailers;**channel members:** the various companies which form a distribution channel; **channels of influences:** ways in which a company can influence consumers to buy their products, i.e., personal influence channels such as salesmen, or non-personal channels. channels such as press advertising; (b)**trading channel:** series of purchase and sales from company-to-company which are made until the finished product is purchased by the customer; **channel power:** the influence which one company in a trading channel has over the other companies in the channel.

Characteristics of Government Undertaking: There are certain features, peculiar to government undertakings and their management: (i) There is a tendency to pioneer into fields of industrial activity which are comparatively new. (ii) The policy of progressive march to socialism. (iii) Government undertakings are usually set-up on a large scale. They involve huge capital investment and are timebound in respect of implementation of their targets. (iv) Social achievement rather than profit maximisation. (v) The executives of public firms are accountable to Parliament. They are directly influenced by the policy of the government, its evolvement and development on the basis of Policy Resolutions announced by the Ministers on the floor of Parliament. (vi) Finance for public sector undertakings derived from government treasury after a number of formalities have been fulfilled and the projects scrutinised even before they are put into action, or gone through experimentation of any kind. (vii) The bigger and larger objectives of the public sector are fulfilled over a longer time as compared with the simple profitability motive of the private sector. **State intervention in economic affairs-:** (i) When the business is of a monopolistic nature. (ii) When private enterprises would not be attracted. (iii) Where the economically week require protection. (iv) In case of social monopolies of public utility services.

Railways, posts and telegraph services, water supply and supply of electricity or gas are generally put under the category of public utilities. (v) Where the consumers need protection. (vi) Where State management and control are dictated by political or social as well as economic considerations.

Charge: A term used in commerce in two major senses, first as a synonym for price. Where sale of goods or services is concerned (though usually one speaks of a charge for services and the price of goods) second in the context of mortgages and the lending of money on security. The creditor is said to have a 'charge' on the property, real or personal, which is provided as security for the loan. **1** (a) money which must be paid or price of a service; **admission charge:** or **entry charge:** price to be paid before going into an exhibition, etc.;**bank charges:** charges made by a bank for carrying out work for a customer; **handling charge:** money to be paid for packing or invoicing or dealing with goods which are being shipped; **inclusive charge:** charge which includes all items; **interest charges:** money paid as interest on a loan;**scale of charges:** list showing various prices; **service charge:** charge added to a bill in a restaurant to pay for service; **charges forward:** charges which will be paid by the customer; a small charge is made which does not cover the real costs at all; **free of charge:** free or with no payment to be made; (b) debit on account; (a): to ask someone to pay for services later; **to charge the packing to the customer:** the customer has to pay for packing (ii) to ask for money to be paid; **she charges 10 an hour:** she asks to be paid Rs. 10 for an hour's work.

Charge Account: Another name for a credit account offered by a retailer, the purpose of which is to attract more trade by giving customers extended credit terms.

Charter: The document creating an organization: a document establishing the accountabilities and functions of an organization or a key position in an organization: a document establishing the purpose, goals, functions, and authority of a programme of work or service.

Chartered Accountant: A member of the Institute of Chartered Accountants or The Institute, being the governing body establishes certain rules of conduct to which the chartered accountant must conform at his peril.

Checklist: List of items which have to be checked, especially as a way of evaluating a promotional campaign or a single advertisement.

Checkout: Place where goods are paid for in a shop or supermarket.

Chemist: A dealer in medicinal drugs.

Cheque: A bill of exchange drawn on a banker payable on demand, a common way of setteling debts.

Cheques may be open (bearer) or crossed. An open cheque is payable over the counter provided it is in order. A crossed cheque has to be paid into a bank account only; **cheque account:** bank account which allows the customer to write cheques; **cheque to bearer:** cheque with no name written on it, so that the person who holds it can cash it; **crossed cheque:** cheque with two lines across it showing that it can only be deposited at a bank and not exchanged for cash; **open or uncrossed cheque:** cheque which can be cashed anywhere; **blank cheque:** cheque with the amount of money and the payee left blank, but signed by the drawer; **pay cheque:** or **salary cheque:** monthly cheque by which an employee is paid; **traveller's cheques:** cheques taken by a traveller, which can be cashed in a foreign country; **dud cheque:** or **bouncing cheque:** or **cheque which bounces:** or US **rubber check:** cheque which cannot be cashed because the person writing it does not have enough money in the account to pay it (b) **to cash a cheque:** to exchange a cheque for cash; **to endorse a cheque:** to sign a cheque on the back to show that you accept it; **to make out a cheque to someone:** to write someone's name on a cheque; **to pay a cheque into your account:** to deposit a cheque; **the bank referred the cheque to drawer:** returned the cheque to the person who wrote it because there was not enough money in the account to pay it; **to sign a cheque:** to sign on the front of a cheque to show that you authorize the bank to pay the money from your account; **to stop a cheque:** to ask a bank not to pay a cheque which you have issued.

Cheque Clearing: A has an account at Bank X and B has an account at Bank Y. When A writes a cheque to B it passes between Bank X and Y; they clear it by debiting A's account and crediting B's Cheque clearing began in the coffee house of London's Lombard Street where bank clerks would meet in order to exchange bundles of cheques among themselves.

Chief Executive: Term used to describe the person who has overall responsibility for the day-to-day running of an organization whether a trading company or some other corporate body. In the case of a limited company the chief executive is normally the managing director, appointed by the board of directors on the authority of the members.

Chilling Effect: Negative effect on workers of regulations or practices that limit freedom and opportunities.

Choice: (a) thing which is chosen (b) range of items to choose from.

Choose: To decide to do a particular thing or to buy a particular item (as opposed to something else).

Circular: (a) sent to many people; (b) leaflet or letter sent to many people.

Civil Service: Organization and personnel which administer a country.

Classification: Arrangement into groups; **Classification of ratios:** Ratios may be classified in a number of ways to suit any particular purpose. Different kinds of ratios are selected for different types of situations. They are: (a) Balance Sheet Ratios (b) Profit and Loss Accounting Ratios (c) Inter-statement Ratios or Combined Ratios (d) Structural Ratios (e) Trend Ratios (f) Primary Ratios (g) Secondary Ratios (h) Liquidity Ratios (i) Leverage Ratios (j) Turnover Ratios (k) Profitability Ratios.

Classified Advertisement: An advertisement in a section of a newspaper of magazine that contains many advertisements, all set in the same simple style, grouped according to a classification scheme say, matrimonial, situations vacant etc., devised by the publisher of the newspaper.

Classified Catalogue: Catalogue which groups articles into certain categories.

Classify: To put into classes categories; classified advertisement listed in a newspaper under special headings (such as 'property for sale' or 'jobs wanted') classified directory book which lists businesses grouped under various headings (such as computer shops or news agents) classified display advertising that, although it is classified may also have individual features such as its own box border or the company logo.

Clearance: Customs clearance passing goods through customs so that they can enter or leave the country; to clear goods through customs; certificate showing that foods have been passed by the customs sale of items at low prices to get rid of passing of cheque through the banking system, transferring money from one account to another.

Clearing Banks: Commercial banks are members of the bankers' clearing house which facilitates the settling of daily balances due between member banks arising from cheque and cash transactions throughout the country, whether by the general public or individual banks.

Clerk: A person concerned with keeping records.

Client: Person who gets help or advice from a professional person or Person with whom business is done.

Clip: Short extract from a film.

Clique: A clique consists of those people who have frequent interactions and observe certain norms and standards. Its purpose is to gain and control power.

Clock Card: Special card which a worker puts into the time clock when clocking on or off.

Clock In or Clock On: To record the time of arriving for work by putting a card into a special timing machine.

Clock Out or Clock Off: To record the time of leaving work by putting a card into a special timing machine.

Close Down: To shut a shop or factory for a long period or for ever.

Closed: (a) shut or not open or not doing business (b) restricted; closed system: work system which is inflexible and does not allow the workers much freedom to work in their own way; closed shop: system where an organization agrees to employ only union members in certain occupations or at certain places of work.

Closing Price: The official stock-exchange price of a share at the end of the exchange's trading day. The price at which shares are quoted at the close of any day's Stock Exchange dealings. The prices can be found in the Official List, published daily by the Stock Exchange.

Cluster: Group of things together, method whereby samples are classified into groups according to certain characteristics; sampling on the basis or well-defined groups.

Cluster Sampling: A term used in market research for the practice of drawing a sample of informants from a geographically localized area (like a single street).

Co-financing: A technique for bringing the international strength of institutions such as the World Bank and the Asian Development Bank together with the financial clout of commercial banks. Project in developing countries are co-financed jointly by the international institution and a group of commercial banks. Co-financing gives the banks the comfort of knowing that borrowers rarely if ever default on loans from the World Bank et al. The World Bank benefits from the extra billions that commercial banks can bring to a negotiating table.

Co-operative Societies—Types of: 1. Consumer's Cooperative Societies—to eliminate middlemen profit supply better quality goods at cheaper prices to the members, an attempt at self-help: surplus used for bonus or for welfare of members. 2. Producer's Co-operatives try to face powerful capitalists: (i) independent production with the help of tools, finances etc. provided by society. (ii) As employees of the society receive wages and bonus. 3. Co-operative Co. Credit Societies try to provide for short-term financial accommodation to their members and encourage thrift, productive loans at cheaper rates of interest. (i) agriculture credit societies. (ii) non-agriculture credit societies. 4. Marketing Co-operatives try to help small producers realize better price for their products, help in processing and grading of output and set-up centralized sales organizations. 5. Co-operative Farming Societies take advantage of economies of large-scale farming to maximize agricultural output by using better seeds, better implements, etc. 6. Housing Co-operatives aim at raising funds for providing houses to members.

Cooptation: It is a process of absorbing new elements into the policy making structure of an organization as a means of averting threats or maintaining its stability in the changed circumstances.

Co-ordination: The process of integrating all the parts and function of an organization.

Co-owner: Person who owns something with another person.

Co-ownership: Ownership by employees of a share in the business which employs them.

Co-efficient of Correlation: Measurement of correlation or relationship between two sets of data on a continuum from +1 to –1.

Coffee Break: Rest time during work when worker can have a cup of coffee.

Cognitive Dissonance: Conflict experienced by a person who cannot resolve apparently contradictory information, as when making buying decisions or evaluating purchases which have been made.

Cold Calling: Calling on a customer without a prior appointment. Many retail business expect sales people to drop in regularly and unexpectedly. For many kinds of selling, however, cold calling is unwelcome, inefficient and time-wasting. Where it is unavoidable, the hit rate (that is, the inverse of the number of calls that have to be made before a customer makes a purchase) is very low.

Cold Storage Training: Training of employees of jobs that will be created in the future.

Collaborate: To work together.

Collar: Part of a coat or shirt which goes round the neck; **blue collar worker:** manual worker in a factory; **white collar worker:** office worker.

Collateral Agreement: An agreement or contract running alongside an existing agreement or contract. If the initial contract is void the collateral agreement is not necessarily void much depends on whether the second contract restates the void agreement.

Collateral Security: Security given for a loan. It is often additional security given over and above assets on which the loan is charged.

Collective Bargaining: An industrial relations process in which employers or their representatives negotiate with employees or their (trade union) representatives on the level of wages and the conditions of employment of a group of employees as a whole, rather than for individuals.

Commerce: Business or buying and selling of goods and services; group of local businessmen and women who meet to discuss common problems and to promote business in their town.

Commercial: Referring to business; person or business selling a company's products or service for a commission; aircraft used to carry cargo or artist who designs advertisement or diplomat who represents and tries to promote his country's business interests; time set aside for commercials on television; college which teaches business studies; person who advises on commercial matters in an embassy; course in which students study business skills; which lists all the businesses and business people in a town; part of a town where most offices and shops are; laws which relate to business; amount of goods or number of passengers which a bus or train or plane has to carry to make a profit; port which has only goods traffic; services which support trade, such as banking and advertising; salesman who travels round an area visiting customers on behalf of his company; van or truck, etc. used for business purposes; not worth anything if sold profitable; not likely to make a profit ; television advertisement which combines still pictures with action shots; guarantee that rival products will not be advertised directly before or after a particular advertisement; time that a television or radio station devotes to advertising.

Commercial Banks: A general term denoting those banks, which conduct a general rather than a specialized type of business. They accept deposits on varying terms, but including demand deposits; and their lending to private sector business for non-fixed capital purposes, generally accounts for the greater part of their assets.

Commercial Bill: A bill which is drawn to finance trade or other commercial or production activities. It has been distinguished from a Treasury Bill or local government bill which have been instruments of public financial operations.

Commercial Paper: A collective term for commercial bills.

Commercial Paper Market: A non-bank short term money market in which corporations lend their surplus cash directly to each other, cutting out intermediate financial institutions.

Commercialization: The launch of a product on to the market; making something into a business proposition; **commercialize:** to make something into a business; **commercially:** as regards business.

Commission: Payment to someone in return for obtaining work, order or sales for others: especially a payment that is a fixed percentage of the value of the business transacted. For example (a) payment to a salesmen of a percentage of the value of the sales he makes, (b) payment to an agent of a percentage of the value of work he procures for others. An action or a document confers authority to perform duties specified in such a way. A task entrusted to someone who is to act as an agent in performing it. A body of people given authority to perform a specific task. Especially a government agency with investigative and administrative duties. A task given to an artist or designer to create something according to outline instructions in return for a fee fixed in advance.

Commission Agent: An agent acting on a commission basis.

Committed Costs: Objects which are produced because of the process of production, goods and services.

Committee: A group of people appointed by an organization to take responsibility for a particular task of function on behalf of the organization as a whole. The committee may or may not be given executive power. It may be permanent standing committee or a temporary ad hoc committee.

Commodity Exchange: It is a market where dealings in a particular commodity are made on a national or international scale. While major capital cities in India are known for commodity exchange. London has been the home of most commodity exchange even though, in modern times, the transactions are no longer in the form of goods themselves but through documents and titles thereto. This process has continued since the introduction of reliable 'grading' services which save the trouble of personal inspection. In fact, commodities can be bought, shipped and sold without the person effecting the transaction ever setting eyes on them. This does not apply to all commodities as some are still auctioned off after inspection, e.g., tea and wool, thus preserving the old personal presence and judgment. Also refered to bulk sale and purchase of financial instruments, for immediate and forward delivery often in the form of a futures contract.

Commodity Futures Contract: Refers to a legally binding commitment to buy or sell a precisely defined quantity and quality of a commodity in a given month, the price of which is determined by the participants at the time of transaction.

Commodity: Thing sold in very large quantities, especially a raw material such as a metal and food such as corn; farm produce grown in large quantities, such as corn, rice, cotton, etc.; basic food or raw material which is vital to a country's economy; place where people buy and sell commodities; trading in commodities for delivery at a later date; person whose business is buying and selling commodities.

Common Market: The European Economic Community organization which links several European countries for the purposes of trade;

the Common Market finance ministers: the finance ministers of all the Common Market countries meeting as a group.

Common Shares: An American equivalent of equity shares, usually of non-par value or of a stated face value of.

Common Stock: US term for Ordinary Shares.

Common Costs: Costs of facilities and services which are being shared by a number of departments.

Communicate: To exchange views or information with someone.

Communication: Effective communication is the medium through which managerial understanding is created. Information, ideas and views are exchanged by the use of verbal and written expression. Therefore, clarity has to be maintained. Orderly construction and direct expression in communication will go a long way in presenting and analysing problems in a business situation. In an organization, a manager has to maintain one-way as well as two-way communication. No interchange is possible in one-way communication and it is in this area that the manager has to be extremely careful in using his ability to avoid conflicts, misunderstandings or misconceptions. Communication is the key to interpersonal competence. A good manager must have immense capacity to listen to others and know how to be 'In' or 'Enter' into the field of others. Two minds can meet only if there is mutual awareness, respect and understanding. Carl Rogers has stated that the maturity of a person is revealed if he does not live behind a mask of fear, frustration, failure and anxiety and therefore intellect, will and feeling are necessary to meet and establish proper communication. The usual barriers to communication are tendency to judge in advance, preconceived assumption, personal viewpoint and one's own feelings. The objective approach to communication includes listening with understanding and expressing ideas with feeling and courage.

Communication Network: A method or form or pattern of communication. The two most frequently studied kinds of networks are wheel-shaped and circle-shaped. The wheel network facilitates quick and accurate communication but is less equipped to handle complexity and change. The circle network adapts well to complexity and change in communication but is less equipped to handle complexity and change. The circle network adapts well to complexity and change in communication and seems to involve and satisfy its members better. These networks are often discussed in the comparison of a mechanistic organization and an organic organization.

Communications Strategy: The

choice of different ways in which marketers set out to communicate with their markets: inevitably a combination of direct face-to-face communication between a sales person and a potential customer, and indirect non-personal communication through advertising and sales promotion. The nature of a product and of its market influences a company's communications strategy. If its products are targeted at mass consumer markets, and if the company can afford it, then its communications strategy need consist of nothing more than a strong dose of media advertising. On the other hand, industrial marketing generally calls for personal selling to meet the often highly specialised needs of industrial customers.

Commutation: The exchange of part of a future pension for cash now.

Commute: (a) to travel to work from home each day; (b) to exchange one form of payment for another.

Commuter: Person who commutes to work.

Companies Act, 1956: The Companies Act, 1956 came into force with effect from April 1, 1956. It is both a consolidating and amending Act. This Act presents the whole body of the company law in a complete form and reveals earlier Companies Acts and their amendments. It contains 651 Sections and XIII Schedules and numerous Forms. This Act is based largely on the report of the Company Law Committee, 1952 (popularly known as 'Bhabha Committee'). With the growing complexities of modern business and with the increasing role of joint stock enterprise in the economic development of the country, the Company Law is fast developing in order to protect the joint stock companies from the inroads of undesirable persons, and to ensure that the activities of the companies are carried on in furtherance of our economic goal of establishing a 'socialistic pattern of society'. The Companies Act, 1956 has been amended for about a dozen times with the last being in the series of the Companies (Amendment) Act, 1977.

Company: It is a legal organization of people for business purposes to buy, sell or provide services. A business that is a legal entity separate from its owners, the shareholders. Thus, companies can own assets, they can sue and be sued at law, they can have 'perpetual succession' (that is, there need be no limit to their lives, irrespective of the lives of, or changes to, the owners). Most companies have limited liability, which means that the owners of the company have limited liability for its debts. In effect the owners' liability is usually limited to their shareholdings. Because owners may be granted limited liability (in the case of the UK from the 1855 Companies Act onwards), many investors are prepared to risk their money and become co-owners. This enables very large amounts of capital to be raised, and therefore, makes very large companies possible. If there were no limited liability (as with a partnership) it would be much more difficult to persuade investors to become co-owners, without their insisting on becoming co-managers so that they could safeguard their own investments and potential liabilities. Most investors have no desire to businesses have no desire for vast numbers of co-managers. Thus, limited liability is essential for large business. Before the 1844 Companies Act in the UK it had been necessary to have an Act of Parliament or a Royal Charter in order to set-up a company. Now companies are commonplace in the UK and throughout the world. They are set-up with a series of legal transactions and registration with government (or state government) offices. In the UK the memorandum of association and articles of association outline the rules of the company; in the USA the analogous documents are the certificate of incorporation and the bylaws. Throughout much of the Western world (though not in the USA) the law distinguishes between a private company and a public company. Table 7 gives abbreviated designations in certain countries which are used as part of the names of companies. It is necessary for a company to be public in order for there to be a market in its securities (share or loans). The extreme example of a public market is a stock exchange listing. Thus public companies. The law impose greater than private companies tend to be larger than private companies. The law impose greater restrictions on public companies. The law imposes greater restrictions on public companies. In the UK, for example, public companies must have a minimum issued capital of £ 50,000. The definition of distributable profit is stricter for them. They are not allowed the exemptions from publication granted to certain private companies. There are around 12,000 public companies in the UK, about half of them listed, and about 950,000 private companies. In some countries, such as Germany and the Netherlands, public companies are required to have two-tier boards, comprising a supervisory board (with some employee representation) and a management board. Proposals like this are contained in the draft Fifth directive of the EU. In the USA there is no such legal distinction between public and private. However, the analogous companies to public ones are those that are registered with the Securities and Exchange Commission (SEC). Companies must register with the SEC in order for there to be a market in their securities. The SEC lays down audit and disclosure requirements. It also provides the backing for accounting standards. Thus, the rules for registered companies are much more extensive than those for unregistered companies. (See also close company and corporation tax). **Company-Definition of:** Section (3)(1)(i) and (ii) of the Companies Act define a company as "a company formed and registered under this Act or an existing company means a company formed and registered under any of the former Companies Acts''. At the time of application for registration, the sponsors must submit the Articles and Memorandum of Association. A company may be defined as an incorporated association, which is an artificial person, having an independent legal entity, with a perpetual succession, a common seal, a common capital comprised of transferable shares and carrying limited liability.

Company and Partnership—Distinction Between: The main points of differences between a company and a partnership firm are as follows: A company is regulated by the Companies Act, 1956, whereas a partnership firm is governed by the provision of the Indian Partnership Act, 1932. The maximum number of members in the case of a firm is fixed at ten for banking business and at twenty for any other business; but no such maximum limit is fixed in the case of a public company. The maximum number of members of a private company, however, must not exceed fifty excluding past and present employees. The minimum number of members in a public company is seven and in case of a private company two. In case of a partnership the minimum number of partners is two. A company is an artificial person and has a distinct legal entity separate from its members. A partnership, on the other hand, does not have a distinct legal entity separate from the members composing it and its existence comes to an end upon the death or lunacy or insolvency of its partners. In partnership each partner has unlimited liability and is personally liable for all the debts of the firm. In a company, on the other hand, a shareholder has limited liability—limited to the extent of the unpaid amount on the shares held by him or the amount guaranteed by him to be his contribution in case the company is wound up. The capital of a firm can be changed by the mutual consent of the partners while such a change in the case of a company involves certain legal formalities. All the partners of a firm are entitled to take part in the management of the business: but in the case of a company the right to control and manage the business invested in the board of directors elected by the shareholders. A partner cannot transfer his interest in the firm without the consent of all other partners. He may, of course, assign his share in the partnership but the assignee merely becomes entitled to the financial benefits in respect of the share and does not become a partner unless the other members of the firm agree. In the case of a private company also the transfer of shares requires the prior permission of the board of directors. But in the case of a public company a shareholder can transfer his shares freely without restriction and the transfer succeeds to all rights of membership. The audit of the account of a company is a legal necessity but it is not so in the case of a partnership. A partnership firm may or may not be registered but in the case of a company registration is essential. A partnership firm can be wound up at any time by any partner and it is 'at will', without legal formalities. In the case of a company, no one member can require it to be wound up 'at will' and winding up involves legal formalities.

Company Law: In some countries, such as Germany, company law has been the main source of general and detailed requirements in accounting. In other countries, such as the USA, there is virtually nothing on accounting in state of federal law; instead accounting rules are set by the securities and exchange commission, by an independent committee, by the profession, or by some combination of these. In the UK, before the EC's fourth directive led to the provisions of the 1981 Companies Act, there were only general requirements in the law concerning accounting. For example, proper books of account had to be kept; annual financial statements had to be audited, to be published and to give a true and fair view; and a number of detailed disclosures has to be made. UK company law really began with the 1844 Act which enabled companies to be easily formed, and the 1855 Act which allowed limited liability. Compulsory independent audit for banks followed in 1979; and for all limited companies in 1900. Not until the 1929 Act did profit and loss accounts become compulsory. Group accounts were required by the 1947 Act (consolidated into the 1948 Act). Company law was consolidated again in the 1985 Companies Act. Before that the principal Act of 1948 had been supplemented by Acts in 1967, 1976, 1980 and 1981. The 1981 Act added requirements for the formats of the balance sheet and the profit and loss account; extended disclosure requirements; provided certain exemptions from publication for smaller private companies; and introduced detailed compulsory accounting principles. Many of these provisions came, via the

Fourth Directive, from German Law (particularly Companies Law of 1965). The 1989 Companies Act amended the 1885 Act be implementing into UK law the requirements of the Seventh and Eight Directives (on group accounting and on auditors). On several matters other than accounting UK law has traditionally been detailed. For example, there are many provisions on audit, directors duties, rights of shareholders and creditors, conduct of the annual general meeting and so on. The law also contains many provisions on business names and insider dealing.

Company Limited by Guarantee: A company which is having the liability of its members limited by the memorandum of association to such amount as the members respectively undertake to contribute to the assets of the company in the event of its being wound up. **Company Limited by Shares:** A company which is having the liability of its members limited by the memorandum of association to the amount, if any, unpaid on the shares respectively held by them.

Company Seal: Every limited company must have a common seal which must be affixed to certain documents. The company must keep a seal book recording details of all these documents.

Company Secretary: The term 'Secretary' has been derived from the Latin word *Secretarius* which stands for a notary, scribe or confidential writer. In fact, the term has been used for a person who keeps the secrets of any venture, public or private. Presently the term 'Secretary' is used to signify an officer who is entrusted with confidential matters by his employer or who conducts correspondence, keeps records and transacts other business for a person or an organization. Whenever the question of defining the secretary comes to our mind, immediately we get the picture of a person of integrity, intelligence and personality moving with grace and discharging his duties to the administration, shareholders, directors and the company law authorities, with unprecedented accuracy and efficiency.

Compassionate Leave: Time off work granted to an employee to deal with personal or family problems.

Compensate: To give someone something to make up for a loss or damage done.

Compensating Errors: A bookkeeping term for two separate errors one in the Debit side and the other in the credit side which happen to cancel out each other.

Compensation: Compensation is the price paid to the employees in return for their effort of work. It represents income to the worker earned by him from his efforts. It must be adequate and equitable to encourage the worker to put in his best performance.

Compensation Management: That face of management concerned with the selection, development and direction of the programmes that implement an organization's financial reward system. (a) compensation for damage: payment for damage done; compensation for loss of office: payment to a director who is asked to leave a company before his contract ends; compensation for loss of earnings: payment to someone who has stopped earning money or who is not able to earn money (b) indirect compensation: non-financial benefit given by a company to employees (such as sports facilities, a company car, health insurance, etc.).

Competent: (a) able to do something or efficient.

Competition: The attempt to do better than other supplying goods and services in the same market. Fostering competition is one of the basic principles of capitalism, which was first formulated in the eighteenth century by Adam Smith; trying to do better than another supplier or to win over some of its customers; **free competition:** being free to compete without government interference; **keen competition:** strong competition; imperfect competition, perfect competition companies which are trying to compete with your product; type of sales promotions which enables consumers who can show that they have brought a certain minimum number of purchases to compete in games; **competitive:** which competes fairly; **competitive demand:** demand for products that are competing for sales; advantage that one company or product has over its rivals in the market; method of budgeting marketing or promotional expenses according to the amounts being spent by competitors; price which is kept low to compete with a rival product; putting low prices on goods so as to compete with other products; to compete with existing products; guarantee that rival products will not be advertised directly before or after a particular advertisement; **competitor:** person or company which competes; **Competitive market:** An open market where goods are freely and voluntarily offered for sale by any number of willing sellers to any number of willing buyers at prices agreed by both parties.

Competitively: Competitively prices: sold at low price which competes with the price of similar products from other companies.

Competitiveness: Being competitive.

Complain: To say that something is not good or does not work properly.

Complement: Purchase of an item compels the purchaser to go for purchase of another items both the items are said to be complementary to each other.

Complementary: Which adds to or

completes something else; demand for two or more products that are needed together; supply of two or more products from the same production process; product for which demand is dependent on the demand for another product.

Composite: Total demand for a product that has many uses.

Compound Interest: Interest calculated not (as with simple interest) as a fixed amount per annum based on the capital to which it applies, but on an accumulating balance which consists of both capital invested and the interest already earned. Thus if a sum of Re. 1 is invested at a rate of interest r, its value after one year will be R (1+r). If the interest gained is now removed, the Re. 1 will remain and will gather r per cent again in the following year. If, however, the R (1+r) is left to secure interest, then it will secure interest in the second year of R (1+r) r, and the original R (1+r) will remain. The total investment at the end of the second year will, therefore, be R (1+r) + R (1+r)r Which reduce to R (1+r) (1+r) = R $(1+r)^2$ At the end of year t, the investment will have a value of R $(1+r)^t$.

Comprehensive Insurance: This term has particular relevance to motor insurance. Any person driving a motor vehicle on public highways must have a current insurance policy that will cover any damage sustained by a third party, irrespective of negligence. Drivers of vehicles may, however wish to cover more than the minimum legal requirements as regards damage. Policies available are many and of different kinds, varying from one company to another according to the insurer's assessment of risk. The greatest insurance cover available is known as comprehensive insurance. This entitles the owner or driver to recompense for all known possible losses from accidents incurred whilst the car is in his possession or being driven by someone else with the owner's permission.

Comprehensive: Which includes everything; comprehensive insurance: insurance policy which covers you against all possible risks.

Comptroller: Traditional form of the term controller, form the French verb comptroller, to check off.

Compulsory: Which is forced or ordered.

Compulsory Winding-Up: A winding-up other than a voluntary winding-up.

Computer-Aided Design: A process in which a designer interacts within computer system to produce a design, from the original idea to the finished product, by electronic manipulation and the use of a visual display unit rather than pencil and paper. Closely associated with computer aided manufacturing.

Computer: A generic term for apparatus which processes information by electronic means at very high speeds. The two principal types are the analog computer and the digital computer. The latter is the type normally met within commerce and can very considerably in both size and complexity depending upon the purpose for which it is designed.

Computer Hardware: Mechanical, magnetic, electrical and electronic equipment that comprises a computer system (or part of a computer system), including the mainframe or central processing unit, input and output devices that communicate with the mainframe or central processing unit and data storage devices.

Computer Language: A system of words and symbols used to instruct a computer in its task of information processing. The most popular computer language in business in COBOL (Common Business Oriented Language): in science and technology ALGOL (Algorithmic language) and FORTRAN (Formula Translation) are commonly used. An introductory computer that combines aspects of all three is called basic.

Computer Package: This refers to the software required for a particular application.

Computer Programme: Set of sequential operating instructions in machine-readable or machine-translatable form which encompasses a particular problem calculation or logic function to be performed by a digital computer.

Computer-Integrated Manufacturing: The ultimate form of automation in which every aspect of manufacturing from the initial design to the delivery of the finished product, is both controlled and coordinated by computer.

Comrade: Friend or fellow worker or fellow member of a union (popularly used to refer members of a left-oriented ideological group).

Comradeship: Feeling of friendship and solidarity with other workers

Concentrated Marketing: Promotion of a product aimed at one particular area of the market.

Concentration: Degree to which a small number of businesses control a large section of the market.

Concentration Ratio: The percentage of the total business of a specified industry that is done by a specified number of the largest firms in that industry. For example, the percentage of the total sales revenue of an industry as received by a few largest firms in that industry. Several different forms of concentration ratio are in use.

Concept: Business idea based on the importance of profit and consumer satisfaction; evaluating a new product idea, usually by consulting representatives from all the main departments in a company and/or by interviewing a sample of consumers.

Concern: (a) business or company

(b) being worried about a problem.

Concert Party: A group of investors who act together (and in secret) to try to gain control of a company. Each buys a small stake which, when combined, gives them control.

Conciliation: Bringing together the parties in a dispute so that the dispute can be settled.

Condition: (a) term of a contract or duties which have to be carried out as part of a contract or which if not fulfilled by the relevant party, allows the other to consider the contract as ended.

Conditional Order: An order given to a banker to pay a certain amount provided a receipt is completed.

Conduct: Way of behaving.

Confer: To discuss a problem with another person.

Conference: (a) meeting of people to discuss problems; (b) meeting of an association or a society or a union.

Confidence: firm trust; feeling of certainity, secret which is told to some reliable person; in strict confidence: as a secret; take into one's confidence.

Conflict: It can be defined as an emotional or physical struggle arising when two or more persons vie for the same resources, activities or goals, but when only one can achieve them at the expense of the other.

Conglomerate: A business organization, usually comprising a group of companies, with diverse and often unrelated financial interests but sometimes trading under the one name.

Consensus: Agreement or approval by a group collectively.

Consider: To think seriously about something.

Consideration: If a contract other than a contract by deed is to be binding the promise of the one party must be supported by the agreement of the other party to do or not do some act or to pay some money. The agreement by the other party is known as the consideration. In simpler term consideration has been defined as the price paid by one party for the promise of the other.

Consignee: In the business of consignment one party, the principal, is called the consignor, whereas the other party, the agent, is called the consignee who carries business on a commission basis.

Consignment Note: A shipping term for a note accompanying a consignment of goods. This is sometimes an alternative to a bill of lading; **consignment:** sending of goods to someone who will sell them for you; note saying that goods have been sent; goods kept for another company to be sold on their behalf for a commission.

Consignor: A term used to indicate a person who consigns goods to another in a contract of sale. The recipient is known as the consignee. In a restricted sense it can mean the person who consigns goods to an agent with a view to his selling the goods. The consignor retains the property in the goods until those goods are sold.

Consolidate: To group goods together for shipping; goods from different suppliers which are grouped together in one shipment.

Consolidated Accounts: Any company which has subsidiary companies or in any other way is legally classed as a holding company must, in addition to the normal requirements of the Companies Acts, file group accounts. These can take various forms but essentially they are intended to show the results for the relevant financial period and the state of affairs at the end of that period, of the group as a whole. The most common form is that of consolidated accounts. The individual final and audited accounts of the various companies in the group are combined into one set of accounts wherein inter-company transactions and indebtedness are eliminated on a self-cancelling basis and the end product consists of a consolidated balance sheet and a consolidated profit and loss account. It should be emphasized that these accounts do not replace but are in addition to the individually filed accounts of each member of the group.

Consolidated Financial Statements: Financial statements which are incorporating the financial position, annual results and funds flow of a holding or parent company and its subsidiaries into one set of statements.

Consolidation: Grouping of goods together for shipping.

Consolidation of Share Capital: The combination of shares into larger units.

Consortium: Large contracts are often tendered for by a consortium (i.e. a group) of companies or firms none of which is competent to fulfil the contract alone. It is generally a rare combination for the purpose of bringing together a number of quite different operative skills or areas of specialized knowledge under one organization.

Consult: To ask an expert for advice.

Consultancy: Act of giving specialist advice.

Consultant: Specialist who give advice.

Consultation: Asking other people for advice before coming to a decision.

Consumable: Goods which are bought by members of the public and not by companies.

Consumer Demand Theory: Refers to that area of economics which defines testable theories of how consumers behave in response change in variables like price, other prices, income changes and so on.

Consumer Durable: A commodity of reasonably long life, like a refrigerator or piece of furniture; as distinct from say, foodstuffs.

Consumer: Person or company which buys and uses goods and services; person who actually uses a product not necessarily the person who has bought it) retailing business owned by consumers who share in its profits; group representing the interests of consumers; credit given by shops, banks and other financial institutions to consumers so that they can buy goods; relatively expensive items bought by the public which can be used for several years (such as washing machines or refrigerators or cookers) goods bought by consumers or by members of the public; published for consumers giving details of product tests special legal problems regarding services offered, etc. customers who buy consumer goods; group of consumers who report over a period of time on products they have used so that the manufacturers can improve them of use what the panel says about them in advertising; index showing how prices of consumer goods have risen over a period of time, used as a way of measuring inflation and the cost of living; legislation to protect the rights of consumers against unfair or illegal traders; research into why consumers buy goods and what goods they really want to buy; lack of interest by consumers in buying a product; type of society where consumers are encouraged to buy goods; the power of consumers to influence trends in production and marketing;spending by consumers; difference between what a consumer is willing to pay for something and what he or the actually does pay for it; survey of existing and potential demand for a product.

Consumer Goods: Goods for direct consumption, like food, clothing and cars, as opposed to things like machinery and tools which are used to make other goods. Traditionally a distinction has been made between 'consumer disposable' (like good) and 'consumer durables' (like care) but this distinction is somewhat blurred by the effects of built-in obsolescence.

Consumer Loyalty: A rather abstract concept in the sense that it cannot be measured in monetary terms even though it is thought of as an asset. It is an adjunct of goodwill and often an integral part thereof.

Consumer Market: The market for consumer goods.

Consumer Profile: A description of the age, social class and other characteristics of consumer of a given product of brand. Drawing up consumer profiles is an essential part of the development of a communications strategy and of market segmentation.

Consumer Protection: Ways in which consumers are protected from sharp, illegal or dangerous practices by manufacturers. Much consumer protection legislation arose as a result of the consumerism movement in the USA and Europe in the 1960s.

Consumerism: In 1962, when John F. Kennedy was the President of the USA, he issued a Consumers' Bill of Rights. It never became law, but it triggered a consumer "movement" for the rest of the decade, based on its recognition of the consumer's four basis rights.(a)The right to safety.(b)The right to be informed. (c) The right to choose. (d) The right to be heard. The birth of consumerism marked a swing away from the overwhelming power of manufacturers, advertisers and retailers. It acknowledged that level of material wealth in most parts of the USA and Europe was so high that consumers could choose which products to buy or indeed whether to buy any. Societies were beyond the stage where almost anything that could be produced be sold. In some respects the Japanese economic miracle was based on an early recognition by Japanese firms of the consumer's new-found power. They recognized that such power would force manufacturers to be much conscious of quality and price.

Consumption: Buying or using goods or services; consumption of goods for show or to get approval rather than because they are useful; use of something in the home or in one's own country.

Contest: Type of promotion where prizes are given to people who give the right answers to a series of questions; incentive scheme that rewards the salesman who has the best results.

Contingencies: The result from conditions that exist at a balance sheet date but where the outcome depends on uncertain future events. As part of conservatism, accountants recognize all reasonable probable losses relating to contingencies in advance. However, some losses are merely possible and are contingent upon some event, such as the loss of a law case of a debtor defaulting on a Bill of Exchange which the company has guaranteed. These contingencies are not accounted for, in the sense of adjusting the financial statements, but notes to the balance sheet will explain the cause of the contingency and the amount (or an estimate) of exposure.

Contingency Planning: The process of developing a series of alternative plans for achieving an objective. Different alternative plans may be implemented according to future events, opportunities or barriers.

Contingency Theory of Leadership: Any theory of leadership which emphasizes the need for flexibility in dealing with any given situation. The complexity of the modern organization means that effective leadership is contingent upon a great many factors; what may be successful in one context may not be successful in another.

Contingent Liabilities: Contingent liability is a liability which has not accrued or become payable at a future date on the happening of a certain event. If the event does not happen, the liability may not arise at all. Thus the liability may not involve payment of money. As it is not a liability at the date of balance sheet it is shown only as a note at the end of the balance sheet.

Contract: A formal binding agreement between two or more parties, presenting pledges of tasks, acts, processes, products or resources to be provided by one party in exchange for a consideration (money or other goods) from another party.

Contractor: An organization or person who takes on work from another organization but generally retains control over his or her own work. Usually, contract work must meet negotiated standards and be done within a specific period of time. Other stipulation also govern the work.

Contribution: Refers to the excess of revenues over variable costs which is available to cover an enterprise's fixed costs and, if sufficiently large, to provide a profit.

Contribution Margin: Sales less all variable costs) whether manufacturing, selling or administrative).

Contribution Margin Ratio: Refers to the total contribution margin divided by the total sales.

Contributor: Person who contributes capital.

Control: 1(a) power or being able to direct people or an organization (b) restricting or checking something or making sure that something is kept in check (c) control group: small group which is used to check a sample group; control systems: systems used to check that a computer system or production process is working correctly 2(a) to control a business: to direct a business (b) to make sure that something is kept in check or is not allowed to develop. In terms of accounting, control refers to the process of checking actual financial performance against planned performance: in general, the power to direct an organization.

Control Chart: Pictorial presentation of data that managers use to compare actual performance with standards.

Controllable Costs: Costs that can be influenced by a given manager within a given time period.

Controller: Usually the person financially in charge of business.

Controlling: Comprises of comparing results with plans in general, appraising results against performance standards, devising effective media, transferring detailed data into form showing comparisons and variances, suggested corrective sections, if needed, informing responsible members if interpretations, and adjusting controlling in the light of control results.

Convertibility: Refer to the freedom to exchange any currency for another currency at the ruling rate of exchange.

Convertible: The capacity of one financial instrument to be converted into another. The expression is usually applied to bonds or preference shares that can be converted into ordinary shares at a specified time, and at the request of the bondholder.

Convertible and Non-convertible Debentures: Convertible debentures are those which have the option of getting a part or full value of their investments converted into equity shares on a fixed date or after some time. They are issued to allow the debenture-holders to participate in the future prosperity of the company. Non-convertible debentures do not enjoy any such right to get themselves converted into equity shares.

Convertible Securities: Refer to the securities which may be converted at given price ratios at the option of the holder at a future date or dates into securities of a different form.

Cooling off Period: During an industrial dispute, a period when negotiations have to be carried on and no action can be taken by either side; period when a person is allowed to think about something which he has agreed to buy on hire-purchase but may possibly change his mind.

Co-operate: To work together.

Co-operation: Working together.

Co-operative Banks: These banks are organized on co-operative lines. They encourage thrift, accept money on deposits and extend loans to the members at a relatively reasonable rate of interest. Co-operative Banks are primarily intended to help agriculturists by providing loans at low rates of interest and on easy terms. They are organized both at State as well as District level.

Co-operative Society: A cooperative society is a voluntary association of individuals, generally belonging to one homogenous group, who associate together to promote their common interests. It is generally formed and registered under the Cooperative Societies Act, 1912. This form of organ can be applied to every conceivable form of economic activity. Nowadays there are a large number of credit societies, retail stores, building societies, marketing societies and producers' societies which are formed and run on the basis of cooperation.

Co-partner: Person who is a partner in a business with another.

Copy Writer: Person who writes copy for advertisements.

Copyright: The legal protection given to artistic, literary, dramatic and musical works to prevent them from being copied without their creator's agreement. In general such protection lasts for the lifetime of the creator and for 50 years after his or her death. Copyright also protects things like distinctive logo design and advertising material. It has been included in a recent international effort to provide greater protection around the world to intellectual property rights. The Berne Convention (set up in 1886) also supposedly gives protection in those many countries that have signed it. But it has no teeth to punish wrongdoers, and no system to arbitrate in disputes. This attempts to protect the work of one writer from being freely copied or in any way reproduced by another. Apart from certain limited exceptions. e.g. short 'quotes' as part of another work the law does not allow an another's work to be used or reproduced without getting prior written permission and will punish all parties to such an offence including the printer as well as the publisher.

Cornering the Market: A firm or company is said to corner a market when it obtains a virtual monopoly over particular goods or services. It is then able to dictate its own price. In the past this sometimes happened in the market of raw materials.

Corporate Conscience: An organizations' obligation to society for humane and constructive policies.

Corporate Identity: The unique characteristics of a corporation together define its identity. These characteristics include obvious things like the design of its officers and the style of its packaging as well as less tangible things its beliefs and the way it conducts its business. Wally Olins, a specialist corporate identity consultant, says that an effective identity depends on two things: credibility and consistency. "It must spring from the organization's own roots, its values and behaviour, its strength and its weaknesses. And it must be carefully and consistently expressed".

Corporate Modelling: The term used for the construction and use of a computer based model of an organization to carry out the calculations required to produce results of business activities based on given sets of assumptions and predictions.

Corporate Planning: Refers to an approach to top level management problems which emphasises: (a) the need for an organization to decide exactly what its objectives are; and (b) the need for long-term planning in every part of the organization to achieve these objectives.

Corporate Raider: A term used with reference to individuals with very large resources of ready money who, either personally or through a company which they control, buy heavily in the equity of a target company with a view to either taking control of that company or, more frequently forcing the directors of the target company to protect their own position and that of the company itself by taking steps that will enhance the attractiveness of the equity to an extent sufficient to dissuade present holders from selling. These measures will usually cause the share price to escalate and enable the raider to resell the shares acquired at a considerable profit.

Corporate: Referring to a large organization.

Corporate Risk: The total risk involved in a business is termed as corporate risk. It mainly comprises two types of risk. Financial risk which is arising out of debt finance and business risk which has been the basic risk involved in the firm's day to day operations.

Corporation Logo: A company's emblems and a powerful part of its corporate identity, logo can become as familiar and as powerful as brand names. When AT&T, the USA's former telecommunications monopoly was forcibly broken up, the courts decided that none of the resulting new companies had the right to use AT&T's logo, a distinctive emblem of a Bell Telephone. The logo was withdrawn from use.

Correlation: Degree to which there is a relationship between two sets of data.

Correspondence: Letters or messages sent.

Cosmetic: Referring to the appearance of people or things.

Cost: 1 (a) amount of money when has to be paid for something; (b) costs: expenses involved in a court case; 2 (a) to have a price (b) to cost a product: to calculate how much money will be needed to make a product, and so work out its selling price

Cost Accountant: Generally an accountant whose job concerns the fixing to monies due for work done in manufacturing a product (i.e. reckoning the cost of material and labour consumer) but who is increasingly called upon to estimate that probable unit cost of a manufacturing process so that a price can be projected for the purpose of making a tender. In this sense the work is closely allied to that of a quantity surveyor.

Cost Accounting: Refers to the accumulation and assignment of historical costs to units of product and departments, primarily for purposes of stock (inventory) valuation and profit (income) measurement. Limitations of cost accounting is the process of accounting for costs. It includes the accounting procedures relating to recording of all income and expenditure and the preparation of periodical statements and report with the object of ascertaining and controlling costs.

Such cost accounting besides being a process for cost finding and cost recording, is good technique for ascertaining profitability, and for decision-making. The main source of cost information for management accounting is cost accounting. However, a limitation of a cost accounting is its emphasis on cost data. Hence, it is considered very narrow in its perspective for it fails to consider the revenue aspect in detail.

Cost Benefit Analysis: The evaluation of the social and/or economic worth of a prospective project. It attempts to measure in monetary terms not only the visible calculable gains and losses of a project but also the abstract benefits of possible detrimental results. If the total projected 'gain' exceeds the foreseeable 'loss' then the project may be approved. Such analyses are not only applied to future possibilities but also to existing situations to decide whether to maintain or scrap them. Cost benefit analyses are viewed with some cynicism particularly in situations which require a number of subjective assessments; they are often regarded as no more than academic games.

Cost Centre: A unit whose direct costs can be ascertained and to which fixed costs can be allocated in the pursuit of effective financial control. This unit may be a department, a place, a person or even a machine. Contrast with profit centre.

Cost Control: Refers to the procedure by which the management accountant evaluated the actual cost of a capital project or a manufacturing operation for the purpose of comparison with the authorized estimates or cost standard.

Cost Effective: Which gives value, especially when compared with something else.

Cost Function: Refers to the relationship, expressed as an equation between a cost and one or more variables.

Cost Minimization: For any given level of output that choice of input combination which provides the smallest possible total cost. The choice of a cost minimizing firm facing fixed input prices and using the two factors inputs. Capital K and Labour L, can be illustrated using isocost lines and isoquants.

Cost of Capital: An average of the costs of a company's various types of capital: ordinary shares, preference shares, debentures, bonds, loans, retained profit and so on. The cost of a loan is the interest paid on it; the cost of a share is the dividend. The tax treatment of these costs (interest and dividends) varies in such a way that it is usually more attractive for companies to borrow than to raise new equity.

Cost of Living: Money which has to be paid for food, heating, rent, etc.

Cost of Sales: The costs associated with making the products that have been sold in a period. This includes the appropriate proportions of production overheads, but not administration expenses. It excludes the costs of unsold production. The cost of sales is deducted from the sales revenue of the period in order to calculate gross profit from trading. The cost of sales is not the same as the purchases of materials for the period for two reasons; first, stocks (inventories) may have been built up or reduced during the period; second, work will probably have been carried out on the stocks during the period. Thus the cost of sales includes the factory wages and overheads. In order to adjust for stock changes, the calculation of the cost of sales is opening stock plus purchases of materials and work done on the stock less closing stock.

Cost Plus Pricing: Refers to a pricing practice whereby firms add a margin on to average variable cost so as to cover fixed costs and some reasonable level of profits.

Cost Push. That increases the cost of the factors of production available for a product, making the product costly. This includes the price of imported raw materials and any rise in property rents. Most importantly, it includes rise in wage costs. Hence employers argue that any wage increase above the rate of inflation is itself inflationary.

Cost-Cutting: Reducing costs.

Cost-effectiveness: Being cost effective.

Costing: Calculation of the manufacturing costs, and so the selling price of a product.

Costly: Expensive or costing a lot of money.

Cottage Industry: Based in the producer's own home.

Counter: Long flat surface in a shop for displaying and selling goods; legal selling of shares which are not listed in the official Stock Exchange list; counter where things are sold cheaply; place where tickets are sold; shop in a factory or warehouse where goods are sold to retailer; section of a shop where gloves are sold; sales staff who serve behind counters.

Counter Advertising: Advertising aimed as a reply to a competitor's advertisements.

Counter Claim: claim for damages made in reply to a previous claim.

Counter-Offer: Higher offer made in reply to another offer.

Counterbid: Higher bid in reply to a previous bid.

Countermand: To countermand an order: to say that an order must not be carried out.

Counterpart: Person who has a similar job in another company.

Countervailing Duty: Or matching duty. A situation achieved when an excise duty on an article produced at home becomes equal to the customs duty imposed on a similar article imported from abroad, neither the home produced nor imported product being given an advantage.

Coupon: A certificate which gives the consumer a price reduction on a specific product. Coupons can be included in print advertising mailed to house holders or they can be enclosed in or printed on a product's packaging. In the USA coupons are heavily used by consumer-goods manufactures, despite the fact that their redemption rates than 5%. City newspapers often have large shopping sections stuffed with coupon offers in their Thursday and Friday editions. Sunday newspapers, too, frequently include coupon inserts. Coupons are commonly used to encourage the purchase of a new product. When used to stimulate sales of a mature product they represent a form of price reduction that is more subtle than straightforward price cutting, and less likely to be noticed by competitors. Low redemption rates can become a problem for manufacturers who use coupons. Retailers may be tempted to redeem the coupons from the manufacturers, but give the price reduction on products other than the couponed ones. In other words, retailers allow the discounted amount to be set off against the total bill, thus destroying the point of the promotion. In finance a slip often attached to bearer bonds, the surrender of which gives right to a dividend at a particular date. There are normally a number of coupons. A coupon is torn off the coupon sheet each year or other period.

Coupon Rate: Refers to the rate of return on a bond or debenture expressed as a fixed percentage of the face value.

Cover Charge: Charge for a seat and a table, in addition to the charge for food and drink.

Covering Letter or Covering Note: Letter or note sent with documents to say why you are sending them.

Craft: Traditional manufacture done by hand.

Craftsman: Person who works in a craft.

Craftsmanship: Skill in doing craft work.

Crash: What happens when a Stockmarket falls unnaturally, and a lot of financial institutions go bust at the same time. The greatest crash this century occured in 1929 in the USA. Since then crashes have been much smaller or the figment of a Writer's imagination. J.K. Galbraith, in his classic book *The Great Crash 1929*, attributed that particular crash to five main causes. (a) The poor distribution of income in American society. The top 5% of the population was reckoned to be receiving 33% of all personal income. (b) Bad corporate structures. The 1920s was a decade of stockmarket fraudsters and crooks who bled corporations of huge sums of money. (c) Bad banking structure. There were too many independent units and the structure was such that the failure of one of them led to others collapsing in a domino effect. (d) The USA's foreign balance. There was a declining trade surplus for the first time in modern history. (e) The poor state of economic intelligence at the time. The government made decisions that were contrary to the best interests of the economy but there was inadequate data on what actually was the state of the economy.

Crawling Peg: Refers to a compromise arrangement between a fixed exchange rate and a floating exchange rate, where the exchange value of a currency has been allowed to alter over time but only by some agreed upon percentage each year.

Creative Accounting: A form of accounting in which the presentation of financial data is manipulated to the advantages of an organization in any way possible within the law (or not as the case may be).

Creativity: Ability to use the imagination to produce new ideas or things.

Credibility: Discrepancy between claims for a product made by the manufacturer and acceptance of these claims by the target audience.

Credit: A wide term which has been used in connection with operations or states involving lending, generally at short-term. To 'give credit' is to finance, directly or indirectly, the expenditures of others against future repayment.

Credit Card: A card which is issued to customers by a bank or group of bodies or other agency (e.g. Diners' Club) which provides the holder direct access to credit, e.g. from a retailer, hotel etc., or in the case of some cards issued by banks, to cash from the banks operating the particular scheme. The credit card is becoming a major instrument in consumer transactions and is replacing the cheque in the payment of everyday debts. In its simplest form it is a method of obtaining credit, i.e., the user can make purchases on credit up to an amount agreed by him with the credit card company merely by presenting the card to the vendor in place of cash.

Credit Insurance: A form of insurance against financial loss incurred through default by debtors in a trading situation. This may involve monies due for goods or services provided, and may arise through the insolvency of the debtor or from protracted default due to economic or political circumstances.

Credit Control: The term which is denoting the set of measures used by the monetary authorities to control the volume of lending by certain groups of financial institutions, e.g., bank credit and hire purchase credit.

Credit Guarantee: Refers to a type of insurance whereby a credit guarantee association offers insurance against default.

Credit Management: Refers to the management of an enterprise's debtors (accounts receivable).

Credit Note: A written message informing a customer that his or her account with a supplier has been credited (and by how much). Credit notes are frequently used when a customer returns goods as being below standard, or when there has been a short shipment.

Credit Rating: A formal assessment of a company's creditworthiness, and of its capacity to meet payment schedules on time. A credit rating is often obtained by a trader dealing with a new customer for the first time. It may come from the client's bankers of existing suppliers, or from one of the specialist agencies (like Dun & Bradstreet) that provide such ratings, for a fee. Therefore it is an evaluation of the soundness of an individual or business firm as a credit risk. It has been usually based on the three 'Cs' of credit: (a) character or integrity: (b) capacity, or earning power, and (c) capital, or the overall financial status of the applicant.

Credit Restrictions: Refer to the measures which are taken or imposed by the monetary authorities; to limit or reduce the volume of credit extended by banks and other financial institutions.

Credit Risk: Companies whose business involves selling on credit, often for extended periods, are prone to incur cash flow problems emanating from the inability of debtors to meet due payment dates, or, in extreme cases, totally reneging on amounts owing for goods or services supplied.

Credit Sale: Refers to a procedure for purchasing goods under which the purchaser is paying deposit on receipt of the goods followed by a number of instalments until the debt gets cleared.

Credit Squeeze: A popular term for the state's interference with normal market forces (through Reserve Bank) in an attempt to regulate the level or economic activity by reducing the money supply.

Credit Transfer: A method of settling a debt. It is often used by persons or business with a great many debts to settle at any one time. A list of the creditors is given to the bank, together with the amounts due, and the name and address of each creditor's bank. The bank then transfers the amounts due and the debtor notifies each creditor that the transfer has been made.

Creditor: Person who is owed money; meeting of all persons to whom a bankrupt company owes money to decide how to obtain the money owed.

Creditors: Amounts representing either cash or a claim to services owed to an accounting entity. A creditor is a "truster". Someone to whom a business owes money. The expression is accounts payable. Creditors are created by purchases "on credit" or by loans of various sorts. Short-term creditors are included under current liabilities on a balance sheet; they are expected to be paid within the year. If credit purchase are the cause, the title used might be trade creditors. Long-term creditors are those who are not expected to be paid within the year. These might be trade creditors but are more likely to be holders of bonds or debentures. The latter would normally be entitled to receive interest, whereas trade creditors are not. However, trade creditors often offer discounts for prompt payment, which is an implied way of charging interest.

Crisis: Serious economic situation where decisions have to be taken rapidly.

Crisis Management: The form of management adopted in an emergency or an exceptional situation which focuses all the resources of the organization on getting through a temporary period of difficulty leaving more fundamental or longer-term issue aside. There is a great temptation for this state of affairs to degenerate is not management by crisis.

Criterion: Standard by which something can be judged.

Critical Path Analysis: An operational research technique used in management. The idea is to examine a project in detail with the objective of (1) breaking it down into component parts, and (2) examining each part both in isolation and in its relationship to the other parts. By this means it may be seen how the project can be completed in the best possible way in the shortest possible time.

Critical Path Method (CPM): Refers to a form of Network Analysis suited to projects where past experience provides a useful guide to the future and the relevant information can be fairly accurately estimated. The activities comprising a project are set out in a network diagram showing the sequence in which each activity can be commenced and its duration. The critical path has been that path through the network that provides the minimum time for the project, obtained by summing the activity times of the path having the longest duration. The only way in which the duration of a project can be shortened has been to reduce the time allotted to activities on the critical path.

Criticize: To say that something or someone is wrong or is working badly.

Cross Elasticity of Demand: Changes in demand for an item depending on the selling price of a competing product.

Cross-Selling: Placing complementary products close to each other in a store. The hope is that the customer who is tempted to buy one will spot the other and fall for that as well. For example, place women's skirts close to their blouses and jumpers: or bacon close to eggs.

Crossed Transactions (or non-complementary): A process in Transactional Analysis, i.e., T.A. These occur when the stimulus and response lines are not parallel. For instance the supervisor tries to deal with the employee on an adult-to-adult basis, but the employee responds on a child-to-parent basis or the supervisor speaks to the worker on parent-to-child basis and the worker responds on a parent-to-child basis (see Transactional Analysis).

Crossing Special: A special crossing is one where words are added to a general crossing specifying by name the bank at which the cheque is to be presented.

Crossing: General: Two parallel transverse lines placed across a cheque with or without the words 'not negotiable'. This makes it necessary for the holder to pay the cheque into an account at a bank rather than being able to obtain cash for it across the bank counter, **not negotiable:** If a cheque is crossed 'not negotiable' the holder cannot give a better title than that which he possesses. This does not stop the holder from transferring the cheque to another party but that other party cannot get a better title than that possessed by the holder himself. The negotiability of the cheque has in fact ceased—it is no longer a negotiable instrument.

Cum: A Latin word meaning with. Thus: cum dividend, cum rights, etc.

Cum All: With all advantages. Refers to a description which may get attached to the sale of a security, implying that any dividend interest, rights, bonus or other benefit, just declared or current has been not being withheld.

Cum Bonus: With bonus just declared.

Cum Dividend: A share is bought cum dividend if the purchaser would receive the next payment of dividend.

Cum Interest: With current interest.

Cum Rights: With 'rights' recently issued.

Cumulative Preference Share: A preference share which entitles the holder to receive not only the current dividend but also any unpaid arrears, before any dividend is paid to ordinary shareholders.

Currency: The coins, notes, cheques, etc., accepted within a country as a proper medium of exchange in the conduct of business.

Currency Depreciation: The extent to which the value of a currency has fallen in terms of its exchangeable value for other currencies.

Current Account: An account kept at a bank on which cheques can be drawn and on which interest is not usually paid; also an account in the books of sole traders and partnerships recording fluctuating amounts of proprietorship interest (i.e. shares of profit less drawings).

Current Assets: An accounting term for assets continually turned over in the course of business. Those assets of the company which have been reasonably expected to be realised in cash, or sold, or consumed during the normal operating cycle of the business.

Current Delivery. Delivery in the current calendar month.

Current Liabilities: Those amounts on a balance sheet that are expected to be paid by the business within a year.

Current Ratio: Refers to the ratio of current assets to current liabilities. It is an indicator of the firm's ability to meet out its short-term obligations.

Current: Referring to the present time.

Curriculum Vitae: Summary of a person's work experience and qualifications sent to a prospective employer by someone applying for a job.

Custom Duty: A tax payable on goods exported or imported from a country.

Custom Permit: The forwarding agent procures a custom permit so that he may not face any difficulty in exporting the goods. He applies to the custom office for granting him a custom permit in regard to the goods he wants to export to any foreign country.

Custom: Made specially for one customer; general way of working in a trade.

Customer: Person or company which buys goods (note that the customer may not be the consumer or end user of the product).

Customer Departmentation: Companies that must provide special services to different groups set up departments by types of customers using customer departmentation. For example, a manufacturer may have both an industrial products division for its industrial customers and a consumer products for other customers.

Customer Profile: A description of a business's customers in terms of their age, income, education, social habits, and so on.

Customer Service: Once upon a time it was thought that goods were goods and services were services and never the twin would meet. Nowadays most people realize that there are few services that do not involve some goods—think of all the paper that comes with running a bank account, for example, and even fewer goods that do not involve some sort or service.

Customs and Excise: The agency responsible for the assessment and collection of Customs Duties, Excise Duties and Value Added Tax in many countries.

Cut-throat Competition: The process whereby the producers of goods systematically reduce their selling prices and maintain them at the lowest level possible for such time as it takes to drive competitors who are insufficiently funded or less efficient in producing the same goods out of business.

Cycle: Events which happen in a regularly repeated sequence; the time between a salesman's visits to the same customer; period during which trade expands than slows down and then expands again; models which are used to explain cyclical change.

D

Damage: Harm done to things, money claimed as compensation for harm done.

Damages: An amount awarded by a court to an appellant who has suffered loss as a result of the actions of another party.

Dangerous: Which can be harmful.

Data: Information (letters or figures) available on computer; data from research carried out with the aim of providing specific information about a certain market segment; data from research which has collected general information with no specific market in mind; getting information; store of information in a computer; selecting and examining data in a computer to produce special information; leaflet with data or information about a product.

Data Base: A large comprehensive central or otherwise significant collection of data; especially when carefully organized and recorded so that information may be derived from it by using electronic data processing.

Data Flow Chart: A diagram of the sequence of operations, both manual and automatic, involved in processing data. A data flow chart identifies the particular items of data at each stage and is normally used to describe a complete data processing system.

Data Processing: Systematically operating of data in order to produce new data according to established rules.

Date Stamping: The marketing of perishable food product with a date by which the product should be sold. Date stamping is a legal requirement in many countries.

Database Management System: A computer software package that manages, updates, secures, and gains computer access to databases: for example, dBaseII, dBase III, and Dataflex.

Dated Security: Refers to any security, like a bond, which has a stated redemption date.

Day Book: A bookkeeping term. Day books are books of prime entry. They record the details of purchases and sales as these take place or rather contain or consist of lists of invoices in and invoices out. The ledger is then written up from these books.

Days of Grace: The additional time allowed by custom for payment of a bill of exchange or insurance premium after the actual date on which the amount was due.

Dead Freight: It is the freight payable where the charterer fails to load a complete cargo and the shipowner tends to charge freight for the space he would have otherwise sold.

Dead Stock: Stock of goods for which no further demand can be foreseen.

Deal: Business agreement or affair or contract; to stop an agreement; sale done for cash; agreement where several different items are agreed at the same time; sales promotion to the trade; sales promotion to consumers to organize; to supply an order to trade or to by and sell; to do business with someone; to buy and sell or options his work involves buying and selling shares for clients on the Stock Exchange.

Dealer Brand: A brand name put on a product by a middleman, usually a retailer; for example, Ann Page at the A&P stores in the USA, or St. Michael at the UK's Marks and Spencer. Sometimes known as 'own label' or 'distributor brand'. The increasing success of these brands reflect the growing power of big retail chains.

Dealer: Person who buys and sells; types of advertising material used by shops to stimulate sales; brand owned by a distributor rather by a producer; advertising which includes the names of local dealers that stock the product being advertised; person who sells to the general public; person who sells in bulk to retailers.

Debenture: A long-term debt instrument, often secured on the general creditworthiness of the issuer rather than on any specific asset. When a company is being liquidated, debenture holders have a right to the company's leftovers before ordinary bondholders.

Debenture Redemption Reserve: Refers to a Capital Reserve which is set-up voluntarily by transfers out of profits. By the date of redemption the amounts transferred should be equal to the redemption value of the debentures.

Debit Cards: In addition to cheque cards and credit cards most banks operating cheque accounts offer debit cards to customers. These are similar in appearance to credit cards and can be used for many of the same purposes. The important difference from the user's point involve the granting of credit facilities by the issuer with the customer settling all transactions by means of a card company, the debit card is merely a substitute for a cheque book and each payment by debit card appears on the user's bank statement as if it had been a cheque payment.

Debit: Money which a company owes and money it receives; balance in an account showing that the company owes more money than it has received; plastic card used to transfer money directly from a customer's account to a retailer's account, without the use of cheques; left hand column in accounts showing the money paid or owed to others; entry on the debit side of an account; note showing that a customer owes money; system where a customer allows a company to charge costs to his bank account automatically and where the amount charged can be increased or decreased with the agreement of the customer; to charge an account with a cost; which can be debited.

Debit Note: A term used in accounting. A debit note is sent to a customer when it is intended to charge his account normally in an unusual situation-say when a person has been insufficiently invoiced for goods.

Debt: A debt is money owned by one person or firm to another. It may carry interest covering the period during which it is due but not paid, although common business usage allows an agreement. It also applies for obligation of goods and services.

Debt Finance: It involves borrowing. It refers to the use of loans by companies to finance their operations, especially capital expenditure through long-term loans.

Debt-Equity Ratio: An accounting ratio obtained by dividing total debt to total equity or fund balances. Debt-to Equity Ratio relates all external liabilities to owners' recorded claims. It is also known as 'External-Internal Equity Ratio'. It is determined to measure the firm's obligations to creditors in relation to the funds invested by the owner. Debt-Equity Ratio: External Equities/Internal Equities.

Debt-Service Ratio: This ratio relates the fixed interest charges to the income earned by the business. It is also known as Interest Coverage Ratio. It indicates whether the business has earned sufficient profits to pay periodically the interest charges. It is calculated as follows: Interest Coverage Ratio: Net profit before interest and tax/Fixed interest charges.

Debtor: The person or organization that owed goods, services or money. The person or organization to whom it is due us known as the creditor.

Debug: To trace and eliminate faults: especially errors in a program for a computer.

Decentralization: Dispersal of the centres of authority and decision-making at various levels of an organization. Systematic and consistent delegation of authority by senior officers to their juniors is an important method of achieving decentralization of authority in an organization. Delegation of authority is the process which leads to decentralization of functions. Centralization, as opposed to decentralization, is the systematic and consistent reservation of authority at central points within the organization.

Decimal System: A system in which everything is calculated by decimal division, i.e., by ten.

Decision: Making up one's mind to do something.

Decision Analysis: One of three techniques suggested by Peter Drucker to help a work organization decide on its most appropriate organizational structure. This technique is to establish what the key decisions to be made in the organization actually are as opposed to unquestioned assumptions about what they are. The other two techniques are activities analysis and relations analysis.

Decision Making: The process or activity of selecting, from among possible alternative, a future course of acting. The process of decision making involves five stages: (i) defining the problem; (ii) analysing the problem; (iii) developing of alternative solution; (iv) selecting the best solution; and (v) converting the decision into action and its follow up.

Decision Model: Refers to a method for deciding among courses of action. A formal decision model requires on Objective Function, a set of alternative actions to be considered, a set of probabilities of each state of nature occurring, and a set of outcomes or payoffs.

Decision Table: Refers to a systematic statement in table form of the contemplated actions, state of nature, probabilities and outcomes contained in a Decision Model.

Decision Tree: A diagram of a sequence of decisions, each of which involves choosing between a known number of alternatives and depends on the results of the previous decision.

Decision-Making Skill: Adequate conceptual understanding is required for taking sound decisions. With the development of intellectual, communication and organizational understanding skills, the manager reaches that stage of awareness when he can take effective decisions. The decisions so made will have to be carried out at the working level and hence the most difficult task is to see that such decisions are carried out at the proper time by the right people.

Declare: To make an official statement or to announce to the public.

Decline: Gradual fall; final stage in the life cycle of a product when the sales and profitability are falling off and the product is no longer worth investing in.

Decruiting: Policy of replacing older workers with younger ones.

Deduct: To take money away from a total.

Deductible: Which can be deducted.

Deduction: Removing of money from a total or money removed from a total.

Deed: A person's statement made in writing on paper, parchment, or vellum bearing the person's seal and his signature, which the person has 'delivered' meaning that he has indicated that the statement is to take effect so that he will have to abide by it.

Deed of Trust: A document that creates a trust: also, a document by which an organization or person transfers ownership of land to an independent trustee for holding until a debt on the land (a mortgage) is paid off.

Deep Discount Bond: A bond which is carrying a low or zero interest coupon and issued at a substantial discount. Tax benefits may arise from lack of symmetry in the treatment of borrowers and lenders.

Default: Failure to repay a loan according to the terms of a contract. Once a borrower is in default there are several legal moves that a lender can make to try and recover the money, or to get hold of any underlying security backing the loan.

Deferred Charge: An expenditure which is carried forward to be written off in future periods.

Deferred Compensation: Payment made by an organization to its employees at some future date, e.g., pensions upon retirement.

Deferred Income: Income which is received or recorded before it is deemed to be earned.

Deferred Shares: These are shares which rank for dividend and return of capital after all other classes of shares have received a fixed rate of dividend or have been paid out in the case of winding-up of the company. These shares are also called as founder(s)' shares having different rights as to dividend, capital or otherwise except the voting rights. Such shares are not allowed to be issued by a company after the commencement of the Companies Act, 1956.

Deficiency Need: Lower -level need that is satisfied by external elements, such as salary, pay and job security.

Deficit: Amount by which spending is higher than income; the accounts show a loss; to put money into an account to balance it; situation when a country imports more than it exports; planning by a government to borrow money to cover the shortfall between tax income and expenditure.

Deficit Financing: Means situation where expenditure exceeds income such that a deficit is operated deliberately. Keynes was the first to suggest that governments should deliberately run a planned deficit as part of monetary policy.

Definitions of Management: E.F.L. Breach defines management as a social process entailing responsibility for the effective (or efficient) planning and regulation of the operation of an enterprise, such responsibility involving (a) judgment and decision in determining plans and using data to control performance and progress against plans; (b) the guidance, integration, inspiration, and supervision of the personnel comprising the enterprise and carrying out its operation. According to Henry Fayol, the main purpose of management is "To forecast and to plan, to organise, to command, to coordinate, and to control: to foresee and provide means examining the future and drawing up the plan of actions: to organise means for building up the dual structure, material and human, of an undertaking: to command means for maintaining activity among the personnel, to coordinate means combining together, unifying and harmonizing all activity and effort: control means seeing that everything occurs in conformity with established rules and expressed command". According to Sprigel, "Administration is a phase of business enterprise that concerns itself with the overall determination of institutional objectives and the policies necessary to be followed in achieving these objectives. Administration predetermines the specific goals and lays down the broad areas within which these goals are to be attained. Administration is a determinative function on the other hand, management is an executive function primarily concerned with coordinating of the broad policies laid down by the administration." Milward says, "Administration is the process and the agency used to establish the object and purpose which an undertaking and its staff are to achieve: secondarily administration has to plan and stablise the broad lines of principles which will govern action. Management is the process and the agency through which the application of policy is planned and supervised." Urwick and Brech have rightly observed: "No ideology, no 'ism,' no political theory can win a greater output with less effort from a given complex of human and material resources, only sound management and it is on such greater output that a higher standard of life, more leisure, more amenities for all must necessarily be founded".

Deflate: To reduce activity in the economy by cutting the supply of money.

Deflation: Means situation in which prices and money incomes have been falling, accompanied by an increase in the value of the monetary units.

Defunct Company: A company that has been struck off the official register of companies because it has ceased to function.

Degree: Qualification awarded to someone who has passed a course of study at a university or polytechnic, amount or level.

Degree of Control: Means how close a control needs to be maintained. Is it necessary to record production every hour, day or week? Must an accurate inventory count be made of all parts at all stages in their processing? It is obvious that there is a point of diminishing returns where the value of such controls no longer justifies the cost of their accumulation.

Delegation of Responsibility: Job enrichment's basis is delegation of more responsibility to the worker. The worker is allowed to take various decisions many of which were previously taken at higher level. Thus more autonomy is enjoyed by the worker as a result of job richment.

Delegation: The act of passing authority and responsibility for a task onto other usually subordinates in the organization.

Deliver: To transport goods to a customer; goods transported to the customer's address at a price which includes transport costs; goods transported free to the ship or plane but not to the customer's warehouse; price which includes packing and transport.

Delivery: The transfer of title in a financial instrument from one owner to another. Hence delivery date, delivery month, and so on, the time when delivery is to be made.

Delivery Note: May take various forms including that of a part copy of the relevant invoice or advice note. It is basically the paper listing and accompanying goods delivered to a customer and is signed by the customer on receipt, when the note is returned to the vendor it is prima facie evidence of delivery both as to place and person.

Delivery Order: An order requesting a warehouse keeper or dock to deliver goods.

Delivery Period: The interval between sending an order for goods and receiving them. The interval between receiving an order for goods and dispatching them.

Delphi Method: A method of obtaining forecasts of future developments in which a number of experts are asked to give their individual forecasts: these are collected, and summarized; a summary of all forecasts is sent to each expert and each is asked whether he would reconsider his views in the light of what others have said; the process is repeated until the predictions are satisfactorily uniform.

Delphi Technique: It is primarily intended for use in long-range forecasting, it also can be used to generate creative solutions to unique problems in an organisation. It is designed to develop a range of possible alternatives that reflect the collective judgement of the participants.

Demand: Refers to the amount of a commodity or service which will be bought at any given price per unit of time.

Demand Deposit: A sum of money deposited by someone in a bank on condition that he can withdraw it on demand.

Demand Pull: That consumers are demanding more than is being produced, and thus pushing up prices. They can only do this if the amount of money in the economy exceeds the growth in production plus the rate of inflation. One theory focuses anti-inflationary efforts on keeping down wage demands; the other on controlling the nation's money supply. Inflation undesirably redistributes wealth and income, hitting hardest those on fixed incomes and benefiting most those heavily in debt. It also undermines the basis for calculating value, and enormously complicates the lives of accountants. It is not in itself, however, necessarily a deterrent to growth. Many developing countries have combined high growth rates with high inflation.

Demarketing: The process of discouraging consumers from buying or consuming. Governments demarket cigarettes by requiring that health warnings be printed on every pack. "Share your bath with someone tonight" was a creative and well received slogan used by a UK water authority to demarket water during a summer drought. Raising prices or restricting distribution in a form of rationing can also be regarded as demarketing.

Democratic Management: A type of management which emphasizes the importances of consulting people about the work of the organization and involving staff at all levels in the process of making decisions usually contrasted with authoritarian management.

Demographic: Referring to demography dividing a market up into segments according to the age, sex, income levels, etc., of the potential customers.

Demography: Study of populations and relevant statistics (such as age, sex, income, education, etc.).

Demotion: Assignment of an employee to a job of lower status, responsibility, or pay. There are three basic kinds of demotions: (1) voluntary demotion, usually the result of a reduction in force, (2) involuntary demotion, which results from a worker's inability to perform adequately on the job, and (3) disciplinary demotion, which usually takes place after an employee has been repeatedly warned to stop some kind of misconduct or disruptive behaviour.

Demurrage: Liquidated damages included in a contract. Normally takes the form of a payment for each day completion is delayed or ships are kept waiting.

Department: Specialized section of a large company.

Departmental Stores: A departmental store may be described as a large retail establishment having in the same building a number of departments each of which confines its activities to one particular kind of trade and forms a complete unit in itself and is centrally controlled. A departmental store implies the opening of a number of shops under one roof and control, each dealing in a certain line of goods. The idea of departmental stores is to provide a large variety of merchandise from a pin to a motor car at one place. It aims at providing convenience in shopping and acts as a universal provider.

The customers can get all their requirements at one place and need not go from place to place making purchases.

Departmental Undertaking: A departmentally managed undertaking managed by the officials of the government under the charge of the Secretary of the Ministry concerned. Such organization do not enjoy any legal entity. They are managed by civil servants who are government employees and who work under the control of a Minister.

Departmentation: Departmentation means divisionalization of work, the desire to obtain organization units to manageable size and to utilize managerial ability. Structure and design of an organization are shaped significantly by the departmentation followed. The chief means of departmentation include by (1) Function (2) Product (3) Territory (4) Customer (5) Process (6) Task force and (7) Matrix. An organizer is free to use any means of departmentation in constructing an organization structure.

Deposit: There are several meanings. (a) Money left as security before receipt of a service, such as a tenant might give a landlord befoie moving into a furnished property, or a telephone company might demand before connecting a line for a new customer. (b) Natural resources found underground, as in "South Africa's rich mineral deposits". (c) Money left with a bank for safe-keeping. Such deposits come in many different forms.

Deposit Account. An account that is always kept in credit, and on which interest is paid.

Depot: Central warehouse for goods; centre for transport.

Depreciation: A charge against the profit of a period to represent the wearing out of fixed assets in that period. So machinery and equipment, vehicles and buildings are depreciated, therefore, accountants do not charge the whole cost of a fixed asset against the profit of the year of purchase, but charge it gradually over the years of purchase, but charge it gradually over the years of its use and wearing out. This fits with the matching concept. The word amortization is also used, particularly in the context of intangible assets.

Depression: Means prolonged and severe slowing-down of economic activity exemplified by mass unemployment and a level of national income well below its potential level.

Deregulation: Reducing government control over an industry.

Derivatives: These are financial instruments which are essentially a by product of the markets in shares, bonds, commodities, etc. They comprise for the most part futures and options which are known as derivative assets in so far as they derive from a more visible series of underlying assets with volatile prices.

Derived Demand: A marketing concept derived from economics. Industrial marketers do not sell directly to consumers but to intermediary manufacturers. The demand for industrial goods and services is thus "derived" from the demand for the consumer goods which require the intermediary product. Thus the demand for the machinery to make tin cans is derived from the demand for products which are packaged in cans.

Determining the Resources: For realistic programming we must recognize the need for facilities, materials and supplies and personnel. Next we should appraise the availability of these necessary resources. If any of them is not available we should set-up another project designed to obtain this resource.

Devaluation: A sudden downward jerk in the value of a currency vis-a-vis other currencies. Devaluations occur when a country's costs have risen faster than those of its competitors, and when its exports are not competitive in price. Devaluations are exacerbated by the activity of speculators in the foreign-exchange markets. They buy and sell vast quantities of currencies in anticipation of a devaluation. Devaluations can result in huge relative changes in a currency's value; 10% overnight, for example. This can wipe out any ordinary exporter's profit at a stroke, which is one good reason why exporters prefer to work within a framework of relatively fixed exchanges rates.

Developer: Person who plans and builds a group of new houses or new factories.

Developing Country: Country which is not fully industrialized.

Development: Planning the production of a new product and constructing the first prototypes.

Development Expenditure: Research and development expenditure.

Development of More Resources: Marketing promotes the development of economic resources of a country and puts it on the road to faster economic development. The revenues generated by business houses are invested in exploiting more and more economic resources of the country.

Difference between Marketing and Selling: "Selling focuses on the needs of the seller, marketing on the needs of the buyer. 'Selling' is preoccupied with the seller's need to convert his product into cash, 'marketing' with the idea for satisfying the needs of the consumer by means of the product and the whole cluster of things associated with creating, delivering and finally consuming it." Theodore Levit. Marketing is customer-oriented, whereas selling is product oriented.

Marketing emphasises long term goals such as growth and stability of business, whereas selling emphasises short term objective of profit maximization. Marketing starts before the product is produced while, selling starts after the product has been produced. Selling ends with the sale of goods. Marketing continues even after sales, e.g., after sale service, study of future demand, etc.

Differential: Which shows a difference; advantage that one product has over rival products in the market; different tariffs for different classes of goods difference in price between products in a range; scaling technique which gives a range of possible answers between two opposite descriptive words; differences in pay for workers doing different jobs in the same industry or profession to reduce differences in pay gradually.

Differential Aptitude Test: Actually a battery involving different tests of aptitudes like verbal reasoning and spatial relations. The test is used to assess educational and vocational performance.

Differentiation: Ensuring that a product has some unique features that distinguish it from competing products.

Diffusion of Responsibility: In social psychology this is the idea that taking responsibility for initiating actions of offering help in an emergency is spread among the people present in the situation. Sometimes the responsibility is so diffuse that no action is taken by anybody. The term can also be used more generally about the diffusion of decision-making responsibility in the presence of other people in a situation.

Dilution: Refers to the decrease in control and earnings per share suffered by existing shareholders on a new issue of shares or a conversion of other securities into shares in which they have a less than proportionate share.

Diminishing Returns: In economics this is the point beyond which any additional input of resources will result in a less than proportionate increase in output. This idea has been borrowed by psychology where it describes an improvement that gets progressively smaller with each succeeding increment. For example, it is used in the study of learning and memory where after a large gain at the beginning extra practice begins to provide less and less gain.

Direct Advertising: Advertisements that are distributed to their audience as individual items and not as part of a publication containing other material. The most common examples are leaflets, brochures and catalogues distributed by retailers, by post or by door-to-door distribution.

Direct Costs: Those costs which can be associated with the production of particular units or types of products, such as manufacturing wages or manufacturing materials.

Direct Expenses: Expenses which can be directly associated with the cost of producing a particular article or service as opposed to overhead expenses.

Direct Labour: Labour which can be directly associated with manufacturing a product or providing a service.

Direct Labour Costs: The costs associated with those members of the work force directly involved in the production of goods and services. Compare with indirect labour costs.

Direct Mail: Selling a product by sending publicity material to possible buyers through the post; advertising by sending leaflets to people by post; single mailing of direct mail advertising literature to send something by post.

Direct Marketing: The shortest channel of distribution, when a manufacturer of a product deals directly with the consumer.

Direct Selling: The selling of consumer goods by the manufacturer, or a wholesaler, directly to the public, i.e., bypassing the retailer methods of direct selling include: mail order through catalogues carried by part time agents; the insertion of an order form in a newspaper or a magazine advertisement' cash and carry warehouses; Sunday markets; door-to-door salesmen; circulation of sectors of the population on the basis of lists of names and addresses sometimes bought from firms specializing in the preparation of such lists; parties at which goods are displayed and ordered custom by telephone.

Direct Taxation: Taxation levied directly on the citizens of a state and paid directly by them to the revenue authorities either personally or through an employer.

Direct-Response Advertising: Advertising that is intended to persuade people to communicated directly with the advertiser as opposed to advertising intended to persuade people to go to buy the advertiser's product.

Director: Person appointed by the shareholders to help run a company.

Director's Fees: Payments made to directors by reason only of their position as directors.

Director's Report: A report to shareholders required by the Companies Acts.

Discharge: Carrying out of a job.

Discharge of Contract: This means the fulfilment of the obligations imposed by a contract, or else an agreement to negate the contract or put one in its place. It can also mean a situation where a party may be released from his obligation by impossibility of performance or by operation of law.

Discipline: Self-control needed to do a job.

Discount: (a) Refers to a reduction in a previously determined price granted to a customer or class of customers, (b) Also, refers to the difference between the price at which a security was issued and the price at which it now stands.

Discount House: A business institution which will buy acceptances from their owners for less than their face value and hold them to maturity.

Discount Rate: Either the relevant rate for discounting future inflows or outflows of cash, for a particular person or business (see discounted cash flow); or the rate at which discount houses or other banks can borrow from the central bank.

Discount Store: A term often used to describe a retail establishment which offers goods on discount.

Discounted Cash Flow: Any profitable investment, whether it be the purchase of shares or an income-earning asset, investor with a cash return over a period, the return being monies earned by the asset after deduction of the costs of making the asset productive.

Discounting the Bills of Exchange: A bill of exchange may be discounted when purchased by a third party for a sum lower than the amount receivable on maturity. The person discounting the bill gains by receiving money at an earlier date. The amount of discount will vary according to the risk the purchaser takes. A good bill is one which is backed or countersigned by a well-known finance house or bank. Bills are normally discounted with banks or on a larger scale with institutions known as Discount Houses.

Discretionary: Which can be done if someone wants powers which the minister could use if he or she wished; income left after fixed payments have been made and whose spending is therefore subject to advertising influence.

Discretionary Costs: Fixed Costs that arise from periodic appropriation decisions.

Discretionary Income: That part of a consumer's disposable income that is not allocated for in advance in the form of mortgage or consumer-credit repayments, school fees, or other standing orders.

Diseconomies of Scale: The disadvantages resulting from a large as opposed to a small-scale of operations in an organization. They include difficulties of co-ordination, communication and adaptability to changing circumstances. Compare with economies of scale..

Dishoarding: Putting goods back on to the market when they have been hoarded or stored for some time.

Dispatch: Sending of goods to a customer; department which deals with the packing and sending of goods to customers; note saying that goods have been sent.

Dispersion Measure: A statistic which indicates the degree to which a frequency distribution or a probability distribution spreads out around its mean. The most frequently used dispersion measure is the standard deviation.

Display Advertisement: A printed advertisement which forms part of a newspaper, magazine, book or similar publication which has been especially designed with the intention of attracting the attention of readers.

Disposable Income: This term is used to describe the amount of a person's wage or salary after all compulsory deductions, such as direct taxating, pension contributions, compulsory savings deposit and national insurance contributions, have been made.

Disposable: Which can be used and then thrown away; income left after tax and national insurance have been deducted.

Dispose: To get rid of to sell cheaply.

Dispute: Disagreement.

Dissatisfaction: Being discontented or not being satisfied.

Dissatisfier: Factor contributing to job dissatisfaction as mentioned by workers responding to a study by Frederick Herzberg, who called these dissatisfiers "hygiene factors".

Distance Freight: Freight charge based on the distance over which the goods are transported.

Distribute: To share out dividends; to send out goods from a manufacturer's warehouse to retail shops.

Distribution: A key marketing function; the process of getting products to consumers. Although some manufacturers can and do sell direct to consumers (see direct marketing), practical considerations require most to use a distribution system composed of independent middlemen, usually wholesalers and retailers. These intermediaries carry out critically important marketing activities, such as buying and selling, sorting and storing, transporting and financing products as they move from producer to consumer, all of which are necessary functions if products are to be found by consumers in the right place at the right time and at the right price. Distribution can also refer to a measure of market penetration; the number of retail outlets which stock and sell a particular that could possibly sell that product.

Distribution Network: The wholesalers, retailers and other firms in an economy that do not manufacture or produce goods but participate in the process of changing the ownership of goods from producer to consumer.

Distributive Industry: That part of a country's industry which is concerned with selling goods and services directly to the consumer, in contrast with the manufacturing sector and the construction sector. Retailers are said to be in distributive trade.

Distributor: A marketing term for a retailer who deals in the wares of certain specified manufacturers, having perhaps the sole agency for an area. He buys and sells on his own account and is not therefore an agent for a single manufacturer.

Diversification: Adding another quite different type of business to a firm's existing trade; adding new types of products to the range already made; diversifying into quite a different type of business.

Divestment: Action or process, undertaken by a firm, of transferring ownership and control of part of its activities to another firm.

Divestiture: Strategy in which a firm sells one of its major divisions.

Dividend: The share of a company's profit paid to a shareholder. The amount he or she receives will depend on the number of shares held. Unlike interest, dividends are optional payments though failure to pay dividend will have an adverse effect on the market value of the shares as very few will be interested in purchasing a non-earning investment.

Dividend Policy: Refers to a company's policy on the division of its profits between distribution to shareholders as dividends and retention for investment.

Dividend Warrant: A document entitling the recipient to a sum of money which can be obtained from a bank. It is similar to a cheque. It states gross amount, tax deducted and net amount paid. The shareholder who is not liable to taxation at standard rate will be able to claim a return (in part of whole) of the tax paid by sending the tax voucher attached to the warrant, to the appropriate tax authorities.

Dividend Yield: Companies usually declare dividends as a percentage on nominal value of shares. This value may be far removed from market value. A company which has been in business over an extended period will, if only because of inflation, find that the current listed market price of its shares is usually well above the price at which they were originally issued, whether this was at the nominal value or at that value plus a premium. This ratio of the dividend to the current market price is referred to as the dividend yield.

Division of Labour: It involves breaking down the work of an organization into a series of tasks or operations which allows specialization by workers in one area of activity.

Document: Any written, spoken, or visual record, contracts, and vouchers useful for future reference.

Domestic: Referring to the home market or the market of the country where the business is situated; consumption on the home market in the country where a company produces goods for domestic consumption for use in the home; electrical machines (such as washing machines) which are used in the home.

Donee: The recipient of a gift.

Donor: A person who gives property or a title to property, to another person. This word is usually applied to gifts, i.e., where no payment is made.

Double-Entry Bookkeeping: A form of bookkeeping devised centuries ago whereby each transaction is entered twice, a transaction being by its nature two sided. The purchase of an asset necessitates the recording of the asset and also separately, of the debt incurred or the money paid. The book in which all the accounts are kept is known as the ledger, though the cash account is normally kept in a separate book, known as the cashbook. At any time the total debit balances in the ledger should equal the total credit balances. If this is so it is an indication that (in the absence of compensating errors) double entries have been properly made. This is because of the two entries made one is always a debit and the other a credit entry.

Double-Taxation: It is fundamental principle of tax law in most nations that the same income should not be taxed twice. In consequence, there is a network of agreements between pairs of nations that seek to avoid taxing income in one country when it has already been taxed in another. This applies in particular to income that arises in one country, but which is remitted to a resident in another. Double taxation can also occur when income passes from one taxable entity (like a corporation) to another (like a shareholder). Attempts to reduce the double taxation of dividends (paid out of a company's taxed income to taxable individuals) have been less widespread than the attempts to eliminate the taxation of the same income in two fiscal jurisdictions.

Down Market: Appealing to a less wealthy section of the population; the company has decided to make products which appeal to a wider section of the public.

Downside: Possibility of making a loss (in an investment) they have been asked for pessimistic forecasts.

Downtime: Period when a machine could be working but does not work because of a fault or because of a break in planned maintenance operations.

Downturn: Movement towards lower prices or sales or profits.

Downward Communication: Information transmitted from higher to lower levels in an organization, also known as vertical communication.

Drawback: Thing which is not convenient or which is likely to cause problems; rebate on customs duty for imported goods when these are then used in producing exports.

Drawee: A person or bank asked to make a payment by a drawer.

Drawer: Person who writes a cheque

or a bill asking a drawee to pay money to a payee.

Drive: Energy or energetic way of working vigorous effort to save money or materials vigorous effort to incrcase sales; he is very energetic in business.

Due: To be ready for payment; bill which as to be paid on May 1st amount owed to us which should be paid expected to arrive; written in the correct legal form after thinking seriously about the problem.

Dumping: Means the sale of a good on a foreign market at a price below its marginal cost and lower than those prevailing in their domestic market. Dumping amounts to prima facie evidence of unfair competition and is against the rules of the General Agreement on Tariffs and Trade (GATT). Proof that dumping has taken place is, however, often difficult to establish. Exchange rate fluctuations, and the use of transfer-pricing methods that might themselves be quite legitimate, can blur the most genuine attempt to compare export prices with domestic prices.

Duopoly: A market in which only two firms compete or which is dominated by two firms.

Duplication: Business transactions inevitable demand a degree of document duplication, whether these be invoices receipts or letters- for every one issued it is imperative that at least one copy be retained by the issuer. Traditionally this was effected by producing carbon copies of all such documents. Whether typed or handwritten. This is still the case with many documents, for example delivery notes, which tend to be printed in triplicate. The sender then retains a copy of the signature admitting delivery. Now-a-days to obviate the need to insert sheets of carbon paper, specially prepared NCR (no carbon required) paper tends to be used. In circumstances where multiple copies of a document are required a photocopier is employed. There are very many photocopying machines now available ranging from the fairly small to the free-standing cabinet variety with varying degrees of sophistication.

Durable Goods: Goods purchased for use over's a period such as washing machines or refrigerators. The consumer's equivalent of a fixed asset.

Duty Free Shop: Where goods are sold usually at airports, on ships, etc., at a cheaper price than usual because you do not have to pay the tax on such goods.

Duty: Moral or legal obligation.

Dysfunctional Stress: Lowered performance by a worker who feels bewilderment, powerlessness, pressure or unfair competition.

E

Efficiency: Means the effectiveness with which existing profitable market opportunities are exploited.

Earn: To be paid money for working.

Earned Income: That part of a person's income which is obtained as a result of the application of their own labour, either as an employee or as a self-employed person.

Earning Capacity: or earning power: amount of money someone should be able to earn.

Earnings: Salary or wages or money received in return for work or investment.

Earnings Per Share (EPS): The earnings of a company which is attributable to the ordinary shareholders (common stockholders) divided by the number of ordinary shares.

Earnings Yield: The earnings yield relates that portion of divisible net profit or earnings of a company applicable to the particular investment to the present market price of that investment and should be contrasted with the dividend yield which relates the dividend paid to that same market price. It is the reciprocal of the price earnings ratio.

Economic: Which provides enough money; concept or formula which indicates the most economic or profitable amount of supplies to order, taking into account stock holding costs and quantity discounts offered for large orders referring to the financial state of a country; state of financial collapse in a country; period during which trade expands, then slows down, then expands again; expansion of the commercial and financial situation; increase in the national income; statistics which show how the economy is going to perform in the short or long term; restrictions on trade with a country in order to make its government change policy; the Common Market.

Economic Appraisal: Means the study of the economic implications of a project,as a first step in assessing its acceptability.

Economic Development: Refers to the process of improving the standard of living and well being of thc population of developing countries by raising per capita income. This is usually realised by an increase in industrialization relative to reliance on the agricultural sector.

Economic Liberalism: Refers to doctrine which advocates the greatest possible use of markets and the forces of competition to co-ordinate economic activity.

Economic Man: An invention of economists to support the belief that the motivation of workers depends solely on rational, financial, reward and punishment. The beauty of the invention is that it saves them from thinking about complicated things like group norms or unconscious motivation.

Economic Sanction: When the government of one nation, or of many acting in concert, want to make a token objection to the policies of another, then a common tactic is adopted to disrupt the economy of the offending nation by the imposition of boycotts and embargoes on trade with that country.

Economic Value: A way of valuing asset at the expected future net cash flows from them, discounted to the present. The "discounting" is designed to adjust for the fact that present money is more valuable than the same nominal amount of future money.

Economical: Which saves money or materials or which is cheap; car which does not use much petrol; using resources as carefully as possible.

Economics: Study of the production, distribution, selling and use of goods and services study of financial structures to show how a product or service is costed and what returns it produces.

Economies of Scale: The advantage resulting from a large, as opposed to a small, scale of operation in an organization. They include lower unit costs, greater purchasing power by buying in bulk, opportunities for training, etc.

Effective Supervision: Supervisor's skill in supervising his subordinates as a group is important to successful performance. The greater his skill in using group methods of supervision, greater are the productivity and job satisfaction of his subordinates. Proper frequency of work group meeting as well as the attitudes of the superior towards the ideas of subordinates promote harmonious group action and group supervision.

Effective: Having an effect; producing the result; making an impression; completely fit for work.

Efficiency: Ability to work well or to produce the right work quickly and precisely.

Efficiency Indicators: In studying specific enterprises, which is the heart of our empirical research, we make use of both overall or aggregate firm efficiency indicators and intrafirm measures. The latter type are the most important. We do, of course, make use of such aggregate firm indicators as total profit, sales, output and/or costs; rate of return; market share; growth rate with regard to the above; and actual versus planned performance. But we have found that it is frequently not very meaningful to focus on such aggregate measures in comparative research particularly when highly diverse countries are involved. More disaggregate measures seem to be more fruitful for analysis.

Efficient Market Hypothesis: Refers to the hypothesis that the stock market is a highly efficient pricing mechanism. Efficiency in this context does not refer to the organizational and operational aspects of the market or to the efficient allocation of resources within the economy but to the capacity of the market to convert information into share prices.

Efficient Portfolio: Refers to a combination of securities which maximized the expected return on the securities for a given variance (standard deviation) or, equivalently, minimizes risk for a given expected return.

Elastic: Which can expand or contract easily because of small changes in price; demand which experiences a comparatively large percentage change in response to a change in price; supply which experiences a comparatively large percentage change in response to a change in price.

Elasticity: May be defined as a measure of the percentage change in one variable in respect of a percentage change in another variable.

Elasticity of Demand: A measure of the sensitivity of demand for a product or service to change in either its price (price elasticity) or in the income of the people demanding the product or service (income elasticity). Price elasticity is the ratio of the percentage change in demand to a percentage change in price.

Elasticity of Supply: Means the response of supply to a change in the price of a commodity. If the price rises, the amount supplied will normally get increased. The elasticity may be calculated as follows: Percentage change in quantity supplied, Percentage change in price.

Electronic Data Processing: Any kind of collection, manipulation or analysis of data that makes use of a computer.

Electronic Funds Transfer: Refers to the systems for the transfer of money in which processes based on paper are replaced by electronic techniques.

Eligible: Person who can be chosen.

Embargo: Any prohibition imposed by government on commerce or freight. When it is forbidden to export goods to certain countries, then goods are said to be subject to embargo. The embargo may be imposed by either side: it prevents the unloading and loading of certain goods. It may also take the form of preventing ships entering or leaving certain ports.

Emoluments: A terms used to refer to the total benefits received by an employee in addition to money paid as salary it includes goods or services acquired as benefits in kind, e.g., private use of a company car free holidays abroad, subsidized accommodation and free meals.

Emotional Appeal: Attempt by advertising to persuade through an emotional rather than a rational massage.

Empirical School of Management: The empirical study is based upon the premise that, if we study the experience of successful managers, or the mistakes made in management, or if we attempt to solve management problems, we will somehow understand and learn to apply the most effective kinds of management techniques. That by finding out what worked or did not work in individual circumstances, the student or the practitioner will be able to do the same in comparable situations.

Employ: To give someone regular paid work.

Employee: Worker or person employed by another.

Employee Booklets: The bigger companies publish well-written and attractive booklets containing company informations. These booklets are supplied mainly to the new employee and also to other. The purpose of providing a booklet about the company is to satisfy the natural desire of the new employee to know the highlights of the company. It is essential to ensure that informal oral communication supplements the booklet in any programme of indication.

Employee Buy-Out: This refers to the control of a company passing to the employees those purchase either individually or through an employee trust a controlling interest in a company's equity share capital.

Employee Profile: Following a job analysis, this is a descriptive list of the background experience and ability considered necessary for the performance of the job.

Employees Development: Each new employee has to be properly trained not only to develop technical skill for the job for which he has been employed but also to make him an integral part of the organization. Increasing skills of the existing employees and shaping the man for new specific jobs through training and other suitable methods is a very important function of the personnel department. This helps not only in keeping the workers' knowledge up-to-date, but also provides them with necessary incentives and opportunities to secure promotions. Provision for the training of the workers assists the management in ascertaining the strength and deficiencies of the employees and enables the management to take suitable action.

Employer: Person or company which has regular workers and pays them.

Employers' Association: An organization of employers within an industry or an economy. It is the organization which engages with trade unions by representing its members in collective bargaining and matters of employment, as well as lobbying on behalf of its members' interests.

Employment Agencies: These are enterprises established either privately or by the state with the object of bringing prospective employers into contact with job-seekers.

Employment Contract: Generally, a promise or set of promises for which, if they are breached, the law offers a remedy. An employment contract is an agreement for work to be done (and other contributions to be made), and total compensation (monetary and non-monetary) to be paid for this, made between an employer and an employee. Employment contracts are legally enforceable.

Employment: Hiring employees being hired as an employee.

Employment Relations: A general term for all relationships that occur in a worker-employer context.

Encourage: To make it easier for something to happen.

End-means Chain: The goals of a company can be structured into an hierarchy. The goals or objectives at the lower levels are the means for the higher levels. The concept of means-ends chain is useful in understanding the relationship between organizational goals and specific activities. In the process, every goal or end requires a decision about the means by which it will be attained. These means then become subgoals for someone else, which in turn, require decisions about their means of attainment.

End-User: The consumer who actually uses a product. This may not be the same as the person who is responsible for making the decision to purchase that product, which is an important point for marketers to remember. For example, babies do not decide what baby food they are to be the end user of; and many men do not decide what suits, socks or shirts they are to be the end-users of.

Endorse: To make an endorsement on a negotiable instrument. To give one's endorsement to a product. To write an endorsement on a licence.

Endorsee: The person designated in an endorsement as the one to whom the endorser is transferring the right to receive money.

Endorsement: A term used with particular reference to bills of exchange. When a bill is negotiated, the person negotiating will write his name on the reverse of the bill. A valid endorsement must be written on the bill itself or on an allied bill. It must be done for the entire bill and by all parties to whom the bill is made out unless one has authority to act for the others.

Endowment: A term used with reference to assurance policies. An endowment assurance is one where the holder of the policy by paying a certain annual premium is entitled to a fixed sum at a stated date.

Enrichment: Making a job more satisfying for the person doing it.

Enterprise Culture: A social climate that encourages private enterprise and the entrepreneur.

Enterprise: System of carrying on a

business; system of business free from government interference; businesses which are owned privately not nationalized; geographical area which is given a special grant by the government towards its industrial and economic development; a small business estate ; a state controlled company.

Entrepreneur: A person who is skilled at identifying products or sometimes new methods of production, setting up operations to provide new products, marketing the products and arranging the financing of the operations. Also a person who risks his or her judgment and often capital in a search for profit from new business opportunities. Such a person is considered to have a high need for achievement.

Entropy: Entropy is a law of nature (normally a concept of physics) which suggests that all organized forms move towards disorganization and demise. If an organization system is to survive the process must be reversed.

Environment: Any or all physical, behavioural, or social characteristics, conditions, elements, or factors that comprise an organization's surroundings and influence its health, growth, development, status, survival, and behaviour.

Environmental Scanning: The systematic examination of the business environment with a view to identifying marketing opportunities and threats. The business environment includes competitors, the domestic economy, trade patterns, cultural and social trends, and technology. Nowadays it also includes attitudes to the environment itself. The powerful Green consumer threats; but it has thrown up many marketing opportunities as well.

Equilibrium: A term used to describe a situation of economic agents or of aggregates of economic agents such as markets. Applied to an individual agent, such as a consumer or firm, it is used to describe a situation in which the agent is under no pressures or incentives to alter current levels or states of economic action, because given his aspirations and the constrains he fails to improve his position in term of any economic criteria.

Equilibrium Price: Means the price at which a market has been in equilibrium. The price at which the supply curve for a good and its demand curve intersect.

Equipment Leasing: It has been common practice for many years to rent very expensive equipment to save a large and immediate cash outlay. The rental agreement is usually accompanied by a maintenance agreement.

Equity Capital: Traditionally this refers to that part of the issued share capital of a company held by those who take the greatest risk and are consequently entitled to all profits and reserves remaining after the contributors of fixed interest or fixed dividend capital have been paid their due. Generally speaking, equity capital is that owned by holders of ordinary shares. The ownership of the company lies with equity share-holders.

Equity Dilution: Sometimes the true interest of a shareholder in a company, as measured by his holding of ordinary shares, may be reduced by the issue of a further quantity of equal ranking shares. Whereas before he may have held shares representing 40 per cent of the equity the new shares may reduce this proportion to say 30 per cent. The new shares usually rank pari passu with existing shares. This is known as equity dilution.

Equity Financing: Financing obtained by selling ownership.

Equity of Redemption: The right of a mortgagor to redeem his property on the repayment of money borrowed.

Equity Shares: All the shares other than the preference shares, are known as equity shares. Equity shares do not carry any preferential rights. All the equity shares shall enjoy the same rights with regard to voting, dividend and return of capital, etc. For the purpose of dividend and repayment of capital, they rank after the preference shares.

Equity Theory: A theory of motivation proposed by Adam that tries to explain the fairness of incentive pay plans. According to this theory of pay, a person looks at the relationship between what he or she puts into work and what he or she gets out of it in comparison with that of other workers. Equity exists whenever the following formula is in balance:

$$\frac{\text{Individual A's Outcome}}{\text{Individual A's Input}} = \frac{\text{Other Workers' Outcome}}{\text{Other Workers' Input}}$$

Errors and Omissions Excepted: These initials are often included at the end of an invoice. The idea is to absolve the person issuing the invoice from clerical errors. (abbr. E. & OE.)

Espionage: Spying on a competitor, trying to find out the secrets of a competitor's work or products, usually by illegal means.

Estate Agent: An agent or broker who is concerned with the sale, letting management and valuation of real and leasehold property.

Esteem Needs: The esteem level represents the higher needs of humans. The needs of power, achievement and status can be considered part of this level. (see Maslow's Hierarchy of Needs)

Estimate: Calculation of probable cost time of something; very approximate calculation; calculation which probably underestimates the final figure these are not the final accurate figures; calculation by a contractor or seller of a service of how much something is likely to cost given to a client so as to get him to make an order; to give someone a written calculation of the probable costs of carrying out a job; to calculate the probable cost or size or time of something; to state in writing the future costs of carrying out a piece of work so that a client can make an order.

Estoppel: A rule of law whereby a person is prevented (or estopped) from denying a statement he has made either orally or in writing (or possibly implied by conduct).

Ethics: A system of behaviours, expectations, and morals comprising standards of conduct for a population or profession.

Euro-Bonds: Euro bond are bonds that arose initially from the need of American industry to raise money abroad for investment there. They are intended as a long terms means of raising funds for the industries of various countries.

Euro-Currencies: A generic term for bank balances within Europe stated in a particular currency but held outside the country of which the particular currency is the monetary unit.

Euro-Dollars: A post the dollar balances in American banks in the names of various persons or companies which are used to finance international trade without ever leaving the banks in which they are held.

Euromarket: A market in financial instruments that are held in countries other than that which issued the currency in which they are denominated: for example, the market for dollar deposits in Europe (that is Eurodollars), or the market for Deutschmarks (Eurodeutschmarks) in the USA. Dollars held in the Far East are more commonly referred to as Asiadollars than Eurodollars. Legend has it that the first Eurodollar was created by a Russian communist eager to own dollars, but not eager to keep them in the USA. The Russian decided to keep them in Europe instead, and a lot of other people soon thought it was a good idea too. The Euromarket today is worth a few thousand billion dollars.

European Currency Unit: The most likely name of a single European currency, if there is ever such a thing. The European currency unit (ECU) is an artificial currency based on a basket of European currencies. It has been gradually expanding its uses since it was first created by the purpose then was to act as a reserve asset and as a means of settlement in the European monetary system.

Evaluate: To calculate a value.

Evaluation Criterion: A standard for judging relative success or failure: a standard for measuring the degree of effectiveness or efficiency with which programme or organizational objective have been met.

Ex Gratia: As a matter of favour often used for payments made where, though not legally bound the payer feels some moral obligation.

Exchange: Means the act of accepting one thing for another, e.g. as in barter or in a transaction involving money.

Exchange Control: Refers to the system whereby the State exercises control over all or some transactions in foreign currencies and gold, undertaken by its nationals.

Exchange Rate Mechanism: A central part of the European monetary system. The Exchange Rate Mechanism (ERM) is an agreement to maintain exchange rates among member states of the European Community within agreed limits, thus guaranteeing a degree of monetary stability within the boundaries of the EC.

Exchange Rate: Refers to the price of a currency in terms of another currency. Exchange rates have been regularly quoted between all major currencies, but frequently one important currency, e.g., the dollar, has been used as a standard in which to express and compare all rates.

Excise Duties: Taxes which are levied on goods manufactured and consumed within a country.

Exclusive Agreement: Where a person is made sole agent for a product in a market; right to be the only person to market the product.

Excuse: Reason for doing something wrong.

Execute: To carry out (an order).

Execution: Carrying out of an order.

Executive: Any of the upper level managers in an organization; person who puts decisions into action.

Executive Committee: A standing committee of the board of directors of an organization, usually comprising the board's elected officers plus a limited number of other board members. The functions and authority of executive committees vary widely among organizations. Some executive committees function as the board of directors between board meetings; they have full authority to make binding decisions for the board range of issues. Some executive committees serve as the president's or executive director's 'kitchen cabine'. Other executive committees are restricted to more routine functions such as creating board meeting agendas and recommending committee appointment.

Executive Director: A company director who is also a working employee of the company in one of a number of executive post.

Exemption Clause: A clause put into a contract particularly a contract for the sale of goods, excluding the vendor from liability for breach of condition or warranty or both. The law is not sympathetic towards exemption clauses and if they are to be effective they must be carefully worded; e.g. a clause exempting implied conditions will not exempt express conditions; a clause exempting conditions will not apply to warranties.

Exercise: Use of something.

Exogenous: A term which describes anything pre-determined or given in a piece of economic analysis.

Exorbitant: Unreasonably high.

Expansion: Increase in size system where money invested in a new company for some years is free from tax.

Expectancy Theory of Motivation: A way of looking at the relationship between motivation and performance of a job. It suggests that people behave in accordance with the expected outcome of their performance and the value they place on that outcome. Thus people would only be motivated to produce more if they expect that their increased performance would lead to greater satisfaction for them.

Expenditure: A relinquishment by a firm of money or some other asset or an incurrence of liability in exchange for a benefit received or to be received.

Expenses: When used by accountants this is a technical term. It means all those payments, whenever physically made, that relate to the period in question. For example, a business may pay its electricity account after the end of the year in which the electricity was used; or it may pay its rent in advance. Such amounts are accrued expenses and prepayments, respectively. Accountants would treat both as expenses of the year to which they relate, showing the accruals or prepayments in a balance sheet. This practice is part of the matching or accruals concept. It is designed to lead to a fairer presentation of profit for a period. Profit is calculated by taking the expenses from the revenues of the period.

Expensive: Which costs a lot of money.

Experience: Knowledge or skill that comes from having lived through various situations; process of learning through activity or observation, having lived through various situations and therefore knowing how to make decisions.

Experimental Method: Use of controlled experiments to discover the influence of various variables in marketing such as types of promotion and sales training.

Expert: Person who knows a lot about something.

Expertise: Specialist knowledge or skill in a particular field.

Exploit: To make unfair use of someone (usually by paying very low wages).

Exploitation: Unfair use of cheap labour to get work done.

Exponential: Typical growth pattern of new products that involves a slow start, followed by acceleration and finally a slowing down; techniques for working out averages while allowing for recent changes in values by moving forward the period under consideration at regular intervals.

Export: The term used for a goods or service which is produced in one country and sold to and consumed in another.

Export House: A general term applied to one of a number of services relating to exports. They are of various types. Some act as merchants buying from manufacturers and exporting on their own account. Others effectively act as the export department of the manufacturers which they represent putting the specialist knowledge which they have acquired over the years at the disposal of their clients and thereby facilitating selling in overseas markets.

Export Incentives: Particular incentives given by the State to promote exports. They may be in the form of grants or subsidies to exporting industries or additional credit facilities or tax exemptions.

Exports: Goods and services supplied to persons or companies in foreign countries for which payment is generally due in the currency of the supplier. This obliges the purchaser to arrange payment in that currency to the immediate benefit of the vendor and the ultimate benefit of his country's balance of payments.

Exposure: Publicity given to an organization or product total number of people who can be reached by a particular advertising medium.

Extension: Allowing longer time for something.

Extinction: Skinner's theory that learned behaviour not reinforced will disappear because of the lack of reinforcement.

External Currency Market: The market for lending to firms outside of a particular country, through deposits of the currency of that country.

ERG Theory (Alderfer's ERG Theory): Alderfer identified three groups of core needs: existence, relatedness and growth (hence ERG). The existence needs are concerned with survival. The relatedness needs stress the importance of interpersonal social relationships. The growth needs are concerned with the individual's intrinsic desire for personal development.

External Sources of Recruitment: External recruitment means the sources through which the personnel management seeks suitable candidates from outside the concern. Selection of the source of recruitment depends on the policy of each individual firm, nature of work, labour supply position, government regulation, etc.

Extrapolation: Forecasting technique which involves projecting past trends into the future;

Extrinsic Reward: Financial or material reward for work.

F

Face Value: The face value of an item is its nominal value, i.e., the value written on it or as in the case of a share contained in the normal description of it. This is a quite different thing from the market value, which is the price that a willing buyer is prepared to pay for it.

Facsimile: Fax or Facsimile machines are now standard office equipment. They are linked to the telephone system and by this means facsimile copies of documents diagrams orders, etc. can be dispatched swiftly for no more than the cost of a telephone call provided the business at the receiving end is equipped with a similar machine.

Factor: A general mercantile agent dealing with a specified category or categories of goods. As an agent he is distinguished by the fact that, provided he has possession of the goods coming into these categories with the consent of the owner, he can sell and give a good title to an innocent purchaser for value, whether or not the true owner has given his permission to sell.

Factor Comparison System: Evaluation of jobs by identifying key jobs and spreading their worth among factor categories, then determining the dollar value for nonkey jobs by comparing them with key jobs.

Factoring: Refers to the sale by an enterprise of its debts to a factor who not only collects the debts but may also provide administrative and bookkeeping services and credit insurance facilities.

Factors of Production: The term used for the resources of society which are used in the process of production. These have been usually divided into three main groups land, labour, capital, but may also include entrepreneurship.

Factory: Building where products are manufactured.

Factory Overhead: All costs which are associated with a manufacturing process other than direct materials and direct labour.

Fad: A product that is suddenly and briefly taken up with great enthusiasm. It is characterised by rapid sales growth and almost equally rapid sales decline. Recent fads include the Rubik cube, the skateboard, the filofax and platform shoes.

Fair: Honest or reasonable.

Fall: Sudden drop or suddenly become smaller or loss of value to drop suddenly to a lower price payment than the earlier one.

Family: Group of products which are linked by a brand name or by their packaging; selling a variety of different products under the same brand name; selling a whole range of products in similar packaging group of people formed of parents and children; stages through which a consumer passes in his or her life such as 'young married' or 'retired' which correspond to different types of buying behaviour.

Fancy: Small attractive items of high prices.

Fashion Goods: Goods where style and design are all-important. Best illustrated by women's clothing, where what starts off in the haute couture salons of Paris and Milan is imitated by mass manufacturers. It then appears briefly in high-street shops before disappearing to make way for the next fashion goods to have been copied from the catwalk, marketing goods with such a short shelf-life requires special skills.

Fast-Moving Consumer Goods: The kind of products that are usually sold in supermarkets and which move off the shelves quickly, like tooth-paste and chewing-gum. Fast Moving Consumer Goods (FMCGS) require in store-stocks of them to be constantly replenished. Hence at any one moment there are more FMCGS on the road than anywhere else.

Favour: To help or to be kind to someone; in favour of: in agreement with or feeling that something is right.

Favourable Variance: A variance in which actual results are better than budgeted results, e.g., actual costs are less than standard costs.

Feasibility Study: Careful investigation of a project to see whether it is worth undertaking.

Feather-Bedding: Heavy subsidizing of unprofitable industry by government, employing more staff than necessary, usually as a result of union pressure.

Feedback: The concept of a return flow of output information which can be used to regulate future input is now widely used in programmed learning and the development of teaching machines. Part of the output of a system that is used to evaluate the performance of the system.

Fictitious Assets: An accounting term for balances which are not strictly assets in the tangible, or even intangible sense, but are nevertheless shown on the asset side of a balance sheet because the rules of double entry demand that they should be so shown.

Field Research: An important part of market research. It involves the collections of data about products or advertising from actual or potential customers, usually by means of interview or questionnaire. The opposite of desk research.

FIFO: A method of processing transactions, materials, or goods on a "first in, first our" basis.

Final Accounts: This term normally refers to annual accounts, i.e., the presentation of the results of the financial year of an organization and the state of affairs at the year end to the members of that organization.

Finance: Finance is the life-blood of every business. Modern money economy is totally based on finance. No business can commence its activities, survive or grow without adequate supply of funds. Finance is needed for the production of goods and services as well as their distribution. A business enterprise needs finance to commence its operations, to continue operations and for expansion and modernization of business. Finance controls the policies, activities and the decisions of every business. Success of a business largely depends upon favourable procurement and economic utilization of finances. Sound financial management is as important in business as the production and marketing of goods.

Finance Act: An annual Act of Parliament which is primarily intended to give effect to the various proposals by the Finance matters in his budget speech which have been debated, amended and passed by Parliament. The Finance Act also states the rates of taxation that will apply in the coming fiscal year.

Finance House: A generic term covering finance companies, merchant banks, industry banks, etc., Many are owned by the clearing banks themselves.

Finance Lease: Sometimes termed as a 'full payout lease', a contract between leasor and leasee for the hire of a specific asset selected from a manufacturer or vendor of such assets by the leasee.

Financial Accountant: A term principally of convenience, to distinguish the accountant responsible for overseeing the financial structure and liquidity of a business as opposed to his counterparts who handle taxation matters and internal audit or costing and budgeting the province of the management accountant.

Financial Accounting: Basically it is a process of systematically recording and analysing information in monetary terms, relating to the transactions of a firm, primarily in order to provide information to people other than the management of the firm, e.g., the owners (stockholders or shareholders) of the firm, creditors, government agencies, or members of the public who might be persuaded to buy the firm's securities. Also the body of knowledge concerning such work. Refers to that part of accounting which is concerned mainly with external reporting to shareholders, government and other users of accounting outside the enterprise.

Financial Analysis: A general term referring to the process of extracting and studying information in financial statements for use in management decision-making. For example, financial analysis typically involves the use of ratios, comparisons with prior periods and with the budget, and other such procedures.

Financial Audit: Determination by examination, review, and verification of financial records of (1) whether the financial operations of a person or organization are properly conducted, (2) whether the financial reports of the audited entity are presented fairly, and (3) whether the entity has complied with applicable laws and regulations.

Financial Centre: Any place in which, for historical or fresh reasons more than an average amount of financial business is transacted. Centres can range from the big and indisputable (like London) to the small and ambitions (like Jersey or the Cayman Islands).

Financial Futures: London International Financial Futures and Options Exchange.

Financial Institutions: Private or governmental organizations which carry out the vital function of facilitating the flow of savings from those businesses and households with surplus funds to businesses and households with insufficient funds to meet immediate needs, or carry out a central role in the supply of money and credit.

Financial Instrument: Refers to any document which is an evidence of debt, and the sale or transfer of which makes the seller to acquire finance.

Financial Intermediary: Any individual or institution that mediates between savers (that is sources of funds) and borrowers (that is users of funds). The chain from original sources to ultimate use can be a long one, with many intermediaries to be found along the way.

Financial Leverage: The ratio of a person's or organization's total debts to total assets. Other measures of financial leverage (such as those comparing cash inflows to committed cash outflows) are used for particular purposes or because of individual preference.

Financial Modelling: Refers to that part of Corporate Modelling which is concerned with the construction and use of computer based models to carry out the calculations necessary to produce financial statements based on given sets of assumptions and predictions.

Financial Planning: Refers to that part of long-range planning concerned with the financial aspects of a company's objectives, and strategies for meeting those objectives.

Financial Ratios: These are ratios used for disclosing the correct financial position of a business enterprise. They may be examined from two angles—short term and long term.

Financial Risk: Risk which results from an increase in Gearing. (Leverage).

Financial Statement Analysis: It is a study of relationship among the various financial factors in a business as disclosed by a single set of statements, and a study of the trend of these factors as shown in a series of statements. By establishing a strategic relationship between the items of a balance sheet and income statement and other operative date, the financial analysis (as it is simply called) unveils the meaning and significance of such items.

Financial Statements: Of the various reports that the companies issue to their shareholders, the annual report is by far the most important. Two types of information are given in this report. First, there is a text that describes the firm's operating results during the past year and discusses new developments that will affect future operations. Second, there are four basic financial statements—the income statement, the balance sheet, the statement of retained earnings and the sources and uses of funds statement. The financial statements, taken together, give an accounting picture of the firm's operations and financial position. The package of financial statements subsumes such schedules as those relating to fixed assets, long-term investments, inventories, long-term debts, accrued liabilities, cost of goods manufactured, selling expenses, administration and general expenses.

Financial Year (Fiscal Year): In this period annual accounts and taxes are calculated. In India, the financial year is from April to March.

Financier: A fairly vague term used to describe those persons with considerable private means or with access to large sums of money whose principal business it is to invest those funds in the energy and innovatory skills of others with the minimum risk and the maximum profit to themselves.

Financing: Providing money planning by a government to borrow money to cover the shortfall between expenditure and income from taxation.

Fire Insurance: Insurance against losses due to fire.

Firm: The name given to a partnership business though more often used for proprietary firms. Any organization or individual person engaged in any form of activity of which an important aim is the production of goods or services for sale to others. Used as an all-inclusive term for units of economic activity. An organization formed to carryout the business of a partnership.

First-in-First-Out (FIFO): One of the many methods accepted by the accountancy profession and the taxation authorities for the valuation of stock-in-trade at a particular date. It adopts the proposition that items of stock are issued to factory or retail outlets in the same order as that in which they were purchased. Items in stock at any time will therefore be valued at the most recent prices at which purchased.

First-Line: The managers who have immediate contact with the workers.

First Line Supervisor: The supervisor responsible for the management of production workers on the shop floor. The term refers to anyone at the level above chargehand and is most often synonymous with the term foreman.

Fiscal Management: Administration of the financial affairs of a care organization or professional practice, including planning, conducting financial operations, exercising controls, and reporting. Activities within fiscal management include resources planning and development, budgeting, accounting, purchasing, billing, investing, and collecting.

Fiscal: Of, or relating to, taxation or government expenditure.

Fiscal Policy: Generally refers to the use of taxation and government expenditure for regulating the aggregate level of economic activity.

Fixed Assets: Assets that are intended for use on a continuing basis in an enterprise's activities those business assets which are purchased for continued use in earning profit (e.g., land, machinery, etc.).

Fixed Capital: Needs relate to the investments that the business is required to make in purchasing real estate or permanent and fixed assets, i.e., land, buildings, stores, plants and machinery, interest during the period of construction of these assets. Fixed assets do not mean that they are immobile or their values will always remain fixed. They only indicate that they will not be resold for profit and will be used by the business for generating profit. They also include intangible asset as goodwill, patent rights, etc. Fixed capital is used in producing commodities continuously over a long period of time.

Fixed Charge: A term used to describe a mortgage of distinct assets which a loan is made. The charge applies to assets specifically identified and is distinguished from a floating charge.

Fixed Costs: In the manufacturing process costs are incurred not only in the provision of the necessary labour and basic matērials but also in a wide range of services and ancillary expenses, e.g., rent rates, depreciation of machinery interest on borrowed capital, etc. These costs tend, by tradition and for convenience, to be separated into two main categories, fixed costs and variable costs. Fixed costs are those incurred irrespective of the volume of production. Variable costs fluctuate with the level of activity.

Fixed Exchange Rates: Exchange rates among national currencies which have been fixed by governments, and have been not free to vary in response to market forces.

Fixed Interest Securities: Those

shares or debentures which carry a fixed rate of interest.

Fixed Rate: A rate of interest which is applied to the original sum in a contract rather than to the reducing balance, and therefore potentially misleading.

Fixtures, Fittings, etc.: An accounting term for immovable assets affixed to a building in some way though not strictly part of that building itself.

Flat Yield: The true rate of interest on a fixed interest security, found by relating actual income to present purchase price, without taking into account any benefit or detriment that might arise from the proximity or redemption date.

Flat Organization Structure: In organizational analysis, the terms flat and tall are used to describe the total pattern of span of control and levels of management. In flat structure there are few levels, which means that both downward and upward communication are simplified.

Flexible Budget: Refers to a Budget that is adjusted for changes in volume over a Relevant Range of activity.

Flexible Budgeting: In financial planning and accounting, adjusting fixed and variable cost to match the level of operations.

Flexible Exchange Rate: Refer the exchange rates among national currencies which have been free to vary in response to market forces, without government attempts to maintain a fixed exchange rate at which one currency gets exchanged for another.

Flexible: Which can be altered or changed.

Float: To make no attempt as a central bank to keep the exchange rates for a country's currency fixed over a period of time. To be free as a currency from action by central bank to maintain a particular exchange rate. To invite the public to buy particular securities or the securities of a particular company of the first time.

Floating Assets: Another term for current assets.

Floating Capital: Financial resources that are readily available for meeting current expenditures. Floor trader A person, usually a member of the stock exchange entitled to trade on the floor of that Exchange.

Floating Charge: When a loan to a business is secured on assets rather than on a particular item, it is said to be a floating charge. The lender has priority of repayment from the fund of assets that exist when even a receiving order is made against the business.

Floating Exchange Rate: Refers to a market situation in which the exchange rate between currencies has been free to change from day-to-day in response to supply and demand, the opposite to fixed parity.

Floating Policy: An insurance policy covering goods not all in the same place and not of constant value.

Floor Trading: At one time most transactions on the major exchanges were effected through floor trading members of the exchanges making deals verbally or by written contract on the floor of the exchange. This was particularly true in the Stock Exchange but recent developments in computer generated price information systems have led to trading being conducted from dealers' offices on the basis of information instantly available on screen.

Floppy Disk: A small magnetic disk inserted into a computer or word processor and used for the storage of data. It is called 'floppy' to distinguish it from a hard disk which is a permanent fixture of much higher storage capacity.

Flotation Costs: The cost which are arising from an issue on a stock exchange of shares or other securities.

Flotation: Traditionally and officially, the establishment of a public company and the raising of the necessary capital for it either by an open offer to the public or by offer for sale or by a placing. Modern usage has slightly altered this meaning, particularly when the company obtains its capital after and not at the same time as its formation a practice now common. The term is now more often applied to the process of floating off capital, either by a new company or a private company which is going public through the medium of a merchant bank or some other intermediary which will offer the shares to the public in the manner it considers most appropriate.

Flow Chart: A graphic device displaying a hypothetical movement of money, goods, credit, or some other element in the economy from one point to another. It is a visual presentation of the controls with the help of symbols and lines. It must be self-contained for each section of the business. It must be able to reflect the control systems in the most rational and scientific manner. Flow chart makes it easier to understand the controls.

Flow Diagram: A diagram or model, to scale showing the location of specific activities carried out in a work-place and either the routes followed by workers or the routes along which materials or equipment are moved.

FOB: Free on Board. Term used of goods shipped where the price is not including shipping or insurance charges; opposite to CIF. An FOB quotation implies that the exporter will deliver the goods free on board a ship in accordance with the contract at the port named; he pays all expenses up to that point.

Focus Group: A group of people together for an informal discussion for the purpose of market research. The interviewer/chairperson has an agenda of topics to cover, but questionnaire are not used. Interaction within the group is designed to encourage wide-ranging exploration of a subject. Focus groups are typically used in new product development in order to test ideas and products. They are also used for qualitative research on existing products, and sometimes by advertising agencies to try out new bits of copy.

Focus Group Survey: Survey method in which a targeted experts are asked to discuss on some issues freely among themselves.

Foolscap: A piece of paper measuring seventeen by thirteen and a half inches.

Force: Strength, group of people.

Forecast: Description or calculation of what will probably happen in the future; forecast of when cash will be received or paid out; calculation of how many people will be living in a country or in a town at some point in the future; calculation of future sales to calculate or to say what will probably happen in the future.

Forecasting: A series of techniques for trying to predict the future based on known data, usually in regard to the economy or some aspect of it like sales demand, or the need for manpower planning. Sometime a qualitative method like to Delphi method may be used, but very often a quantitative method is used employing a mathematical or statistical technique like regression analysis.

Foreign Bond: A bond denominated in a currency foreign to the issuer, and sold in the domestic market of the currency of issue. Thus a Swiss franc bond issued by a Japanese company and sold in Switzerland is a foreign bond on the Swiss market. (See also EUROBOND).

Foreign Company: A foreign company means a company incorporated outside India but having a place of business in India.

Foreign Exchange: Currency or interest bearing bonds of another country.

Foreign Exchange Market: The market where dealings are made which in the absence of controls, determine the rate of exchange of one currency with another. The market is not in any particular place but consists of a wed of dealings between banks and various dealers in bills of exchange and foreign currency.

Foreign Exchange Risk: Refers to the risk of loss from carrying out operations, or holding assets and liabilities, in a foreign currency.

Foreign Exchange Transaction: An accounting transaction which is involving a currency other than that in which an enterprise's accounts are kept.

Foreign Investment: Refers to any investment in another country which is carried out by private companies or individuals as opposed to government aid.

Foreign Payments: Refers to any payment that has to be made to a foreign country whether in return for goods and services or as repayment of debt.

Foreign Trade: Trade with foreign countries. It implies buying and selling of goods between two countries beyond its national borders. Mutual advantage is the basis of all internal trade. Theory of comparative costs gives rise to trade between different countries. Every country tries to produce those goods which it can produce at a cost which is not higher than that at which it can obtain them from other countries. It will obtain all these goods from other countries which it cannot profitably produce at home, and will give in exchange those things in which it has got an advantage over other countries. It is always carried on wholesale basis.

Foreman or Forewoman: Skilled worker in charge of several other workers.

Forex Markets: Foreign exchange markets including forward foreign exchange markets.

Forfeit: Taking something away as a punishment; clause in a contract which says that goods or deposit will be taken away if the contract is not obeyed; the court said that the goods had to be taken away from their owner to have something taken down as a punishment; to lose a patent because payments have not been made; to lose a deposit which was left for an item because you have decided not to buy that item.

Forfeited Shares: The shares forfeited, in accordance with a company's Articles of Association, for non-payments of calls.

Forfeiture: Act of forfeiting a property.

Forfeiture of Shares: Shares, forfeiture of.

Forged Transfer of Shares: Where a transfer is forged, registered, and a share certificate given to a transferee, the true owner is entitled to be reinstated on the register.

Forgery: A counterfeit coin, note or document that tries to pass as something that it is not. Forgeries often involve the copying of other people's signatures. To make forgery as difficult as possible, the printing of notes has become a highly specialized task. It involves the use of a number of technical devices, and most of the world's currencies are now printed either in the UK or the USA.

Formal Communication: Communication between people through the official channels of an organization, following the official procedure. Usually contrasted with informal communications.

Formal Group: A group set-up by the management of an organization with written mandate and a well-defined purpose. Usually compared with an informal group.

Formal Organization: It refers to the

structure of jobs and position with clearly defined functions and relationships. In formal organizations, every subordinate must obey his superior, whether he likes it or not. As such everybody becomes responsible for the performance of a given task.

Forward Contract: Refers to a futures contract to by or sell a specific physical commodity at some time in the future.

Forward Dating: The practice of dating commercial documents in advance. Invoices may be dated forward, perhaps to give the customer additional time to pay or where delivery has been delayed. Cheques may be forward dated where the drawer has no present funds but expects to be able to meet the cheque at the date specified.

Forward: In advance or to be paid at a later date; buying shares or currency or commodities at today's price for delivery at a later date; agreement to buy foreign currency or shares or commodities for delivery at a later date at a certain price; expansion of a business by becoming its own distributor (as opposed to backward integration, where the company expands by becoming its own supplier) market for purchasing foreign currency or oil or commodities for delivery at a later date; price of goods which are to be delivered in the future; rate for purchase of foreign currency at a fixed price for delivery at a later date; sales for delivery at a later date; a put a later date than the present one on a cheque; deal where the customer pays for transporting the goods; charges which will be paid by the customer to buy foreign currency before you need it, in order to be certain of the exchange rate; to sell foreign currency for delivery at a later date balance which is entered in an account at the end of a period and is then taken to be the starting point of the next period to sent something to someone; words written on an envelope, asking the person receiving it to send it on the person whose name is written on it.

Forward Dealings: Agreements to buy or sell specific quantities in goods, currencies, etc., at a stated price and time in the future. Such dealings are common in international trade where although both price and exchange rate are subject to frequent variations, contracts need to be made well in advance.

Forward Exchange Contract: An agreement to exchange different currencies at a specified future date and at a specified rate.

Forward Exchange Market: The term used for a market in which currencies are bought and sold at rates of exchange fixed now for delivery at specified dates in the future.

Forward Market: Any transaction involving a contract to buy or sell commodities, or securities at a fixed future date at a price agreed in the contract, has been part of a forward market.

Forward Rate: Means the rate of exchange at which a currency may be bought or sold for future delivery, on the forward market.

Forwarding Agent: A general agent who specializes in moving goods from a factory or port of entry to their proper destination such an agent normally owns the transport necessary for this work and often arranges freight and customs formalities for his principal.

Foul: Bill of lading which says that the goods were in bad condition when received by the shipper.

Fractionation: Charging separately for several services or components of a service that were previously subject to a single charge or not billed at all. The usual effect is to increase the total charge.

Fragment: To split into sections; market which is split into many small segments, which are more difficult to sell into.

Franchises: Licences given by manufacturers who wish to limit the distribution outlets of their products or who wish all their sales in one area to be handled by specified persons. The terms also applies where a patent holder licenses a foreign manufacturer to produce the goods covered by the patent. The person giving the licence is known as the franchisor and the person receiving it is the franchisee.

Franking Machines: Businesses with a heavy outflow of mail often wish to bypass the necessity of buying and sticking on stamps. They apply to their nearest Head Post Office for permission to obtain a franking machine.This prints the value of the stamp on each letter, retaining the total cost within the machine.

Fraud: Harming someone by obtaining property or money after making him believe something which is not true. If a contract is made as a result of fraud by one party, i.e. a fraudulent misrepresentation the injured party may rescind the contract and also obtain damages. To be fraudulent the misrepresentation must be made either with an attempt to deceive or without caring whether the statement was true or false.

Fraudulent Misrepresentation: Making a false statement with the intention of tricking a customer.

Free Enterprise: Production of goods and provision of services by private individuals and corporations owned by private individuals for profits in which individual producers act according to own judgment and not under the direction or influence of government; thus the government provides no subsidies or price controls.

Free Exchange Rates: Rates of exchange in the foreign market which are governed only by normal forces of supply and demand with no interference or supervision by State authorities whether at a national or an international level. Free exchange rates are the opposite of fixed rates. When a country decides to abandon fixed rates of exchange in favour of a free market it is said to float the currency, i.e. leave the rate of exchange to float within the supply and demand market until its true level is determined.

Free Float: The length of time for which an activity in a network may be delayed or extended without delaying the start of any succeeding activity.

Free Good: A good which at, a given time and place is either in such abundance that any one can obtain it without cost (e.g. air) or is incapable of being sold (e.g. sunshine).

Free Market: Refers to a market in which there is an absence of intervention by government and where the forces of supply and demand are permitted to operate freely.

Free Trade Zone: Area on seaports and airports when goods of foreign countries may be brought in and reexport without payment of customs duty.

Free on Board (FOB): When an exporter delivers goods 'free on board' he pays all charges involved in getting them actually on to the ship. His responsibilities include putting the goods in a condition for shipping, taking them to the ship and loading them. The buyer must provide the ship, and the seller's responsibility ends when the goods are on board.

Free Port: To facilitate the flow of international trade, and to help to balance of payments of the countries operating them, a number of free-port have been established throughout the world. The advantage of a free-port is that goods can be moved through the area of the port without being subject to any customs or tariff charges or barriers.

Free Reign Leader: A free reign leader (or Laissez Faire leader) does not lead, but leaves the group entirely to itself. The free reign leader avoids power. He largely depends upon the group to establish its own goals and work out its own problems.

Free Trade: A condition where no restrictions by way of tariffs or quotas exist to limit the trade between countries.

Free Trade Area: A group of trading countries, normally inspired by geographical proximity, sometimes join to create an area of free trade by scrapping tariff barriers between themselves. By doing this they hope, through the pooling of knowledge and the growth in mutual understanding to increase not only mutual trade but also the internal efficiency and economic expansion of each individual country.

Freight Forwarder: Person or company which arranges shipping and customs documents for several shipments from different companies, putting them together to form one large shipment.

Frequency: Number of times an advertisement appears in a specific period; number of times a person sees an advertisement during a campaign (as opposed to the reach, which is the number of people who see the advertisement once) the number of times a salesman visits a particular customer during a certain period.

Frictional Unemployment: Unemployment due to unforeseen circumstances, such as changes in technology or in the demand and supply of certain products.

Fringe Accounts: Accounts or customers that are not very profitable for the supplier items given by a company to workers in addition to a salary (such as company cars, private health insurance).

Fringe Benefit: A reward beyond the basic pay for the job. Example can range from subsidized meals and travel to pensions, holidays and sickness benefits.

Frozen Assets: Assets tied up so that transactions in them are restricted or impossible.

Fulfil: To complete something in satisfactory way.

Fulfilment: The process of fulfilling orders received through direct-mail selling. In the case of a magazine subscription, for example, fulfilment will involve sending magazines to the subscriber for the period of time paid for; sending reminders as and when the subscription needs to be renewed leaving a trail so that any problems with a particular subscriber can be followed up. Most such fulfilment systems nowadays are computer-based. (See key code).

Full Cost Pricing: Basing prices on the full costs of products, i.e., on product costs based on Absorption Costing and Normal Volumes, plus a mark-up.

Full Employment: In economic theory this term describes a situation where, within an economy, the total available labour force is being used in activities that contribute to the well-being of the nation and add to the gross national product-allowing for a measure of unemployment necessarily arising as persons move from one job to another. Alternatively, it can be defined as an economic situation where the demand for labour of all sorts equals or exceeds the supply.

Full Timer: Person who works full time.

Function: Duty or job to work.

Functional Organization: A form of organizational structure in which specialists carry out their own particular function in an organization (like research and development or quality control) but without any authority over people in line management.

Functional Stress: A healthy level of individual stress that benefits the organization.

Functions of Management: There are four fundamental functions of management: (i) Planning; (ii) Organising; (iii) Motivating; and (iv) Controlling. Regardless of the activity to be performed and its sphere, the management of any and every level performs its following five basic functions: (i) Formulates the objectives and the course of action to achieve the desired objective, i.e., planning, (2) Establishes the structure, systems, and the procedures of operation to achieve the objectives, i.e., organizing, (3) Place the men, machines and methods in proper positions and contexts for accomplishing the overall objectives, i.e., staffing and coordinating, (4) Implements and transmits the plan into actual action, i.e., directing and communicating, (5) Checks, evaluates and makes corrections as and when required to bring performance in line with the actual plan, i.e., control and review, i.e., controlling.

Fund: Money set aside for a special purpose, money which is available for spending, to provide money for a purpose.

Funding: A term used in connection with a variety of operations concerning the replacement of short-term loans by longer term ones.

Funds Flow Analysis: It is an invaluable analytical tool for a financial manager or a creditor for evaluating the employment of funds by a firm, and in determining the sources for such funds. In addition to studying past flows, the analyst can evaluate future flows by means of a funds-statement based upon forecasts. Such a statement provides an efficient method for the financial manager to assess the growth of the firm and its resulting financial needs, and determine the best way to finance those needs. In particular, funds flow analysis is very useful in planning intermediate, and long-term financing.

Funds Flow Statement: It is a statement in summary form that indicates changes in terms of financial position between two different balance sheet dates showing the different sources and applications of funds. The major purpose of the funds statement is to provide a detailed presentation of the results of financial management, as distinguished from operating management.

Funds, Unrestricted: Money donated, granted, or received from general revenues that can be expended at the discretion of the administration or the governing board.

Future Costs: Cost which are based on expectation of the future costs, not past costs, have been relevant in decision-making, although the latter often form the basis for prediction.

Future Options: An option in a contract that gives a buyer the right, but not the obligation, to buy something at a stated price within a certain time.

Future: Referring to time to come or to something which has not yet happened; delivery at a later date.

Futures Dealing in: Buying and selling by middlemen of options to purchase shares, stocks, or goods, or to sell them. This helps to put forward buyers in touch with forward sellers. The dealer, of course, takes a commission.

Futures Market: An organized market for buying and selling futures contracts.

G

Gain: Increase or becoming larger, to get or to obtain.

Gambling: An agreement whereby one party pays a sum of money if an event occurs on consideration of the other party paying a fixed sum if it does not neither party has a personal interest in the event nor stands to lose anything other than the money which is the subject matter of the agreement.

Game Theory: Principles, developed from business games, which relate to making the best choice from a number of possible strategies in various hypothetical situations conflicting interests are involved.

Gantt Chart: A type of bar chart developed by Henry Gantt which is widely used in the planning and control of production. The chart depicts the progress of a project over time in term of scheduled performance as compared to actual performance.

Gap Analysis: A procedure for discovering marketing opportunities represented by gaps in a market. There are three important areas in which to look for gaps; a neglected consumer group; a deficiency in existing product offerings; an area suitable for exploitation because of some new technological development. Market researchers have developed sophisticated techniques for conducting gap analysis (see perceptual mapping).

General Agreement on Tariffs and Trade (GATT): An agreement signed in 1947 by more than forty countries, to campaign against the imposition of tariff barriers and quota restrictions, and progressively to liberalize trade between the participant countries. There are provisions to discourage blocks within the group, and to insist on most-favoured nation treatment for all members and to desist the members from making frequent changes in tariffs. (see WTO)

General Manager: The manager responsible for the whole range of administration in an organization and not just a specific function.

General Meeting: A meeting which may be attended by all the members of an association and which gives them some opportunity to control the association's affairs.

General Policy: An insurance policy that gets around a trader's need to insure every single shipment separately. The trader and the insure agree in advance on cover up to a certain ceiling. The trader then merely advises the insurer on the nature and value of shipments when they are made and until (in total) they reach the ceiling.

Generics: Goods that are sold with little or no advertising or promotion, and usually in plain, undecorated packaging. Generics have made strong inroads into commodity-type grocery products like soap and lavatory paper. In general, generics refers to goods that are nonproprietary, in particular to drugs and pharmaceuticals that have come 'off patent', like Anacin and Paracetamol. Genetic drugs can be manufactured and sold by anybody.

Geographical: Referring to a certain area; degree to which consumers in a market are concentrated or dispersed in a country or area; dividing of a market according to areas or regions.

Geometric Mean: A statistical term and a form of average, obtained by multiplying together numbers in a series and then finding the root.

Get Along: To manage.

Gift: A voluntary transfer of property real or personal by one person to another without that other being required to give any consideration whatever.

Gift Cheques: Decorative cheques sometimes made available by certain banks for use on festive occasions. Visual delights apart, the only real beneficiary is the bank, which will make a special charge to the account of the donor.

Gift Token: Can be of various kinds but is basically a means of giving another person a predetermined sum in the form of goods which the recipient may choose for himself.

Gilt Edged: Refers to a high-grade bond issued by a company which has demonstrated its ability to earn a comfortable profit over a period of years and pay its bondholders their interest without interruption.

Gilt-Edged Securities: The term is used to describe stocks and bonds issued by the government and quoted on the stock exchange. Theoretically they are non-risk investments as it is assumed that the state will never retreat on its debts. In fact, the low capital risk makes the market value of such securities totally dependent on prevailing interest rates, and, consequently, an investor may be forced to sell them at a price lower than the one paid for initially. These are government stocks, and marketable loans raised for public corporations where repayment is guaranteed by the government.

Global Market: A market for goods or services that attracts buyers from all over the world, the idea that there might be a global market for a very wide range of products and services (from Mars bars to mortgages) was popularised in the 1980s by a marketing professor from Harvard called Theodore Levitt.

Go Public: To become listed company on a stock exchange for the first time usually by making a public offer of securities.

Go-Slow: A form of industrial action, short of as strike, where workers do not withdraw their labour but slow down the rate at which the work is done instead, usually by meticulously following the rule book.

Goal-Setting: Process of establishing what a person or an organization should achieve at some time in the future.

Goal: A desired result of activity by an individual or an organization. The end result of a plan. A state which an individual consciously or unconsciously, strives to achieve.

Goal: Aim for something which you try to do; aim of an organization.

Goal Congruence: Coordination of the personal and group goals of subordinates and superiors with those of the organization of which they are a part. **Goal setting:** Process of establishing what a person or an organization should achieve at some time in the future.

Going Concern: An important underlying concept in accounting practice. The assumption for most business is that they will continue for the foreseeable future. This means that, for most purposes, the break-up or forced-sale value of the assets is not relevant. Particularly for fixed assets, what they could be sold for may be a severe underestimate of their value to a business in terms of replacement cost or economic value. Their net realisable value is, therefore, ignored in most systems of accounting, including the conventional system, historical cost accounting. Companies do not need to disclose that they are following the going concern convention. However, if there are doubt that a business is a going concern, the convention should be abandoned in order to show realisable values, where appropriate.

Going Rate: The current price for a product or service.

Gold and Foreign Exchange Reserves: All nations have what might be called last ditch reserves with which to pay their international debts. They tend to be accumulated in the natural course of foreign trade. However, when it comes to settling a particular debt it is obviously necessary to have the appropriate currency. For this reason national reserves need to be held in a currency that is internationally recognized and the only commonly accepted currency is traditionally, gold; thus gold producing countries have valuable natural source of international exchange, though they have to take care not devalue that asset by overproduction. After 1945 and until relatively recently the American dollar was virtually on a par with gold in the international exchange market as it was a currency that was always acceptable, particularly as its value in exchange was more likely to increase than to fall in recent years the dollar has lost a great deal of its attraction due to lack of confidence in the stability of the American economy and the emergence of other currencies backed by the economic strength of their countries of origin, e.g. Germany and Japan. At one time the reserves were referred to as the gold and dollar reserves. The changing tides of fortune have led to this title being discarded in favour of gold and foreign exchange reserves. Considerable attention is paid to the level of these reserves and any tendency for them to fall calls for government action.

Gold Coins: The use of gold in the making of coins for common currency is a practice dating back countless years. In more recent times the international exchange value of gold has increased so substantially and paper currency has become so widely accepted that the need to use precious metals in minting coins has virtually disappeared.

Gold Standard: A country on the gold standard agrees, by definition, to convert its currency freely into gold through its central bank.

Golden Handcuffs: A practice frequently adopted to deter competitors from poaching senior executives by devices such as golden hellos. Attractive remuneration packages are offered to senior management figures particularly those with specialized knowledge, which make it more worthwhile for them to remain with present employers than to succumb to offers made by rival organizations. Generous but delayed share option schemes can form a helpful ingredient in preparing these inducements known colloquially as golden handcuffs.

Golden Handshake: A very generous payment to employees to persuade them to leave without making a fuss, even if they have not completed their contract. Senior managers in the past have been known to write the terms of their own golden handshake.

Golden Hello: A variation on the golden handshake theme but to welcome the arriving executive rather than speed the departing one. When a major firm or company is looking for new and experienced executives it may try to poach those working for other companies by the offer of very attractive initial remuneration packages. In addition to high basic salaries these might include special bonuses and valuable share options.

Goods: Movable personal possessions which can be moved and are for sale; imported goods held by the customs until duty is paid; machinery buildings and raw materials which are used to make other goods; goods bought by the general public and not by businesses cloth and clothes; manufactured goods which are ready to be sold; items which are used in the home expensive items which are not basic necessities; items which are made by machine; value of goods being manufactured which are not complete at the end of an accounting period; goods which are in the process of being transported; goods kept for another company to be sold on their behalf for a commission central warehouse where goods can be stored until they are moved; train for carrying freight.

Goods on Approval: A person may ask for goods on approval if he wishes to see them before deciding whether to buy, and the vendor will usually allow him a stated number of days in which to make a decision. Equally, a vendor may also send goods to a selected number of persons in the hope that they will purchase them. In the first instance, the purchaser has a duty to take care of the goods and to return them as directed. In the second instance, the person is a quite involuntary bailee and has no responsibility toward the goods unless custom dictates otherwise. He may not destroy them but may demand that the vendor retakes them immediately and at his own expense or simply redirect them to the vendor.

Goods on Consignment: Goods sent to an agent for sale. The agent has possession but not title though he may be able to give a good title to a bonafide purchaser even when acting outside his authority. The goods are usually returnable by the agent, who works for a commission. The venture is normally made for a limited period only.

Goodwill: Good reputation of a business considered as an intangible asset. Goodwill may arise from the good reputation of the business or the fact that it is making profits above the average due to some particular advantage of location.

Government Company: A government company is defined as any company in which not less than 51 per cent of the paidup share capital is held by the Central Government or by any State Government or Governments.

Government Securities: Fixed interest securities issued by the government. They may be in the nature of bonds or other types of security and may or may not be redeemable.

Grade: Level or rank (in a structure), US mark given in a test, to make something rise in steps according to value or quantity.

Grand: Important major plan; final total made by adding together several subtotals one thousand pounds, dollars.

Grapevine: The informal communication network of an organization. Often much more efficient than the formal one.

Gross National Product (GNP): The total value of all goods and services that are produced by the residents of a specified country over a period (usually one year). Unlike gross domestic product, GNP includes income that a country's own residents derive from assets owned abroad but excludes the income of foreigners within the country.

Grapevine: It refers to informal communications. Such informal channels may be resorted to by the managers when they find that it is not possible to gather information through the established channels of the formal communication system in the organization. It is important to note that grapevine is a natural and normal activity as it arises from social interaction of people.

Gratis: Free or not costing anything.

Gratuitous Guest: An individual transported in a vehicle, such as a bus or ambulance, with permission of the operator but without payment.

Gratuity: A sum paid without obligation for services rendered or bonus given to someone at the end of a fixed term contract of employment.

'Great Man' Theory of Leadership: Under this theory leaders were felt to be born, not made. This so-called great man theory of leadership implied that some individuals are born with certain traits that allow them to emerge out of any situation to become leaders.

Green Paper: A publication of the government with a green cover-usually a proposal to which the government is not committed but would like public comment on.

Grey Market: Trading in shares ahead of the official start of dealings. Shares are traded in the grey market before they have been allocated. They are traded on a basis of 'when issued', denoted by the letters WI.

Gross Cash Flow: The sum of net profits after tax has been paid, and the amount of expense determined as depreciation of a firm over a period.

Gross Domestic Product (GDP): The total value of goods and services that are produced within a specified country (including those produced by non-residents) over a period (Usually one year) excluding all goods and services used during that period to produce further goods and services. Like gross national product, GDP may be measured at 'market prices' or at 'factor cost'.

Gross Income: Revenues from services, investments, contributions, and all other sources, prior to any deductions such as expenses or the funding of reserves.

Gross Profit: Where the buying or selling of goods is concerned. It refers to the proceeds of sale, less the cost of putting the goods into a condition for sale. Where the goods are also manufactured this cost will include part of the overhead expenses. Otherwise, overheads concerned with distributing or selling the goods and administering the business generally are charged after gross profit to produce net profit on trading. This will then be adjusted for exceptional items not connected with the major objects of the business to produce the actual net profit.

Gross: Total or with no deductions; total number of people who have seen an advertisement multiplied by the number of times it has been run; total sales of a publication before adjusting for error or discounting unsold copies; the number of times a television or radio spot has been seen based on television ratings total earnings before tax and other deductions; salary before tax is deducted, gross profit shown as a percentage of sales.

Gross Working Capital: The total value of the current assets of a firm.

Group Insurance: Insurance obtained by an individual as a member of a group rather than as an individual. For instance, an insurance company might offer favourable car-insurance terms to accountants (as a group), on the grounds that they drive more carefully and are less prone to accidents than the population as a whole.

Group: Several things or people together survey method in which a sample of people are asked to discuss some issue freely among themselves; interview with a group of respondents in order to discover the views of the group as a whole such as a family; several companies linked together in the same organization; results of a group of companies taken together to put several items together.

Growth: Expansion of a business organization of the economy in general. The rate of growth in the latter is usually measured by the rate of change in the gross domestic product.

Growth Stocks: Market jargon for stocks or shares which are judged, either on past performance or on future prospects to be worth investing over a period. The term is usually reserved for those without immediate income earning capacity but which promise to be good long-term investments offering sustained capital growth.

Guarantee: A promise by one person (usually called the 'Guarantor') that he will make good any failure by a second person (called the 'principal debtor') to meet financial obligations owned to a third person. A promise, given by a manufacturer will correct any defects in the goods found by a purchaser within a certain time.

Guaranteed Bond: A bond issued by one company to another company (e.g., the parent company) guaranteeing that interest will be paid on the capital borrowed from the parent company.

Guarantor: A person who promises that if a second person fails to fulfil some obligation then he will fulfil it instead or pay money up to a specified limit to compensate for any loss caused by the second person's failure.

H

Hallmark: Mark put on gold or silver items to show that the metal is of the correct quality; reputation that a brand name has for high quality to put a hallmark on a piece of gold or silver.

Halo Effect: Series of positive impressions of a product which consumers retain and which can be revealed by a respondent when questioned in a survey.

Halsey Premium Plan: Under this plan for completing the job or a unit of work a standard time is determined. If the worker completes the job in the time allowed or in more than the time allowed he is paid at his time rate. But if he can complete the job in less than the standard time then he is paid at his time rate for the actual time taken to complete the job and is rewarded at his time rate for a definite percentage of time saved. This percentage usually varies from 33-1/3 to 70% but the most common percentage being 50% with the other 50 shared by the employer.

Handle: To deal with something or to organize something.

Harass: To worry or to bother someone, especially by continually checking on him or her or making sexual approaches.

Hard Currency: In the world of foreign trade this term is commonly used to be scribe any currency which is generally safe, i.e., in no apparent danger of losing its value by loss of confidence or by devaluation. The demand for a hard currency will, almost by definition. Exceed the supply.

Hard Funding: Money obtained from an organization's regular sources of operating funds that is budgeted for activities. In contrast, soft funding implies that the money comes from a grant or other source that will not continue indefinitely.

Hard Money: Revenue from an assured, continuing source that is set aside for the operation of a specific programme, service, or facility. Examples include state and local government financing, endowments, and long-term contracts for health care delivery.

Hard Sell: Anything that is deemed to be aggressive selling. That can vary greatly depending on the market in which the selling is taking place. In a high-class boutique a hard sell can be as soft as a silk blouse. At a fruit stall in the street it may be as hard as a plum stone.

Hardware: Physical apparatus used for some purpose (especially computers) as opposed to 'software' i.e. the instructions for using the apparatus.

Haulage: The charge made for carrying goods, though not usually for loading or unloading them; is the business of transportating goods by road.

Hawker: A person who sells goods which he carries round with him.

Hawthorne Effect: The finding in industrial psychology that paying attention to people at work improves their performance. Part of the series of Hawthorne studies done at the Hawthorne works of the Western Electric Company in Illinois between 1927 and 1932. Various attempts were made to improve workers' conditions including changes in lighting, rest breaks, hour of works and method of payment. Each of these changes resulted in an increase in productivity—and so did a return to the original conditions of work. The investigators concluded that the change in the external environment had not influenced the worker's performance so much as their perception that the management of the organization was interested in them and their work.

Hazard: Fire hazard: situation or goods which could start a fire.

Health: Being fit and well, not ill.

Heavy Industry: The term applied to traditional industries like steel-making, coal-mining and ship-building which were the basis of western industrialization in the nineteenth century and have always required heavy physical labour.

Hedge: To protect oneself against financial loss; especially to make a transaction in a futures market for a commodity or for foreign currency which reduced the risk of loss from a commitment one already made in connection with that commodity.

Hedging: A trader, particularly if buying or selling forward in the commodity exchanges, may 'hedge' to protect himself from losses arising from variations in price. For instance, a dealer who has sold a large quantity of goods forward may want to insure against the possibility of heavy losses through a rise in price by buying early or passing some of his forward sale to other dealers.

Herzberg Two-Factor Theory: A theory of motivation proposed in the late 1950s by Fred Herzberg, an American psychologist. Herzberg's theory resulted from a study of job satisfaction in which he found that satisfaction and dissatisfaction with work were caused by different factors. Satisfactions resulted from motivators like, recognition and increased responsibility, but dissatisfaction resulted from the working environment itself and factors like poor physical conditions or relatively low pay. Herzberg referred to these as 'hygiene factor'. Thus, neither interesting work nor a good working environment were sufficient by themselves—though each was necessary—to ensure job satisfaction. Herzberg's work led to an emphasis on job enrichment schemes.

Hidden Reserve: Secret reserve.

Hierarchy: Any organizational structure containing different levels of authority and often responsibilities. Any arrangement of things in succeeding levels, each one subsuming all preceding levels.

Hierarchy of Effects: Model showing stages in the effects of advertising on a consumer (awareness, knowledge, liking preference, conviction, and purchase).

Hierarchy of Needs: A theory of motivation, developed by Abraham Maslow, based on five ascending levels of needs: physiological, security, social, esteem and self-actualisation.

Hierarchy: Organizational structure with several levels of responsibility or authority.

High Quality or High Grade: Of very good quality.

High-Involvement Product: A product over which consumers take time and trouble to reach a purchasing decision, goods for which they shop around, comparing prices of financing arrangements. Consum ers take this sort of trouble over their purchase when there are elements of self-image, cost or product performance involved. Cars, homes, fitted kitchens, hi-fi systems and package tour holidays are some examples of high-involvement products.

High-Level: Involvement of senior people: high-level ranks.

Hire: Paying money to rent a car or boat or piece of equipment for a time.

Hire Purchase: A form of consumer credit that involves an agreement that is both a hire and a purchase agreement, in effect, the consumer hires the product and pays rent regularly (for the hire) for a pre-arranged length of time. With the last rental payment the hitherto hired goods become the property of the consumer.

Hiring: Employing for specific jobs.

Historic Cost: The cost of something on the day it was purchased; its original cost, as opposed to its replacement cost, or its inflation-adjusted cost. Accountants like historic cost because it gives them a real figure to play with. It is not very helpful, however, to claim in a company's accounts that the value of its premises is the historic cost that was originally paid for them (may be 100 years ago) This bears little relation to what it will cost to replace them today, or to their value in the market.

Historical Cost Accounting: The traditional method of book-keeping whereby all values, whether attributable to assets and liabilities or income and expenditure, are expressed in terms of the original amount expended. This means that published accounts are of historical relevance only and do not represent the real cost in terms of the contemporary value of money or level of prices. In times of inflation this practice can lead to a misleading picture of the health of business.

Hoard: To buy and store food in case of need or to keep cash instead of investing it.

Hoarding: Buying large quantities of money or food to keep in case of need; large wooden board of posters.

Holding Company: A company which is either a member (share holder) of another company and controls its board of directors or which holds more than half in nominal value of the Equity Share Capital of the other company.

Holiday: A period of time during which you are not working, e.g. Bank holiday: weekday which is a public holiday when the banks are closed.

Honorary Secretary: A person who takes on the secretarial duties of a club or organization without payment or for a nominal ex-gratia sum known as an honorarium.

Horizontal Integration: Horizontal Integration is said to take place if two firms at the same stage of the production process merge to form a single business organization.

Hot Money: Apart from its use in the world of crime to describe stolen or counterfeit money, hot money is a term sometimes used in the sphere of international payments. It refers to funds that move quickly from one country to another in search of the highest rate of interest.

Household: A group of people who all live regularly at the same address and can be treated as a unit. There are two basic methods of identifying households; by defining 'housing units' and treating all the people living in one housing unit as household; by identifying groups of people who regularly live together as a family usually defined as a group who are all catered for by one person for at least one meal a day.

Human Behaviour School of Management: According to this school, since managing involves getting things done with and through people, the study of management must be centred on interpersonal relations. Popularly called the 'human relations', "existing and newly developed theories, methods, and techniques of the relevant social sciences upon the study of inter and intrapersonal phenomena, ranging fully from the personality dynamics of individuals at one extreme to the relations of cultures at the other." In other words, this school concentrates on the "people" part of management and rests on the principle that, where people work together as groups in order to accomplish objectives, "people should understand people".

Human Capital: That part of an organization's capital represented by the ability, experience and skill of its workforce.

Human Engineering: An American term for Ergonomics.

Human Relations in Management: Management's task in harnessing human energy to organizational requirements involves a process of directing their efforts, motivating them, controlling their actions and modifying their behaviour to fit the needs of the organization. Without this active intervention by management people would be passive, even resistant to organizational needs. They must, therefore, be persuaded, rewarded, punished, controlled and their activities must be directed. This is management task. We often sum it up by saying that management consists of getting things done through others.

Human Relations: The discipline concerned with the application of the behavioural sciences (e.g., psychology, social psychology, sociology, and cultural anthropology) to the analysis and understanding of human behaviour in organizations.

Human Relations Skills: The managerial abilities needed to resolve conflict, motivate, lead and communicate effectively with other workers.

Human Resource Accounting: A concept that views the employees of an organization as capital assets, like plant and equipment. While the concept is intuitively attractive, calculating the value, replacement cost, and depreciation of human assets poses significant problems.

Human Resources: All the people who work for an organization in any capacity.

Human Resources Management: The responsibility for making the best use of an organization employees. The HRM is the planning, organizing, directing and controlling of the procurement, development, compensation, integration, maintenance and reproduction of human resources to the end that individual, organizational and societal objectives are accomplished.

Hygiene: Being clean or careful that every thing is clean and conditions are healthy.

Hyper-Inflation: A term applied to inflation when it is running at extremely high levels. Extreme inflation.

Hypermarket: An increasingly popular term for those very large supermarkets which offer a wide range of goods including consumer durables such as 'T.V.'s, videos, furniture, refrigerators, etc.' Occasionally these large indoor marketplaces concentrate on a limited range of durables. In this way they can offer customers an immense choice and, due to savings on rent, rates, bulk- building etc., afford to sell at concessional prices.

Hypothecation: Hypothecation is a charge against property for the amount of debt where neither ownership nor possession is passed to the creditor. In hypothecation, goods are in the possession of the borrower, but are charged equitable to the bank. Usually the hypothecation deed empowers the bank to require possession of goods to be handed over to him.

Hypothecation Letter of: Exporters may borrow from a bank, using the goods they are shipping as security. Until repaid the banker has a lien on the goods as they are listed in the bill of lading. The lien, which of course is not a possessory lien, is conveyed by a letter of hypothecation.

Hypothesis: A testible assertion, statement, or preposition about two variables which are in some way related to each other.

I

IFCI: In India the process of institutionalized industrial development financing dates back to 1948 when with its establishment the Industrial Finance Corporation of India (IFCI) was enjoined to assist industrial development particularly in the less developed areas in the country. In providing assistance the (IFCI) alongside the IDBI, the National Small Industries Corporation and organizations at State levels has not only emphasised the technical, financial and economic viability of projects but also the managerial capability of the promoters. It has been conscious of the need to ensure that its assistance while being of financial advantage to its beneficiary should fit in the economic strategy of the country and seek a social impact.

Illegal: An illegal act is one which is forbidden by law. An unlawful act on the other hand, is one which though not forbidden by law is not given the protection of the law.

Illegal Partnership: Partnerships formed for illegal purposes are void ab initio.

ILO: International Labour Organization.

Image Consult: A public relations practitioner who specialize in teaching executives how to project a more impressive image (both inside and outside their organizations) by dressing, speaking, socializing, and otherwise behaving in a more 'executive like' manner.

Image: General idea that the public has of a product or a company; qualities which people tend to associate with a particular brand name or branded product; idea which a company would like the public to have of it; to publicize a company so that its reputation is improved.

Immediate Annuity: An annuity which is designed to provide immediate benefits.The assurance company commences payments as soon as the sum agreed as the cost of the annuity is paid over to it.

Immediate Holding Company: A legal and accounting term for the company which actually holds the controlling interest in another company even though the first company may itself be controlled by yet another company.

Impact Analysis: Forecasting method designed to predict the effect of technological breakthrough on specific industries.

Imperfect Competition: (1) Refers to any form of market structure other than perfect competition and would thus include monopolistic competition, oligopoly, and monopoly. (2) Refers to any market structure other than perfect competition and monopoly.

Impersonal Accounts: A term used in double entry book-keeping to describe those accounts in the ledgers which are kept for recording capital, assets, expenses and income.

Impersonality: A form of management that is mechanical in its approach and lacks the personal involvement of a human relations emphasis.

Implied Consent: The apparent acceptance of a proposed condition, course of action, or promise of outcome. Actions, and expressions can lead to the assumption of agreement to or acceptance of a proposed action or condition.

Implied Terms: Terms which are not included in a contract but which the law considers would have been included had the parties remembered or thought it necessary to do so or which any reasonable man would have taken for granted.

Import: Goods brought into a country from abroad for sale; services (such as banking, tourism, etc.) which are paid for in foreign currency; real goods which are imported; government measure to stop imports; tax on goods imported into a country; tax on imports, especially a tax imposed by the EC on imports of farm produce from outside the EC; government licence or permit which allows goods to be imported; fixed quantity of a particular type of goods which the government allows to be imported; extra duty charged on imported goods, to try to prevent them from being imported and to encourage local manufacturers to bring goods from abroad into a country for sale.

Import Duty: A tax imposed on the importation of goods into a country.

Import Licence: A licence given by a government to a trader which permits him to import specified goods into his country.

Imports: Goods or services purchased from other countries involving the use of foreign exchange. Imports, like exports, may be visible or invisible.

Imports-Restrictions on Trade: Various restrictions apply to imports. Duty rates on some goods vary according to the type of product and the nature of any existing agreement with the supplying country. Tendencies to impose restrictions are countered both by fear of reprisals by the other country and by the general agreement on tariffs and trade. Other goods may be the subject of quotas, i.e., only a certain quantity may be imported in any one year. All nations have a list of goods, the importing of which is prohibited. Such lists vary widely from country-to-country.

Impoverished Management: Style of a manager who has little concern for either people or productivity.

Imprest: The term denotes a particular system of accounting for petty cash within a business. Under the imprest system, the petty cashier receives a fixed float for sundry expenses over a certain period. At the end of that period, or when the float is exhausted, vouchers for all expenses will be presented and the expenditure reimbursed, theoretically returning the float to its original level. The person responsible for petty cash has little opportunity for misappropriation because the reimbursement depends on the production of the couchers: this gives the employer a reasonable degree of control over sundry disbursements.

Impulse Buying: A term used to describe the very human tendency to spend first and think afterwards. It is often heartlessly exploited by the owners of large stores and supermarkets, where goods are displayed in such a way as to tempt customers to buy them irrespective of a real need for the particular goods and regardless of their ability to afford such purchases.

In Service Training: Training that is relating to the trainees current employment and takes place where the trainee is employed.

Incentive Scheme: A scheme whereby employees are offered benefits (usually monetary) as a reward for increasing efficiency by their own efforts. In the case of non-productive work force whose efficiency cannot directly related to output, the incentive may take the form of a special bonus determined by overall profit.

Incentive: Thing which encourages a customer to buy or staff to work better; extra pay offered to a worker to make him or her work better; additional incentives to buy apart from advertising such as free; plan to encourage better work by paying higher commission or bonuses.

Income and Expenditure Account: This, as its name suggests, is an account of income received and amounts expended by an organization or a person over a given period. It is similar in form to a profit and loss account but with the emphasis on cash, rather than credit transactions.

Income Bonds: Bonds or investments in unit trust where the prospect offered is a relatively high annual income, not merely capital growth.

Income Elasticity of Demand: Refers to a measure of the responsiveness of the quantity demanded of any goods to a change in the level of income of the persons demanding the goods.

Income Fund: A mutual fund whose prime objective is to maximize current income (not, for example, to maximize future growth).

Income: Money which a person receives as salary or dividends or it refers to the wealth, measured in money, which has been at the disposal of an individual or a community, per year or other unit of time.

Income Return: Either the annual gain from an investment or the percentage figure found by dividing the annual gain by the initial price of the investment.

Income Statement: Presentation of a firm's revenues and expenses for a given period.

Income Tax: From a business perspective, a tax on profits from business or work, but not on growth in the value of investments of property. For an individual, an income tax is a tax on personal income from work, less allowable deductions, credits, and other factors.

Income Tax Allowances: These are various deductions from income which can be claimed when calculating tax payable.

Incompetent: Who cannot do a job well.

Incorporation: A company has no legal existence until properly incorporated according to provisions set out in the Companies Act.

Increase of Capital: A company may increase its authorized capital where the articles of association so permit, notice must be given to the Registrar of Companies.

Incumbent: Person currently filling a position.

Incur: To make yourself liable to.

Indemnity: An agreement whereby one person agrees to make good any loss suffered by a party to a contract of which he himself is a stranger.

Indemnity Policy: Contract that provides cash payments limited by a fixed schedule of payments for covered services, groups of services.

Indent: An order stating goods required.

Indenture: A property deed between two or more parties.

Index Number: A number which measures relative changes. It may be used with reference to price or quantity or anything which can be stated numerically. One specified point of time or quantitative level will be taken as a base (usually given the value of 100) and each subsequent measurement will be expressed as number above or below this figure, to be determined by the percentage change during the interval.

Indifference Curve: Line on a graph that joins various points, each point representing a certain combination of two commodities each combination gives equal satisfaction to customer.

Indirect Costs: The costs of a business that cannot be directly associated with the production of a particular unit or type of product. Examples are machines used for the production of a variety of products at different times of the day; the supervising staff in a factory who look after several product lines; and the heating and rental costs of a manufacturing unit that produces several products.

Indirect Expenses: Expenses incurred in producing goods or services though not attributable to any particular item produced.

Indirect Labour: Labour needed in producing goods or services though not attributable to any particular item produced.

Indirect Manufacturing Costs: Synonym for factory overhead.

Indirect Tax: Refers to a tax that is not assessed on and collected from those who are intended to bear it. Examples are value added tax, sales tax, payroll tax and exercise duties.

Indirect Taxation: That part of total tax revenue collected by means of a levy attached to expenditure on goods or services.

Individual: One single person belonging to one person; demand from one single consumer.

Inducement to Break a Contract: In this context to induce is to bring pressure to bear or to offer a bribe to effect the breaking of the contract.

Induction: A process of introducing or orienting new employees to the environment of the organization. It is very much a socialization or personalization problem. A new employee must be made to feel at home after he has been placed on a particular job. He must get himself challenges. This will generate in him a sense of belonging and self-confidence.

Industrial Development Bank of India (IDBI): IDBI came into existence in July, 1964 by an Act of the Parliament, for (i) co-ordinating and supervising the activities of other financial institutions providing term finance to industry, (ii) enlarging the usefulness of these institutions by supplementing the resources of other financial institutions, (iii) providing direct finance to key industries and, (iv) diversifying and speeding up the industrial growth according to national interest.

Industrial Dispute: A dispute between one or more employers or organization of employers and, one or more employees or organizations of employees.

Industrial Engineering: Activity, process, or study of designing as means of production, taking account of men, materials, tools and plant, in order to produce required quantities of a product to a specified design in the most satisfactory manner.

Industrial Espionage: It is the activity of finding out the industrial secrets of your enemies or rivals by using spies.

Industrial Finance Corporation of India (IFCI): IFCI was established on 1st July, 1948 by a special Act of the Parliament. The object of the corporation is to provide long term and medium term finances to the industry for a period not exceeding 25 years. It gives guarantee for loans which may be raised by industrial enterprises from other sources in the open market. This corporation also underwrites the issue of shares, bonds and debentures of the industrial concerns.

Industrial Goods: Goods that are normally bought for incorporation in, or to aid the production of other goods or services.

Industrial Psychology: The branch of psychology that deals with the world of work, including counselling, the environment, human relations, job analysis, job satisfaction, motivations, recruitment, selection, training, and especially, ergonomics. The term is now used interchangeably with occupational psychology.

Industrial: Referring to industry or manufacturing work.

Industrial Relations: Relations between trade union and employers or between an employer and the unions representing his employees. Relations between employers and employees both as individuals (employee relations) and as members of organized unions.

Industrial Revolution: The industrial revolution is the name given to the historical process, beginning in the late eighteenth century that led to the industrialization of the United Kingdom, making it the first industrialized nation and the richest economy the world had ever seen.

Industrial Sociology: The study of the effects of social processes on the environment of work and on the economy, e.g., the black economy or social change and its effects on economic life.

Industrialization: The term used to describe the process of change of society from being a lárgely agricultural economy to an economy dominated by machined with a concomitant change in the way of work is organized, featuring a division of labour, mass production and standardization.

Industry: The activities of processing of manufacturing goods on a large scale using extensive plant and equipment. A class of firms that are sufficiently similar in their main activities or products to be grouped together for purposes of description, analysis or classification.

Inefficient: Not efficient or not doing a job well; unable to work efficiently and correctly.

Inelastic Demand: Demand which experiences a comparatively small percentage change in response to a percentage change in price; supply which experiences a comparatively small percentage change in response to a percentage change in price.

Inexperienced: Who does not have much experience.

Inferential Statistics: Statistical procedures by which generalizations can made from findings on representative samples of the large groups from which they are drawn.

Inferior: Not as good as others; product which consumers buy less of as their incomes rise.

Inflation Accounting: Refers to techniques for dealing with the impact of inflation on accounts and accounting procedures.

Informal Organization: Unlike the outward face of the formal organization, this reflects the inner life of the organization where communication proceeds via the grapevine, where life is lived in informal groups and productivity is determined by the group norm of a particular work group.

Information: Generally, knowledge provided by the specific arrangement of language or data elements (or both) in a medium of communication. This definition precludes the use of 'data' and 'as synonyms'. Information is the content of a communication, and a communication system is the vehicle for its delivery. The interrelationship between content and communication assures that information is not conveyed without both being present.

Information Management: The planning, development, organization, structuring, and transmission or sets of language symbols which, when properly received and interpreted, provide knowledge and influence human endeavour through comprehension and understanding the value of the added knowledge. Information management includes the processes of analysing and resolving problems and administering or facilitating technical, semantic, and effective communication.

Information Retrieval: Activity or process of obtaining specific information from a store of data.

Informational Role: Role in which a manager serves as monitor, disseminator or spokesperson.

Information System: Any systematic way of organizing the handling of information, from information gathering to information retrieval and use.

Information Technology: A relatively new field that combines the technology of the computer with that of communication. It is concerned with the gathering, recording, storage, processing and dissemination of information and represents the latest form of man-machine interface.

Infrastructure: The network of essential services supporting a modern society that has undergone industrialization, especially education, gas, electricity and transport.

Infringement: A breach or violation of a right: also, the unauthorized making, use, selling, or distributing of something protected by a patent, copyright, or trademark.

Ingredients of Leadership: There are five ingredients which determine the quality of an individual leadership ability. An effective leader in one who can: (i) Make other people feel strong; help them to feel that they have the ability to influence their future and their environment; (ii) Build others trust in the leader; (iii) Structure co-operative relationship rather than competitive relationships; (iv) Resolve conflicts by mutual confrontation of issues rather than by avoidance or forcing a particular solution; and (v) Stimulate and promote goal-oriented thinking and behaviour.

Innovate: To bring in new ideas or new methods.

Innovation: New idea or new method or new product.

Innovations: Often used to cover both technological advances in production processes as well as the introduction of different attributes and attribute combinations in marketable products.

Input-Output Analysis: Means the quantitative analysis of inter industry relations. All transactions that involve the sale of products or services within an economy during a given period have been arranged in a square indicating simultaneously the sectors making, and the sectors receiving delivery.

Insider Dealing: Generally refers to the use of information not publicly available to acquire shares at less than their 'real worth'. These are dealings in stocks and shares by an individual who has access to special knowledge of facts which might influence the value of those shares. Such dealings have been expressly prohibited.

Insolvency: A person or organization is insolvent when he or it is unable to pay debts when they become due. Insolvency is not the same as bankruptcy or liquidation of a company though they may.

Instalment: Part of a sum owed which is paid regularly until the total amount is paid; the last of a series of payments should be paid now; not to pay an instalment at the right time.

Instalment Plan: System of buying something by paying a sum regularly each month.

Instalment Sale: Refers to a credit sale in which payments are made by instalments.

Institution: Organization or society set-up for a particular purpose; bank or investment trust or insurance company whose work involves lending or investing large sums of money.

Institutional: Referring to a financial institution buying or selling shares by financial institutions advertising; an organization rather than a product financial institutions who invest money in securities.

Institutional Advertising: Advertising that is intended to create a favourable estimation of the advertiser rater than of any particular product of the advertiser. It is also called goodwill publicity. In India, for example, SAIL advertises the fact that it is linked with people in their daily life.

Institutional Finance: Large number of financial institutions started after the independence of the country to provide medium and long-term funds to the industries. They are providing secured funds at reasonable rates of interest both for fixed and working capital requirements.

Institutional Investors: The term used for the shareholders other than persons, industrial and commercial companies, the public sector and the overseas sector, i.e., financial institutions such as insurance companies and pension funds.

Instruct: To give an order to someone, to teach.

Instructor: Person who shows how something is to be done.

Insurable Interest: A financial interest in a person, organization, services, or goods for which there is a possibility of financial loss that can be actuarially determined and rated, and which warrants the purchase of protection, i.e., to insure any property or insure against any particular event, one must have an insurable interest, i.e., must stand to lose from the destruction of the property or from the event.

Insurable Risk: A risk that is one of a large, homogeneous group of similar risks that would incur a definable and quantifiable loss, for which the loss is large enough to cause hardship.

Insurance: A contract between two parties (the insure and the insured) in which the insurer (usually an insurance company) agrees to reimburse the insured for clearly defined losses. It does so in return for the payment of a regular premium. In essence, this is a method of transferring risk from an individual to a larger group (the group of all those who are paying premiums to the insurer).

Insurance Broker: This is a person employed to negotiate a contract of insurance. He is an agent for both parties but a principal for the purpose of receiving payment from the insured.

Insurance Company: Any corporation engaged in the business of furnishing insurance protection to consumers and corporate or group purchasers.

Insurance Premium: What the insured agrees to pay to the insurer. It is payable on a stated date though a number of days of grace are normally allowed.

Intangible Assets: An accounting term for those unseen assets which have a value to the business and perhaps also a saleable value. Assets that are not physical or tangible. Intangible assets that may be shown on a Balance Sheet include patents, licences, trade marks and goodwill.

Integrated Action: Bringing several businesses together under a central control; process of expansion in which a business becomes its own supplier; process of expansion in which a company becomes its own distributor; joining similar companies or taking over a company in the same line of business as oneself; joining together businesses which deal with deferrer stages in the production or sale of a product.

Intelligence Test: A test that is supposed to measure intelligence whatever that may be. Its purpose is to discriminate between people who score high and people who score low (e.g., high and low Intelligent Quotient (IQ)) for the purpose of assigning them to various educational, occupational and social categories. High scores are supposed to denote high intelligence, and vice versa, but in the absence of an agreed definition of intelligence the operational definition becomes circular—people score high on intelligence tests because they are highly intelligent and these people score high on intelligence tests. There is also a great deal of evidence that intelligence tests, which are usually highly verbal, tend to be biased in favour of white, urban people in their selection of test items. They measure the IQ of the candidates regarding their reasoning, perception, numerical ability, etc.

Intensive: Use by a producer of as wide a network of distributors as possible to sell products; industry which needs a large amount of capital investment in plant to make it work; industry which needs large number of workers or where labour costs are high in relation to turnover.

Interaction: Contact between individuals or groups.

Interest: The amount paid by a borrower to a lender in payment for a loan. Interest may be simple or compound also, a broad term for any right in property. For example, both an owner who mortgages land and the person who lends the owner money on the mortgage have an interest in the land. Interest is usually a contractual payment, so an unpaid lender can take legal action against the defaulting borrower. Interest may be paid at a fixed rate of at one that varies with prevailing rates (a floating rate). It is part of the expenses of a business, and is tax deductible.

Interest Group: An informal group of people whose primary purpose is to advance the position of their members.

Interface: Link between two different computer systems or pieces of hardware, point where two groups of people come in contact; to meet and act with.

Interim Dividend: Dividends are paid on shares when the profits for the year are known. This may be some time after the end of the year. When dividend is declared and paid before the accounting year is ended, such dividend is called interim dividend, i.e., in between the two dates of Balance Sheet.

Interim Financing:A short-term construction loan, preceding the final financing, which is provided at a later time by a mortgage: any form of bridge financing. Particularly for non-profit organizations, the situation in which one funding source provides interim of bridge financing for an agency until it receives funds from another source (private or public).

Interim Report: It is becoming increasingly common for public companies to issue interim reports to shareholders and the press with a view to keeping them informed of the progress of the business and preparing them for the final audited annual report.

Interim Reporting: This includes the preparation of quarterly, half-yearly, and other interim reports and income statements, cash flow and funds flow statements, scrap reports, etc.

Intermediary: Person who is the link between parties who do not agree or who are negotiating.

Internal Audit: The audit of a business conducted by the business itself on a continuous basis. This is a part of the general system of internal control. This may be distinguished from external auditing which involves checking, by or for the owners of resources or companies, on the stewards or managers of those resources. This is called an external audit because it is done by professional accountants who are not day-to-day employees of the company. To some extent internal audit may duplicate or preempt the work of external auditors, and may reduce the work and fees of the latter. However, internal audit tends also to be actively concerned with the discovery and prevention of fraud and with the design and effectiveness of system of Internal Control.

Internal Communications: Their primary function is to bring about understanding. The greater the sensitivity of an issue the more important the need to communicate effectively. The internal communication programme must make available to all affected employees the information that will enable them to understand not only what is happening and what they are expected to do about it but why the new policies have been adopted. The initial message must be followed by ample continuing communication to indicate how the programme is progressing.

Internal Controls: Accounting procedures for protecting a non-profit organization's assets and ensuring the accuracy and reliability of its accounting data, promote operational efficiency, and encourage adherence to prescribed managerial policies.

Internal Funds: Companies have mainly three sources (banks, financial markets and shareholders) from where they can get external funds. Internal funds, that is, the fruits of their own labour; cash retained in the business and not distributed to shareholders. Companies in different countries have traditionally had very different ratios of external to internal funds.

Internal Rate of Return: The Rate of Interest which documents the flow of revenue generated by an investment, so that the Net Present Value of the flow is equal to the capital sum invested.

International Marketing: Companies are increasingly selling products outside their domestic market. Some foreign brands have become so familiar that consumers assume they are manufactured by indigenous companies. For example, who knows that Nescafe is made by a Swiss company; Baskin and Robbins ice-cream by a British company. The evolution of international markets is one of the most significant trends in contemporary marketing. The marketing knowledge and ability possessed by multinational firms can aid immensely in the development of balanced economies in the both new and changing politico-economic systems. Marketing managers must recognize, analyse and adjust to the marketing systems of each international market.

International Stock Exchange: The London Stock Exchange changed its name to the International Stock Exchange in the 1980s to match what is saw as its new role as the premier Stock Exchange in Europe. For many years the London Stock Exchange was second only to the New York Exchange, but in recent years it has been overtaken by Tokyo. It is still by far the largest exchange in Europe, however, and it has traded an increasing volume of non-UK shares. On some days, for example, its volume of Dutch and Swedish shares has been half as much as the volume traded on the Dutch and Swedish domestic markets. These days all trading is done via television screens and telephones. The floor (where brokers used to meet market makers and scream out their client's orders) has been converted into office accommodation.

International Trade: The term used for the trade which is carried out between nations in goods and services.

Internship Training: This method of training refers to a joint programme of training in which the technical and business houses co-operate. The object of such cooperations is to provide such training as will bring about a balance between theory and practice. For this purpose, students may be sent from their schools to factories for practical training during vacations.

Interview: Talk with a person who is applying for a job; contact between a person looking for information or opinions and a person giving them either through a meeting or by telephone or by post; sales interview meeting between a salesman and prospective customer in which the latter may find out relevant information about a product or service in order to make a buying decision to talk to a person applying for a job to see if he or she is suitable; to try to get information or opinions from someone,either through a meeting or by telephone or post.

Interviewee: Person who is being interviewed.

Interviewer: Person who is conducting the interview.

Interviews: Kinds of (i) **Patterned of guided interview.** Personality, motivation and interest are measured through a common standard of questions asked to each candidate. It avoids personal prejudices or bias in the interview. (ii) **Unpatterned or non-directed interview.** Questions are not planned in advance. Searching questions are asked providing full opportunity to the candidate to prove his worth and suitability for the job. (iii) **Stress interview.** Awkward questions are asked to the candidates to test their will-power, resistance to stress, power to maintain balance of mind, etc. (iv) **Group interview.** Several candidates are asked to discuss a topic in a group. It facilitates the employers to assess the comparative merit, communication skill and qualities of leadership of the candidates.

Intestate: Dying without making a valid will.

Intrinsic Rewards: Non-material rewards of working in a job (such as challenging nature of job).

Intrinsic Value: The value contained in the substance from which an article is produced as opposed to the stated value or price of the end product if put on sale in an open market. In commerce the term is often used in connection with metallic currency.

Introductory: Special price offered on a new product to attract customers.

Intuition: Intuition is characterised by the use of hunches, inner feelings, or the "gutfeeling" of the person reaching a business decision. Preferences and the psychological make up of the deciding individual play an important part: the subject element is vital. It is believed by many that the intuitive decider has more "precognitive" ability and is better able to anticipate the future instances where reliable data are lacking.

Intuitive Decision-Making: Decision-making based on the belief that good decision-making is an art, not a science.

Inventories: The normal US term for raw materials, work-in-progress and goods ready for sale. In the UK the word "stocks" is generally used.

Inventory Control: Discovering and maintaining the optimum level of investment in inventories (stocks). The main problem of inventory control is balancing ordering costs (which decline in total as stocks increase) against carrying costs (which increase as stocks increase), in order to calculate the economic order quantity (EOQ) which minimized total costs. There are two techniques of inventory control: perpetual and periodic. Perpetual inventory control is a continuous method of stock taking by means of records as well as physical verification. The periodic control system is carried out at the end of a period, generally one year.

Inventory: The sum total of all items in a group of items (e.g., office supplies, brochures, souvenirs for sale, etc.) or their value, usually based on cost: also, the process of counting, listing, and pricing such items: also, a questionnaire designed to obtain non-intellectual information about a subject. Inventories are often used to gain information about an individual's personality traits, interests, and attitudes, and other features.

Inventory Valuation: The methods of valuing inventories (Stocks) either under historical cost accounting (HCA) or under some form of inflation accounting.

Investment: The use of money to make money by, for example, lending it for interest, buying property for gain in value, leasing property, and other ways.

Investment Club: A voluntary association of persons who pool their savings, or part of them to build up in investment portfolio, which gives them a better return per person than each could expect separately.

Investment Company: Any company which uses its funds to acquire shares or securities rather than engage in business on its own account.

Investment Grants: Refers to a segment of a business that is held responsible for investments as well as revenues and costs.

Investment Income: In the context of business accounts this refers to income from outside investments, as opposed to income from normal trading operations.

Investment Trust: An institution that issue shares to investors, and reinvests their money in a diversified portfolio of securities. An investment trust thus gives the small investor the benefit of diversification with-out the enormous transaction cost usually associated with it. For some reason investment trusts often trade at a substantial discount to the value of the shares in their portfolios. This leaves them vulnerable to takeover by an Asset Stripper. Unlike Unit Trusts these are "close-ended funds" in that there are no extra regular contributions from participants. If shareholders wish to extract their funds they must sell their shares to another investor. This would have no direct effect on the trust.

Investments: Refers to shares, loans, bonds and debentures held either as a Fixed Asset, i.e., to provide a continuing source of income and in some cases control or significant influence over the activities of another enterprise, or as a Current Asset, i.e., as a temporary means of earning income on funds eventually intended for other use.

Invisible Trade: The part of international trade which relates more to services rendered that to transactions in visible goods. Earnings from invisible trade are a very important factor in balance of payments. This could be true of any nation that relied heavily on other countries for both its food and raw materials.

Irredeemable Debentures: Securities are irredeemable if there is no provision for their holders to be paid back by the issuing company. Normally loans are redeemable but shares are not. However, there are exceptions to both these rules; and in the UK there are loans called irredeemable debentures.

Issue: The sale of a new Security. An issue can be made in several ways: through an Offer For Sale in which the issuing house (that is a Bank) buys the securities from the company and then sells them to the public; through a direct sale by the company itself; through a Private Placement with a limited number of investors. A company's issued share capital is the face value of all the issues of shares that it has made. Issued capital is to be distinguished from Market Capitalization, which is the value put upon all these issued shares by the stockmarket (that is, the share price multiplied by the number of shares in issue).

Issue Price: Refers to the price at which a share, bond or debenture is issued. It is not necessarily equal to the Par Value since shares can be issued at a premium and bond and debentures at a premium or at a discount.

Issued Capital: The amount of capital actually issued by the company.

Issued Share Capital: The amount of share capital of a company, at Nominal Value, that has been issued to the shareholders. Sometimes not all of this has yet been called up. Its Memorandum of Association specifies the maximum share capital that is authorized for a company, although this can be changed by the shareholders. Often a company will not have issued as many shares as are authorized. The issued capital will be shown in the Balance Sheet, and the authorized share capital will be shown in the notes to the financial statements.

Item: Thing for sale; goods sold for cash; for goods which are not in stock; items in accounts which do not appear each year and need to be noted; goods or services which have been paid for and appear in the accounts point on a list; we will now discuss the fourth point on the agenda.

Itinerant Worker: Worker who moves from place-to-place, looking for work.

Itinerary: List of places to be visited on one journey.

J

Jargon: The language, lexicon, or vocabulary peculiar to a particular trade, profession, or group: speech abounding in uncommon or unfamiliar words, often vague in meaning.

Jingle: A catchy little tune which when played as part of a television commercial can be a powerful marketing tool. Jingles use to be written and commissioned especially for particular advertisements, and a very small number of them would subsequently become popular hit songs. In recent years, how ever, advertisers have increasingly used snippets of popular old songs as jingles. In particular, they have used songs which evoke nostalgia among Baby Boomers—today's big spenders—for the years of their youth, the 1960s. The trend was led by Levi Strauss, which has always (and very successfully) put nostalgia at the centre of its advertising message.

Job: A piece of work or an order for a piece of work to be done. The term is also used more widely to describe one's livelihood. A job is, therefore, a unit of work large enough to be the basis of an occupation.

Job Analysis: Job analysis is a method used by management for the determination of specific tasks and their requirements and is the most important function of the personnel department. It refers to the detailed study of the job in order to determine the tasks and responsibilities involved in a job and the personal abilities required to perform that job. According to G. Terry, job analysis consists of the study of "the make up of a job in relation to other jobs and its requirements for competent performance and essential information." Detailed information regarding the nature and requirements of each job may be collected either from the employees who actually perform the jobs or their supervisors who watch the employees doing the work or outside observers or trained job. Job analysis, which is the first step in the job evaluation process consists of analysing the job in detail. The idea of such analysis is carried out by gathering information in respect of the job either through interviews or questionnaire. Where the workers are illiterate or unable to express themselves in written language, pertinent job information is collected through interviews.

Job Costing: A method for calculating cost in an area where each job constitutes a separate order or finite unit of work. This is considered particularly appropriate for consultancy work, e.g., in building or qualitative market research.

Job Description: It is desirable to define the responsibilities of a job

(job description), and to specify the qualification necessary to fill the particular job (job specification). At one extreme top management might appoint a general sales manager and just leave it to him to sell the product. At the opposite extreme, before looking for a general sales manager, a careful job description may be drawn up of what the job involves and from that a specification made of the kind of man needed to fill it.

Job Design: One of the central concerns of industrial society. In addition to providing all of our goods and services, work provides our social identities, and is the single most significant determinant of our physical and emotional health. Organising work in a manner consistent with societal goals has always been the basic task of management. The scientific management movement, has concerned itself solely with the physical considerations of work: it was human engineering. A modern-job design purview seeks to address the totality of these concerns.

Job Enlargement: Expanding the content of a job to include new responsibilities that will usually require training and the acquisition of new skills.

Job Enrichment: A term often confused or used interchangeably with job enlargement. Enlarging a job adding additional but similar duties to the job—does not substantively change and by no means enriches it: it is nothing more than horizontal loading—laying similar tasks alongside one another. Job enrichment is based on the theory that job satisfaction and interest is the function of job content. It is applied as motivational tool whose basis is 'motivator' which satisfy higher order needs of the worker. It improves both efficiency and satisfaction by making the job meaningful. The job becomes meaningful to the worker when it provides a sense of achievement, recognition and an opportunity to use his skill, knowledge and ability and help personal growth and advancement. It makes the job challenging and full of responsibility.

Job Evaluation: A method of comparing jobs for their relative value to an organization and then determining on the basis a hierarchy of pay appropriate to each job. The method uses such factors as complexity, experience, responsibility, skill, etc. or job rating process is a systematic method of appraising the worth of each job in relation to other jobs in the organization. It is used both for factory jobs as well as for desk work. Job evaluation is the systematic and orderly process of measuring the worth of a job in terms of money within an organization. The immediate objective of job evaluation process is to obtain internal and external consistency in wages and salaries but the ultimate objective is employee and employer satisfaction with wages and salaries paid.

Job Modification: An adjustment to a job to make it more efficient, more interesting or less tiring.

Job Redesign: Doing a new job design as part of wider process, like job enlargement or job enrichment, and preparatory to job restructuring.

Job Rotation: The systematic moving of people at the same level in an organization from one job to another. On the shop floor it is done to relieve boredom and monotony: as part of the organization of transferring an employee from one job to another of a similar level in an organization in order to give him experience before promotion.

Job Satisfaction: The extent to which a worker is content with the rewards she gets out of her job, particularly in terms of intrinsic motivation.

Job Security: An attitude of helpfulness on the part of superior is essential to promote job security. The lack of security besides being a worry cuts down initiative, develops resistance to change and unwillingness to take responsibility. On the other hand, excessive job security is likely to develop indifference and indiscipline, as the employee knows that he cannot easily be removed from his job whatever be the justification for such a drastic action.

Job Sharing: The procedure whereby two (or more) part-time workers make up one full-time job between them and share the accompanying pay on a pro-rata basis.

Job Specification: A much more detailed version of a job description stating as exactly as possible what a job entails. It is usually drawn up on the basis of job analysis. It will not be possible for any manager to recruit the correct type of persons unless he is able to specify the requirements of each job clearly. This would help him in increasing the efficiency of the employees by giving them only those duties which exactly fit their abilities and capacities. He would be able to put"round pegs in round holes and square pegs in square holes".

Jobber: A merchant middleman who buys from an importer or manufacturer or some large wholesaler and sells to retailers. It is a Stock Exchange term used to refer an independent dealer in securities. He buys and sells securities in his own name and is not allowed to deal with the public directly. A jobber can deal with a broker or another jobber only.

Jobbing: Doing small pieces of work.

Joint: Refers to the costs of two or more products of relatively significant sales value that are simultaneously produced by a process or series of processes.

Joint Account: In banking an account opened in the names of more that one person.

Joint and Several: A legal term referring particularly to partnerships. Partners are said to have joint and several liability for their firm's debts. This means that in addition to all partners being jointly responsible for debts incurred by the firm each partner is individually, or separately, liable for all debts. This point is especially important when a partnership firm becomes bankrupt.

Joint Consultation: This refers to employer-employee discussion either within a single business entity or over many productive units within an industry.

Joint Holders: Where shares are held jointly the holders may have them registered jointly, in which case only the first named receives notices.

Joint Products: Two or more products ordinarily produced under a given process. Production of one product also gives by products of some kind. It is possible, however, to have alternative processes which yield differing quantities of the two products.

Joint Sector: That sector in an economy in which public and private sectors collaborate.

Joint Sector Undertaking: Joint company enterprise system is common in France, Italy and India. Under this system public and private ownership over the companies is combined and the government invests money with private investors and also can control as well as supervise the working of the organization.

Joint Venture: A business contract or management effort between two persons, companies, or organizations involving risk and benefit sharing often set-up for a specific purpose and a limited time.

Journal: A book-keeping term for the book or books where details of transactions are first entered. A business usually has many transactions each day. The Double Entry system has to record all these. However, there is a danger that the main books of Account would get swamped with information if each one were recorded separately. Thus for some very frequent events, such as Sales, there are special Day Books. The journal, as its name suggests, is also a day book. It contains a record of the creation of double entries for those types of items that are not sufficiently frequent to have their own specialized day book, such as year-end entries and the correction of errors. Every Debit or Credit that is recorded can be traced to back to their source, where a description and date can be found.

Judgment Sampling: The selection of respondents for a survey on the basis of criteria judged by the researcher to be the most appropriate for the purposes of the research. Judgment sampling is most frequently used in Industrial Market Research. In an industry dominated by a few manufacturers, the researcher may decide that a sample which is representative of those few is more significant than one which attempts to embrace all manufacturers in the industry.

Junior Level Management: The term applied to managers who are relatively low in the hierarchy of an organization because they are junior in age and/or level of responsibility and authority.

Junk Bonds: These are bonds of a company or corporation with a low credit rating which therefore carry correspondingly high rate of interest which is part compensation for the high degree of risk attached to the capital subscribed, that are frequently used to finance takeovers of companies.

Junk Mail: Promotional and Advertising material of all kinds that arrives, unsolicited, in the daily mail. The judgment that term implies is picturesque, but not entirely accurate. (See Direct Mail). Philip Kotler, One of the USA's most famous Marketing *gurus*, and author of the classic standard textbook *Marketing Management*, has been something of a counterweight to the Theodore Levitt school of global marketing arguing that markets are becoming more fragmented, not less. For instance, he was written: The heart of modern strategic marketing can be described as STP marketing, namely segmenting, targeting and positioning. This does not obviate the importance of LGD marketing—lunch, golf and dinner marketing—but rather provides the broader framework for strategic success in the marketplace. Today's companies are finding it increasingly unrewarding to practice mass marketing or product variety markets are becoming "demassified". They are dissolving into hundreds of micromarkets.

Jury of Executive Opinion: Using a panel of executives to contribute to forecasting.

Just-In-Time Production: A Japanese approach to the process of production which emphasizes tight scheduling of materials into and out of the process, with a very low inventory of stock carried on-site. The aim of the processes to prevent bottlenecks in production and ensure a smooth flow of throughput. It is also claimed that this approach reduces costs, increases job satisfaction and improves quality.

Justice: Fair treatment in law, fairness and reasonableness.

Juvenile: Young (person), juvenile labour: children and other young people employed under special conditions (as in films, etc.).

K

Keen: Active; strong competition prices which are kept low so as to be competitive.

Key Result Area: A major area of grouping of activities and their results that are "Keys" to an organization's survival and success. Key result areas are integral to organizational planning, management, and evaluation, and are absolutely essential for managing by objectives.

Kickback: Part of a person's payment for doing a job that he gives to someone else for getting him the job.

Knockdown: Goods sold in part which must be assembled by the buyer; very low prices.

Know-How: A term used to describe saleable knowledge of technique or special skill which have been developed within an industry for use on certain projects. This may be the result of many years of intensive research and development in the manufacture of a valuable product.

Know-How Agreement: An agreement by which the possessor of know-how promises to disclose it to someone else. When the disclosure is made to enable the other person to perform his own research or to evaluate the usefulness of the know-how, the agreement is called a 'secrecy agreement'. When the disclosure is made so that the other can use it in commercial production, the agreement is called a 'know-how licence'.

L

Label: Piece of paper or card attached to something to show its price or an address or instructions for use; label which you wet to make it stick on the item; sticky label ready to stick on an item; label with a piece of string attached so that it can be tied on to an item; label with an address on it; label which states the quality of something such one showing that a product meets government standard goods specially produced for a store with the store's name on item to attach a label to something parcel with the wrong information on the label.

Labour: All human resources which are available to society for use in the process of production. International Labour Organization (ILO): Section of the United Nations which tries to improve working conditions and workers' pay in member countries.

Labour Force: The people in an economy who are available to perform work. The collection of people who perform the work of an organization.

Labour Intensive: It is an activity requiring a large proportion of human effort relative to capital investment.

Labour Management Relations: A general term referring to the formal and informal dealings and agreements between employees or employee organizations and managers.

Labour Market: The market for labour in a particular area: the available workers, the firms that wish to employ them and the kinds of contracts they enter into including rates of pay.

Labour Mobility: Movement of workers from job-to-job.

Labour Organization: Any organization of any kind, or any agency or employee representation committee or plan, in which employees participate and which exists for the purpose, in whole or part, of dealing with employers concerning grievances, labour disputes, wages, rates of pay, hours of employment, or conditions of work.

Labour Relations: Relations between trade unions and employers, or between an employer and the unions representing his employees. The collective bargaining process today is responsible for the so-called myth that management, representing capital, sits on one side of the table, with labour leaders, representing organized workers, on the other. Since the respective interests are alleged to be contradictory, public policy is now increasingly directed to equalizing the bargaining strength of the respective parties. When successful, the result of any collective bargaining process best serves the interest of the state as well as the working classes.

Labour Welfare: Labour welfare work is necessary not only for the workers' benefit but all the more so in the employer's own interest. Welfare work has beneficial effects on the work. The welfare measures influence the sentiment of the workers and contribute to the maintenance of industrial peace. When the worker feels that the employer and the government are interested in his day-to-day life he would like to take advantage of such facility and make his lot happier. Thus his tendency to grouse and grumble are likely to be reduced to a minimum.

Labour-Intensive: The term used for relying mainly on labour in the production of goods and services as opposed to the investment of capital in the process of automation, e.g., as in teaching or tailoring. It is, therefore, the opposite of capital intensive.

Labour-Turnover: The percentage of the total labour force of an organization leaving its employment and being replaced over a given period of time, usually a year.

Labourer: Person who does heavy work.

Lag Time: The number of days between the date a service is rendered and the receipt of a claim by an insurer, service plan, prepaid plan, or other third party for processing and payment.

Laissez Faire: The doctrine that government need not interfere in economic affairs.

Laissez-Faire Economy: From the French for "let". This is the term used in economics for the traditional doctrine that a government should not intervene in the workings of its country's economy. The basis for the free enterprise system.

Last In First Out: (LIFO) In the context of Inventory Valuation, the calculation of the cost of inventories (stocks) on the basis that the quantities in hand represent the earliest units purchased or produced. This is one of the methods available for the calculation of the Cost of Stocks (Inventories) in those frequent cases where it is difficult or impossible to determine which specific items remain and which have been used. When prices are rising, last in, first out (LIFO) will lead to more up-to-date costs for the inventory used (Cost of Sales) and, thus, lower profits than would be shown by other methods, such as FIFO. It is, therefore, popular with many companies in the USA, where it is allowed for tax purpose (as long as it is also used in the income statement). However, the inventory value shown in the Balance Sheet may be seriously misleading as it will be based on very old prices. The methods is, therefore, discouraged by the appropriate Accounting Standard (SSAP 9) in the UK, and is rarely found. Nevertheless, it is allowed by the Companies Act, although it is not accepted for tax purposes.

Latent Demand: Situation where there is demand for a product but potential customers are unable to pay for it.

Latter of Regret: A letter sent to applicants for a new issue of shares informing them that their application has not been accepted.

Launch: To put a new product on the market (usually spending money on advertising it) act of putting a new product on the market. The gradual launch of a product by releasing it in selected areas over a period.

Laundering: The process of passing "dirty" money through clean places (like Switzerland) in order to hide it from the tax inspector, or to disguise from the police where it came from (as with drug money). Laundering is often accomplished by introducing dirty money into legitimate business (like construction where costs cannot always be clearly identified.

Lawyer: Person who has studied law and practices law as a profession.

Laying-Off: A business may need to reduce its level of operations and in doing so it may be necessary to reduce its workforce. Employees can be laid off either temporarily or permanently and in the latter case it may be necessary to make statutory redundancy payments.

Lead Time: The length of time between ordering the supply of something and receiving it. Also an estimate of such a length or time.

Leader: Person who managed or directs others; product which sells best; product which sells most in a market or company which has the largest share of a market; cutting prices on some goods in the hope that they attract customers to the shop where more profitable sales can be made; article which is sold very cheaply to attract customers main article in a newspaper or magazine.

Leader Behaviour Description Questionnaire (LBDQ): It is used to analyze leadership in numerous types of groups and situations. The LBDQ can be administered in a variety of situations. In order to examine how the leader was described, the answers to the questionnaire were then subjected to factor analysis. The Ohio state leadership studies by using this technique, found the popular two-dimensional aspects of leadership, i.e., consideration and initiating structure.

Leadership: A widely-applied term that usually refers to the personality characteristics and the behaviour of people with authority and influence and responsibility for leading groups. The term is also used to refer to the group of people officially responsible for running an organization.

Leadership Function: Leadership

function embraces those activities related to supervising, leading, and motivating personnel so that they will perform their tasks in desired ways. The function entails human communication, man-to-man relationships and the use of incentives or penalties to motivate people in desired directions. As with other managerial and enterprise functions, the way in which this function is performed makes a considerable difference in the efficiency of the firm. However, what motivates men to better performance in some cultures may not work very well in other cultures. While leadership may prove quite difficult to define precisely, most perceptive observers can readily detect a situation characterized by weak, vaccinating and ineffective leadership as compared to one in which the leader is competent, respected, and effective.

Leadership Quality: Personnel Manager is responsible for guiding the human resources in handling the jobs properly. He must possesses the quality of leadership, a sense of social responsibility and a standard of social justice. He must possesses better communication skills, art of persuasion and adequate patience and tolerance. He should have initiative and ability to take right decisions at the right moment. He must be able to impress and convince others by his arguments and logic. He must never be afraid of criticism and should in all circumstances be prepared for compromise. He must be good in negotiations.

Leadership Style: An imprecise term that refers to the blending of person's knowledge of leadership theory and skills with his or her own personality and values under different organizational circumstances to yield a "style" of leadership behaviour. Some people are relatively rigid and can use only one or two leadership styles; others are more flexible and may have many style options available to them. This term usually refers to the adoption of an authoritarian management or a democratic management style by an individual in organization, depending on which style is more comfortable to his or her personality.

Lease: A contract whereby a person or a company (the lessee) is granted the exclusive right to the use of an asset owned by another (the lessor). In return the lessee makes periodic payments throughout the agreed term of the lease. For a lease that lasts for most of the expected useful life of the asset, the act of leasing is very similar to hire purchase, or to a purchase made with a loan from the lessor. In this case, accountants treat the item as an asset and record the future liabilities as if they were loans, despite the fact that the assets are not owned by the lessee. This is an example of the application of the principle of Substance Over Form.

Lease Back: Sale and lease back.

Lease-Purchase: A lease that includes a provision whereby the leaseholder may purchase the leased asset during the term of the lease—usually at a favourable price, or that a portion of the lease payments that have been made up to the time of purchase may be applied against the purchase price.

Leasehold Land: Land rented from the true owner. The lease may be for a long or short period. At the end of the period it must be handed back, together with all buildings, whether these were on the land originally or not.

Leasehold Property: Land and buildings or merely buildings in the possession of a person or a business and subject to the laws regarding a lease or lease hold land.

Leasing: The hiring of capital goods or equipment by manufacturing companies in order to avoid the all-at-once cost of purchasing them. A financial institution buys the capital goods, sets the capital cost off against its taxable income and leases the goods to manufacture is passed on to the lessee in the form of lower charges. Leasing is particularly attractive when the lessee has used up all its available capital allowances (because of its own heavy expenditure on capital goods); the lessee does not have thc cash to make a straight-out capital purchase; the lessee does not want to be burdened with the chores of ownership. Leasing rather than outright purchase is preferred by many companies because it reduces the demand on cash flow in the short-term (there is no capital outlay), and it may guarantee service from the lessee (important in the case of complicated equipment). It also offers the prospects of updating products on favourable terms. Firms leasing computers or company cars, for example, have exploited this marketing opportunity.

Leave: Permission to be away from work.

Ledger: A business account book, usually recording day-to-day transactions, and usually showing debits and credits separately. In practice a business of any size will subdivide its ledger into a General or Nominal Ledger and several Subsidiary Ledgers.

Legal: According to the law or allowed by the law, referring to the law.

Legal Tender: Money which, if offered at a proper time and place in settlement of a due debt, must be accepted by the creditor in satisfaction of that debt. If the offer is refused then, although the debt is not extinguished, the creditor will lose his right of lien and will not be allowed to charge any further interest.

Legislation: The process of creating

laws: legislative bills (proposed statutes or ordinances) proposed or in the process of being considered for enactment: also, inaccurately used to mean laws or statutes.

Legitimate Power: This power source, identified by French and Raven, stems from the internalized values of the other persons which give the legitimate right to the agent to influence them. The others feel they have the obligation to accept this power. It comes from three major sources. First the prevailing cultural values of a society, organ or group, second, from accepted social structure, third, being designated as the agent of a or representative of a powerful person or group.

Lender of Last Resort: Within the financial structure of any economy there are many institutions prepared to lend money. In order to lend these institutions must first borrow must themselves to have sources of funds on which to draw. There must then obviously be a lender who can in the last resort, create or originate funds. This role is usually played by the central bank of a country, in India the RBI.

Lessee: One who is given possession of someone else's property by means of a lease. or the person to whom a lease is granted.

Lessor: One who gives possession of his property to someone else by means of a lease or the person granting a lease.

Letter of Allotment: Letter issued indicating allotment of shares to the applicant.

Letter of Credit: An arrangement with a bank to make money available to a customer abroad. The customer's account then debited with the required amount, and the bank then instructs its relevant Correspondent Bank to make the money available wherever the customer wants it. As a security check, the bank will send its correspondent a copy of the customer's signature.

Letter of Indemnity: When a manufacturer export goods he sometimes sends a letter of indemnity agreeing to make good any loss due to faulty packing, short loading, etc. In doing this he ensures a clean bill of lading.

Letter of Intent: A preliminary understanding that forms the basis of an intended contract.

Letter of Renunciation: This applies to a rights issue of shares where the holder who does not wish to take up the new shares may renounce his rights either absolutely or in favour of another person by means of a letter of renunciation.

Leverage: Means an indicator of the relationship between long-term debt and capital employed. It is measured by the ratio, long-term debt, total capital employed.

Leverage Ratio: An organization's total debt divided by its total assets: one of many accounting ratios used for assessing an organization's financial health.

Leveraged Buy-Outs: Means business acquisition in which the managers of the business successfully did and take control, in a transaction financed largely by borrowing the debt is ultimately paid either out of the earnings of the business, or from the sale of its assets.

Leveraged Lease: In general terms, a finance lease to which there are three parties: a lessee, a lessor and a lender who provides financing to the lessor.

Lewin Model: A process of planned change in three stages: Unfreezing the status quo, moving to a new level and refreezing at the new level.

Liabilities: Amounts of money that must be paid by a business at some future date. Many liabilities are of known amount and due date of payment. They include long-term loans, bank overdrafts and amounts owed to suppliers. There may be current or non-current liabilities: the former are expected to be paid within a year from the date of the Balance Sheet on which they appear. The difference between the Current Assets and the Current Liabilities is described as Net Current Assets. Liabilities are valued at the amounts expected to be paid at the expected maturity date. In some cases amounts that are not quite certain will be included as provisions for liabilities; they will be valued at the best estimate available. The convention of conservatism suggests that amounts are called contingencies.

Liability: An obligation, which arises from a transaction or other event that has already occurred and that involves an enterprise in a probable future transfer of cash, goods or services, or the foregoing of a future cash receipt, the amount of which and the date of settlement of which are measurable with reasonable accuracy.

Licence: A document permitting its holder to do something otherwise forbidden and usually obtainable by paying a fixed sum. Licenses are means of raising revenue and of controlling the use or abuse of certain rights.

Licensee: A person who is entitled to do something under the terms of a licence. A person who is entitled to use someone else's property under the terms of a licence.

Licensing: Selling the right to use some process, trademark, patent, and so on, in return for a fee or for the payment of royalties. Licensing is a relatively low risk way of entering a foreign market: the licensee (the purchase of the right) bears most of the risks incurred. If the licensee is an effective marketer, the licenser (the seller of the right) can reap a rich reward for little risk. Licensing is often used to enter markets where direct entry is difficult; for example, in Japan or to manufacture television tubes to a Yugoslav State Corporation; while Massey Ferguson gave a Polish company the right to manufacture its brand tractors.

Lien: Means a claim against property; a bond has been usually secured by a lien against specified property of the company.

Life Style Selector: A company based in Denver, has a Database of 10 m names and address, each identified by demographic and consumption information. Such firms make it possible for marketers to select carefully the most likely buyers of virtually any product. Although direct mail is sometimes disparagingly referred to as 'junk mail', research suggests that less than one mailing in five goes into a waste bin unread.

Lifc: In which the thing insured against certain to occur: the death of the insured. The only uncertainty is when. This sort of insurance is usually refered to as life assurance because the event is assured of happening. Life assurance is traditionally sold directly by sales people to customers in their homes; casualty insurance is usually sold by insurance agents who match a customer's needs with insurance policies available on the market. Agents are widely used because the terms and conditions of different policies vary greatly and can be extremely complicated. It is difficult for individuals to shop around for a policy as they would for a cream cake.

Light Industry: The term applied to industries like electronics or clothing which tend to be smaller in scale and the require less physical labour than heavy industry.

Light: Not heavy; shares lost value on a day when there was little business done on the Stock Exchange; industry which makes small products (such as clothes, books, calculators, etc.) person who watches little television; type of pen which when passed over a bar code, can read it and pass information in it back to a central computer.

Limitation: Act of allowing only a certain quantity of something; making someone liable for only a part of the damage of loss; limiting the amount of time available; law which allows only a certain amount of time (a few year) for someone to claim damages or property.

Limited Liability: This is a privilege extended to companies registered as limited companies under the Companies Acts. It means that members of those companies.i.e. those providing the share capital cannot be asked to contribute more than the nominal value of the shares registered in their names.

Limited Liability Company: A company whose owners have limited liability for the debts of their business. The owners of partnerships and sole trader businesses are fully liable in law for the debts of those business. Thus the providers of ownership finance for such businesses tend to be few in number, and restricted to those who are able and willing to become managers of the business in order to protect their interests. For really large business with thousands of owner another legal form is necessary, so that the owners (or shareholders) may have limited liability for the debts of their business, and therefore be prepared to delegate management to directors. In 1855 in the UK a Companies Act introduced the possibility of registration of companies in limited liability form. The liability of shareholders is limited to their share capital. This, of course, may damage the interests of lenders. Thus companies are generally not allowed to pay back capital to shareholders, and have to notify lenders of their status by putting after their names such warnings as Ltd.

Line and Staff: The work of a company after being divided into the main functions, such as production and sales, is further sub- divided into, what are usually called, line or operational and staff or specialist jobs. In designing the structure for a new company, management has to decide which will be line and which staff functions. Line functions are those which have direct responsibility for achieving the objectives of the company. Staff activities are those which primarily exist to provide advice and service. Whether a function is line or staff should depend on the company's objectives.

Line and Staff Concept: A term used in organizational theory to denote the different functions performed in an organization by managers who are directly responsible for achieving the organization goals ('line') and those who perform supportive functions like marketing or personnel ('staff'). Line and staff conflict arises because of sharp differences in the training, experience and outlook of the two groups. Staff, because of their specialised knowledge acquired by training or experience, tries to assume the role of an expert Line manager because of his broad responsibilities and general competence takes pride in what he calls a common sense view of things. Thus, staff-men faced with opposition to their ideas, tend to see the line managers as basically stubborn, resistant to change and improvement and not appreciative of their special qualifications and capabilities. Line managers, on the other hand, often regard staff proposals as impractical to academic or building castles in the air. They see personal staff as interested only in their techniques and procedures, talking a professional jargon which no one else can understand.

Line and Staff Conflict: The line and

staff departments of an organization are generally found to be at loggerheads with each other. The line department complains that: (i) The staff people encroach upon their authority and prerogatives: (ii) The advice given by staff people is mostly academic and unhelpful in achieving production goals: (iii) When a project is unsuccessful it is the line people who are blamed and held responsible for its failure but when it is successful staff people receive credit. Staff departments complain that: (i) Line people are generally ignorant and bull-headed. They resist new ideas: (ii) Line people distrust, non-co-operate and even sabotage staff plans: (iii) Staff has not enough authority to translate its advice into action: (iv) Line departments receive preferential treatment in matters of staff allowances and other facilities on the basis that they are earning departments.

Line and Staff Organization: The line and staff type of organization in its simplified form is shown in the figure. One can see that the only difference between this and the line type of organization is the addition of some specialists. In this case the specialists are the chief engineer and the sales manager who are added in order to relieve the chief executive of some of his burden.

Line Assistant: The line assistant in an organization assists his chief in the whole range of his duties, except where a more limited delegation is made. He helps the principal to manage the function: that is, he assists with overall planning, organizing, direction, co-ordination and control. Although the line assistant is in the direct chain of command, he is staff to his superior because he exists only to advise, counsel and act for his principal. The line assistant has no responsibility apart from that of his principal, therefore, he has none to redelegate.

Line Extension: Increasing a Product Line by adding variations of existing brand. When a company has a successful brand there is a temptation to use the brand name on other products. Thus a well-known brand of hand lotion might have variants for dry skin, sensitive skin, detergent-damaged skin, and so on. The successful Hob-nob biscuits added a chocolate-coated Hob nob to its range. One of the most successful extension of recent years was the launch of the Mars bar in ice-cream form. Line extension runs the risk of weakening the brand name. If the lotion for sensitive skin is no good, then the original lotion's image suffers. It also runs the risk of consumers substituting the new product for an old one: buying the chocolate-coated Hob-nob instead of (not as well as) the plain Hob-nob.

Line Management: Line organization within industry is an arrangement wherein the roles of individual managers are related to the roles of those directly above and below them. Line management is consequently, management where executives are directly responsible to the person above them in the management scale. It is in effect the organization of management by delegation. The term used to describe managers who are responsible for an organization carrying out its basic functions, e.g., marketing, production, etc. and who give and receive orders via the chain of command, within the organizational hierarchy.

Line of Command: The sequence of people in an organization through whom instructions from the chief executive pass before reaching a particular employee.

Line Organization: Line organization, also known as military or departmental or scalar type, is the oldest form of organization structure. It is called military system for the reason that it was being followed till recently in the army in its pure form.

Line Relationship: A line management relationship between a superior and a subordinate in the hierarchy of the organization.

Line-Staff Relationships: Study of company organization brings to light frequent instances of friction and conflict between line and staff. What is at the root of the difficulty? Both line and staff have their view-points. Line managers most often have these complaints about the staff organization: Staff tends to assume line authority. Staff does not give sound advice. Staff steals credit. Staff fails to see the whole picture.

Linear Programming: A mathematical technique employed to pick the best choice from among several alternatives. The economic theorists approach to the analysis of business behaviour and business problems is based on the concept of optimization. This, however, does not mean that in applied operations research work the analyst pretends to be able to find the best of all possible decisions.

Liquid Assets: Assets that are in cash and immediately available or that are easily convertible into cash, like securities or bank deposits. Refers to current assets other than stocks and work in progress (inventories). They are also referred to as Quick Assets.

Liquid Ratio: This ratio is also called Acid-test Ratio or quick ratio. Liquid ratio is ratio of liquid assets to liquid liabilities or current liabilities. It is concerned with the relationship between liquid assets and liquid or current liabilities. For the purpose of computation, the current assets and liabilities could be classified as follows: Current Assets (a) Liquid Assets and (b) Deferred Assets. Current Liabilities (a) Liquid Liabilities and

(b) Deferred Liabilities.

Liquidation: The distribution of a company's assets after it has ceased trading. The assets are divided among the company's creditors. Preferential creditors or various sorts (like the tax authorities and unpaid employees) get first priority. What is left is then divided among the rest, each according to the amount it is owed. This term is applied to the winding up of the affairs of a company when it ceases business. In most publicized instances it indicates bankruptcy, but it is equally applicable to the winding up of a company by its shareholders when the purpose for which it was initially founded has been completed.

Liquidator: An official who supervises the winding up of a company. He takes over the company's property though it does not vest in him unless a court says so. He acts rather as a receiver and manager. Generally speaking, he does any thing necessary to conduct the winding up operation.

Liquidity: An expression denoting the cash resources of a business. Thus, a company with ample cash may be said to have good liquidity. Poor liquidity may lead to difficulties in paying debts as they fall due, and to inability to undertake profitable projects due to lack of funds. Of course it may be possible to solve this in the long run by being profitable; or in the short run by selling assets or by issuing more shares or long-term loan stock. One measure of liquidity is the net Current Assets or working capital of a business. Which is the Current Assets less the Current Liabilities. Other measures include the Liquidity Ratios: the Current Ratio and the Quick Ratio (acid test). However, all these measures are most useful when seen in the context of similar companies and when looking at a trend for a particular company.

Liquidity Ratio: Refers to the ratio of the total assets of a bank which are held in the form of cash and liquid assets.

List Price: Usually the manufacturer's recommended retail or wholesale selling price.

Listed Company: A company of which the shares are listed on a recognized Stock Exchange. Such companies are always public companies.

Listed Securities: Refers to any securities of a company listed on a recognized stock exchange.

Listing: The addition of a company's capital to the list of other shares and Debt instruments that are traded on a particular Stock Exchange. The obtaining of a listing can be expensive. As a general rule, the higher the status of the exchange the more the listing costs. It can also involve the company in disclosing information that it would prefer to keep to itself.

Lloyd's: A London insurance market which began in the eighteenth-century coffee house of a man called Edward Lloyd. The market which started as an association of London underwriters, has grown into a complex and unique organization. At its centre are more than 25,000 names, wealthy folk who pledge their wealth, without limit, to under write insurance risks (see Name and Underwriter). In recent years the market's considerable reputations has been tarnished by a series of scandals and heavy losses that have discouraged individuals from becoming names. Without a continuous flow of new names the market itself is in danger. To compensate for the loss of names, the market has recently introduced the concept of limited liability. In its early years, Lloyd's was almost exclusively involved with marine insurance and it still produces Lloyd's Register of Shipping, the most authoritative listing of the world's merchant fleet, and of its seaworthiness. (See also Lutine Bell.)

Load: Goods which are transported; goods carried by a lorry or container; amount of goods carried on a lorry or container; amount of goods or number of passengers which a bus or train or plane has to carry to make a profit; largest weight of goods which a lorry or plane can carry; amount of goods which a lorry is capable of carrying; number of seats in a bus or train or plane which are occupied by passengers who have paid the full fare amount of work which a person has to do; to put goods into a lorry or a ship for transporting; ship which is full of cargo to take on cargo; to put a program into a computer; price which includes an unusually large extra payment for some services.

Loan: A transaction in which the owner of property (usually money) allows somebody else (the borrower) to have use of that property. As part of the transaction, the borrower usually agrees to return the property after a certain period, and to pay a price for using it. In a case where the property lent is money, that price is called Interest. For accounting purposes, a loan is an account receivable by the lender and an account payable by the recipient.

Loan Capital: A company's long-term sources of funds raised from creditors rather than shareholders. That part of the capital of a company or other organization subscribed for a fixed period or for a period determinable by either party or on the happening of a stated event. It is entitled to fixed interest and may be secured on the property of the business or on a guarantee by a third party. It must be distinguished from share capital. The most common form of loan capital is a debenture. There are many expression for long-term loans: Debt Capital, Loan Stock, Debentures, Fixed Interest Capital. Loans may be made by private persons, other business or banks. In many cases there is a market in loan securities, so that they can be sold to other investors by the original lender. The loans will usually have a fixed repayment, redemption or maturity date, and a fixed interest entitlement until that date. Loans will normally be recorded in the borrowing Company's Balance Sheet, at the repayment amount, as long-term liabilities. However, their value in the securities market at any moment will depend upon their interest rate and maturity date, and upon the market rate of interest at that moment.

Lobbying Groups: Organizations try to influence political and legal trends because they are so important to business operations.

Local: Referring to a small area of a country or part of a large town; newspapers which are sold in a small area of the country; radio station which broadcasts over a small area of the country.

Localization: Originally this referred to the tendency of industries to stick together: jewellers in one district, lacemakers in another, hosiers in yet another. In modern parlance localization has come to have a very specific marketing meaning, the exact opposite of globalization: the tailoring of goods and services for small local markets, fully taking into account a market's geographical and cultural differences. The debate between those marketers in favour of globalization and those in favour of localization has not been resolved other than by the creation of the slogan: "Think global act local". But Procter & Gamble, which once believed that its great marketing prowess could brush aside all cultural differences, has now taken on board that it must account for local differences and must fine-tune its "world products" accordingly.

Location: Place, especially a site where still photographs or films are made.

Lock-In: A loan that does not permit prepayment. The borrower is "locked-in" for the period of the loan.

Lock Out: Action by employers equivalent to a strike by employee. It occurs when an employer refuses to allow employees entry to their place of work unless they agree to certain terms that have been put to them.

Logo: A distinctive symbol used repeatedly by an organization for identifying itself. Often consists of the organization's name in distinctive lettering. Short for logotype, the trademark or other identifying symbol of an organization, often including the name.

London Inter-Bank Offered Rate (LIBOR): This is the rate of interest at which banks will lend to each other in the inter-bank market. It is a benchmark rate for wholesale money transfers and is quoted for both sterling and other currencies. As a constantly changing measure of the cost of money in large quantities as it moves between banks themselves. It is a more exact indicator of current interest rate movements than the bank base rate.

Long-Term: For a long period of time; debts which will be repaid many years later or over a period of many years; forecast for a period of over three years; loan to be repaid many years; aims which will take years to achieve.

Long-Term Unemployment: A term normally reserved for a period of unemployment of one year or longer.

Long-Term Financing: Any loan that has a term of more than ten years.

Long-Term Liabilities: An accounting term for amounts borrowed by a business and not repayable within the next accounting period.

Lose Leader: Something which a retailer sells at a loss in order to attract customers to his shop where they will buy (other goods on which he hopes to make a large profit).

Loss: Loss of an order: not getting an order which was expected; compensation for loss of earnings: payment to someone who has stopped earning money or who is not able to earn money; not keeping customers because of bad service or high prices, etc. not getting an order which was expected; the company found it has a smaller share of the market; having less money than before or not making a profit; the company did not make a profit; not to show a profit in the accounts at loss made by selling assets; the car was so badly damaged that the insurers said it had no value; loss made when an asset has fallen in value but has not been sold; situation where the company's receipts are less than its expenditure; making a loss or not making any profit; to stop doing something which was losing money being worth-less or having a lower value; goods which weight less than when they were packed; amount or weight which is lost while goods are being transported.

Low-Grade or Low Quality: Unimportant or poor quality.

Low-Involvement Product: A product purchased without much deliberation or forethought that involves neither ego nor much money; in other words where a poor purchasing decision does not have very significant consequences. The challenge for marketers is to try and make low-involvement products more interesting to consumers. Heavy advertising to develop Brand Loyalty is one device; for example, the old Lux soap advertisements that used to use film stars' endorsements. While soap is not something that consumers want to become involved with film stars.

Loyal: Who supports the company he works for.

Loyalty: Inclination of a customer to keep buying the same brand of product; inclination of a customer to keep shopping at the same shop; inclination of a person to keep reading (and buying) the same publication.

Lump: The lump labour: self-employed workers who are paid a lump sum for a day's work or for the amount of work completed (often with a view to avoiding tax); lump sum: money paid in one single amount, not in several small sums.

Luxury: Expensive thing which is not necessary but which is good to have; product which people buy more of as their incomes rise.

M

Machine: Device which works with power from a motor.

Machine-Hour: A unit for measuring the usage of machines which is equivalent to the use of one machine for one hour. Thus a use of 3 machines for 1 hour each or 6 machines of 1/2 hour each, etc., are measured as 3 machine hour.

Macroeconomics: The overall working of an economy and the interrelations between its different factors, including gross domestic product and gross national product, employment and unemployment, investment patterns and national markets.

Magazine: Paper, usually with pictures, and printed on glossy paper, which comes out regularly every month or fortnight or week; special colour supplement published with a newspaper; magazine with articles on computers and programs; with articles on work which the average person can do to repair or improve the house; magazine produced for the workers in a company to give them news of the company's affairs; magazine produced for people or companies in certain trades; magazine with articles on holidays and travel; aimed at the women's market; advertising sheet put into a magazine when it is mailed or to put an advertising leaflet into a magazine before it is mailed or sold; sending of copies of a magazine by post to subscribers.

Mail Order: A form of trading conducted mainly through a postal or delivery system which connects buyers and sellers.

Mail Order Advertising: Advertising intended to persuade people to buy goods by mail order. Note that mail order advertising may or not be direct mail advertising.

Mail Order Business: Mail order business is a kind of retail trade where business is done through post. From the buyers point of view it may be described as 'shopping by post'. The seller approaches the customers by post, by sending them circulars, catalogues, price lists, samples, etc. When the buyers are convinced, they place orders for the supply of goods through post. The goods are usually supplied though value payable parcel. But if the price of goods has been received in advance, then they are sent by registered parcel post. In the case of costlier goods, a certain percentage of the price is always required to be paid in advance.

Mail Order Firm: A firm selling a wide variety of customer goods but operating through post or parcel service rather than through retail premises.

Mail Transfer: As applied to banks, Mail Transfer is an advice sent by one branch of the bank by mail to another branch to credit the account or pay amount to the beneficiary of the transfer.

Mailshot: Printed material that is sent by mail to consumers in order to persuade them to purchase something.

Maintain: To keep something going or working.

Maintenance: This term has several quite distinct meanings: (1) It refers to the cost of maintaining something. Considerable expense may be incurred within a business through the continual maintenance of items of plant and machinery. Costs of maintaining equipment are normally treated as expenses incurred in earning the profit for any given period.They are allowable as deductions for tax purposes (2) The term has an equivalent meaning when applied to persons rather than object. A man divorced from his wife may be ordered by the court to pay both her and their children, if any, fixed sums each week or month for their maintenance, i.e., living expenses. Amounts payable on a court order are taxable in the hands of the recipient and are tax deductible for the person making the payment. (3) Maintenance has a specific meaning in the law of contract. It is applied to payments made to the plaintiff or agreement to make such payment by third parties where the particular third party has no legal or moral interest in the action or insufficient interest to satisfy the court that his offer of financial backing is justified. Where payments of this type are not seen as representing a justified interest they are illegal and any contract connected with their payment would be treated as illegal.

Man-Hour: A unit for measuring employment equivalent to the employment of one person for one hour. Thus employment of 3 men for 1 hour each, or 6 men 1/2 hour each, etc., are measured as 3 men-hours.

Man-Machine Chart: A multiple-activity chart that shows the activities of a machine and the worker who operates it.

Man-Machine Interface: All those points of contact in the workplace between people and the equipment they use. The term now has a particular reference to information technology.

Management: Directing or running a business; way of organizing a business where each manager is responsible for doing what his superior tells him to do; buying and selling shares by a specialist on behalf of a client; directing the making and selling of a product as an independent item; accountant who prepares specialized information for managers so that they can make decisions; financial information sales, cost, credit, profitability, etc.; prepared for a manager; committee which manages a club, a pension fund etc; person who gives advice on how to manage a business; training course for managers; selection and training of potential managers; management system whereby deviations from plan are located and corrected; **management by objectives:** way of managing a business where the managers work according to a plan and checks are made periodically to see whether their work is completed correctly and on time; a group of managers working together; ways of managing a business; training managers by making them study problems and work out ways of solving them; young person being trained to be manager; the main directors of a company; the department managers of a company who carry out the policy set by the directors and organize the work of a group of workers.

Management Consultant: A person whose business is to advise on management problems, on making more effective use of resources employed and also on problems involving basic organization administration and reorientation.

Management Accountant: Management accountant plays a significant role in the decision-making process of the organization. He is variously known as Controller of Finance, Financial Controller, Financial Adviser or Chief Accounts Officer, etc. He is responsible for the installation, development and efficient functioning of the management accounting system. He plays an important role in gathering, compiling, reporting and interpreting internal accounting information. He designs the framework of the financial and cost control reports in order to satisfy the information needs of different levels of management.

Management Accounting: A system designed specially to serve the needs of the managers of a business, distinct from other work done by accountants, such as Auditing or financial accounting. Financial accounting and reporting is required by law (and is intended for shareholders and creditors) or by the need to deal with other parties such as customers or suppliers. Thus it has to obey many rules and has to strive for objective. Management accounting, on the other hand, can be tailor-made for a particular company and will be designed to help managers to make decisions. It may involve many estimates and forecasts. This is primarily concerned with providing information relating to the conduct of the various aspects of the business, the cost or profit associated with same portions of business operations, is called Management Accounting. Management accounting provides assistance to the management in all of its functions. By providing the accounting information in the required form, and at the required time, it enables management to perform its functions effectively. It makes available the relevant information after modifying the same suitable for effective planning and decision-making. It helps to replace intuitive decision-making system with scientific decision-making ones. Control refers to observing whether the actual results correspond to plans, and taking suitable action if there are deviations. Management accounting helps to prepare accounting information for the use by managers of an organization in budgeting, decision-making, planning and formulating policy. Management accounting includes such tools as budgetary control, standard costing, etc., which greatly help the management to exercise its control function effectively.

Management Audit: A review designed to evaluate management efficiency and to identify areas in need of management improvement within an organization. Management audits are used to ensure effectiveness in meeting organizational goals. It is an inspection and evaluation of organizational performance, including one or more of the following:; organizational structure and compensation, operational effectiveness, quality of services and products, market effectiveness, fiscal performance and integrity, customer (client or patient) relations, professional relations.

Management Buy-Out: Refers to a transaction by means of which a team of managers acquires a substantial holding in a company.

Management Buy-Outs: When a company is in difficulty or when it faces the possibility of a takeover bid by another company senior executives of the first company may obtain substantial institutional backing with a view to taking over the company themselves.

Management by Objectives: A term proposed by the American management specialist Peter Drucker in the 1950s to emphasize the importance of setting objective for and by each individual member of an organization as well as the various branches of the organization. Drucker also emphasized the element of self-control and taking responsibility for one's own work. As an objective and a quantifiable measure of performance this technique has since become very popular with senior management, though its application in practice has often been more top down and formalized than Drucker has intended.

Management Control: Control is one of the five managerial functions. It involves the setting up of processes and machinery to find out whether the organization is carrying out its four functions of organizing planning, deciding and implementing the objectives of the company in the best manner and whether it is moving satisfactorily towards the goals set, management development. Any conscious effort on the part of an organization to provide managers with skills they need for future duties, such as rotational assignments or formal educational experience. The semantic difference between training workers and developing managers is significant. A manager is trained so that he or she can be of greater organizational value not only in present but also in future assignments.

Management Development: The process of identifying training and generally equipping relatively junior managers with the experience or skill necessary for senior management positions with an organization in the future. It is a process that, ideally, should be an integral part of a coherent personnel policy going from initial recruitment to ultimate retirement.

Management by Exception: A philosophy of supervision that encourages lower-level managers to make decision on routine matters within set guidelines.

Management Education: Any course of introduction in management and related field-which is often know as business administration. Success in such a course is usually rewarded with an academic qualification whether the setting is an institution of higher education or an in-house programme tailored to a particular organization. The term is often used interchangeably with management training, though the emphasis of management education is generally more formal and academic.

Management Game: Often synonymous with 'business game' this is an educative exercise beamed at schools, colleges, etc. The games attempt to simulate real life theoretical situations which present management problems or business situations requiring one of a variety of decisions. Contenders attempt of maximize real profits by the solutions or decisions they choose. Any number of variables may be introduced into the situations and the problem may be complicated by new factors being introduced after each of a series of separate decision.

Management Information System (MIS): Any formal process that provides the managers in an organization with facts they need for interpretation and decision-making. Most management information systems use computers to collect, store, manipulate, and retrieve information for planning, organizing, directing and controlling administrative activities (and sometimes clinical activities) concerned with the provision and utilization of services, programmes, projects, and products, tools and incorporate relational approaches for examining data, in order to create options for administrative and clinical decision-making and evaluate probabilities and risks of decision alternatives. Many management information systems also automate routine decision processes and the rules and procedures by which decisions are made and actions taken.

Management Making: The most effective use of available resources, whether in the form of machines, money or people, can be ensured if The people responsible for the management of an organization direct their efforts towards the attainment of its objectives.

Management Process School: Management theory perceives management as a process of getting things done through and with people operating in organized groups It aims to analyse the process, to establish a conceptual framework for it, to identify principles underlying it, and to build up a theory of management from them.

Management Science: The application of scientific methods, and particularly quantitative methodology to the practice of management. The application of a behavioural science or social science perspective to the study of management.

Management Strategy: Management strategy of convincing divisional executives that the objectives we have jointly agreed to are both desirable and attainable. We are deadly serious about our responsibility to persuade— so serious, in fact, that when our plans go away, we charge the failure to our lack of salesmanship, not the division's lack of implementation.

Management Style: The general approach a manager has to dealing with other people at work, and in particular the exercising of his or her authority with subordinates. This style is often characterized as tending toward authoritan management or democratic management, depending on the personality of the individual manager, but people can also have somewhat different approaches when faced with different situations.

Management Team: A vague term generally referring to a group of managers who, in addition to their distinct responsibilities, are held jointly accountable (by a senior manager or governing body) for an organization's performance in meeting established goals or providing services that fulfil the mission of a programme within budgetary and revenue constraints.

Manager: Anyone involved in the administration of an organization with the authority to use organization resources, whether money, labour or equipment in furtherance of the organization's objectives, i.e., person who administers an organization or a department.

Managerial Economics: The application of economics to the kind of practical business decision that a manager has to take. As well as economics the field draws on operational research, management accounting and marketing.

Managerial Grid: A technique used in management development that was devised by two American organization psychologists, Robert Blake and Jane Mouton building on previous contribution to the study of human relations by psychologists like Argyis, Lewin and Likert. The technique consists of scoring management on two dimensions at right angle to each other, a grid. The dimensions are concern for procurion (or the task in hand) and concern for people. Each individual scoures are then plotted on this grid to see how much of each concern they express. The grid also forms the basis for a seminar exploring various aspects of the work group.

Managerial Psychology: The systematic study of the role of the manager in an organization and in particular the relationship between supervisors and supervisees. This area of study is a part of industrial psychology.

Managerial: Referring to managers; to be appointed a manager; decisions taken by managers.

Managing Director: The director of a company who generally ranks first in seniority under the chairperson or president and being normally the chief executive, he will be the key figure in the running of the business with ultimate responsibility for all decisions that are made in the area of management.

Mandate: A document giving one person authority to act on another person's behalf with the backing of the law.

Manpower: Number of workers in a country or industry or organization.

Manpower Analysis: An analysis of the employees in organization that attempts to identify patterns and trends in their employment. It will examine, for instance, the distribution of employees by age, sex, skill, job title and length of service. It is the first stage of systematic manpower planning.

Manpower Needs: Different business enterprises may need different types of people at different times. To maintain continuous supply of the required kind of people for a business, the personnel department may undertake a study of the present and future requirements of the concern to determine its manpower needs. It is also required to ascertain the different sources of supply of labour and must keep in touch with the general factors effecting the supply of labour.

Manpower Planning: The process of forecasting both the numbers and the kinds of employees that an organization will be required over a given period of time and taking steps to ensure their supply. Ideally this should be an integral part of an organization's personnel policy from recruitment to retirement, including selection, promotion and training.

Manual Worker: Someone employed on the shop floor of an organization doing physical rather than mental work. Whether the work is skilled or unskilled.

Manufacture: To make a product for sale, using machines; making a product for sale, using machines; products made in foreign countries.

Manufacturing Industry: That branch of industry concerned with the manufacture of goods by the application of labour to raw materials.

Margin: A margin is strictly the difference between the cost of an asset of investment and the amount that one is willing to advance for its purchase.

Marginal Analysis: A tool of analysis which is found in all branches of economic theory. It is concerned with the relationships between marginal changes in related economic variables; marginal changes being very small increments or decrements in the total quantity of a variable.

Marginal Cost: The extra cost that would result from producing one extra unit of a product (strictly speaking an infinitesimally extra amount). For the purpose of calculating marginal cost, all the Fixed Costs should be ignored; only those extra costs that are related to the small production increase should be measured. For decision-making purpose it is often useful to compare the marginal cost of extra production with the marginal revenue that would result.

Marginal Pricing: Basing prices on the marginal costs of.

Marital Status: Condition of being married or not.

Mark Down: To make the price of something lower; to lower the price of a company's shares following an announcement of bad news, or of bad results by the company or to make the price of something lower.

Mark Up: Increase in price amount added to the cost price to give the selling price; we take the unit cost and multiply by 3.5 to give the selling price, mark up expressed as a percentage either of the cost price or of the selling price.

Mark-Up Pricing: A pricing technique, widely used by retailers, whereby a product's selling price is set by adding a certain percentage to its cost price (that is, marketing it up).

Market: A situation where buyers and sellers are in communication with each other. This may take several forms, e.g., in person (as in a cattle auction) or electronically (as in the Stock Exchange) or through the mass media as in newspaper advertising columns: the nature of the demand for a particular product. In marketing terms, a group of consumers who share some particular characteristic which affects their needs or wants, and which makes them potential buyers of a product. For example:—**The Soap Market:** All those people who share an enthusiasm for personal cleanliness.-**The Teenage Market**. Anyone between their 13th and 20th birthday. **The Housing Market**: Everybody who wants to own a roof over their head. **The Leisure Market**: All those with spare time on their hands.

Market Analysis: The process of systematically determining the characteristics of a market and the measurement of its capacity to contribute to or buy a service or product.

Market Capitalization: The total market value at current Stock Exchange list price of a specified category of issued shares in a particular company.

Market Economy: Means an economy in which the crucial economic decisions and choices have been made in decentralized manner by numerous private individuals and firms, operating through a free price and market mechanism.

Market Forces: The underlying forces in an economy, which affect the levels of prices through exerting pressures on the demand for or the supply for various goods and services.

Market Leader: The firm or company which has the biggest share of the available market for a specified product.

Market Maker: The market maker is the person, or organization who undertakes to make an ongoing market in the securities in which he elects to deal either with investors or other dealers. He must retain stocks of those securities and must make a two-way price on a continuous basis in each at which price he is then committed to deal.

Market Mix: The combination of different aspects of an organization strategy for marketing a product, e.g., advertising market research, production and public relations. The guidelines for the most appropriate mix are sometimes expressed as the 'four Ps'—project, price (market), position and place.

Market Price: In a stock exchange context, the price at which a listed company's securities can be bought and sold. In general terms it is the price at which specified goods can be sold in the market.

Market Research: Marketing decisions can be no better than the facts upon which they are based importance of market research has increased very much with the widening of markets and increasing competition. Nowadays goods may be manufactured for stock rather than to order. It is necessary to manufacture goods by keeping in view the future trends of demand.

Market Risk: Synonym for Systematic Risk.

Market Share: Refers to the proportion of total market sales accounted for by one firm.

Market Structure: Refers to the economically significant features of a market which affect the behaviour of firms in the industry supplying that market.

Market Value: It is the amount that an asset would realize if sold in the free market. The market value of something at a particular time is the price that any buyer might reasonably be expected to pay for it at that time if he was able to make a considered judgment of its value and was not influenced by any special relationship with the seller.

Marketable Securities: US term for investments held as Current Assets.

Marketing: Marketing implies the process of moving the goods and services from the producers to the consumers. It involves all the activities from product development to storage, transportation, sales promotion, pricing and financing. It creates utilities of time, place and possession. Marketing is a creative, dynamic and challenging socially useful activity, which every business has to undertake. Marketing is generally concerned with the creation of place and time utility, and included in this enterprise function are such problems as pricing and price policies to be pursued as well as channels for distribution of products. This function interlocks closely with production. Environmental differences of many kinds become relevant in the sphere of international marketing. For example, problems of design can assume great importance, as supported by the fact that most American and European automobiles have special radiators for marketing in tropic countries, and heavy duty springs if they are to be sold in countries with poor roads. Marketing is the performance of business activities that direct the flow of goods and services from producer to consumer or user. Marketing is a total system of business activities designed to plan, price, promote and distribute want-satisfying goods and services to present and potential consumer—William J. Stanton. Therefore, the process of identifying needs and satisfying these with suitable goods or services, through, product design, distribution and promotion either as a business or as a non-profit making organization; contract by which one company undertakes to market another company's products; organization set-up by the government or by a group of producers to help producer; market a certain type of product; money set aside by an organization of its marketing activities; all methods of communicating used in marketing such as television, radio and sales literature. The activities, of a firm, that are concerned with acquiring and maintaining markets for the firm's products and for ensuring that the firm's output reaches those markets in time and with needed supplies.

Marketing Audit: There are two not unrelated meaning. 1. Extensive productivity analysis, a process that judge how well resources are being used in a company's Marketing Department. In this context the term is used in an accounting sense; it is an investigation enabling the auditor to draw conclusions about the stewardship of the marketing management. 2. One of the critical steps in the planning process, in which the existing marketing situation and the company's marketing capability are assessed.

Marketing Budget: A financial statement about the level of Marketing effort to be undertaken by a company. The marketing budget represents the cost of achieving the company's marketing objectives as described in the Marketing Plan. The budget is expressed as a profit and loss statement, showing both the revenues anticipated from sales and the costs of the marketing resources that will be put into the marketing mix.

Marketing Department: The department in a company that is responsible for Marketing; to some extent its size and form will depend on the size and nature of the company (whether it is in consumer goods or industrial goods, and so on). In a not untypical company the director of marketing will answer to the managing director, and will have various divisions under him or her; for advertising and sales promotions; for sales; for marketing research; for Product Planning; for Administration.

Marketing Environment: The set of external factors that affect the market in which an organization operates, i.e., cultural, economic, legal, political, geographical, etc.

Marketing Function: The functions of marketing management are marketing opportunity assessment, marketing planning and programming marketing organization and leadership and evaluating and adjusting marketing efforts. The marketing management team must perform these four entrepreneurial functions if the firm is to develop an efficient corporate marketing system.

Marketing Management: Marketing management is primarily concerned with the stimulation of sales and promotion of consumers satisfaction. It includes analysis of markets, determination of marketing goals, sales forecasting and formulation of marketing plans, policies and procedures. An important function of marketing management is to evolve an appropriate marketing mix, i.e., planning and development of a satisfactory product for a particular market demand and fixation of its prices.

Marketing Mix: A description of the various elements of the marketing process that must be co-ordinated to make up the total marketing effort. These elements are often crudely summarised as the Four Ps. 1. **Product**. What product is going to be offered to the customer? What are its characteristics; its Brand name; its Packaging? What additions can be made to the Products Line? 2. **Price**. How much is the customer going to pay for the product? How are price levels to be adjusted in the light of consumer's responses and of competitor's behaviour? 3. **Place**: How is the product going to get to where the customer is when the customer wants it? What type of wholesale and retail outlets are to be used? What is to be the geographical coverage? What sales force is needed and what will be its size, territories and style of selling? 4. **Promotion**: How is the customer going to know about the product, and be persuaded to buy it? What Advertising is to be used and what will be its nature, content, frequency and reach? How much sales promotion, publicity and personal selling are there to be? To reflect many companies' growing customer orientation, there is a tendency to refer less to the Four Ps, and more to the Four Cs. 1. **Customer value** (From the buyer's point of view.) This replaces product. 2. **Cost to the customer:** This is more than the price charged because it includes the cost of the customer's time and energy; it replaces price. 3. **Convenience for the buyer**: This replaces place. 4. **Communication:** This is a dialogue which replaces promotion (a monologue by the seller).

Marketing Plan: The plan drawn up by managers of products, brands or markets to define their objectives and strategies. Typically, a marketing plan will consist of the following sections. An analysis of past marketing (size, growth, consumer behaviour, trends); the product (sales, prices, profits); the competition (size, market share, strategies); distribution and the environment (demographic, economic, political and technological trends); This leads to a statement on the company's strengths and weaknesses and the opportunities and threats facing it. The formulation of marketing objectives, in relation to financial objectives (profits, sales revenues, return on capital, and so on); The marketing objectives might be to increase the Product Line's market share by 3% over the planning period, or to increase the sales revenue of the Brand by 5%. Whenever possible marketing objectives are stated quantitatively, with a given time period for their achievement. The development of marketing strategies. For each objective, managers have to decide which of many possible strategies to follow. If the aim is to increase the product line's market share, a brand might be selected for increased marketing support, or another brand might be added to the line. The brand's sales revenues might be increased by using a special sales promotion. Or the price of the brand might be raised. The preparation of action plans setting out what is to be done, who will do it, when and at what cost.

Marketing Research: Marketing research is distinguished from market research in that while the former deals with problems involved in marketing a particular product. It start with market research and then studies practical difficulties in selling and deciding for instance what lines might be pushed in particular areas and what special problems might be met in any particular region. It is concerned with the problems attached to selling a particular product for a particular manufacturer, while market research on the other hand would tend to study the state of consumers' demand in relation to perhaps a group of products of a very similar kind. Thus market research might be used by a group of manufacturers to obtain a field study whereas marketing research would be used by a particular manufacturer to discover the best way of selling his own particular goods.

Marketing Segmentation: It is generally more satisfactory to market products to a group of consumers who have similar characteristics, wants and needs than to the general, undifferentiated public. The match between what the consumer wants and what the manufacturer offers is then likely to be closer. Groups of consumers with quite detailed characteristics in common are called 'market segments', and the process of identifying them is called 'market segmentation'. Markets may be segmented in many different ways, depending on the insight or perceptiveness of the marketer. Consumer market segments are commonly based on the following kinds of characteristics. **Demographic:** sheltered housing targeted at the over 60s; **Geographic:** country, state, region. A company may choose to sell its products in selected areas, or it may sell different products in different areas. Nestle markets Nescafe in India, USA and the UK; but its decaffeinated freeze-dried Taster's Choice brand is not distributed in the UK, although the company does market a (different) decaffeinated coffee there. **Psychographic:** social class, lifestyle, personality. Manufacturers of clothes, furniture, food products, cosmetics, drinks and cars give great attention to market segments based on these variables. **Use:** occasion, user status, user rate. There is a hot-drink before bedtime market, as well as a summer-barbecue market, a charter-flight market, a health-food market, and so on. There are potential user, first-time user and regular-user markets, and there are markets segmented into light, medium and heavy users. Industrial markets are frequently segmented by type of organization (such as manufacturing, governmental, agricultural) or by type of goods required (such as raw materials, installations, services). A market segment must meet certain standards if it is to be the focus of a Marketing effort. Its size and purchasing power must be substantial enough to promise a profitable return. It must be accessible. It must have future as well as present viability.

Marketing-Objectives of: (i) Securing consumer satisfaction, (ii) Coordinating production with consumption, (iii) Maximization of profits without unfair trade practices, (iv) Service to the society, improving quality of life.

Market Place: Open space in the middle of a town where a market is held, situation and environment in which goods are sold.

Mass Media: Forms of communication that large—usually nation wide audience, i.e., radio, television and newspaper.

Mass Production: The production of identical items on a very large scale.

Master of Business Administration (M.B.A.): The academic qualification in management education which is generally accepted as a prerequisite for a professional career as a manager. The qualification is also becoming increasingly sought after in India but not in other industrialized countries like Germany and Japan which have alternative routes into management.

Matching Concept: A convention that the expenses and revenues measured in order to calculate the profit for a period should be those that relate to the period, rather than those for which cash has been paid or received. This is sometimes called the Accruals Concept. For example, accountants record a sale on credit when it would be legally enforceable or on delivery of goods, not at the later date when cash is received. Similarly, the electricity expense of a business will be the amount that relates to the period not what happened to be paid in the period. Depreciation is a good example of the matching concept in action. When a fixed asset is bought it will normally be used for several years. Thus, accountants do not charge an expense equal to the cost of the asset in the year of purchase. Instead the asset is capitalized, recorded in the Balance Sheet and gradually charged as an expense, called depreciation, over the years of its use.

Material Management Department: An organizational unit that orders, supplies, materials, furniture, and equipment. The unit also purchases, receives, maintains, and stores the supply inventory, and usually delivers supply items to other units, departments or services.

Material: Substance which can be used to make a finished product; bricks, cement, etc., used in building; substances which have not been manufactured (such as wool, wood, sand, etc.) substances made as products of a chemical process; system to check that a company has enough materials in stock to do its work; moving materials from one part of a factory to another in an efficient way; posters, photographs, etc., which can be used to attract attention to goods which are for sale.

Maturity: The time at which a debt or other obligation becomes due or a right becomes enforceable. It is usually the date on which the borrower of a loan note, or bond must pay the full amount of the debt for the instrument.

Maturity Date: The date when a debt for which an extended time for payment has been given, must be settled.

Maximization: Making as large as possible; business strategy based on achieving as high a profit as possible.

Mean: A form of average used in statistics. It is a weighted arithmetic mean where each digit included in the summation is multiplied first by a factor representing its relative frequency or statistical importance.

Mean Deviation: A simple and easy measurement of dispersion used in elementary statistics. When considering a series of values the arithmetic mean is first determined. Then the differences between the actual and that mean value are added together and divided by the number of items in the series. The result is the mean deviation.

Mean Price: Often referred to as the middle-market price, it is the arithmetic mean of two given prices, e.g., the buying and selling price quoted by a market maker.

Media: Means of communicating a message (about a product or service) to the audience; means of communicating information to the general public (such as television, radio, newspapers); types of media used as a vehicle for advertising; advertising media such as television, radio and teletext services; various types of media used together in a promotional campaign; advertising media such as magazines and newspapers; examining different types of media and their audiences (such as the readers of newspapers, television viewers) to see which is the best for promoting a certain type of product; business which offers organizations a media buying service and possible additional services such as media planning; person in an advertisement in the media on behalf of an organization; placing advertisements in the media on behalf of an organization; basic type of medium such as TV, radio or the press-report about something in the media; document giving basic data or information about a publication such as circulation readership and geographical distribution; happening which is staged by, or organized so as to attract the attention of the mass media; business which offers organizations a media buying service but without the creative services usually offered by advertising agencies; single unit of advertising space or time; person or company that owns a magazine or newspaper, or radio or TV station; strategy concerned with what type of media should be used and how much advertising should be done and when; study or investigation of a target audience in order to improve an organization's promotional activities; all the details of advertising to be used in a promotional campaign, such as the timing and positioning of advertisements; choosing the right type of media for a promotional campaign; media independent (a business which offers organizations a media buying service but without the creative services; usually offered by an advertising agency).

Media Analysis: The study of the effectiveness of various media in reaching an audience. Finding answers to questions like: How many people who buy a magazine look at the back cover, the inside front cover, the centre-spread, and so on? How many people driving past a Billboard at 100 kph can read print 2 meters high? How many people stay awake long enough to see the credits to the late-night movie?

Media of Advertising: Mural or Outdoor Advertising: Poster Advertising, Hoardings, Vehicular Advertising, Sandwich Board Men, Electronic Displays. Press Advertising: Newspaper, Magazines, Trade Journal's Professional Journals. Direct Mail Advertising: Sales Letter, Circular Letters, Catalogues and Price Lists, Pamphlets, Dealers' Aids. Audio-Visual Aids: Radio, Television, Film, Window Display, Fairs and Exhibitions, Bonuses and samples, Personal Approach. Advertising is thus the modern means of informing the consumers about the products made available by the manufacturer or seller. Advertising has become a specialized branch of management. It is through advertisement that firms increase the sale of their products. The purpose of advertising is to inform, to persuade and inspire the consumers to buy the goods.

Media Planning: Activity or process of choosing the media that are to carry specified advertising.

Median: Another form of statistical average used where the mean does not give a fair picture, due to the presence of a few extreme values in a series the inclusion of which gives an unrepresentative average. The median is arrived at by putting the series in an ascending scale. If the number of items is even, the two middle items are taken, added together and halved.

Mediation: Any attempt by a neutral third party to help settle disputes. A mediator has no power but that of persuasion. A mediator's suggestions are advisory only, and may be rejected by either or both parties to a dispute. Mediation and conciliation tend to be used interchangeably to denote the entrance of an impartial third party into a dispute. However, conciliation is the less active term. Technically, it refers simply to efforts to bring the parties together so that they may resolve their problems themselves. Mediation, in contrast, is a more active term. It implies that an active effort will be made to help the parties reach agreement by clarifying issues, asking questions, and making specific proposals.

Medical: Referring to the study or treatment of illness.

Medium-Term Capital: Funds raised for a stated and limited period, not repayable at call. The period is normally less than five years.

Memorandum of Association: A legal document drawn up as part of the registration of a company. The memorandum includes a record of the company's name, its registered office, its purpose and its Authorized Share Capital. The other document drawn up at the birth of a company is the Articles of Association. These are rules concerning the relationships of the company to the shareholders, the shareholders to each other, and so on. Every limited company when formed must file with the Registrar of Companies a document known as its memorandum of association which is open to public inspection. It must contain certain statutory clauses, though others may be added to suit the whim of individual companies.

Memorandum or Memo: Short message sent from one person to another in the same organization.

Menu: A list of computer programmes, operations, options, instructions, files, questions, and other functions displayed on a computer monitor in order to assist an operator.

Mercantile: Commercial person who sells for a business or another person and earns a commission; country which earns income from trade; laws relating to business; all the commercial ships of a country; negotiable document used in commerce.

Merchandise: which are for sale or which have been sold; goods sold off cheaply to pay a company's debts to sell goods by a wide variety of means; including display advertising sending samples, etc.

Merchandising: A smart for selling.

In some industries (like the rag trade) sales people are called merchandisers. Merchandising implies rather more than selling; unlike selling, it is not, for example, done door-to-door. Merchandising involves the whole range of activities that can be used to increase the sales of goods through retail outlets.

Merchant: Businessman who buys and sells, especially one who buys imported goods in bulk for retail sale; bank which lends money to companies and deals in international finance; person who as a high position in a merchant bank; all the commercial ships of a country; commercial shop or ship which carries a cargo.

Merchant Bank: A UK Bank engaged in corporate finance, investment banking, Portfolio management and a few other banking services. Unlike a Clearing Bank it is not involved in running personal bank accounts, or in issuing and clearing cheques. Some merchant banks are the offspring of eighteenth and nineteenth century immigrant families such as the Hambros, the Schroders and the Rothschilds-who founded them as financial arms of their big merchant trading houses. The power of these institutions in the UK is still considerable; many become home to retired senior ministers, Treasury mandarins and heirs.

Merger: Action by which two firms come under common ownership or control. Similar terms include 'acquisition', 'amalgamation', 'consolidation' and 'take over' merger tends to be the term with the most general meaning. 'Amalgamation' and 'consolidation' tend to indicate agreement between the original owners of the merged firms: 'consolidation' implies a completely new firm being created from the merged firms.

Mergers and Acquisitions: Mergers between companies, and acquisitions of one company by another; also the name given to the department of an Investment Bank charged with handling them. Mergers and acquisitions (M&A) activity is more prevalent in economies with strong, egalitarian stockmarkets (like the UK and the USA) than it is in Japan or continental Europe.The level of M&A activity is a mirror of the general states of an economy, and is determined by three things in particular. Confidence as to the future level of business activity. The Rate of Interest. The availability of funding.

Merit: Quality which deserves reward.

Merit Rating: Assessing an employee's performance and personal qualities by which his pay can be determined. Also such an assessment of an employee.

Metamarketing: US marketing applied to all kinds of organizations, such as hospitals, churches and religions as well as to profit making concerns.

Metric System: The system of measurement in multiples of ten in use in most countries. The system was proposed for international use at a conference in 1960. It is derived from the French metric system and is known as the Sl (Systeme Internationale d' Unites).

Microchip: A tiny piece of silicon, containing a complete electrical circuit used extensively in the manufacture of the microcomputer.

Microeconomics: The part of economics that deals with small-scale issues like the prices of individual products, the performance of individual companies, or even a family budget.

Microprocessor: The microchip containing the central processing unit of a microcomputer. Also used of the microcomputer itself.

Middle: In the centre or between two points; middle management: department manages in a company, who carry out the policy set by the directors and organize the work of a group of workers.

Middleman: A person who puts producers in touch with consumers. In the sale of goods, both wholesalers and retailers are middle-men.

Middle Management: The level of management that includes all managers above the supervisory level but below the level where overall company policy is determined.

Middle-of-the-road (organization man) Management: Style of a manager who has limited concern for both people and productivity.

Milking: A short-sighted marketing strategy that aims to make as much profit from a product in as short a time as possible, with no regard to the long-term future of the product. This is often an appropriate strategy with a FAD like toys, dolls and various accessories.

Minimize: To make something as small as possible; to make something seem not very important.

Minimum Subscription: The amount stated in the prospectus which the directors consider the minimum that must be raised for the company to be launched successfully.

Minor: A person under the age of eighteen.

Minority Shareholder: Members of a company in which the controlling interest, i.e., the majority of the equity share capital, is held by another company—a holding company, Minority shareholders have little or no say in the conduct of the affairs of the company.

Mint: The organization authorized by the State to manufacture and issue, on a monopoly basis, the bank notes and coin which make up the legal tender of nation.

Minute Book: A book containing the minutes of meetings specifically one containing the minutes of meetings of directors off a company or of general meetings of a company.

Miscellaneous: Various or mixed or

not all of the same sort.

Mismanage: To manage badly.

Misrepresentation: Making a wrong statement in order to persuade someone to enter into a contract (such as to buy a product or service); false statement made wilfully to trick someone.

Mission: The long-term of an organization; group of people going on a journey for a special purpose; visit by a group of foreign businessmen; visit by a group of businessmen to a foreign country; visit to an area to search for information about a problem.

Mistake: Work action or wrong decision.

Mix: Arrangement of different things together; combination of all the elements that make up marketing, such as price distribution and promotion; combination of products made or sold by the same company; different elements used in a company's promotion.

Mixed Economy: In economics, this refers to the kind of economy in which the ownership of the means of production is partly in the private sector and partly in the public sector.

Mobile Shop: A retail outlet which takes goods to potential customers rather that wait for them to come to the shop.

Mode: Another form of average used in statistics, though not as common as the mean or the median as its application is of only limited use. It is the value which occurs most frequently in a given series.

Modern Management-Approaches to: (1) The operation approach; (2) The empirical approach; (3) The human-behaviour approach; (4) The social-system approach; (5) The decision-theory approach; (6) The communication approach; and (7) The mathematical approach.

Monetary Assets: Those Assets that are denominated in money terms or have a face value. Cash or Debtors (accounts receivable) are examples of monetary assets. Non-monetary assets include land, buildings, etc. Monetary and non-monetary assets are important for some systems of Foreign Currency Translation and Inflation Accounting

Monetary Policy: In economics this refers to a government's position on the regulation of the amount of spending power available in an economy and the cost of borrowing money, e.g., deciding whether or not to impose a credit squeeze.

Monetary: Referring to money or currency; the government's policy relating to finance (bank interest rates, taxes, government expenditure and borrowing) fixing of fixed exchange rate for a currency; methods of controlling and exchanging currencies between countries; system of controlled exchange rate between some member countries of the Common Market; (part of the United Nations) a type of bank which helps member states in financial difficulties gives financial advice to members and encourages world trade; standard currency in a country (the pound, the dollar, the franc, etc.).

Money: Coins and notes used for buying and selling; to have a salary or wages; to have a large salary or high wages; to make a loss or not to make a profit; the company has been working at a loss; to earn enough to cover your original investment; to make a profit; to deposit money into a bank account; to invest money in a business; to pay cash especially as a deposit; money which can be borrowed at a low rate of interest; extra salary paid to workers in dangerous jobs; money which has to be borrowed at a high rate of interest; money which can be earned with no difficulty; money which is moved from country to country to get the best returns; money in notes not coins; cash or money which is immediately available; money not being used to produce interest amount of money which exists in country; markets for buying and selling short-term loans; rates of interest for borrowers or lenders; document which can be bought for sending money through the post; money order in a foreign currency which is payable to someone living in a foreign country; sums of money.

Money Making: Which makes money.

Money Market: A market in which banks and other financial institutions buy and sell short-term financial instrument such as bills and Commercial Paper (that is money) among themselves.

Money Measurement Convention: Traditionally accountants only include items in accounts and financial statements that can be measured in money terms with reasonable objectivity. Thus the value of a skilled management team, or of loyal staff or customers, is not normally shown in financial statements. This is because it is difficult to measure reliably its worth in money terms. This convention is linked to the use of Historical Cost Accounting, where Assets are measured at their purchase price or production cost.

Money Supply: In economics this refers to the total amount of money circulating within an economy at any given time, whether in the form of notes, coins, bank deposits, etc.

Money-Market Fund: A fund which gathers individuals' small savings and invests them in the Money market. Money market funds were particularly popular in the USA when US Interest-rate controls restricted the amount that banks could pay on regular deposits. The funds gave individuals a chance to circumvent the controls by giving them indirect access to the (uncontrolled) money markets.

Moneylender: One of those persons

whose business is lending money.

Monopolist: Business which is the sole seller in a market.

Monopolistic Competition: Refers to a market situation in which competition exists between each of two or more (perhaps numerous) sellers whose products are close, but not perfect, substitutes for one another.

Monopolistic: Situation where there are only a few producers who, therefore, control the market among them.

Monopoly: A market structure having a single seller of a commodity or service dealing with a large number of buyers; the seller has complete control over the quantities of goods offered for sale and the price at which the goods are sold. A situation in which a market is under the control or domination of a single organization. This condition is generally considered to be met at one quarter to one-third of the market in question. Monopoly is contrary to the deal of free trade and is therefore subject to legal sanctions in all industrialized countries with a capitalist or mixed economy. Monopolies can occur in both the private and public sectors.

Monopsony: The reverse of a monopoly, it is an industry in which there are many willing sellers but only one buyer. The buyer can, therefore, set each seller against the others and obtain supplies at the lowest possible price, i.e., situation where there is only one buyer for a particular product.

Moral Obligation: Acts of payments arising from feelings of moral obligation do not constitute good consideration for the formation of a contract.

Moratorium: A period agreed between a borrower and a lender in which repayments of principal are allowed to lapse. Banks do not like to give moratoria on interest payments because it forces them to do nasty things to their accounts, like increasing provisions against bad debts.

Mortgage: The transfer of an Interest in real estate to some one else as Security for a loan. This transfer most commonly takes place between a house-buyer and the financial institution that is financing the purchase. In many countries such institutions are very specialized. In the UK they are called building societies. A second mortgage is a second loan secured on the same price of real estate.

Most-Favoured-Nation Clause: This concerns international bilateral trade agreements where each country offers most favoured-nation status to the other and a clause is inserted to this effect in the trading agreement. To give such status is to agree that each will afford the other best available tariff and quota terms in the course of international trade.

Motion Study: This is a study in management that is complimentary to time study. Study of the movements of an operator on machine is called Motion Study. It is undertaken to eliminate useless motions and to find out the best method of doing the work. According to Galbraith, "Motion Study is the science of eliminating wastefulness from using unnecessary, ill-directed and inefficient motions. The aim of motion study is to find and perpetuate a scheme of best method of work. It means elimination of unnecessary and wasteful movements." E.A. Farmer defines motion study as "the study of movements involved in a task with a view to eliminating such movements as are unnecessary and improving the others".

Motivate: To give someone a good reason or incentive to do something.

Motivation Skill: It is only through proper understanding of the hopes, fears, aspirations, disappointments and failures of a person that a Manager can decide as to how to motivate his subordinates. He must find out why people behave as they do. The needs of every person can be classified broadly under bio-genic group, socio-genic group and ego group.

Motivation: The causes of particular behaviour by an individual especially causes (e.g. emotions) related to the internal state of the individual. Process or study of motivating people to behave in a particular way.

Motivation, Psychology of: When we manage a business we are not managing just a department or an organization but primarily the people who compose the department, the people who are part and parcel of the organization, the people who were managed by our predecessors and they will be managed by the posterity as well. How do these react to varying situations, phenomenal changes in systems conventions, tastes, habits, aptitudes and in essence the totality of the enormous changes that envelop them? The changes brought about by social, political, economic and other factors may have a salient effect on the people, may even change the orders of priority which they fix for themselves but it is quite doubtful whether the people will change basically.

Motivational: Research into the psychological reasons behind buying behaviour.

Motivator: An aspect of a job that can contribute to the satisfaction but not the dissatisfaction of the job-holder according to the motivation-hygiene theory.

Moving Average: A statistical term used to show trends in a series of figures. It attempts to iron out casual fluctuation by showing the movement in an n year average;

for example, if total asset are shown for fifty years, the average for the first, say five years would be taken. The next figure would be the average after dropping the first year and adding in the sixth, the process continuing until the fiftieth year is included. This type of average is rather rudimentary and tends to be of value only when the series is particularly long. In any event the initial figures are not true averages.

Multi-Brand Strategy: The practice of carrying many brands within one Product Line; a strategy developed and practised by Procter & Gamble with, for example, its 24 different brands of fabric-washing products. The strategy has several objectives. It is a means of obtaining greater shelf space in retail outlets, relative to competitors. It is a way of dealing with "Brand Switchers", customers who like to try a different brand from time-to-time. It is a way of dealing with would-be competitors, leaving them no gaps in the market. It is a way of segmenting the market, providing brands which may develop their own loyal followers. It is a strategy that can be used to create a degree of competition among a company's brand managers, and to keep them on their toes.

Multi-Pack: A package containing several separate items which are sold out as one unit.

Multilateral Trade: Whereas bilateral trade describes trading agreements between two countries, multilateral trade is international trade carried on with many different countries and involving many currencies, which often benefits from the setting up of international clearing houses for mutual indebtedness.

Multimedia: Referring to several media used in a project.

Multinational: An abbreviation for a discriminate multilateral trade.

Multinational Corporation: Means a corporation or company which is operating in a number of countries with production or service facilities outside the country of its origin; the principal decisions of the company are taken in a global context. Often called international corporations, these are very large business enterprises, normally of a corporate nature, with interests (e.g. subsidiary companies) in businesses situated throughout the world. They are structured on a global basis and although they may originate from, or be registered in, a particular country, they rarely acknowledge allegiance to any one country unless it is convenient to do so.

Multiple: Many type of question used in a survey which allows the respondent to choose a single answer from several possible ones.

Multiplexing: Simultaneous or almost simultaneous transmission of a number of different messages through a single communications channel.

Mutual Bond: An open-end Investment Trust that continually issues new shares as it receives new capital, and redeems the shares of owners who want to sell. The capital is invested in stocks and shares by the fund's managers, who are paid a commission for their services.

Mutual Funds: The name for financial institution that use money provided by investors to own and manage a portfolio of investment in other Stocks and Shares.

N

Narrow Market: A market in which there is only a small supply of goods or services being sold. The expression is applied particularly to financial markets (such as the Stockmarket) where there is a shortage, for example, of a particular company's shares on offer.

National: Referring to the whole of particular country; customer with branches or locations all over the country; advertising in every part of a country, not just in the capital sales or publicity campaign in every part of a country; value of income from the sales of goods and services in a country; newspapers which sell in all parts of a country; annual value of goods and services in a country including income from other countries.

National Debt: A term used to describe the estimated total indebtedness of the central government to its own nationals and, to a lesser extent, persons or bodies overseas. Although the greater part of the debt is permanent and irredeemable, the identity of the persons to whom it is owed is by no means constant as the slips of paper which comprise it are constantly being bought and sold in the market.

National Development Finance Industries: In the private sector have on the whole done progressively well. Regional figures for amount of funds invested by them in industry would not be very meaningful because the productivity potential of a given amount of money differs from country and situation to situation. Nevertheless quantitatively the NDDIs have been the source of a major portion of the funds that have gone into industrial development in the private sector as well as in some countries in the small and medium reaches of the public sector.

National Income: Refers to a measure of the money value of the goods and services becoming available to the nation from economic activity.

Nationalization: State ownership and control of any of the means of production, distribution or exchange. The taking over and running of commercial companies by the state. The financial sector frequently has a high degree of nationalization. In India, for example, the largest commercial banks and many large insurance companies are controlled by the state. In the 1980s there was a widespread political reaction against nationalization (see privatization). Nationalized industries were frequently seen as inefficient and uncompetitive. In many cases they were, but not entirely because they were owned by the state. The process by which a state takes over the ownership of a private company or industry and brings it within the control of the public sector. This may be due to practicing the ideology of socialism or to the attempt to save a strategic part of the economy from collapse of foreign ownership.

Nationalized Industries: These are industries owned by the public, i.e., in the control of the government through a semi-autonomous Board of Management. There are no shareholders apart from the government.

Near-Market Research: Scientific research with an evident potential for commercial applications.

Nearby Delivery: Delivery in the next calendar month.

Needs: What is necessary needs assessment or assessment of needs-analysis of an organization's manpower requirements which can form the basis of training plans.

Needs Theory: Motivational theory focussing on the internal stimuli that cause people to take action.

Negotiable Instrument: A document of title that can be freely negotiated. Title can be transferred by delivery, and no particular form is necessary. Normally a financial instrument that can be handed from one owner to another without informing the original issuer of the instrument; for example, a bank note, a bearer bond or a cheque. A cheque may be made non-negotiable by the addition of the words "not negotiable" between two lines across the front of it.

Negotiate: To negotiate with someone=to discuss a problem formally with someone, so as to reach an agreement.

Negotiation: Discussion of terms and conditions to reach an agreement; contract which is being discussed; something which must be discussed before a decision is reached; to start discussing a problem; to start discussing a problem again after talks have stopped for a time; to refuse to go on discussing a problem; to negotiate discussions stopped because no agreement was possible; discussions between management and workers about pay.

Net Assets: The total of fixed plus net current assets, or fixed plus current assets less current liabilities. The worth of a business in accounting terms, as measured from its Balance Sheet.

Net Book Value: The different between the cost of an asset and its accumulated depreciation.

Net Current Assets: The current assets or working capital of a business is the excess of the Current Assets (such as Cash, Stocks and Debtors) over the Current Liabilities (such as Trade Creditors and Overdrafts). This is one measure of the Liquidity of the business. However, the movement of the total from year to year, or of the Current Ratio (of Current Assets to Current Liabilities) might be more useful information.

Net Present Value: An estimation of

the value today of a payment that is to be made (or received) tomorrow. The payment is discounted by an amount that takes into account in the time between now and the day that the payment is due. This amount is calculated having regard to expected interest rates and the degree of risk involved in the payment. The net present value of an investment project is the differences between the present value of the future revenues of the project, and the present value of its future costs.

Net: The balance of items or amounts remaining after some items or amounts have been removed; also, the amount or number of items free from encumbrances or obligations: also, the considerations that remain after discounting or removing those that have little or no bearing on the issue or problem at hand.

Net Price: The amount which a buyer pays after all discounts, etc., have been deducted.

Net Profit (or Net Income): It is the excess of 'revenue and gains' over 'expenses and deprival'. It results in an increase in the proprietor's equity. 'Net Loss is the deficiency of revenue and gains' as compared to 'expenses and deprival', and leads to decrease in the owner's equity.

Net Profit Ratio:NP Ratio: Net profit / Net sales × 100. This is used as a measure of overall profitability and is useful to the owners. It is both an index of efficiency as well as profitability when used along with GP Ratio and Operating Ratio.

Net Realisable Value (NRV): The amount that could be raised by selling an asset, less the costs of the sale. NRV usually implies a sale in the normal course of trade. Thus there would also be a deduction for any costs to bring the asset into a saleable state. The normal rule for the valuation of Current Assets, such as Stocks, is to use the Lower of Cost and Market, where the latter means the NRV (except that, in the USA, it can mean the replacement cost, where lower). The use of NRV has also been proposed for some systems of Inflation Accounting, either as the main valuation basis or as a basis for those Assets that are about to be sold.

Net Sales: Total sales less amounts given as discounts, and amounts coming from goods returned.

Net Weight: The actual weight of goods after deducting the weight of all packing materials.

Net Worth: An accounting term for the total of share capital and reserves or rather the difference between total assets and outstanding liabilities. It generally refers to the market value of owners' equity.

Network: A diagram, used in project network techniques, that represent the component activities and/or events in a project and shows their interrelationships. A network consists of lines, called 'arrows', that joint points (or circles or rectangles) called 'nodes'. A network is a graph but users of project network techniques have developed a terminology that is almost entirely different from that uses by mathematicians who have built up the theory of graphs.

Network Marketing: A new method of selling that is, basically, a way of taking the well-known "Tupperware party" formula to the streets. Particularly appropriate for selling costume jewellery, one practitioner described network marketing as having three essential elements. 1. The sales person wears the product. 2. He or she carries the catalogue with them. 3. He or she talks about the business everywhere and all the time. This practitioner claims to have sold jewellery this way even at a supermarket checkout and in a doctor's waiting room.

Network Designs: Organization design that takes into account a unique combination of strategy, structure and management process. It goes beyond the matrix structures and totally abandon the classical hierarchical, functional structure of organization. The emphasis, under this structure, is given on the achievement of team goals, broader competencies, leadership, etc.

Network Planning: Using a project network technique for planning.

New: Recent or not old; type of organizational buying where a completely new type of product is bought; group of people from different departments in a company who work together on a new product development project; improving excising products or developing completely new ones; electronic instruments which have recently been invented

New Product Development (NPD): The range of activities involved in conceiving, developing and launching a new product into a market. NPD is a critically important process since most firms have to introduce new products frequently and continually in order to retain their competitive advantage. Failure rates are high. Only about half the new products placed on the market become commercially viable, and only one in 40 new product ideas ever becomes a successful product.

New Push Theory: Budgets play an important part in the "Push" Finance people are usually asked to scrutinize all budgets. They are directed to cut out all "the lace and niceties" and "get down to essentials". In short a new pressure upwards is expressed somewhere in the budgets in terms of a "tighter" figure. The results may be as expected. Human efficiency rise say 10% and production is increased. A new level of efficiency is stabilized at 80%.

Niche Marketing: The systematic search for a market niche usually by a small specialist organization. Its basic principal is the attempt to create a new market rather than increase market share of an existing market.

Niche: Special place in market occupied by one company.

No Claims Bonus: Motor insurance policies usually incorporate a substantial no claims bonus which is set against the annual premium where the insured has satisfied the conditions written into the insurance contract. This normally applies where no claim has been made on the insurer for a specified number of years.

Nominal Price: A quotation for a futures contract during a period when no trading is actually taking place.

Nominal Value: The current exchange value of an item.

Nominee: Someone whose name is used in place of somebody else's. To ensure greater secrecy for a Swiss bank account, beneficiaries of the account often open it in the name of a nominee. The nominee then passes on all the interest (minus his fee) to the true beneficiary, whose name need never be known to the bank. A recent agreement between Swiss banks says that they will always try to find out who is the true beneficiary of an account before they allow it to be opened.

Non-Operating Expenses: Expenses that cannot be associated definitely with the principal activities of the business are non-operating expenses; for example, interest paid etc.

Non-Payment: Not paying a debt due.

Non-Returnable: Which cannot be returned; packing which is to be thrown away and not returned to the sender once it has been used.

Non-Executive Directors: As the name implies these are directors who although they have seats on the Board, are not working or executive directors.

Non-Operating Income: Incomes that cannot be associated with the principal activities of the business are non-operating incomes, for example, rent received, dividend on past investments in charge, etc.

Non-Price Competition: Attempt to compete in a market through other means than price such as quality of product and promotion

Non-Profit Making Organizations: Organizations which do not exist to make a profit but to provide some sort of service to the socity or to their members. These are concerns like clubs. Education institutions, charitable hospitals, societies for the promotion of art and culture etc. Most of their transactions are for cash and the use of credit is very limited.

Non-Taxable Income: Incomes not liable to income tax.

Non-Union: Company using non-union labour: company employing workers who do not belong to trade unions.

Non-Verbal Communication: Communicating a message, using facial expressions or body language (body gestures, body postures, eye contact), but without speaking. Normally refered as 'knesics'

Non-Voting Share: An ordinary share in a company that carries no entitlement to vote at shareholders' meetings.

Norm: In statistics this is value representative of a whole set of numbers, such as one of the measures of central tendency (mean, median and mode).

Normal: Usual or which happens regularly; if things work in usual way; term used in sampling theory referring to the results of a sample and meaning a symmetrical distribution of values around a mean or average so that one can be confident that the sample is properly representative of the population of universe; price that can be expected for a product under normal market conditions; product which people buy more of as their incomes rise and less of as their incomes fall; minimum profit that can motivate a business to carry on a certain type of production or selling.

Normative: Establishing, or seeking to establish, norms: attempting to set out the proper course of action; stating what should be rather than what is, what was or what will be.

Not Negotiable: If the words 'not negotiable' are written across a bill of exchange, a person taking the bill cannot get a better title than the person from whom he took it. This does not prevent the bill from being negotiated, but the bill is no longer a negotiable instrument.

Notary Public: Usually a solicitor and someone specifically appointed to deal with such matters as the noting of bills of exchange, attesting deeds, etc. A notary's word is acceptable as evidence in most courts.

Note: A Written acknowledgement of a debt, in two slightly different forms. **Paper money**: As "in pound note" and "notes and coin". **A type of security**: As in floating-rate note and promissory note.

Nullification: Act of making something invalid.

Nullify: To make something invalid or to cancel something.

Numbered Account: The term used to describe a bank account which is identified by a number only and where the bank is not free to give the name of the account holder to anyone. These accounts are usually in Switzerland. Where the laws governing banking allow the high degree of secrecy necessarily involved and are frequently used by those who wish, for reasons ranging from tax evasion to shady or plainly crooked dealing to hide the existence of large sums of money. The Swiss banker is not necessarily thereby willing to become an accessory to crime, but tradition precludes asking a customer the source of the money which that customer wishes to deposit, or disclosing either the names of specific depositors holding numbered accounts, or the amounts in them at any time, except in very strictly defined circumstances.

Numeric: Referring to numbers; in the order of figures (such as 1 before 2, 33 before 34) in the form of figures; part of a computer keyboard which is a programmable set of numbered keys.

Nutrient: A food substance that is digested and absorbed by the body and utilized as food and energy to sustain life.

O

Object Program: The result of translation by a computer using a translating routine, of a source program. The object program is in a form more readily usable by the computer than the source program.

Objective: Something which you hope to achieve; aim which you hope to achieve within a few years or a few months; way of managing a business where the managers work according to a plan and checks are made periodically to see whether their work is completed correctly and on time; method of calculating an advertising appropriation by basing it on the actual amount needed to achieve the objectives; considered from a general point of view not from that of the person involved.

Objectivity: An accounting measurement is said to be objective if it is reasonably independent of the judgment of accountants. There is much to be said for objectivity in accounting, because it reduces the time taken both to arrive at figures and to check them. It also means that the easily reassured that the figures contained in them are not arbitrary. The most obvious result of this desire for a simple, verifiable system is the conventional use of Historical Cost Accounting. The original purchase price of an asset is much more objective than its current selling price, replacement cost or the value of future benefits expected to flow from it. However, such techniques as Depreciation and Provisions for Bad Debts do add subjectivity, even to historical cost accounting. The main problem with greater objectivity is the possible sacrifice of relevance. The price of a machine eight years ago is objective, but irrelevant for a knowledge about how much the machine is worth or for a decision about what to do with it. A well-known saying in accounting is that it may be better to be approximately right than precisely wrong. Nevertheless, at present, most of the world settles for a system that might be said to be not precisely wrong.

Objective Function: A mathematical expression of the relatioship between a dependable variable and some other measure of output.

Obligation: Duty to do something.

Observation Method: Market research method of obtaining information by observation rather than interviews.

Obsolescence: Act of going out of date because of advances in design or technology and therefore becoming less useful and valuable; deliberately making old models seem out of date by bringing out new ones with changes and additional features which will attract the customer; method of ensuring continuing sales of a product by making it in such a way that it will soon become obsolete; redesigning a company's product to make other products in the market obsolete.

Occupation: Job or work.

Occupational Mobility: Occupational mobility is mobility prevalent in an economy that provides for inter-change of work force from one occupation to another. Occupational mobility is very much less in an underdeveloped country compared to a fully developed country, where occupations of different sort have a tendency to merge into each other at higher management levels.

Occupy: To live or work in a property (such as an office); to occupy a post: to be employed in a job, to take up a certain amount of time.

Odd-Even Pricing: A pricing convention used in retailing whereby a product's price is not rounded up, but left as a figure ending in a five or a nine (both 'odd' numbers). Thus 99p is used in preference to 1; and Rs. 24.95 in preference to Rs. 25. This odd convention persists even though it has never been proved that consumers actually think, or even feel, that 'odd' priced goods are better value than 'even' priced goods.

Off Balance Sheet: Any transaction by a financial institution that does not have to appear on the institution's balance sheet; for example, a fiduciary deposit of advisory business. Such transactions are particularly attractive to banks, which have to pay an additional price (in the form of extra reserves) for every extra cent that they put on to their balance sheet. In the advertising industry such off balance sheet business is described as being below the line. Leasing is off balance sheet business for the lessee, but not for the lessor.

Off Balance Sheet Financing: Financing assets by 'borrowing' in such a fashion that the debt does not appear as a balance sheet item.

Off the-Job Training: Any training that takes place while the trainee is not performing his responsibilities of the normal job.

Off-The-Job: Off-the-job training: training given to workers away from their place of work (such as at a college or school).

Off-The-Peg Research: Market research that uses old data collected by someone other than the researcher. The four main types of material taken off-the-peg are: published sources; data regularly collected and sold by market research companies (see syndicated research); data on specialist subjects regularly collected and sold by market research companies (see under specialist research); data commissioned from syndicated surveys (see omnibus research).

Offer: A term used in the law of contract. The offer is the first step.

Other things being equal, acceptance of the offer can bind the offeror. The offer may be conditional or unconditional. The acceptance must be in the same terms as the offer.

Offer Price: Bid price.

Office: Building or set of rooms where a company works or where business is done.

Office Bearer: Person who holds an office, especially person who is a member of a union council handles the office of secretary or treasurer, etc.

Official Reserves: Gold and foreign exchange reserves.

Oligopoly: A situation in which a few sellers can control or dominate a market. Such a situation is widely regarded as an incentive for the sellers to form a cartel.

Oligopolistic Industry: Market structure characterized by a few very large sellers and by interdependency. The pricing policy of one or more firms prompt reactions from other firms in the industry.

Oligopsony: Means a market in which a few buyers have to face a very large number of sellers. This type of market is comparable to that of oligopoly.

On Demand: A bill of exchange is payable on demand when it is payable on presentation. An uncrossed cheque is a bill payable on demand.

On Line: That part of a computer system which is under the immediate control of the central processing unit and can make information immediately accessible to the user by being linked directly to a mainframe and operating in real time. Most common example is that of an airline seat reservation system.

On the Job-Training: On the job training involves assignment of a new employee to a specific job at a machine or workplace in the shop, office or laboratory. The worker is trained while he is engaged in the work by utilising the actual work situation for the purpose. He is instructed by an experienced employee, special instructor or his superior.

On the Job Test: It is on the basis of the result of various tests that a candidate is finally selected, but before he is given a job on permanent basis, it would be better to try him out for a few weeks in the factory itself. It is only by observing workers actually at work that one can find out whether he can work harmoniously with his fellow-workers and his behaviour towards the higher management. It is then that he can be finally selected or rejected.

On-the-Job: Training given to workers at their place of work.

One-Stop Shopping: A strategy that is commonly found among financial-service firms and consultants in the 1980s, based on a belief that customers like to buy services as they buy groceries: all in one place.

So groups like Saatchi & SaatchI ballooned, believing that clients who popped in for a spot of advertising might also buy, say, a bit of market research and a human-resources consultant while they were on the premises. For the most part it did not work like that. Customers remained faithful to specialist providers of services, and many one stop shops have been disbanded.

Open: At work or not closed; ready to accept something; anyone can apply for the job; ready to accept a reasonable offer; the company is ready to discuss an offer which is lower than the suggested price; unsecured credit amount owed with no security; cheque which is not crossed and can be cashed anywhere; bank credit given to good customer without security up to a certain maximum sum; import licence for all goods which are subject to special import restrictions; market where anyone can buy or sell to start a new business working; to be at work.

Open Cover: Open policy.

Open Door: A term used to describe unscheduled and unlimited access or admission to, or availability of a person, service, or facility, a policy adopted by a manager to assure open feedback and the participation of all employees in issues relating to management actions, policies, organizational performance, and employees beliefs and attitudes.

Open Door Policy: Policy of a country to accept imports from all other countries on equal terms.

Open Ended: With no fixed limit or with some items not specified; question in a questionnaire which allows a respondent to answer as he or she likes without having to choose from pre-set answers.

Operate: To work to be in force; to make a machine work.

Open General Licence: Importers must obtain licences. There are usually restrictions on some goods imported from certain areas, but where no restrictions apply, open general licences are available.

Open Market: Open market in the context of world economy implies that a country permits international exchange of goods and services and currencies without much restriction. Open markets are those where offers to buy or sell are made to the public at large and not to a restricted number or behind closed doors.

Open Market Operations: These are referred to as operations by the central bank of a country with a view to stabilize interest rates, or adjust the quantity of money in circulation. The Reserve Bank of India may increase the quantity of money enormously by buying securities on a large scale in the open market. The money it spends will increase the balances of the clearing banks, and enable them to lend an even greater amount to the public for development of trade and industry. Similarly, if it tries to contract the supply of money in circulation, it will sells securities in the open market.

Opening Prices: These are the prices at which transaction begin in a market from the start of a firm. In the Stock Exchange for instance, at the time of official opening dealers begin by quoting prices before they have a full appreciation of the relative strength of supply and demand. If they have any reason to think that demand will be heavy where favourable trends have been released overnight, then they will mark up their opening prices compared with the closing prices of the earlier day.

Operating: General running of a business or of a machine; forecast of income and expenditure over a period of time; costs of the day-to-day organization of a company; book which shows how to work a machine; profit or loss made by a company in its usual business; financial statement which shows a company's expenditure and income and consequently its final profit or loss; low priced industrial products that are normally bought by producers; the main program which operates a computer.

Operating Income: The income which arises out of the normal business of a firm.

Operating Leverage: Refers to the Gearing (Leverage) which results from an enterprise's asset structure as distinct from its Capital Structure.

Operational Planning: Planning that is directed towards the fulfilment of departmental goals, carries out a tactical plan.

Operating Profit or Loss: An accounting term that has been given more significance by the terminology adopted in the formats for the profit and loss accounts of limited companies.

Operating Profit: Refers to that profit which would be earned if no resources get diverted to the future expansion of the firm.

Operating Ratio (OR): This is the ratio of cost of goods sold plus operating expenses to net sales. This is closely related to the ratio of operating profit to net sales. For example, if the Operating Ratio is 80% then the Operating Profit Ratio would be 20%.

Operating Statement: A imprecise term for a statement showing the cost of running a business and the profit earned by a business or one of its departments.

Operating System: The internal programmes of a computer that allow it to respond to the user's commands and to run "application programmes".

Operation Research-Basic Concepts of: There are four concepts of fundamental importance to the practice of operations research: (a) the model, (b) the measure of effectiveness, (c) the necessity for decision, and (d) the role of experimentation. This concerns the development of procedures in the various disciplines with the object of maximizing efficiency in the use of resources and time available. It is necessarily much concerned with management techniques and is, to this extent, a tool of management.

Operations Research Models: An exact model is used in operations or processes where chance plays a small role, where the effect of a given action will be reasonably closely determined. Exact models can be used, for example, in long-range production scheduling problems in the face of known or committed demand. The probabilistic model, contains explicit recognition of uncertainty. Such models are of great use in the analysis of advertising problems, where the unpredictability of consumers plays a great role. They make extensive use of the highly developed theory of probability, which has come to be such great value in the physical sciences.

Opportunity: Chance to do something successfully; possibilities for making investments or sales which will be profitable; possibility on-going into a market for the first time; number of opportunities an average member of the target audience will have to see an advertisement; jobs which are available; possibility for a customer to make a purchase; company's analysis of both the advantages and disadvantages in its environment in order to ensure sound strategic planning; cost of a business initiative in terms of profits that could have been gained through an alternative plan.

Opportunity Cost: A hypothetical measure of the monies forfeited by using one alternative use out of two possible uses. It is the amount that, in theory, that asset would have earned in the other use. In economics this refers to the last income, profit or time involved in foregoing an alternative course of action, e.g., this is an economic cost and would not be included as an accounting cost. There are two definitions: 1. What investors lose by not having put their money into the highest-yielding asset that had been available. 2. The maximum amount of profit that could have been produced if factors of production had been put to others uses.

Optimal: Best combination of elements or activities that can be achieved in a marketing mix.

Optimisation: A key concept in micro economics; the consumer is assumed to maximum utility or satisfaction, subject to the constraints of income, while the producer is assumed to maximise profit and minimise costs, subject to the technological and legal constraints within which it operates.

Optimum Order Point: The level of

inventory at which an order should be placed in order to minimize costs associated with procurement.

Optimum Order Quantity: The quantity of an item that should be purchased in order to minimize procurement costs.

Option: An agreement whereby one person grants another the right to buy or sell certain goods at an agreed price, or within a stated future time. The term is usually used with reference to dealings on the stock exchange. Options to sell are known as deals for the 'put' options to buy as deals for the 'call'. It is also permissible to have the double option, i.e., to buy or sell. An option is essentially an agreement giving one person the right to buy or sell a given quantity of specified goods services or choses in action at an agreed price at any time within a stated period.

Orange Goods: A category of consumer goods-things like clothing-that because of wear-and-tear or because of changing fashion. To be contrasted with fast moving consumer goods whose turnover is much quicker.

Order Control: A method of production, planning and control involving receiving the customer's order to following up.

Ordinary Resolution: A resolution passed at a meeting of the shareholders of a company usually at the annual general meeting. A simple majority of those present is sufficient for the passing of such a resolution, unless the articles of association of the company say otherwise.

Ordinary Share: The basic type of share, with no bells and whistles attached other than a voting right and dividend. Contrast with preference share.

Organizing: Organizing comprises of: (i) Breaking down work into operative duties, (ii) grouping operative duties into operative positions, (iii) assembling operative positions into manageable and related unit, (iv) clarifying position requirements, (v) selecting and placing individuals on proper jobs, (vi) utilising and agreeing upon proper authority for each management member, (vii) providing personnel facilities and other resources and (viii) adjusting the organization in the light of control resources.

Organization: A group of people brought together for the purpose of achieving certain objectives. As the basic unit of an organization is the role rather than the person in it the organization is maintained in existence, sometimes over a long period of time, despite many change of members.

Organization Audit: An audit of all aspects of an organization operations. In practice this is usually the same as a management audit.

Organization Chart: A chart outlining the relationship between the different functions, responsibilities and titles in an organization and often the people who actually perform them.

Organization Convenience: A course of action that meets the (usually financial) interests of the organization as a whole as well as its individual members. It involves the application of behavioural science to process the functioning and the management of the organization, especially in response to changes in the environment.

Organizational Change: Any adjustment made by an organization in responding to environmental forces or anticipating future events.

Organization Man: A term, used both approvingly and pejoratively, applied to someone who has the kind of personality which allows him to fit relatively, comfortably into an organization, particularly a formal organization with some degree of bureaucracy.

Organization Size: The number of members an organization has can have a direct effect on its organizational structure. The larger the number the greater the pressure to operate as a formal organization with a high level of bureaucracy, a relatively fixed chain of command and increased levels in a hierarchy of authority.

Organizational Behaviour: The behaviour of an organization acting as an entity, rather than that any individual member.

Organizational Buying: Buying by a large organization such as a company or government department, as opposed to purchases by individual consumers.

Organizational Culture: This term denotes 'culture' as the term is not only the shared beliefs, value, attitudes and expectations of its members to make up the culture of an organization, but also the unquestioned assumptions about its traditions and ways of doing things.

Organizational Development: It stresses the concept of improving or developing the existing personnel to their full potential. It can be viewed as more personnel oriented than structure oriented. Formally defined organizational development includes efforts to improve by getting the best from employees individually and as members of working groups.

Organizational Goals: The normally stated objectives which are the basis for the existence and the maintenance of an organization.

Organizational Loyalty: The basis of the contract between an organization and its members. It is usually assumed to be something the individual owes the organization—rarely the other way round.

Organizational Pathology: Writers on organizational theory from a human relations viewpoint have proposed that an organization can be healthy or unhealthy, just like any of its individual members.

Organizational Shape: The profile

of the levels of hierarchy in an organization, the extent to which it is a flat organization or a tall organization.

Organizational Structure: The arrangement of the work of an organization into the different functional roles and management roles.

Organizational Theory: The systematic study of the organization, its structure and functioning and its relationship to the people who comprise it. This area of study draws heavily on psychology and sociology.

Organize: To arrange something so that it works efficiently; workers who are members of trade unions; market controlled by regulations set down by government or an official organization.

Organizing Function: Organizing function involves the determination and enumeration of activities, the assignment of such groups of activities to units headed by managers, and the delegation of authority to carry them out. It is the totality of such activities and relationships that make up the function of organization. All enterprises have some form of organization, however, simple or informal.

Orientation: Introduction of new employees into an organization.

Original Maturity: . The length of time from the issuing of a security or loan to the date of the last repayment.

Out-of-Stock: With no stock left.

Outlays: Actual expenditures of funds, including checks issued, the payment of interest accrued on debt, and other payments (minus refunds and reimbursements).

Output: Amount which a company or a person or a machine produces

Output Contract: An agreement to purchase the entire production or output of a particular items.

Over the Counter Market: A secondary market in which unquoted shares are purchased and sold to the general public by jobbers and finance brokers outside the Stock Exchange.

Over-Capitalized: A business is overcapitalized when it has more capital than it can profitable use.

Over-the-Counter (OTC): An open market for securities that are not listed on a regular Stock Exchange. OTC markets enable smaller companies that cannot afford the full expense of a major market listing to establish a free-market price for a company's founders to recoup some of their investment. OTC markets exist solely on computer screens and telephone lines; they have no physical trading floor.

Over-the-Counter Securities: A method of allowing the exchange of securities for those companies that are not large enough for a full listing on a Stock Exchange, or for companies that would prefer not to obey the listing requirements of an exchange.

Overcompensation: Producing a

greater effort than is needed to overcome a difficulty or resolve a defect. The term is often used in connection with attempts to overcome an inferiority complex.

Overconforming: This term is sometimes used to describe a person who is excessively slavish to the demands of authority or the convention of social norm.

Overdraft: Refers to a system of bank lending, by which the client is permitted to draw cheques beyond the credit balance in his account, up to an agreed limit, and to pay interest only on the daily amounts by which his account is overdrawn.

Overfunding: There are two meanings: 1. A pension fund is overfunded when it has received so many contributions that it is (actuarially) able to repay more in the future than it is contractually to. 2. A government is said to be overfunded when it has issued more bonds in a particular financial year than it needs to finance its debt.

Overhead Expenses: Expenses incurred in manufacture, though not directly identified with any particular item produced.

Overhead: Money spent on the day-to-day cost of business; plan or probable overhead costs of the day-to-day running of a business; Expenses of a business that cannot be traced to units of production or to processes that produce particular single products. The term "Indirect Costs" has the same meaning. There will be production overheads, administration overheads, distribution overheads and possibly others.

Overproduction: Manufacturing too much of a product.

Overseas: Across the sea or to foreign countries; phone call to another country; section of a company dealing with trade with other countries; markets in foreign countries; trade with foreign countries; to sell more than you can produce; stock market prices are too low, because there have been too many sellers.

Overstock: To have more stock than is needed; to have too many spare parts in stock more stock than is needed to supply orders.

Oversubscribed: Shares are said to be oversubscribed when more are applied for than are offered. In these cases, applications are usually scaled down prorata, though sometimes small applications are met in full and only large ones (above a stated limit) are scaled down.

Overtime: Any time worked outside normal working hours, for which people are paid at a higher rate than the basic level of pay, usually double or time-and-a-half.

Own Label Goods: Goods specially produced for a store with the store's name on them.

Owned Funds: These funds are those that have been contributed by the owners of the business, i.e., proprietors, partners or shareholders as the case may be. Ownership funds are the real risk capital. Generally, it remains invested in the business as long as the business continues to exist. Owners of business can withdraw these funds from the business only at the risk of the closure of the business.

Owner: Person who owns something; person or company that owns a magazine or newspaper or radio or TV station; person who owns something on his or her own, without any partners; person who owns and lives in a house; situation where goods shipped or stored are insured by the owner, not by the transport company or the storage company; situation where the owner has to insure the goods while they are being transported.

Owners' Equity: That part of the finance of an enterprise provided by its owners. Also referred to as Shareholders' Fund.

Ownership: Act of owning something; common or collective ownership: situation where a business is owned by the workers who work in it.

P

P/E Ratio: Price Earnings Ratio.

Package: Goods packed and wrapped for sending by mail; group of different items joined together in one deal; salary and other benefits offered with a job; agreement which covers several different items; holiday or tour where the hotel, travel and meals are all included in the price; to wrap and pack goods in an attractive way to sell a holiday package including travel, hotels and food; Group of different items joined together in one deal.

Packaged Goods: Consumer goods that are packaged by their manufacturer, and not sold loose. Such goods include most food, cosmetics and cleaning products. Despite the hygienic advantages of packaged goods, many consumers still seek out unpackaged alternatives; of fruit and vegetables, for example, and of sweets.

Packaging: A marketing term for the presentation of goods, i.e., the manner in which they are wrapped or displayed. The wrapper can be a vital selling factor apart from being a platform for advertising. The packaging of many products today has become an integral part of the product. It may have been originally designed to protect the product, but it now carries out a range of other functions as well. A convenient means for dispensing its contents (liquid soaps, glue or toothpaste, for example). A means for carrying important information about the contents (sometimes required by law). An important means for promoting and advertising the product itself. Through design and labelling it can become as important as what it contains, people may still like to by boiled sweets in brown paper bags, but they want their designer chocolates in something a bit more glamorous.

Paid-Up Share Capital: The Issued Share Capital to the extent that it has been called up from the share holders and cash or other consideration has been received from them.

Paid: With money given.

Paid-In Surplus: A US expression for part of the amounts of money paid by investors when they purchase a Company's Shares. Most shares in the USA have a Par Value, which is a short of label. Usually shares are issued at above par value, in which case the Capital paid is divided into share capital (at par) and paid-in surplus (the excess above par). For most purposes paid-in surplus is treated exactly as if it were share capital. There are several alternative titles for these amounts, including paid-in capital. In the UK the equivalent term is Share Premium.

Paid-Up Capital: That part of the capital of a company, both called-up and paid-up. The difference between called up capital and paid-up capital will represent calls in arrears.

Paired Comparisons: Method of assessment where items to be assessed are each compared with all others and a final score for each obtained.

Pamphlet: Small Booklet of advertising material or of information.

Panacea: A universal remedy for all problems in an organization: ideally it should be cheap, painless and change nothing important, which is why reorganization is such a great favourite.

Paper Profit: Strictly speaking increases in value of unrealized investment or assets not sold.

Paperwork: Office work, especially writing memos and filing in forms.

PAR: The nominal or face value of a security. In the case of stocks and shares this is almost always well below the market price of the stock. A security is at par when it is selling at its face value.

Par Value: The face value or nominal value of a share or a debenture.

Paradigm: A detailed example or model of a particular process.

Parallel Market: A market in a particular finance instrument that develops outside the standard channels for such a market. For example, the market in ADRS, or the parallel money markets to be found in the Euro market.

Parallel Pricing: Practice of increasing the price of a product that is sold by several manufacturers by the same amount at approximately the same time by all the manufacturers.

Parent Company: A company which controls another company.

Pareto Effect or Pareto's Law: Situation where a small percentage of customers may account for a large percentage of the value of a company's sales or profits (also called the **eighty-twenty rule**). Terms which start to operate on January 1st; new prices will apply from January 1st continue to be applied; we have put into the contract terms which will make this work personal belongings to carry out; to make a payment; to clear something through customs; to bring two parties together and make them agree to a settlement.

Pari Passu: A legal term meaning 'ranking equally'.

Parity Check: An internal computer check to ensure that data are not distorted during processing. Each unit of data is required to have an even number of I's in its binary representation (an additional I being added during coding if necessary) and the number of I's in each unit of data is checked during processing (On some computers a unit of data is required to have an odd number of I's).

Parity: The perceived fairness of equal rates of pay between individuals or groups of people.

Parkinson's Law: An unofficial law,

proposed by C. Northcote Parkinson in his book entitled *Parkinson's Law*, which has been generally accepted as a very relevant half-truth. It claims that work expands according to the time available in which to perform it.

Part Payment: Part payment of monies due under a contract or a debt.

Part-Time: Not working for the whole working day.

Part-Time Job: Any job that takes up less than the normal full-time hours of work in any given situation.

Participate: To take part in an activity or enterprise.

Participation: Payment by the insured person, under an insurance policy provision, of a certain percentage of any loss: also, a mortgage agreement in which the lender receives a share of the profits of a venture in addition to interest on the loan.

Participative Management: As organizations have proliferated in size and specialization, the problem of control and integration of supervisory and staff levels has become increasingly worrisome. The best answer until now has been participative management. But information technology promises better answers. It promises to eliminate the risk of less than adequate decisions arising from garbled communications, from misconceptions of goals, and from unsatisfactory measurement of partial contributions on the part of dozens of line and staff specialists.

Participative: Where both sides take part.

Partner: A person who is associated with another (or other) in an organization, activity or endeavour. A full partner exercises authority and makes decisions which commit and are binding on the resources of the organization, activity, or endeavour. A silent partner is one who is not publicly known to be a partner. A limited partner is a partner with limited authority to participate in operating decisions or to commit the partnership's resources.

Partnership: Two or more people involved in the ownership and control of a business. This form of organization is governed by the Partnership Act. The relationship between partners and their individual rights and duties are governed by the agreement that they draw up. In the absence of an agreement all partners are equal as regards profits and losses.

Party: Company or person involved in a legal dispute or legal agreement; any third person, in addition to the two main people involved in a contract group or people who meet to celebrate something or to enjoy themselves; selling by salesmen who present their products at parties organized in their homes.

Patent: A monopoly right, awarded by law to an individual or a group, granting sole right to make, use or sell an article or process they have invented. In India a patent normally lasts for twenty years during which time the patent holder is protected from any attempts by others to copy their invention.

Patron: Regular customer; person who gives an organization or charity his or her financial support.

Pay: Salary or wage or money given to someone for regular work.

Pay Slip: A slip of paper included in a pay packet, giving details of how the net pay has been calculated.

Pay-Back Method: A popular technique for appraising the likely success of projects, or for choosing between projects. It involves the analysis of their expected future net cash inflows, followed by a calculation of how many years it will take for the original capital investment to be recovered. It is popular because it is simple to use and, perhaps more importantly, simple to explain to non-financial managers. It may be a reasonable way of choosing between projects which have similar initial investments. However, there are drawbacks to the more general use of the method: 1. It ignores the net cash flows that arise after the pay-back period; the quicker pay-back project may actually be far less profitable in total. 2. It ignores the time value of money, that is, it ignores the fact money received in two year's time is less valuable than an equal amount received in one year's time. More sophisticated methods of investment appraisal, such as the Net Present Value method, adjust for both the above problems by discounting these methods are not popular with business people, presumably because they are more difficult to understand and involve many more judgments. The pay-back method is often used in conjunction with others.

Pay-Back Period: The period over which the discounted net income from an investment amounts in total to its original cost.

Payable to Bearer: A bill of exchange is payable to bearer when no particular payee is named, or where it is endorsed in blank.

Payable to Order: A bill of exchange is payable to order when the name of a payee is stated, and where there are no restrictions on transfer.

Payable: Which is due to be paid; which has to be paid before the goods are delivered; which has to be paid when the goods are delivered; which must be paid when payment is asked for; which has to be paid by sixty days after the date of invoice; cheque which will be paid to the person who has it, not to any particular name written on it, shares which must be paid for when you apply to buy them; money owed by a company; bills which a debtor will have to pay; the tenant (and not the landlord) must pay for the electricity.

Payback Period: Refers to a method of Capital Investment Appraisal, which measures the expected length of time over which the undiscounted cash receipts of a capital project equal the undiscounted outlays.

Paycographics: Study of the life style of different sectors of society for marketing purposes; dividing a market in to segments according to the life styles of the customers.

Payee: A person to whom a negotiable instrument (such as a check) is made out, for example, "pay to the order of John Smith".

Payee's Account Cheque: This type of crossing a cheque is a direction to the collecting bankers that the proceeds of the cheque are intended to reach the hands of the payee. He should, therefore, collect the cheque only by credit into the account of the payee. It is also a term used in double-entry bookkeeping to indicate the records of the amounts charged to others for goods and services sold, and the amounts received.

Paying Agent: A financial institution that is appointed by a borrower to be responsible for paying the interest and principal on the borrowing instrument (a bond of a syndicated loan) as and when it is due.

Payment in Advance: Money paid for goods or services not yet received.

Payment in Kind: Remuneration for work done or for services rendered.

Payment of Bonus Act, 1965: The Act applies to every factory and other establishment in which 20 or more persons are employed during an accounting year. The Act also applies to an employee drawing Rs. 1,600 per month as salary or wages. According to this Act every employer is bound to pay to every employee who is qualified for the minimum period of service of 30 working days during an accounting year a minimum bonus of 4 per cent of the salary of the wages earned by the employee during the accounting year or Rs. 40 whichever is higher irrespective of whether the employer has had any profit or not. The bonus is to be paid within a period of 8 months from the close of the accounting year. This Act also lays down a limit of maximum of 20 per cent of the total salary which may be paid to the employees as bonus.

Payment of Wages Act, 1936: The major provisions of this Act relate to: (i) Fixation of wage periods and time for payment of wages: the Act stipulates that the wage period shall not exceed a month and undertakings employing less than 1,000 persons shall pay wages before the expiry of seventh and other undertakings before the expiry of the tenth day after the last day of the wage period for which wages are paid. (ii) Deductions from wages: Deductions from wages are permitted in certain cases like (a) fines (b) absence from duty (c) damages and loss, and (d) recovery of advance, recovery of loan, etc. Deductions from wages of person in a wage period is limited to 50 per cent of the wages. (iii) Levy of Fines: the Act provides for the manner in which and the extent to which the fines can be imposed. The fines collected are to be maintained under a separate fund and to be applied for welfare purpose of the workers. If there are any unauthorised deductions or any undue delay in the payment of wages claim application can be presented to the authority appointed under this Act within one year.

Payoff: The actual result of some past action, or the estimated result of some possible future action; especially when expressed quantitatively. In game theory, a measure of the value to a player of an outcome of a game.

Payroll: The list prepared by a firm giving details of wages and salaries. It states the name or number or both, of the employee and the amounts paid. It may also give information on how the net pay is calculated.

Payroll Deduction: A specified amount of money withheld from the earnings of an employee to finance a benefit. A payroll deduction may be a set payroll tax, such as the Social Security tam, a required payment for a benefit, such as a health insurance premium, or a voluntary deduction, such as a fixed amount for a savings account.

PD: Physical distribution.

Pedlar: Someone who sells from door to door for cash.

Penalty Clause: A clause in a contract stating that a certain sum should be paid by any party breaching the contract.

Penetration: Percentage of a target market that accepts a product; (ii) percentage of a target audience reached by an advertisement; the selling of more of a company's products into a market segment, shown as a percentage of the total market; pricing a product low enough to achieve market penetration.

Pension: A sum of money paid periodically to an individual who retires from employment (or simply from a particular organization) because of age, disability, or the completion of a specified period of service. Such payments usually continue for the rest of the recipient's life, and sometimes extend to his or her legal survivors.

Pension Fund: A fund set-up by a company or other organization to manage the savings of employees, and so on, and to pay the pension benefits to which those savings entitle them. Pension funds are among the biggest investors on the stockmarket, but they have traditionally kept a low profile in the affairs of the companies that they own. That may be changing. Pension funds played a big role in a number of recent cases where top management was removed, or its decisions reversed. However, they have not yet sought what some think is their rightful place on the boards of major corporations.

Perception: The process by which an individual receives, selects and interprets information. Marketers and advertising specialists are particularly interested in the phenomenon of perception; they want to find the signals that will produce in the consumer a favourable view or perception of their product (its image). When the signals are right, advertising can be very powerful; for people's perceptions of products owe very much more to skilful advertising than they do to any intrinsic or exclusive qualities that the products may possess.

Perfect: A market structure is considered to be perfectly competitive if the following conditions hold; there are a large number of firms each with an insubstantial share of the market. These firms produce a homogeneous product using identical production processes and have perfect information. It is also the case that there is free entry to the industry, that is new firms can and will enter the industry if they observe that greater than normal profits are being earned. The main effect of this free entry has been to push the demand curve facing each firm downwards until each firm earns only normal profits, at which point there exists no further incentive for new entrants to come into the industry. Further since each firm produces a homogeneous product, it cannot be able to raise its price without losing all of its market to its competitors. Hence the demand curve facing each firm in the long-run will be horizontal and tangential to the minimum point of the long-run average cost curve of the firm, as shown in the diagram.

Performance: The way of job or task is done by an individual, a group or an organization.

Performance Appraisal Interview: An interview between an employee and his or her line manager, usu ally conducted once a year, at which an assessment is made of the individual's job performance and how it relates to training needs, promotion opportunities, etc.

Performance Appraisal: Performance appraisal is the systematic periodical evaluation of the performance of an employee on his present job and also relation to future jobs that he may be required to take up. It measures and evaluates the results of the performance of the workers. It points out their potentialities and deficiencies.

Performance Appraisal—Methods of: Important methods of performance are as follows: (i) Ranking under this method, employees are compared with one another on the basis of their overall performance. (ii) Graphic rating scale. It is the most popular and the oldest method of performance appraisal. A graphic rating scale chart is prepared to indicate the different degrees of various qualities on which the employees are to be appraised. (iii) Check-list method. Here a list of statements is prepared. Each statement is given a weight or scale value. (iv) Field review appraisal of the employees is done by the personnel officer by collecting oral ratings about their performance from the supervisor at the place of work. (v) Confidential reports: A confidential report by the immediate supervisor is prepared for the determination of promotions or transfers. The format and pattern of this report varies with each organisation.

Performance Bond: A guarantee from a bank to an importer (often provided by the exporter's bank) that the exporter will fulfil a contract according to its terms and conditions. Performance bonds are often used in the construction industry, particularly in the Middle East, when the buyer wants to ensure that a contractor completes a contract on time, and as promised. Failure to perform according to the terms of the bond gives the buyer some degree of financial compensation for delay of failure to meet specifications.

Performance Evaluation: The assessment by a superior of a subordinate and an important part of any Management Control System.

Performance Rating: Production is achieved in any organization with the association of Men, Machine and Raw Materials and it is the responsibility of the Management to provide for best possible interaction of the same so that productivity is maximized. Variables affecting ultimate output are numerous and all of them are not equally important.

Perishable Goods: Goods which deteriorate if not used within a specified time, e.g., food.

Perpetual: Going on for ever. Thus a perpetual debenture is a debenture that never gets repaid.

Perpetual Succession: One of the attributes of a corporation. Any corporate body, whether a corporation sole or a corporation aggregate, has a legal existence quite distinct from the person or persons of which it is composed. For this reason its lifespan is not limited by that of its member(s) and it is therefore said to have perpetual succession, it continues to exits until wound up in the manner prescribed by law.

Perquisites: The special benefits, frequently tax-exempt, made available only to the top executives of an organization. There are two basic kinds of executive perquisites: (1) those with "take home" value (such as company cars, club memberships, etc.) and (2) those that have no "take home" value, but serve mainly to confer status (such as the proverbial executive washroom, office size and decor, etc.). Perks.

Persistent Demand: Continuous or stable demand for a product.

Personal Accounts: An accounting terminology representing a person, institution or artificial person, such as company, etc.

Personality: The sum total of all factors that make an individual human being both individual and human: the thinking, feeling and behaving that all human beings have in common, and the particular characteristics pattern of these elements that makes every human being unique.

Personnel Department: A department of an organization that provides for the planning and management of the organization's human resources, including recruiting, interviewing, and screening of job applications, planning and classification of new positions, compensation and benefits planning, implementation and maintenance of compensation schedules and job classifications, providing new employee orientation.

Personnel: People who work in a certain place or for a certain organization.

Personnel Management: This is a branch of management that is primarily concerned with the management of human relationships within an organization. Its objective is the maintenance of those relationships on a basis which, by consideration of the well being of the individual, enables all those engaged in an undertaking to make their maximum personnel contribution to the effective working of that undertaking. Personnel management maximises the contributions and the satisfactions of the employees of a business. Activity, function or study of helping managers in an organization to make the best use of the human resources of the organization.

Personnel Manager: A personnel manager is expected to be a leader with high intellectual powers and a philosopher who gives to the organization a vision of future for leading human relations in an organization towards more prosperous and progressive policies.

Personnel Policy: Formulation and development of personnel policies becomes important to a company when: 1. The organization has reached a size that requires many decision-making centers that will act consistently. 2. Situations requiring decisions occur frequently. 3. A record of decision-making criteria is needed to evaluate the effectiveness of the criteria as the results of decision become known. The process of developing a personnel policy involves assessing its appropriateness to the organization. It must be acceptable in all the situations in which it might be used as basis for decision testing against each of the organization's major functions to make certain that all operating, legal, financial, marketing, and public relations considerations had been taken into account. The policy should also be tested against community practice to assure that the reputation of the firm is being maintained at as high a level as its business and financial situation will permit. The maintenance of a competitive position in the community in these matters can assist the organization with its employees, its public, its bankers, its stockholders, and its customers, and thereby facilitate the survival and growth of the organization.

Personnel Records: Personnel records are maintained for the following objects; (i) to provide complete information on demand about the employees of the organization; (ii) to enable the personnel managers to find out most suitable staff for different departments and decide about their promotion and transfers; (iii) to serve as authenticated basis for the calculation of super/annuation or retirement benefits of the employers.

Peter Principle: Managers tend to be promoted to the level of their incompetence. Specifically, if a manager succeeds in a position, this very success may lead to promotion to a higher position, often one requiring skills that the person does not possess.

Petrodollers: Money received by governments as royalties for petroleum oil extracted from their territories. Such royalties are normally payable in US dollars.

Petty Cash: This refers to ready money kept within a business for the purpose of meeting small incidental expenses on a day-to-day basis, and also perhaps for reimbursing staff for minor costs incurred on behalf of the business.

Petty Cash Book: A book recording Petty Cash transactions. It is usually kept by the imprest system, in which a fixed sum or 'float' is allocated as sufficient to meet petty cash expenditure for an agreed period of time.

Petty Cashier: A person responsible for keeping petty cash and the petty cash book.

Philanthropic Voluntarism: The issue facing managements today is not one of philanthropic voluntarism and not one of superficial public relations. As Professor Baumol of Princeton University, U.S.A. observes, business organizations will not serve the national interest (must less their own) by undertaking to behave like philanthropic institution. Such a transformation is neither feasible nor desirable.

Physical Distribution: The process of moving goods from the producer to the end user.

Physiological Needs: Man's needs are organized in a series of levels—a hierarchy of importance. At the lowest level but prominent in importance when they are denied with. For a hungry man what is important is bread. Unless the circumstances are unusual his needs for love, for status, for recognition, are inoperative when his stomach has been empty for a while. But when he eats regularly and adequately hunger ceases to be an important motivation. The same is true of the other physiological needs of man, for rest, exercise, shelter, protection from the elements.

Pie Chart: A popular manner of presenting statistical information. A circle is drawn representing a pie or cake and slices are cut in the 'cake' to represent the contribution of various ingredients to the whole.

Piece-Work: Wages are often paid on piece-work principle. It means that a person's pay is directly related to the number of units produced in the period covered by that pay.

Pilferage or Pilfering: Stealing small amounts of money or small items from an office or shop.

Pioneer: First person or company to do something; project or development which is new and has never been tried before; hard intensive selling in new markets.

Piracy: Unauthorized use of someone else's production, invention or conception; especially infringement of copyright or patent right. Video piracy is a problem facing the firm industry where commercial recording films has been indulged in by video distributors.

Placement: Putting someone in a job; placement service: office which specializes in finding jobs (such as for students leaving college).

Planned Change: A proactive approach to planning that tries to see the organisation as it should be in future.

Planned Economy: An economy under the central direction and control of the state, e.g., under the ideology of socialism, which would decide on matters like pay and production in the absence of market forces.

Planning: Organizing how something should be done, especially how a company should be run to make increased profits; planning the future financial state of group of companies; planning the future financial state of the country for the government; planning the calls which a salesperson will make and how he or she will reach them most efficiently; planning to get the right number of workers for each job; deciding what media should be used in a promotional campaign. A manager is said to be planning when he decides which objectives or goals he will pursue, when they will be achieved, and exactly how his resources of manpower, equipment and time will be devoted to their achievement. To help or make easier the realization of the results intended he will decide to follow existing policy or make new policy about such matters as pricing, competition etc. The planning process is logical because it reflects the successive steps and conditions required to reach an objective. The plan itself may be either formal or informal. This means that while the process and the importance of objective may be the same in either event, it is sometimes advantageous to reduce some plans to writing or illustration while other plans may not require this treatment. The decision to formalize a plan depends on the presence of a large number of actions that must be taken over a fairly long period of time and, consequently, are likely to be overlooked. Planning is done: 1. By clarifying, amplifying and determining objectives. 2. By forecasting. 3. By establishing the conditions and assumptions under which the work will be done. 4. By selecting and stating tasks to accomplish objectives. 5. By establishing an overall plan of accomplishment, emphasising creativity to find new and better means for accomplishing the work. 6. By establishing policies, procedures, standards and methods of accomplishment.7. By anticipating possible future problems. 8. By modifying plans in the light of control results.

Planning Function: Comprises Offsetting uncertainty and change: focusing attention on objectives: gaining economical operations and facilitating control. Planning comprises of: (i) Clarifying. amplifying and determining objectives, (ii) Forecasting, (iii) Establishing the conditions and assumptions under which the work will be done, (iv) Selecting and stating tasks to accomplish objectives, (v) Establishing an overall plan of accomplish, emphasising creativity to find new and better means for accomplishing the work, (vi) Establish policies, procedures, standards and methods of accomplishments, (vii) Anticipating possible future problems, (viii) Modifying plans in right of control results.

Plant: Plant is an industrial establishment that is either a factory, a mill or a workshop concerned with some type of operations. It refers to a place where goods are produced, such as sugar factory, iron and steel factory, or from where distribution of goods takes place such as a departmental store or from where services are supplied such as transport depot, etc. The term plant includes not only the equipment installed in the factory, but also the workers who are engaged therein. Prof. Sargent defines "plant" as `a congregation of body or persons assembling together at a certain time and place'.

Plant Layout: 'Plant layout' means the arrangement and location of different departments and of the machinery and equipment within a department. Every entrepreneur has to give thought not only to the question of localization of plant but also of its proper housing and arrangement before starting a new enterprise. Efficiency of a manufacturing enterprise depends upon the planning of the layout, and the design for the factory. A better plant layout must provide for all future developments in the processes and techniques of production or the changes that may become necessary because of changes in management policies.

Ploughed-Back Profit: That part of the profit for the year not distributed but retained in the business, normally for development by reinvestment.

Point of Sale: The place where the whole marketing effort-the sale-culminates. The term usually refers to a retail store, but with the advent of self-service and the technological revolution, it may now mean a checkout counter or a through-the-wall bank teller machine. It can also be inside the customer's own home. So called "home shopping" allows customers to make purchases in their pyjamas, via an interface with their television screens.

Point of Sale Advertising: A form of advertising material that is below the line and placed in retail outlets, i.e., the point at which the sale is actually made.

Point System: Evaluation of jobs by assigning points to each job and converting these points to wages.

Policy: A statement of an organization's intention to act in certain ways when specified types of circumstances arise. It represents a general decision predetermined and expressed principle or rule establishing a normal pattern of conduct for dealing with given types of business events usually recurrent. A statement of policy is useful in economizing the time of managers and in assisting them to discharge their responsibility equitably and consistently.

Policy Formulations for Planning: The use of policies assists manufacturer in answering what to plan. At all organizational level better understanding of what is to be accomplished as well as the means of accomplishment is fostered by the use of sound policies. Confidence of the manager is enhanced since a manager operating with a policy gains assurance that one's actions are in keeping with the wishes of and will be backed up by one superiors.

Population: Number of people who live in a country or in a town; total number of people in a group under study in a survey, from which a sample is chosen.

Portfolio: A collection of financial assets belonging to a single owner. A well-diversified portfolio contains a mixture of things, like shares, bank deposits, gold and government bonds. Institutions offer management services to customers who want their portfolios to be trouble free. The institution keeps the assets somewhere safe, and carries out tasks like the collection of dividends, and the claiming of rights or scrip issues.

Portfolio Risks: A risk that depends not only on the riskiness of the individual securities or other assets on a portfolio but also on the relationship among those securities.

Position: Situation or state of affairs; what's the state of the company's current account? (a) statement of position by one group during negotiations; (b) place where something is; place in a publication where an advertiser asks for his or her advertisement to be put.

Poster: Large notice or advertisement to be stuck up outdoors; place reserved for posters.

Potential: Possible, a person's ability to become something in the future.

Power of Attorney: A legally binding document that empowers on person to act on behalf of another. A power of attorney may specify that the power is for a limited range of purposes of for a limited time; or it may be given unconditionally. Use of the power of attorney is increasing with the rise in the number of elderly people no longer capable of managing their own affairs. A general power of attorney gives the holder fairly exclusive rights to act for another person. A special power of attorney is of a more limited kind, perhaps for acting on one occasion only.

Power: The ability to make things happen for exerting influence over people or things. The most commonly recognized sources of power are physical strength, knowledge, or position in hierarchy of an organization. But there are also less concrete sources of power such as exist in personality factors like charisma or the relationships between people in an organization.

Pre-Coding: Assigning codes to items on questionnaire in order to facilitate reference and evaluation.

Pre-Testing: Testing or evaluating a product or advertising campaign before it is launched or run.

Preference Shares: Preference shares are those which carry with them certain preferential rights in priority to the equity shares. They enjoy: (a) preferential right to receive dividends before they are paid to ordinary shares and (b) preferential right as to return of capital in the event of the winding up of the company. Preference shares may be cumulative or non-cumulative. They may be redeemable or irredeemable.

Preliminary Expenses: These are the

expenses necessarily incurred in the formation of a company for instance the expenses of promoting the company, publishing a prospectus, issuing shares, obtaining the statutory books, etc.

Premium Offer: A form of sales promotion that offers a customer the opportunity to obtain one product, either free or at an attractive price, by purchasing another. It is a device that is particularly popular with cosmetics manufacturers; purchasers of a new after shave, for example, often walk away from the shop with a piece of luggage or a towel that dwarfs their genuine purchase.

Premium: There are two meanings. 1. A regular payment to an insurer for providing insurance cover 2. The amount paid over and above some calculated value. For example, the amount paid for a company over and above its market capitalization, or the amount paid to an auctioneer (like Sotheby's) on the sale and/or purchase of antiques.

Prepaid Expense: Any expense or debt paid before it is due: for example, a travel advance to an employee.

Prepayment: Payments in advance. Amounts recorded in a Balance Sheet which show that certain payments have been made in advance, perhaps for rent, property taxes of insurance premiums. Conventional accounting uses the Accruals Concept or Matching principal, which is that only the expenses that relate to a period should be charged against profit for that period. Thus prepayments will have been paid in the period leading up to the balance sheet, but will not be treated as expenses until a subsequent period. Technically, instead of the debit being treated as an expense, it is treated as an asset. The parallel treatment for expenses paid late gives rise to accrued expenses on the balance sheet.

Presence: Measurement of an advertisement's real audience as opposed to its potential audience.

Present Value: The future net cash inflows expected from an asset or a proposed project, discounted to reflect the fact that money is more valuable if received now rather than later. For the valuation of an asset it might be more normal to refer to the method as the Economic Value. This makes an appearance as a possible valuation in unusual circumstances under some systems of Inflation Accounting. When choosing between investment projects, these concepts are normally considered under the heading of Net Present Value.

Presentation: Showing a document; cheque which will be paid when it is presented; you do not pay to go in if you show this card demonstration or exhibition of a proposed plan; demonstration by a salesman of a product; standard sales presentation which some salesman use all the time instead of adapting their presentation technique to different customers.

President: In commercial parlance, the title president is sometimes accorded to the most senior executive in a public company.

Press: Newspapers and magazines; newspapers which are sold in a small area of the country; newspapers which sell in all parts of the country; meeting where reporters from newspapers are invited to hear news of a new product or of a court case or of a takeover bid, etc., reports about something in the press; cutting out pieces in newspapers and magazines which refer to items of particular interest; (ii) piece cut out of a newspaper magazine which refers to an item of particular interest; date on which a publication is printed; part of the public relations activity of an organization aimed at building up good relations with the press; sheet sent to newspapers and TV and radio stations giving news about something.

Prestige: Status or reputation achieved because of being successful or wealthy or powerful; advertising in high quality magazines to increase a company's reputation; expensive luxury product; expensive officer in a good area of the town.

Price Control: Direct intervention by the government to keep prices stable.

Price Discrimination: When intermediaries or industrial buyers purchase products of similar quality and in similar quantity they expect to buy them on the same terms. If the seller favours one or more of its customers, and the terms, then under the law of the USA an offence has been committed. This is not usually the case in other countries where, for example, a professional firm of builders will usually obtain lower prices from a builder's merchant than will an odd-job home builder.

Price Earnings Ratio: The ratio between the market value to share capital and the profit for the year.

Price Leader: A firm that is one of suppliers in an obligopoly and usually is the first of the suppliers to change its price the other suppliers making similar changes soon after the price leader.

Price Maker: A firm that produces goods and sells them at prices which it can determine itself.

Price Sensitive: The effect that an increase (or decrease) in price has on the sales of a product of service. A product is said to be "highly price sensitive" if a small change in price results in a large change in sales. In general, low-price, commodity-type goods are very price sensitive; high-price, luxury goods are not.

Price: The total amount of money that must be handed over in exchange for an article or service that is being purchased.

Price War: A situation in which competing suppliers of a goods reduce their prices drastically in the hope that the competitor will find it impossible to continue supplying that goods and will then leave the market.

Price/Earnings Ratio: The market price of a stock divided by its reported (or anticipated) earning per share. When divided by its reported earnings it is known as the historic price/earnings (P/E) ratio; when divided by its anticipated earnings it is known as the prospective P/E ratio. P/E ratios listed in newspapers are of thc historic variety. The P/E ratio is a measure of the number of years it will take for a share purchased now to repay its purchase price to an investor if all its earnings are paid out as dividends. The average P/E ratios on different stockmarkets vary greatly. In Tokyo, where investors are happier than elsewhere to receive their reward in the form of capital gain, P/E ratios tend to be high (often over 30). In Anglo-Saxon countries, where (higher) dividend payments are excepted, P/E ratios tend to be lower (in single figures).

Pricing: Giving a price to a product; a company's policy in giving prices to its products; illegal fixing of prices by several businesses so that they all charge the same price; putting a low price on a product so that it competes with similar products from other companies; setting a price for a product so as to maximize its contribution to fixed costs; making the selling price the same as the cost of a single extra unit above the number already planned; setting a low price for a product to try to penetrate the market; setting a medium price for a product where the raw materials used in making it are subject to wide price fluctuations.

Primacy Effect: The finding that, under certain conditions in the process of learning, the first one of a series to be learned is remembered best.

Primary Market: A market for a goods in which the sellers are the producers of the goods. A market for securities in which the sellers are the issuers of the securities.

Primary Product: An economic good that is a result of agriculture forestry, fishing, mining or quarrying and has been subjected to little or no processing or transformation by humans part from the activity involved in extracting it from its natural source.

Prime Costs: The prime costs of production are direct materials, direct labour and direct expenses, i.e., materials, labour, and expenses that can be directly associated with the cost of producing a specific item.

Prime Lending Rate: This is the American equivalent of the British banker's base rate.

Principal: Person or company which is represented by an agent; most important.

Principal Sources of Funds of a Public Limited Company: Issue of shares and debentures, long and medium-term borrowings, Sales of fixed assets, and long-term investments. Funds from operations or trading income, non-trading income, such as income from investments, gifts, damages awarded in legal action, etc.

Private: Belonging to a single person, not a company or the state; letter which must not be opened by anyone other than the person it is addressed to; client who has dealings with a company as an individual not as the representative of another company; income from dividends or interest or rents which is not part of a salary; ordinary person with money to invest; property which belongs to a private person or company not to the state or to a local authority; brand owned by a distributor rather than by a producer company with a small number of shareholders whose shares are not traded on the Stock Exchange; businesses which are owned by private shareholders not by the state; all companies which are owned by private shareholders not by the state.

Private Bank: A bank that is owned by a limited number of partners, each of whom bears unlimited liability for the debts of the bank. Private banks of this sort are popular in secretive Switzerland. In recent years the expression has come to refer to any bank that offers services predominately to wealthy individuals. Most large commercial banks now have private-banking divisions.

Private Company: A company which isn't a public Company. A private company is not permitted to issue shares or debentures to the public.

Private Placement: The sale of a large part of a new issue of shares (or of a chunk of existing shares) to a small group of investors, usually big institutions like insurance companies and pension funds. The sale is private in the sense that it is not offered to the general public, and is not sold through a recognized stock exchange.

Private Sector: The 'private sector' of the economy has been the combination of elements in the economy which have been not organs or agencies of central or local government and therefore includes the company sector and the personal sector.

Privatization: The process of transferring the ownership of an organization or an industry from the public sector to the private sector, usually by the public sale of shares.

Privilege: Advantage associated with a certain position or situation.

Proforma Financial Statements: Financial statements prepared for future periods on the basis of assumptions contained in Budgets.

Proforma Invoice: Where a vendor requires payment before delivery of goods, he issues to the prospective purchaser a proforma invoice giving details of the payment necessary to obtain them. This will be the selling price of the goods plus, where applicable, additional charges for postage and packing.

Problem: Thing to which it is difficult to find an answer.

Problem Identification: Problem identification is a major task case studies. Frequently, it requires deep and concentrated thought. A common criticism by the non-professional is that the case does not include all the facts. This is true: few case studies can include all the facts. But managers seldom have all the facts, a concept itself subject to wide interpretation by the researcher. So while not perfect case studies do have a definite sense of reality. Attempting to determine a solution without full knowledge may be frustrating but actually it is part of the essence of managerial problem solving.

Procedure: A discrete operation, frequently consisting of a set of closely related tasks producing a single desired result or discernible service.

Process: Series of steps or stages that make up an activity.

Procurement: The activity of buying.

Producer: Person or company or country which manufactures; customers who buy goods to be used in production; amount by which the actual price of a product is more than the minimum which the producer would accept for it.

Product: Anything that can be offered to a market that might satisfy a need or a want. It may be an object, a service, a place, an organization, or an idea. Products can be thought about on three levels. Every product has a core benefit (for example, soaps and detergents make things clean). This is known as "the core product". Products also have brand names, packaging, quality and style. Beyond these direct attributes there is the "augmented product", which includes guarantees, after-sales service, installation, delivery, credit terms, and so on.

Product Differentiation: The practice of making one product distinguishable from others. Products may be differentiated by quality, price, styling and service. In virtually every product class there are many products performing similar functions, needing to be differentiated from each other. Not only must one company's brands be distinguishable from the brands of competing firms, but they also frequently need to be distinguished from each other too.

Product Line: A group of closely-related products marketed by the same company. Companies can have one or many product lines; and product lines can contain few or many products. Heinz has a product line with more than 57 varieties, while Procter & Gamble has something like 57 product lines including beauty care products, chemicals, detergents, disposable nappies, and so on. The number of products within a product line is related to the number of different consumer segments that a company has been able to identify and supply.

Product Life Cycle: A concept that suggests that all products pass through a series of growth curves until they reach a point where demand either levels out or begins to decline.

Product Market: A company's product line is frequently sold to several different classes of customer. Each of these classes (or "product markets") has distinct requirements. A line of food products, for example, may be sold to the retail market (grocery outlets), to the catering market (restaurants and hotels), and to the institutional market (schools, hospitals, military installations or prisons). Each product market requires a different marketing approach.

Product Mix: This is the whole range of products offered to consumers by a single company at any given time. The product mix is described in the following terms. **Width**. The number of product lines a company offers. **Length**. The number of brands of each product; Procter & Gamble, for example, has several brands of soap. **Depth**. The number of variants that each brand has; soap may come in hand size, bath size, guest size, family size, and so on. **Consistency**. The extent to which the product lines are related.

Production: All the process involved in providing goods and services to the market, from the extraction of raw materials to the retailing of finished products. Making or manufacturing of goods for sale; production in batches; production of goods in the home market; manufacturing of large quantities of goods; speed at which items are made; cost of making a product; section of a company which deals with the making of the company's products; system of making a product, where each item (such as a car) moves slowly through the factory with new sections added to it as it goes along; person in charge of the production department; separate small group of workers producing a certain product.

Production-Operations Management (POM): Management concerned with the provision of goods and services.

Productivity: A measured relationship between the quantity (and quality) of results produced and the quantity of resources required for production. Productivity is, in essence, a measure of the work efficiency of an individual, work unit, or entire organization. Productivity can be measured in two ways. One way relates the output of an enterprise, industry, or economic sector to a single input such as labour or capital. The other relates output to a composite of inputs, combined so as to account for their relative importance. The choice of a particular productivity measure depends on the purpose for which it is to be used.

Profession: An occupation requiring specialized knowledge that can be gained only via intensive preparation. Professional occupations tend to have three features: (1) a body of erudite knowledge that is applied to the service of society, (2) a standard of success measured by accomplishments in serving the needs of society rather than serving purely personal gain: and (3) a system of control over the profession that regulates the education of its new members and maintains both a code of ethics and appropriate sanctions. The primary characteristic that differentiates a profession from a covation is its theoretical commitment to rendering a public service.

Professional Ethics: The rules of conduct of a profession.

Profile: Description of the characteristics of something; description of an average customer for a product of service; basic characteristics of a particular market.

Profit: The gain made by the sale of goods or services after deducting the value of the labour, materials, rents, interest on capital, and other expenses involved in the production of the goods or services. Economists define profit as return on capital investment. It is what is left over from an enterprise after all bills have been paid. Profit is the entrepreneur's reward for the risks he or she takes. To more practical accountants, profit is the difference between the revenue from sales and the total cost tax is what is left after all money costs have been deducted from sales revenue, that is, wages and salaries, rent, fuel, raw materials, interest and depreciation. Gross profit is net profit before tax, and before interest and depreciation.

Profit and Loss Account: The results of all trading organizations and businesses operated for profit are usually shown in a profit and loss account. By tradition this account tends to be in three parts; the trading account, the profit and loss account proper and the profit and loss appropriation account. Such an account is usually prepared on an annual basis.

Profit Centre: A unit of organization which is treated as a separate entity for purposes of financial control and which is allocated designated income targets with its profit to be calculated over a given period of time. This unit may be a department, a place, a person, or even a machine.

Profit Impact of Market Strategy: Commonly known by its acronym PIMS. An extensive database that throws some light on the factors that bring about different rates of return on investment (ROI) in different industries. The database arose out of a series of studies undertaken by the US company General Electric in the 1960s.

Profit Making: A business is the only human organization whose existence depends on profit. As Ells and Walton point out governments can tax churches, can call on members for support, and the family can survive without profits, but a business requires profits to justify its existence. Profit making is a basic goal of business and the profit concept underlies marketing. Profit goals are achieved in the market place and the basic task of the marketing manager is to serve consumer needs profitably in a way which will be consistent with long range survival goals.

Profit Margin: Refers to profit per unit of output which is expressed as a percentage of price.

Profit-and-Loss Statement: The operating statement used by profit making companies, the equivalent of a profit-and-loss statement for non-profit organizations is called an operating statement or a statement of activity.

Profit-Sharing: A system that allows employees to participate in the profit of the organization that they work for. Profit-sharing schemes are designed to motivate employees without actually giving them a share in their company. These schemes often fail because workers cannot see the correlation between their own efforts and the company's profit. Profit-sharing comes to them like manna from heaven and is something that feel powerless to influences.

Profitability: Ability to make a profit amount of profit made as a percentage of costs; way of calculating how profitable something is.

Profiteering: Making too much profit.

Program: The set of linked instructions given to a computer in order that it may systematically perform a given task.

Programme Evaluation and Review Technique (PERT): Closely related to critical path analysis, this is a continual review of the procedures developed by critical path analysis, with a view to maximizing efficiency and making necessary alterations at the earliest opportunity.

Programming: A fairly general term concerning data processing by computers. A computer will only do what it is told to do. The instructions given to a computer are known as a program, and devising these instructions is known as programming.

Project: Particular job of work which follows a plan; examining all the cost or problems generated by a project before starting work on it; engineer in charge of a project; manager in charge of a project.

Project Finance: A method of finance big capital projects—like the building of a dam or the digging of a mine—that depends for collateral on the expected cash flow of the project. It does not rely on guarantees from third parties.

Project Management (Matrix Structure): An organizational arrangement whereby specialists from functional departments are assigned to special projects under the direction of a project manager.

Promissory Note: An 'unconditional promise' in writing made by one person to another, signed by the maker, engaging to pay, on demand or at a fixed or determinable future time, a certain sum in money to, or to the bearer.

Promoter: The person responsible for the formation of a company.

Promotion: A word with several meanings: (1) increasing sales of specific goods or services by means of marketing research, advertising, etc.; (2) upgrading in individual in his employment; (3) forming a limited company; (4) All means of conveying the message about a product or service to potential customer (by publicity or sales campaign or TV commercial or free gifts).

Promotional: Used in an advertising campaign; discount which is offered to a buyer in return for some promotional activity in connection with the product sold; forecast cost of promoting a new product; combination of all the elements that make up a company's promotion; reduced price offered in order to maximize sales (often when a product is launched) material used in promotion such as display material and sales literature.

Proposed Dividends: Dividends proposed to be paid. When the annual accounts of a company are printed they usually contain an item for dividend on ordinary shares. This is the amount recommended by the directors, but it does not become payable until it has been approved by the shareholders at the annual general meeting.

Proprietary: Owned, as in the case of property: private: profit- making: owned and operated for the purpose of making a profit, whether or not one is made.

Proprietary Ratio: This is a variant of the debt-equity ratio. This ratio relates the shareholder's funds to total assets. It is calculated by dividing the shareholder's funds by the total tangible assets. This ratio indicates the long-term or future solvency position of the business.

Proprietor: The sole of an establishment or business.

Prospect: Possibilities for the future; sales in the market are likely to be lower than they were last year; person who may become a customer; potential customers who are very likely to buy.

Prospectus: Refers to any prospectus, notice, circular, advertisements or other invitation, offering to the public for subscription or purchase of any share or debentures of a company. Whenever an offer of shares or debentures for sale to the public is made, the offering company must issue a prospectus and file this with the Registrar.

Protocol: The minutes or records of a diplomatic conference; especially a note of agreement on subsidiary matters which supplements a treaty. A code of diplomatic etiquette and precedence.

Prototype: First model of a new product before it goes into production.

Provisions: Money that a bank sets aside out of its profit to compensate for its doubtful debts, that is, loans that it feels might never be repaid in full. Banks in different countries set aside more or less money depending on their prudence. In the UK there are two types of provisions. *Specific Provisions*: These are set against specific identifiable borrowers who look unlikely to pay. *General Provisions*: These are not linked to individual borrowers but are based on a hunch about what expected market conditions might mean for borrowers who have not yet been identified.

Proxy: A person acting in place of another. A member of a company can nominate another person (who need not be a member) to attend a meeting and if necessary vote.

Psychological: The retail price of an item that is generally accepted without question by the consumer, though it may be a relatively higher one largely because of its familiarity. This term is generally applied very broadly to include any procedure or technique for assessing any aspect of mental or emotional functioning. It would thus include both projective techniques and psychometrics.

Psychological Test: Way of assessing the principal traits of a person's character. Business psychologists have devised certain tests which seek to measure the psychological characteristics of individual applicants for a position. A psychological test is an objective and standard measure of a sample of human behaviour. It consists in giving to the applicant a task which is representative of the job for which he is being considered. His performance of the task is evaluated in relation to that of the other candidates.

Public: Referring to all the people in general; idea which the people have of a company or a person; nationalized industries and public services; advertising a public service or cause such as famine relief; transport (such as buses, trains, etc.) used by members of the public warehouse which stores goods awaiting shipment or which have just been landed, groups of people that are identified of marketing purposes.

Public Corporation: A quasi-autonomous body similar in function to a company but set-up by the State to run either public services or a industry which is in the hands of the or by the process of nationalization.

Public Gelatins: Every modern business house maintains a Public Relations Department to obtain the goodwill of the public. The ultimate idea of any business is serving the public. Therefore, the goodwill and cooperation of the public is absolutely necessary for any business house to succeed and prosper. The Public Relations Officer is appointed to keep the company's liaison with the public at large and with strategic clients.

Public Goods: Commodities typically provided by a government that cannot, or would not, be separately parceled out to individual since no one can be excluded from their benefits. Public goods such as national defence, clean air, and public safety are neither divisible nor exclusive.

Public Interest Group: An organized pressure group seeking to develop positions and support causes relating to a broader definition of the public good as opposed to any specific social or economic interest.

Public Offer: A new issue of securities offer to the general public.

Public Relations: "The means by which an organization tries to develop a mutual understanding between itself and its public", according to the Institute of Public Relations. Contrary to popular belief, public relations (PR) is a two-ways means of communication, as much about listening; as about telling. While much (PR) work is concerned with handling press conferences and press release, (PR) covers a wide range of activities, from preparing in-house newsletters to negotiating sponsorship deals. A company's relations with government, with consumer groups, with trade unions and with investors may all appropriately involve (PR). Public relations can either be carried out by in-house public-relations officers (PROS), company employees specifically charged with the task, or it can be subcontracted to a firm of PR specialists.

Role of: Public relations play a vital role in this image-building. It is not a matter of make believe but a matter of calculated political well-planned public relations activity would, therefore, be the key to the political performance problem. In our industrial development so far, we have concentrated essentially on technical performance. It is now high time that we apply ourselves to the political performance and it is in this effort that the public relations will play a vital role in the years to come.

Public Sector Objectives: Public sector come into being for a variety of reasons, such as: (a) Inability of private sector to muster enough venture capital; (b) Inability, of private sector to attract capital in projects which have long gestation period and which involve much capital and complex technology; (c) to develop backward regions, and thus correct of chronic unemployment; (e) To provide infrastructural facilities for economic development; (f) For strategic reasons; (g) To develop self-reliance in technologies; (h) To implement labour-intensive technology wherever appropriate; (i) To prevent concentration of economic power in private hands; (j) For revenue motives; and (k) To produce consumption items at cheap prices, and so on.

Public Sector: The part of a mixed economy which is controlled by the state rather than by individuals or private companies. Compare with private sector.

Public Utilities: These organizations, sometimes in the form of public corporations, are essentially managed or supervised by central or local government to supply fundamental services to the public in cases where a natural monopoly usually exists.

Public Utility: An organization that provides an essential public service, like the supply of water or electricity, whether it is part of the private sector or the public sector.

Publicity: Attracting the attention of the public to products or services by mentioning them in the media; office which organizes publicity for companies who do not have publicity departments; money allowed for expenditure on publicity; organized operation to publicize something over a period of time; text of an advertisement before it is printed; section of a company which organizes the company's publicity; money spent on publicity; person in charge of a publicity department; sheets or posters or leaflets used for publicity.

Publicize: Attract people's attention to a product for sale of a service or an entertainment.

Pull Strategy: Attempt by a producer to persuade final users to buy a product and so "pull" the product through the distribution channel to the point-of-sale; combination of both pull and push strategies.

Purchase: Thing which has been bought; to buy something; records of purchases; book in which expenditure is noted; official order made out by a purchasing department for goods which a company wants to buy; price paid for something; tax paid on things which are bought; buying of large quantities of goods at low prices purchase made in cash; system of buying something by paying a sum regularly each month; contract to pay for something by instalments; thing bought as soon as it is seen to pay cash for something.

Purchase Journal: A bookkeeping term for the book in which details of all credit purchases are first entered.

Purchases: A person who buys goods from another. Generally any person taking a title to goods from another person, whether cash passes or not.

Purchasing: Buying; section of a company which deals with buying stock, raw materials, equipment, etc.; head of a purchasing department; person in a company or organization who is responsible for buying stock, raw materials, equipment, etc.; possibility for a customer to made a purchase; quantity of goods which can be bought by a group of people or with a certain amount of money; purchasing organized by the main office for all departments or branches; frequent buying of a low price product for house hold use.

Purchasing Power Parity: Means a theory having little practical validity which considers the equilibrium exchange rate between two currencies to be when they have equivalent domestic purchasing power.

Pure Competition: Hypothetical model of a market where all products of a particular type are identical where there is complete information about market conditions available to buyers and sellers and complete freedom for sellers to enter or leave the market.

Push and Pull Strategies: Two different ways to move consumer goods through a distribution channel. Most companies have to use a push strategy to move their products, persuading each member in the distribution channel to stock them. Large and rich companies, on the other hand, may be able to choose a pull strategy. By investing large sums of money in advertising and sales promotion they can create consumer demand for their product. That demand then acts as a pull to draw the product through the distribution system.

Pyramid Selling: Method of selling based on selling franchised to distributors at various levels in the distribution channel, each of whom buys goods from another distributor at a higher level.

Q

Qualification: Formal document or proof which recognizes that a person has completed a specialized course of study or has a special skill.

Qualitative: Referring to quality; data found in qualitative research; survey based on finding the opinions of respondents rather than any scientifically measurable data.

Quality: What something is like or how good or bad something is; we sell only farm produce of the best quality; newspapers aiming at the upper end of the market; checking that the quality of a product is good; person who checks the quality of a product. When a product is being manufactured in quantity it is necessary to ensure that each item is up to the specified quality.

Quality Circles: Small groups of workers who volunteer their time and energy to identify, analyse and solve quality related problems in their areas of responsibility.

Quality Control: When a product is being manufactured in quantity it is necessary to ensure that each item is up to the specified quality. In order to keep a check on this standard it is common to introduce a statistical method of quality control which relies on the taking of random samples from the production line and subjecting them to intense scrutiny. The result of such test (allowing for a predetermined margin of failure) will determine whether or not the total output is of an acceptable quality.

Quality Forecast: A forecast based on opinions, sometimes combined with statistics.

Quality Market: A market in which the quality of a product is more important to the customer than the price.

Quantitative: Referring to quantity; information gathered in quantitative research; survey based on measurable data.

Quantitative Methodology: The use of research methods in behavioural science or social science which are concerned more with the precision and generalizability of the data being collected than their richness of content or complexity, e.g., having a narrower but sharper focus than qualitative methodology. The experiment and the structured questionnaire are the most common methods used.

Quantity: Amount or number of items; discount based on quantity bought or on the value of total purchases.

Quantity Discount: Additional discount obtained in bulk-buying.

Quantity Rebate: Quantity discount.

Question Marks: In the Boston matrix products which are not very profitable having a low market share but a high growth rate.

Questionnaire: Any set of written

questions used in the collecting of information of purposes of comparison. It is widely used in market research and is the basis of all work in survey research.

Queueing: In ergonomics this term is used to describe a way of dealing with sensory overload in which all the stimuli but one are 'put on hold' by the brain unit that one has been processed.

Queueing (Waiting Line) Model: Quantitative control tool used by firms to determine the optimal methods for serving customers or for scheduling the flow of material through various manufacturing processes.

Quick Ratio: A company's quick ratio (or acid test) is a measure of its liquidity. The ratio is normally measured by comparing the cash plus debtors of a company with its current liabilities. An alternative measure (of all current assets to all current liabilities) is called the current ratio.

Quorum: The number of person who must be present at a meeting in order that the meeting can officially be declared in order. In case of companies the quorum for member's meetings is fixed by the articles of association. The Companies Act specifies that, 'three members should be present in person in the meetings, however, even one member could be a quorum if the articles so allow.

Quotation: Estimate of how much something will cost; putting them on racks in retail shops.

Quoted Investment: An accounting term for investments in shares or debentures which are quoted on a recognized Stock Exchange.

Quoted Price: It is the price of a share commodity as stated in the official list of the Stock Exchange commodity market.

R

R & D Organization in Management: Creative, qualified, and productive personnel is the most important asset of an R & D organization. An effective recruitment programme based on the specific requirements of the organization is the only way of securing adequate personnel. The selection process must be followed by orientation and integration of the individuals into the organization. Management should use adequate means to obtain this necessary organizational socialization. The main objective is to get the professional to understand, accept, and support the company environment and goals and at the same time be able to contribute to the advancement of his scientific field.

Random Sampling: The process of sampling data at random from a population so that inferences can be made about the population from findings about the sample. The crucial condition is that each individual in the total population has an equal of being chosen.

Rank: To list or arrange things in order of importance (according to some concept of what makes them important) or order of the degree to which they possess some specified attribute.

Ranking Method: Method to job evaluation in which all the jobs to be evaluated are ranked according to some consistent system, e.g., by asking someone to put the jobs in order of importance after considering job descriptions.

Rapport: Good communication and understanding between two people.

Rate Card: A list of advertising prices charged by a television channel, a radio station, a newspaper of a magazine. A television rate card typically includes the cost of a 30 second slot at different times of day. A newspaper of magazine rate card includes the cost of a full-page or half-page advertisement, plus special rates for the back page, or for the "inside front cover". Rate cards are used by advertising agencies in planning their use of the media. They are also of considerable interest to marketing managers with advertising budgets to prepare.

Rate: Degree or level; money charged for time worked or work completed.

Rate of Exchange: The price of the currency of one country in.

Rate of Interest: The cost of money over time. The difference between the rate of interest paid by banks to their depositors and the rate of interest that borrowers pay to banks for their loans is called the bank's turn. Rates of interest are influenced by three main factors: 1. The rate of inflation, which acts as a floor, only in very exceptional circumstances can a central interest rate fall below a nation's rate of inflation. 2. The degree of risk run by the lender, thus blue-chip companies will be charged a base rate plus, say, two percentage points; an entirely new electronics company will be charged several percentage points more. 3. The demand for money. After integration of the eastern part of Germany, the demand for money there increased greatly. The bundesbank had a choice between printing more money in order to dampen demand. Each national financial market has its own distinctive key rate (or rates) of interest.

Rate of Return: A measure of the profitability of a business. It normally compares the annual profit of the business with the amount of capital invested in it. The rate of return may be measured before tax or after tax, and it is important to be clear which one it is. Such a measure will normally be used to compare one company with another. Thus it is also important to define the profit figure and the capital or asset base carefully.

Rating: Assessing something by assigning a certain grade, merit rating: judging how well a worker does his work, so that he can be paid according to merit.

Ratio Analysis: Ratios are invaluable aids to management and others who are interested in the analysis and interpretation of financial statements. Absolute figures may be misleading unless compared, one with another. Ratios provide the means of showing the relationship which exists between figures. Though there is no special magic in ratio analysis, many prefer to base conclusions on ratios as they find them highly useful for making judgments more easily. However, the numerical relationships of the kind expressed by ratio analysis are not an end in themselves but are means for understanding the financial position of a business. Generally, simple ratios or ratios compiled from as single year's financial statements of a business concern may not serve the real purpose. Hence, ratios are to be worked out from the financial statements of a number of years.

Rationalization: Streamlining or making more efficient.

Rationing: The term used for any method of allocating a scarce product or service other than by means of the price mechanism.

Ratios: Ratios analysis is a popular sport of investment analysts, financial journalists, textbook writers and examination setters. It involves the comparison of a company with its past or with other companies, by setting one piece of financial data in the context of another. For example, comparison of the absolute levels of profit for two companies of different sizes would obviously be meaningless. However, it may be valuable when the profit of the two companies can be set in the context of their total assets or capital figures. This would lead to a comparison of profitability ratios. There are also the gearing ratio, which measures the proportion of debt finance; the liquidity ratio, which measures the size of current assets in the context of the debts of a company; and the frequently used price/earning ratio, which sets in the context of its part of the annual earnings of the company. Like most useful simplification, ratio analysis contains great dangers. First, it is important to ensure that there is consistency of definition from year to year and from company to company. When international comparisons are being made ratio analysis is especially dangerous because there are major differences in the methods used for valuing assets and measuring profits. Another danger is that ideal ratios may be thought to exist. An example is the liquidity ratio. There are textbooks that suggest that a current ratio (that is, current assets: current liabilities) should be above 2: 1. However, it is nonsense to regard this as a general rule. For some companies in some industries (possibly heavy engineering), this level might be dangerously low; for other companies (such as supermarket chains) it would suggest exceptional inefficiency in the use of resources.

Reactive Change: An organization's adapting and changing, sometimes grudgingly, because it can no longer ignore external or internal pressure.

Re-Advertisement: Second advertisement for a vacant post; fit to be used to be sold; money which is immediately available for payment; these items sell rapidly or easily in the Middle East; market with a high turnover of goods; sale that is easily achieved.

Re-Employ: To employ someone again.

Re-Engage: To re-employ a person but not necessarily in the same job.

Re-Export: Exporting of goods which have been imported; export something which has been imported.

Real Value: It is mostly in making comparisons over a period when prices have reacted to arbitrary and artificial pressures which do not reflect genuine worth.

Real Wages: Disposable income left after paying taxation, etc., the buying power of a certain income as opposed to the actual money received.

Realisable Profit: A profit is realisable, but unrealised, if productive activity of price rise mean that assets could be sold for more than they were previously recorded at in a company's accounts. Conventional Historical Cost Accounting ignores realisable profits until they become objective and easily measurable by being realised, basically by sale. This is partly due to traditional conservatism, and partly to the much greater simplicity and auditability of objective, realised amounts. However, the problem that results from this Realization Convention is that the profits recorded for any year are a very incomplete indication of what happened in that year. To take a simple example, suppose that an asset is bought as an investment and that it is sold after ten years. In the first nine years no gains will be recorded, but in the tenth year the full gain will be recorded, and treated as profit even if the asset had actually lost value during that year.

Realization Convention: A well-established principle of conventional accounting, that gains or profits should only be recognized when they have been objectively realized by a sale being agreed. This is consistent with the all-pervasive concept of conservatism, which anticipates losses but never profits.

Rebate: A rebate is similar to a discount in so far as it reduces an amount payable. Sometimes it is used as a synonym for discount in a trading situation. However, a discount is strictly a reduction allowed by the payee, whereas a rebate is an amount returned to the payer-often at a later date.

Rebuy: Act of buying a product again; buying decision where either the product or the supplier has changed from the time of the previous purchase; buying decision where the same product is bought again from the same supplier.

Receipt: A document issued by a creditor to acknowledge payment of debt. At one time a stamped receipt was demanded as proof of payment. Now if payment is by cheque made out to the creditor and paid into his account, no other receipt is legally necessary.

Receivable Turnover Ratio: Receivable or Debtors normally include both Debtors and Bills receivable and represent the uncollected portion of credit sales. Receivables constitute an important component of current assets and therefore the quality of receivables to a great extent determines the liquidity of a firm. This ratio can be calculated in two ways as follows: Receivables Turnover Ratio (Receivables velocity): Credit Sales/Average Accounts Receivable. Receivable Turnover Ratio: Average Accounts Receivable/Credit Sales per day. where, credit sales per day: Total credit sales/360 or 365.

Receivables: Money owing to a company but yet received. A figure closely watched by accountants and bankers.

Receptionist: He or she represents the company to callers of various types. Callers may include customers, prospective customers, sales representatives, solicitors and promoters, creditors, applicants for positions, and friends of the employer. It is the receptionist's job to handle each visitor in a manner that will build goodwill for the firm and conserve the time and energy of the person or persons for whom he or she works.

Recession: A lack of growth or a decline in trading or in the economy generally though not as seriously as in a depression.

Recognition: Ability of the consumer to recognize a brand on sight; advertising research test to see how well someone can remember an advertisement either with or without prompting or aided recall official approval given by the controlling media organizations to an advertising agency so that the agency can receive commissions from media owners.

Recommend: To say that someone or something is good.

Recommended Retail Price (RRP): Price at which the manufacturer suggests the product should be sold on the retail market though this may be reduced by the retailer.

Recruit: New member of staff, to search for and appoint new staff.

Recruitment: Is the process of searching for prospective employees and stimulating and encouraging them to apply for jobs in an organization. Detailed and systematic study of manpower requirements, both operative and executive, will materially assist in the execution of the recruitment function. A logical sequence of events would be: (i) the determination of the need for a new employee through organization, growth or replacement, (ii) preparation of an employee requisition (iii) recruitment of applicant and (iv) selection.

Recycle: To take waster material and process it so that it can be used again; paper made from waste paper.

Red Tapism: Means delaying tactics used by the officials in disposing of management questions. Departmental management is usually taken to be a synonym for redtapism. Rules, regulations and procedures are rigidly followed and the officers are discouraged from taking quick and independent decisions. They lack initiative and settle down as mere cogs in the huge machine.

Redeem: To end an obligation to someone else by making a suitable payment. Specifically to buy back a security, to end a mortgage by paying off the relevant loan.

Redeemable Shares: The shares, whether preference of ordinary, which are specifically redeemable under their terms of issue.

Redemption: Refers to the repayment of shares and debentures (stocks and bonds), usually at prearranged amounts and times.

Reduction: Lowering.

Redundancy: The dismissal of someone from his employment either because his job ceased to exit or skills are no longer required.

Reemployment: Employing some again.

Reference Group: A reference group may be a bunch of friends, neighbours, or colleagues, or it may be a distant group that the consumer admires for aspires to belong to, such as movie stars of pop singers. The influence of reference groups is strongest where highly conspicuous products are involved, such as clothes, cars, drinks or high-tech equipment. Marketers attempt to associate such products with appropriate reference group.

Registered Office: The official residence of a company. Any document which the law requires to be delivered to the company must be delivered to the Registered Office. The Registrar of Companies must be notified of any change of address.

Registrar of Companies: The government officer with whom Annual Reports (including financial statements) and other documents must be filed.

Regression Analysis: Method of discovering the relationship between one dependent variable and one or more independent variables.

Regulate: To adjust something so that it works well or is correct to change or maintain something by low prices are regulated by supply and demand prices are increases or lowered according to supply and demand.

Regulation: Regulations: laws or rules.

Reimburse: To reimburse someone his expenses: to pay someone back for money which he has spent.

Reimbursement, Retroactive: Additional payment by a third party to an institution for services not identified at the time of initial reimbursement.

Reimportation: Importing goods which have been exported.

Relations: Dealing with other people or other organizations.

Relation-oriented Need: Need that can be satisfied on the job through interaction with other workers.

Relief: Person who takes the place of another, who is sick or on holiday.

Remittance: A sum of money that has been sent from one place to another.

Remnant: Odd piece of a large item sold separately.

Remunerate: To pay someone for doing something.

Rent: The sum received by a person who hires his property out to another.

Renunciation: The decision by shareholders not to take up their rights to a new issue of securities. After shareholders have renounced their rights, the rights can be sold to somebody else. (See Rights Issue.)

Repackaging: Splitting a security into different bits (its interest payments and principal repayments, for example) and reselling them as separate financial instruments.

Repertoire: The group of brands

within a product class which a consumer considers to be acceptable; in other words those brands that he or she will purchase occasionally. Complete Brand Loyalty (in which a consumer never buys anything but one particular brand of a product) is very rare.

Replacement Cost: The cost of replacing any asset that is wasting over time. For companies to ensure that they have thought capital to replace old plant and equipment as and when needed, they make a suitable charge against profit every year.

Report: Statement describing what has happened or describing a state of affairs; document sent each year by the chairman of a company or the directors to the shareholders explaining what the company has done during the year; document which says if something can be done; document which describes what progress has been made; official document from a government committee; make a statement describing something; to be responsible to or to be under someone.

Repositioning: Changing or adjusting the consumers idea of a product by a change in its advertising.

Represent: To act on behalf of someone.

Representative: A person authorized to act or speak on behalf of others.

Reprimand: Formal censure for some job-related behaviour. A reprimand is less severe than an adverse action, more forceful than an admonition.

Requisition: Official order for something.

Rescheduling Debts: Business entity has serious liquidity problems which it convinces creditors are a temporary phenomenon only. Creditors for loans due for payment in the near or immediate future agree to convert the outstanding loans into others which are not repayable until some more distant date. In return they may obtain better interest rates or repayment in the form of stated instalments at staggered dates.

Rescission: In insurance, the cancellation of a policy with repayment of the premiums.

Research and Development (R&D): Activities that are directed towards finding improvements or innovations in a firm's products, by solving the technical problems of producing such improved or new products. The 'research' aspects may involve any efforts to increase knowledge about natural phenomena like new raw materials that may be relevant to the activities of the firm.

Research and Development Expenditure: This is often referred to by the abbreviation R & D expenditure. Most companies, are continually researching into and developing better ways of achieving their stated objectives. They may be looking for new methods of producing old lines, or discovering and elaborating techniques for the production of new items either to replace or to compete with products already marketed by others. R & D is, therefore, an integral part of the world of competition and enterprise.

Research: Trying to find out facts or information; research into why consumers buy goods and what goods they may want to buy; looking for information that has already been compiled; research to find information which has not been published and has to be found through surveys; examining the possible sales of a product and the possible customers of it before it is put on the market; examining the reasons for the good or bad sales of product after it has been launched; research carried out in the interests of successful marketing including market research, media research and product research; study or evaluation of a target audience in order to improve an organization's promotional activities; research carried out to examine various competing products in a market and the potential market for such products; scientific investigation which leads to making new products of improving existing products; study to try to find out information; section of a company which does research; create small group of research workers; person who works in a research department study or to try to find out information about something.

Resentment: Feeling of annoyance at something.

Reserve: An amount of money or other negotiable instrument set aside by an insurance company to assure the fulfilment of its commitments to pay future claims.

Reserve Bank of India: Prior to the establishment of the Reserve Bank of India in 1935, the Imperial Bank of India, through primarily a commercial bank, carried out certain central banking functions and in particular acted as a banker to the Government.

Reserve Capital: A company may pass a special resolution stating that a portion of its capital not already called up shall not be capable of being called up except in the event of the company being wound up. This capital is called the reserve capital.

Reserve for Obsolescence: A sum of money set aside by a business out of profits to guard against the possibility of sudden obsolescence of fixed assets.

Reserve Price: A term used with reference to auctions. A lot which is subject to a reserve price is one which the owner does not wish sold below this price.

Reserves: An amount notionally set aside out of profits (after the latter have been calculated), often to register the fact that they are voluntarily or compulsorily undistributable.

Reserves should be distinguished from the latter are charged in the calculation of Profit, and represent reductions in the value of Assets or anticipations of future liabilities. Of course neither reserves nor provisions are amounts of cash. A provision involves an accounting expense, and a reserve is an accounting allocation of undistributed profit from one heading allocation of undistributed profit from one heading to another. Reserves belong to shareholders, and are part of a total of shareholders' equity, resented by all the assets of the business, less the liabilities owed to outsiders. It should be noted that this terminology is used somewhat loosely by some accountants. Balance-sheet accounts that identify the liabilities faced by an insurance company. Reserves attempt to present as true a picture as is possible of an organization's financial condition by reporting disbursements on an accrual basis. Reserves are estimates of obligated sums of money and are of four principal kinds: (1) reserves for known liabilities not yet paid, (2) reserves for losses incurred but unreported, (3) reserves for future benefits, and (4) reserves for various special purposes, including contingency reserves for unforeseen circumstances.

Residual Maturity: The time left from today until the final repayment.

Residual Value: The difference between the original worth of an asset (for example, the purchase price or fair market value of a donated automobile) and that portion of it that has been amortized or written off (as a depreciation expense or loss).

Resign: To give up a job.

Resource: Strengths or advantages of a person or organization.

Respondent: Person who answers questions in a survey.

Responsibilities of Management: Management carry all the responsibilities and duties that are incumbent upon it as a leader of the growth and planning process. It is management's job to see that conditions conducive to rapid growth are created, for there in lies the destiny of the country. This imperatively imposes upon management the responsibility to develop people. As a very vital part of this responsibility, management must multiply itself for taking on the responsibility, for higher growth. Another important responsibility of management is innovation which only means more and better people, goods and services. The innovation always results in creating new conveniences, new wants, lower prices, new techniques, better and new product, new designs, efficient and effective methods, better uses of capital, materials, machines and people and a development of better human beings.

Responsibility: Being responsible for doing a job or for the care of someone or something.

Responsive: Who listens and does what someone asks.

Restrain of Trade: Any activity which interferes with the operation of a free market process fixing or preventing a new competitor from entering the market.

Restraint: Control; wages under control; situation where a worker is not allowed to use his knowledge in another company if he changes jobs; attempt by companies to fix prices or create monopolies or reduce competition which could affect free trade.

Restrictive Covenants: Terms in a contract which restrict the right of one party to contract freely after determination of the contract or during its continuance.

Restrictive Endorsement: Bill of exchange may be endorsed in a way which restricts the freedom of the endorsee to negotiate them.

Restrictive Practice: This term usually refers to a work practice supported by a trade union in the interest of job security for its members which limits the scope of management especially in the allocation of particular kinds of work. The practice may not be officially agreed through collective bargaining.

Retail Price Index: The index number which attempts to measure changes in the cost of living. It is quoted with reference to inflation and can be used to evaluate real as opposed to nominal changes in prices.

Retail: Sale of small quantities of goods to ordinary customers; market research method by which a research company regularly checks a sample of retailers for unit sales and stock levels of different brands; person who sells to the general public; full price paid by a customer in a shop; index showing how prices of retail goods have increased or fallen over a period of time; shop which sells goods to the general public; all people or businesses selling goods retail; the value of the goods if sold to the public is fixed, before discounts etc are taken into accounts; he buys goods in bulk at a wholesale discount and sells in small quantities to the public to sell goods direct to the public to sell for a price; the retail price these items is 25p.

Retailer: Person who runs a retail business selling goods direct to the public; group of retailers who buy together from suppliers so as to be able to enjoy quantity discounts or the place where products and consumers finally get together, the last stop on the **Distribution Channel.** Retailers come in many different shapes and sizes, from department stores to corner stores, from hypermarkets to flea markets.

Retailing: Selling of full price goods to the public.

Retained Earnings: Amounts of

profit, earned in the year and former years, that have not yet been paid out as dividends.

Retained Profits: That part of the earnings or net profits of a business not distributed to the owners-shareholders in the case of a company but reinvested in the business.

Retention Money: In certain types of contract, particularly building contracts, part of the price is kept back for a period after the contract is complete in order to give the purchaser time to inspect the work done and discover any bad workmanship.

Retire: To stop work and take a pension.

Retirement Fund: A fund established and maintained to pay employees following their retirement, under terms specified in the employing organization's retirement plan. Retirement funds, established in conformity with qualified retirement plans, may be tax-exempt or tax deferred.

Retirement: Voluntary or involuntary termination of employment or voluntary service because of age, disability, illness, or personal choice. Also, completion of the monetary obligation for a bond or a loan note, thereby ending its functional existence.

Retrain: To train someone for a new job, or to do the same job in a more modern way.

Retrenchment: Reduction of a company's expenditure or expansion plans by means of reducing surplus staff for cutting the size of the operating activities or because of technological upgradation.

Return Load: When a vehicle is hired to carry goods to a particular area, the haulier, rather than bringing the vehicle back empty, will advertise for return loads. Part load.

Return on Capital: The profit earned by capital.

Return on Investment (ROI): Ratio of net income after taxes have been paid of a firm or a division of a firm over a period to the average value during that period of the operating assets of the firm. Synonym for rate of return.

Return: Yield or profit; for example, the return on a public relations campaign.

Revaluation: Action by the government of one country to change a peg for its currency in terms of the currency of another country so that in future a unit of the first currency will be exchanged for more units or the second currency. A fresh valuation of assets.

Revaluation of Assets: The fixed assets of a business are frequently subject to change in value, both real and nominal. Real value can change where the asset is of a durable type, e.g., land the demand for which has forced up the market price. Nominal values rise continually in times of inflation, where the fall in the value of money is reflected in higher replacement costs. Some increases in value are often acknowledged in the published accounts of the business, where the asset value is restated in terms of current prices.

Revenue Expenditure: Expenditure that is written off completely in the profit and loss account in the accounting period in which it is made.

Revenue: Money received from all sources. Unless otherwise stated, gross receipts represent receipts prior to the deduction of expenses.

Review: General examination.

Revolving Credit Agreement: A written contractual agreement which is made between a commercial bank and a customer for the bank to offer short-term funds up to a specified limit for a stipulated period of time at an interest rate generally tied to the prime rate.

Reward: Money or other gains from effort, to give a person something in return for effort or achievement.

Rigging the Market: Operations designed to create an artificial market to benefit the operator.

Rights Issue: An Issue of shares which gives the right to existing shareholders to buy the issue at a favourable price within a specified period of time. Rights that are not exercised can usually be sold on the open market before they expire.

Risk Capital: Capital invested in an enterprise with a high degree of risk, though usually with the possibility of a large financial gain.

Risk Management: The function of planning, organizing, directing, and evaluating a comprehensive programme of activities to identify, evaluate and take corrective action against risks that may lead to patient injury, employee injury, and property loss or damage with resulting financial loss or legal liability; all of an organization's efforts to protect its assets, reputation, and human and physical resources against loss.

Risk: Possible harm or chance of loss or suffering harm; to do something which may make you lose money or suffer harm; possibility of losing money; analysis of how much can be lost and gained through various marketing strategies; capital for investment which may easily be lost in risky projects, but which can also provide high returns; situation where the carrier is responsible for loss or damage to goods being transported; situation where goods shipped or stored are insured by the owner, not by the transport company or the storage company; loss or damage against which you are insured; situation or goods which could start a fire it is not likely or it is very likely that the insurance company will have to pay out against claims where he is concerned or refers to a situation in which future events are not known with certainty but an array of alternative outcomes and their probabilities can be estimated. The danger of making a loss. Investors are rewarded for taking risks; in general, the higher the risk, the greater the reward. Investors who play safe (only buying government bonds, for instance) are said to be risk averse. Risk takes several forms. **Exchange-rate risk**. The danger from borrowing in one currency and lending in another, or of having receipts denominated in one currency and payments in another. **Interest-rate risk**. The danger from, say, taking fixed-rate deposits and making floating-rate loans. **Maturity risk**. The danger which arises when payments are due in seven days and receipts are not coming in for eight. **Political risk**. The danger of a change of government in the country of the borrower. This change may compel the borrower to renege on the Debt, or somehow to reduce its value.

Risk Premium: 1) An addition to the 'pure' discount rate so as to take account of the uncertainty associated with the future benefits of revenue from a project. 2) In an uncertain world, refers to that part of the return to capital which compensates the owners of capital for the risk involved in its use in business ventures.

Risk-Taking in Business: In a business. In earlier day, status and prestige in society accrued for the most part to the civil service and to the military to government officials. The operator in the market place was definitely second class. Also, stability of the society was the desideratum, certainly not change in any disturbing degree. Development, however, does involve, and more that depends upon economic promotion and management and the changes in society which such activity entails. A development responsibility of the government therefore includes support, recognition, and encouragement of business managers. The significance of this point becomes even more clear when it is remembered that the government's intervention in the economic matters frequently involves the use of public officers in business activity. These specialized officers in economic affairs, like the specialists in science and technology, should receive the status and recognition and compensation due to the importance of their functions in comparison with the administrative class in the civil service.

Role: A term widely used in social psychology to refer to the kind of behaviour expected of a given person in a given situation. The term has been applied generally to the organization and the workplace.

Role Ambiguity: A situation in which an individual is unclear about the role expected.

Role-incongruency: Conflict experienced within a worker when social pressures on the worker are at odds with the organization's goals.

Role and Responsibilities of Personnel Manager: Differing according to size and nature of the enterprise, taken as a specialized function: (i) formulation of personnel policies, plans, programmes, and procedures, (ii) undertaking personnel research for better advice to management, (iii) developing an effective system of recruitment, selection, training, placement, appraisal etc., (iv) designing schemes of motivation and welfare, (v) establishing effective communication system, (vi) advising management in negotiating with employees, (vii) facilitating the growth of cordial work relationships.

Role Conflict: A situation in which an individual is expected to play two or more roles which are in conflict or in competition with each other.

Role-negotiation: A technique in which managers discuss what they want from one another and explain why.

Roll-Over: The extension of a loan beyond its original final payment date. Many so-called short-term loans get rolled over so many times that they eventually become long-term loans.

Rolling Launch: The process of gradually introducing a new product into the market. The first stage might consist of putting the product through a market test. If it is successful then distribution might be extended, perhaps to another test area. This way the whole market gradually be covered.

Royalties: The sum paid for the right to use another person's property for productive purposes.

Royalty: A fee paid to an author or composer on each sale of published work for which he holds the copyright, or to an inventor for the use of an invention for which he holds the copyright, or to an inventor for the use of an invention for which he holds the patent.

Run-of-Paper: Advertisements that appear in newspapers or magazines in no particular order, that is, they do not have a specified position (such as "facing contents page"). Run-of-paper (ROP) advertisements are less expensive than those that want to be in a particular position. But there is a risk that the advertiser will end up somewhere near the back of the magazine facing an article that nobody wants to read.

Rural Market Potential: Marketing in India has been essentially urban based since it has been assumed that the buying power exits only in the urban areas. The rural sector has largely been neglected. But companies, both private and public have now realized the potential that exists in the rural market and have started to move towards tapping this vast market.

S

Safe Custody: This is service offered by most commercial banks. They volunteer to accept deeds, documents, jewellery and other items of property for storage in safe custody on behalf of customers.

Safety: Freedom from danger or risk.

Safety Margin: Sales of a product in excess of its break even point.

Safety Net: The capacity of social programmes to supply a subsistence standard of living to people lacking adequate essentials of daily living.

Safety Provides: The condition where the probability of accidents is minimum. Every accident is the result of a set of unsafe conditions and acts. It is the cumulative effect of this set of conditions that acts over a period of time and an accident occurs. But if the unsafe conditions or acts are removed before the event's arrival at a point of time when the accident takes place, the accident could be prevented. Safety, therefore, means elimination of unsafe conditions and acts.

Salary: A fixed regular payment to an employee for work done usually restricted to payments to non-manual workers and payments made at intervals of a month or longer. Also the amount a person receives as salary in a particular period.

Salary Administration: Activities concerned with fixing and sometimes paying salaries in an organization.

Salary Structure: The principles, rules and procedures by which the salaries of an organization's employees are determined.

Sale: Act of selling or of giving an item in exchange for money; selling something for cash; selling something for credit, using a credit card; selling something because a court orders it or because it is the only thing to do to avoid a financial crisis; sale with no guarantee of quality; sale on condition that the goods match the description of them given by the seller; system where the retailer sends goods back if they are not sold, and pays the supplier only for goods sold; document which the seller gives to the buyer to show that a sale has taken place; agreed ways in which a sale takes place (such as discounts and credit terms), to announce that something is ready to be sold; being sold in a shop; money received for selling something or number of items sold; person who sells for a business or another person and earns a commission; various tools used for selling, such as samples, display cases and sales literature; examining the reports of sales to see why items have or have not sold well; quality which makes customers want to buy; analysis of a company's sales in terms of such factors as product revenue and area; record of sales; sales as recorded in the sales book; plan of probable sales; visit to a prospective customer in order to make a sale; planned work to achieve higher sales; meeting of publicity staff etc. to discuss results and future sales plans; scheme that rewards salesmen with the best results and so encourages effort and initiative; contract between a buyer and a seller, whereby the former agrees to pay money to the latter in return for goods; all the costs of a product sold including manufacturing costs and the staff costs of the production department; section of a company which deals with selling the company's products or services; sales in the home market; vigorous work to increase sales; person in a company in charge of sales; total sales or sales broken down by category; group of salesmen; calculation of future sales; sales for delivery at a later date; meeting between a salesman and a prospective customer in which the latter obtains all information about a product necessary from him to be able to make a buying decision; information which may lead to a sale; book in which income from sales it recorded; office worker who deals with the sales ledger; printed information which helps sales; person in charge of a sales department; different elements used in selling a company's products; talk by a salesman to persuade someone to buy; promotional and sales techniques aimed at short-term increases in sales, such as free gifts, competitions, and price discounts; sales targets given to salesmen which are based on either unit sales or revenue; report made every month showing the number for items or amount of money received for selling stock; person who works for a company, selling its products or services to customers; lack of willingness by the public to buy a product; degree to which customers buy a product in response to the promotion of it; money received from sales; methods used by a salesman to persuade customers to buy such as presentation of goods demonstrations and closing of sales; number of units sold selling of goods at specially low prices; sale of all goods in a store at cheap prices; sale of items at low prices to get rid of the stock; sale of items at half the usual price; sale of old used household goods; period when major stores sell many items at specially low prices. In the sale of goods act a contract of sale is defined as a contract whereby the seller transfers, or agrees to transfer, the property in goods to the buyer, for a consideration called the price.

Sale and Lease-Back: An increasingly common commercial phenomenon whereby a company, or other business organization which needs the cash tied up in to found every day activities makes a contract with an insurance company, to sell the relevant to that investor on condition that the sale in accompanied by a document leasing the same property back to the business for an agreed term.

Sales: The figure for sales, recorded in the financial statements for a period, will include all those sales agreed or delivered in the period, rather than those that are paid for in cash. The sales figure will be shown net of sales taxes (VAT in the UK). In the UK the word "Turnover" is used in the financial statements, although "sales" is generally used in the books of account.

Sales Agent: A person employed by a company or manufacturer to control or supervise the distribution of his goods in a particular area.

Sales Forecast: An estimate of how much a company hopes to sell to a Market, calculated separately for each Product. A sales forecast forms the basis for establishing a Sales Quota. Forecasting for new products is not easy: it may have to depend on extrapolating from demand for similar products, or on market tests of the product. Forecasting sales for existing products is considerable easier, but still depends on analysing the dynamics of markets that are constantly changing. Statistical tools such as Time-Series Analysis and multiple-regression models (which identify the factors that influence sales) can be employed. But despite these sophisticated techniques, the fingers-in-the-wind judgments of managers and sales people are still widely used.

Sales Journal: In which details of a sale are first entered. In form it is similar to the purchase journal. It is also referred to as a sales day book.

Sales Ledger: A book or other record having a chronological list of credit sales.

Sales Promotion: Any attempt to increase the sales of a particular product by raising public awareness of it through advertising or public relations.

Sales Representative: A person employed by an organization to sell its goods and to make contracts on its behalf concerning these.

Sales Response Function: The relationship between likely sales volume during a specified period of time and different levels of marketing support. Other things being equal, the higher the level of marketing support (particularly of advertising and sales promotion), the more of the product is likely to be sold. Marketing managers try to calculate sales response functions (albeit imprecisely) using a mixture of judgment, statistical analysis of past sales and marketing expenditure, and occasional experiments, perhaps in a smallish television region where the results of an increase in advertising expenditure can be more easily measured.

Sales Tax: A tax which is levied on a market transaction. There have been many types of sales taxes but they may be divided between those which apply to a large range of expenditure and those which apply to the sale of a specific goods or services.

Salesman: Man who sells goods or services to members of the public; man who goes from one house to the next, asking people to buy something; man who encourages clients to take out insurance policies; person who represents a company selling its products or services to retail shops.

Salesmanship: It is a virtue that brings potential buyer into contact with a seller in such a way as to affect the transfer of goods. It is an art of creating demand for goods, which one has to sell. Salesmanship performs the function of feedback from consumer to manufacturer. It minimises the gap between the products and the consumer. 'Salesmanship is the science and art to selling your point of view, starting with the other man's viewpoint and lending his mind to the point where he will accept the goods. Salesmanship involves winning the buyer's confidence and permanent customer. It is a face to face persuasive communication between a seller and prospective buyer. Salesmanship is advantageous to both the seller and the consumer. The sellers gain as their sales increase and the buyer's benefit through expert advice in regard to choice of goods. The salesman helps the consumers by explaining to them the various attributes and uses of the product. He also helps the dealers by giving them timely information regarding market conditions.

Sample: Specimen or a small part of an item which is used to show what the whole item is like; sample to be used to see if a whole consignment is acceptable; sample given free to advertise a product; book showing samples of different types of cloth or paper, etc.; small group taken to show what a larger group is like; a sample chosen without any special selection method; to test or to try something by taking a small amount; representative group of people questions to find out what the reactions of a much larger group would be.

Sampling: Testing a product by taking a small amount; testing a small sample of a batch to see if the whole batch is good enough to be accepted testing the reactions of a small group of people to find out the reactions of a larger group of consumers; choosing samples for testing without any special selection method; difference between the results achieved in a survey using a sample and what the results would be using the entire population or universe; proportion of a population or universe that is chosen as a sample; definition of the population or universe out of which a sample is to be taken.

Satisfaction: Feeling of being happy or good feeling; making a customer pleased with what he has bought; a worker's feeling that he is happy in his place of work and pleased with the work he does.

Satisfier: Factor contributing to job satisfaction as mentioned by workers responding to a study by Frederick Herzberg, who called these satisfiers 'motivators'.

Saving Account: An account designed specifically to assist customers to accumulate large sums by means of small and regular savings.

Savings Bank: A Bank whose raison d'etre is (or at least was) the gathering of deposits from small savers. At such a bank the withdrawal of savings on demand is limited. Traditionally, savings banks do virtually no business with industry, and provide no money transmission services. In many countries savings banks have strong local roots, either as national banks with a regional structure, or as separate regional institutions. They are often set-up as mutual institutions (whose depositors are also their shareholders), recent years and become more like full commercial banks.

Scenario: Possible future sequence of events.

Schedule Planning: Planning concerns scheduling which is affixing time value to each needed activity and to the total project. Scheduling gives vitality and a practical meaning to a plan.

Scheme: Plan or arrangement or way of working.

School of Management Theory: Frank P. Carracciolo has specified 6 main classes of management theory: (i) The Process School. According to this school management means (a) analysing processes, (b) establishing conceptual framework of process and (c) identifying principles underlying the process. (ii) The Empirical School. This school believes that by analysing the experience of successful managers or the mistakes of unsuccessful managers, management can learn about applying the most effective techniques. This school recommends case study approach for drawing general conclusions and enumerating principles. (iii) The Human Behaviour School. The exponents of this school of thought suggest the application of existing and newly developed theories, methods and techniques of the relevant social science to the study of human relations from personal dynamics or cultural heritage. This school puts more emphasis on motivation of the individual and on human psychology and sociology. (iv) The Social System School. The theory was founded by Chester Barnard who went into the co-operative, biological, physical and social aspects of the individual's environments. This theory emphasises formal organization concept which consists of a cooperative system in which individuals not only communicate with each other but are also willing to contribute action towards a conscious common purpose. It is under this theory that managements are said to perform highly effective functions in socialist societies, where workers are motivated by a determination to show result and are fixed with the zeal to achieve common purpose.

(v) The Decisional School. This School emphasises on rational approach to decision-making through the selection of a course of action from various possible alternatives. The theory can be expanded to examine the nature of organization, structure, psychological and social reactions of individuals, and groups in order to provide the bases for decisions and value judgements.

(vi) The Mathematical School. According to the exponents of this school, mathematicians provide the people in management the means of seeing many problems more clearly, the need for establishing goals and measures of effectiveness. They are helpful in getting people to view the management to review and reorganize information systems, so that mathematics can be given sensible quantitative meaning.

Scientific Management: School of management which believes in the rational use of resources in order to maximize profits. This school of thought was originated by F.W. Taylor.

Scope: Opportunity or possibility; the sales performance could be improved.

Scrap: Residue from a manufacturing process which can be either sold or re-used. It has a small but measurable value.

Scrap Value: Synonym for the Residual Value of a fixed asset.

Screen: To examine something carefully to evaluate or assess it; to examine candidates to see if they are suitable.

Screening: A process of analysing what chances a new product has of success by considering the extent to which the product has (or has not) got those elements that will determine its success. For instance, screening a new pizza would involve considering how acceptable things like the thickness of its crust, the variety of its topping, or the flavour of its cheese were to the market at which it was to be aimed.

Scrip: A popular term for share and bond certificates.

Scrip Issue: A free handout of shares to company's existing shareholders in proportion to their stake in the company; a capitalization of a company's reserves. Also known as a bonus issue. There is no such thing as a free lunch. A scrip issue is little more than an accounting device; it does nothing to increase the value of the company. After it has taken place, the shareholder's equity is worth the same. It has just been divided into more little pieces of paper (that is shares). A scrip issue is a useful way of reducing the market price of a share that is too high (and harmful to its marketability).

Search: Executive search: looking for new managers for organizations, usually by approaching managers in their existing jobs and asking them if they want to work for another company.

Seasonal Index: An index number that shows the relative sizes of the figures in a monthly time series which is used to produce seasonally adjusted data.

Seasonal Variations: In statistics variations often occur seasonally and are deliberately allowed for. Employment figures, for example, may offer more employment, for instance, in the catering industry, during the summer, and in the retail trade, around Deepawali or Durgá Puja.

Seasonal: Which lasts for a season or which only happens during a particular season; changes made to figures to take account of seasonal variations; demand which exists only during the high season; discount offered by media owners to advertisers at certain times of the year; unemployment which rises and falls according to the season.

Secondary Banking: Allied closely with the secondary market of which it forms a part, secondary banking is concerned less with banking service to the public, but more with transacting the type of business that clearing banks prefer not to dabble in, such as the granting of second mortgages and other high risk operations.

Secondary Market: A market in secondhand financial instruments. When first issued, instruments like shares, bonds and certificates of deposit are sold in the primary market. Much of their attraction to investors lies in the liquidity provided by the secondary markets in which they can be sold thereafter.

Secondary: Second in importance; people who read a publication after the original purchaser has finished with it; companies which provide money for hire-purchase deals; data or information which has already been compiled and it therefore sound through desk research; industry which uses basic raw materials to make manufactured goods; nickname given to a brand deliberately by the producer or by the consumer.

Secret Reserves: Kept by a company or business but not disclosed to the public in the balance sheet, being hidden in the wrongful valuation of assets or liabilities.

Secretary: The person who deals with the general administration of an organization, particularly with clerical work such as correspondence, taking minutes at meetings and keeping records correspondence and other matters no needing the employer's personal attention.

Secretary, Personal: A person employed as an assistant to deal with correspondence and other matters which does not require the employer's personal attention.

Secretary, Private Confidential: A private secretary with greater responsibility than normal and so allowed to deal with confidential matters.

Secretary, Private: A personal secretary but acting for one person only in stead of many people within an organization.

Secured Creditor: A creditor whose debt is secured, e.g., by a charge on the property of the debtor.

Secured Loan: A loan which provides a lender with the right to take over certain prescribed assets of a borrower if the borrower fail to repay. The assets given as security for the loan may be physical (like property or goods), or they may be documents entitling the holder to certain payments. As a result of their secured lending, banks have ended up owning all sorts of things, from airplanes to fish 'n' chip shops.

Securities: A charge by way of mortgage, to the lender as collateral for the money lent. In more recent times the term securities has become the generic term for virtually all stocks, shares, bonds, etc., traded on the Stock Exchange including derivatives such as futures and options.

Security Market Line: Refers to the linear relationship between the expected return of a security and its Systematic Risk, the expected return comprising a risk-free return plus a risk premium.

Security: There are two meanings. 1) Something of value given by a lender to a borrower to support his or her intention to repay. 2) In the case of a mortgage the security is the property that the mortgage loan is being used to purchase. (See also collateral).

Seed Capital: A term applied to the minimum amount considered necessary to set-up a new business, sufficient to conduct some preliminary research and fund initial equipment required.

Segment: A section of a market defined by certain criteria to divide a potential market into different segments.

Segmentation: Division of the market or consumers into certain categories according to their buying behaviour.

Self-Evaluation: In management self-enrichment can be achieved through self-disclosure and group feedback, sensitivity analysis tests, management affectiveness seminars, self-analysis etc. If a manager adopts the following five steps to maturity, he could successfully operate an organization: 1) Self-examination 2) Self-expectation 3) Self-realisation power 4) Self-deduction 5) Broadened perception. The answer to the various questions we ask ourselves in the above areas will disclose the extent to which we differ from others.

Self-Regulatory: Which regulates itself.

Self-Employed: Working for yourself or not on the payroll of a company.

Self-Enrichment: It is a virtue which can be achieved through self-disclosure and group feedback, sensitivity analysis tests, management effectiveness seminars, self-analysis, etc. If a manager adopts the following five steps to maturity, he could successfully operate an organization; self-examination: self-expectation: self-realization power: self-education; and Broadened perception.

Self-Image: Idea that a person has about himself or herself.

Seller: Person who sells; market where the seller can ask high prices because there is a large demand for the product thing which sells.

Seller's Market: A market situation in which sellers have more power to influence prices and conditions of sale than buyers, usually because demand exceeds supply. Always contrasted with buyer's market or a situation in which consumers want to buy more of a particular type of goods or services than are being supplied. Economists say that in such a situation the price of the goods or services will rise, and that will attract other players into the market. That, in turn, will increase the supply to such an extent that it might become the exact opposite: a buyer's market. Such logic does not apply in case like telecommunications, where the initial capital investment required to become a supplier is prohibitively high. It does not apply either when there are things like import controls that prevent competitive products from entering a market.

Selling Price: Generally the cash price which a customer must pay for an article.

Selling Short: A term used in the Stock Exchange where stocks or shares are sold which a person does not own but anticipated acquiring at a favourable price prior to the date of settlement.

Selling: The process of exchanging goods or services for money; the functions in an organization which are most concerned with this process. These now include advertising, distribution, marketing and quality control as well as sales promotion.

Semantic Differential: Scaling

technique which provides a range of possible answers between two opposite descriptive words.

Semantic Problem: A communication problem arising when readers or listeners do not understand the use of words or phrases.

Semi-Skilled: Semi-skilled workers: workers who have had some training.

Semi-Structured Interview: Interview using some pre-set questions out allowing some questions of the interviewer's choice as well.

Semi-Variable Costs: Costs which are fixed for a given level of output and vary as different output levels are reached.

Semiotics: Use of such promotional tools as package design, logos and slogans in marketing.

Seniority: This term refers either and/ or greater length of service in an organization.

Sensitivity Analysis: Varying the data in a calculation so as to ascertain which variables have a material effect on the results.

Sensitivity Training: A technique for trying to improve 'interpersonal communication and the quality of interpersonal relations in small groups. The orientation of this technique is based on the method and experience of group therapy. Group leaders try to facilitate open and honest discussion of feelings within the group. The hope is that any new-found sensitivity to one dealing with other people will carry over to other areas of life, such as work groups.

Sequential Sampling: Carrying on the process of sampling until enough respondents have been interviewed to provide the necessary information.

Service: Businesses have service functions to perform besides profit-making. Timothy E., Shea Vice-President in Charge of Engineering of Western Electric Company has said: "Business is a vehicle through which man serves society". Such a view of service and profits requires a balancing of functions by managers. Customer service is one of the keys to survival and profit. The serving of customer needs profitably is the basic concern of marketing executives. Service to customers and to society concepts rests on the ethical view of business practice or work done by an employee for his or her employer or company.

Service Industry: Organizations offering services.

Services: In an economic sense, they may be defined as any functions or tasks that are performed, for which there is a demand and hence a price determined in the relevant market. They are sometimes referred to as intangible goods.

Set: A collection of objects of some sort is defined by a rule which unambiguously determines whether or not something is included in the collection. A state of psychological preparedness, of limited duration, which is characteristically taken up in anticipation of a particular type of stimulus or situation.

Set Up: To begin or organize or to start a new business or company legally.

Set-Off: A right of set-off can occur when two parties are indebted one to the other. One debt can only be set off against another when the parties concerned are acting in the same capacity. For instance, a personal debt from A to B cannot be set off by B against monies he owes to A acting as trustee for a third party.

Settle: To solve a problem or dispute.

Settlement: On the Stock Exchange the date on which various transactions made during one period.

Share Account: A type of account offered by a credit union that is similar to the time and savings accounts offered by commercial banks and thrift institutions.

Share: An expression of a proprietary relationship in a company. Shareholders are proportionate owners of a company but the company's net assets belong not to them but to the company as a separate and independent legal entity. The most common types of shares are Ordinary Shares and Preference Shares.

Share Broker: Stockbroker.

Share Capital: The total of shares issued or authorized to be issued by the company.

Share Certificate: This is evidence of ownership of shares but not a negotiable instrument nor strictly a document of title. Ownership is determined by the entry in the company's share register.

Share Index: An index number based on the prices of a particular of shares supposed to be representative and intended as a guide to overall market fluctuations.

Share Option: Options to purchase shares.

Share Premium: A sum over and above the nominal value may be charged on an issue of shares if their profitability indicates that their real value is in excess.

Share Register: The register kept by a limited company giving the names and addresses of members and particulars of their share holdings.

Share Transfer: When a company's share is sold or otherwise disposed of to another person it is necessary to transfer formally the right of ownership. This is effected by the completion of a transfer form which is then sent, together with the share certificate to the company. On receiving the transfer form, signed by the seller, the company will enter the buyer's name in its share register and delete that of the seller.

Share Warrant: A share certificate that does not contain the name of the member, so that title is transferable by delivery, it is not a negotiable instrument. Warrants can only be issued when shares are fully paid. The member's name is struck off the register when the warrant is issued.

Shareholders' Funds: The total of the shareholders' interest in a company. This will include the original share capital, amounts contributed in excess of the Nominal Value of Shares (that is, Share Premium), and Retained Profits and other Reserves. In the USA this total is sometimes, called Stockholders' Equity. The shareholders' funds will equal the Net Assets or net worth of the company.

Shares; Forfeiture Of: When a shareholder does not pay the calls due on his shares, they may be declared forfeit by the directors, provided that the articles of association of the company allow. Forfeited shares may be reissued.

Shares; Preference: These shares have a preferential right to dividend, i.e., they are entitled to a fixed sum before anything is paid to holders of ordinary shares. The dividend may or may not be cumulative. In any event, dividends are paid at the discretion of the directors and the shareholders cannot insist on them. The voting rights of preference shareholders are normally strictly limited; they can usually only vote when their dividends are in arrears.

Shares; Qualification: Shares taken up by the directors of a company as a qualification for directorship. The Companies Act does not insist on a director to hold the qualification shares to be a director but the articles of association often provide such kind of provision on qualification shares.

Shares; Cross Holding: This situation occurs when Company A holds shares in Company B, which itself holds shares in Company A.

Shares; Nominal Value: The nominal value of a share is the value stated in the memorandum of association and on the share certificate. The market value of the share may be quite different.

Shares; Ordinary: These have no particular right to dividend but are entitled to all the profits after prior demands, such as preference dividends. The ordinary shareholders are the true owners of a company.

Ship Broker: Person who arranges shipping or transport of goods for customers on behalf of ship owners.

Shipment: Goods sent; shipment of a large quantity of goods; goods from different companies grouped together into a single shipment; delivery of a large order from a manufacturer direct to a customer's shop or warehouse, without going through an agent.

Shop: A department of an enterprise where manufacturing or a specific manufacturing process is carried out. An establishment where retail business is carried on. An advertising agency.

Shop Floor: A term originally applied to the area of a factory in which production took place. It has been widened in its application to indicate the blue collar workers in an organization as opposed to the white collar workers or even the work force in general as opposed to the management.

Shoplifting: Stealing or picking stealthily goods from a shop without intending to pay for them. This is a major problem with which shopkeepers have to contend and the larger stores, which rely greatly on impulse buying and put or display goods within easy reach of customers, accept shoplifting as something which can be controlled but not eliminated 100% and 'budged' for it accordingly. The gains from the high turnover are considered a reasonable price to pay for losses by shoplifting, some modern department stores employ special security personnel or automatic equipments or wall mirrors to keep watch on customers.

Short Staffed: With not enough staff.

Short-Range: Forecast which covers a period of a few months.

Short-Term: For a short period; debts which have to be repaid within a few weeks; forecast which covers a period of a few months; gains made over a short period loan which has to be repaid within a few weeks; planning for the immediate future.

Short-Term Capital: Capital raised for short periods to cover temporary fluctuations bank overdraft are an example.

Short-Term Deposits: Monies deposited with banks, finance houses, etc., on terms which allow them to be withdrawn at short notice.

Short-Term Money Market: Refers to a market in which large borrowers and lenders of money and large buyers and sellers of securities come together to transact their daily business dealings.

Sick: Ill or not well, sick leave: time when a worker is away from work on full pay because of illness or injury.

Sick Pay: Pay given to workers who are off work for reasons of illness or injury. As well as statutory provisions there are many occupational schemes and these are sometimes regarded as a fringe benefit of a job.

Simple Interest: Interest calculated on the original sum (principal) invested and not also on interest reinvested. It can be calculated from the formula l = Pai, where l=the amount of simple interest, P=the principal, n=the number of periods, and i=the simple rate of interest per period.

Simulation: The acting out of a real-life marketing situation for the purpose of testing a product.

Simulation Exercises: It is a method of imparting training and quite popular for management development. Under this case studies, decision games and role play methods are adopted so as to provide work type situation to the trainee, possibly, to acquaint them of ground realities.

Single Market: Wherein trade between member nations would be as free and unencumbered as that between two cities in any one nation.

Sinking Fund: An account into which monies are paid at regular intervals in order to meet a large payment that is expected at some future date, such as the replacement of an asset, or the maturing of a liability (such as a fixed-term Bond).

Situation: State of affairs; stage in marketing planning concerned with investigating the organization's strengths and weaknesses.

Skill: Ability to do something because of training.

Skilled: Having learnt certain skills, skilled workers or skilled labour: workers who have special skills or who have had long training.

Skimming: Fixing a high price on a product in order to achieve high short-term profits (the high price reflects the customer's appreciation of the added value of the new product, and will be reduced in due course as the product becomes established on the market).

Slack: The amount of time that events of a project can be delayed without affecting the outcome of the project.

Slogan: A memorable and approsite saying about a product that helps to keep it at the forefront of consumers' minds. The best slogans are sometimes witty, and often simple. For example, Heineken refreshes the parts other beers cannot reach. Persil washes whiter. Put a tiger in your tank. (Esso petrol). It may be December outside, but it's always August under your armpits. (US deodorant). Hands that do dishes can be soft as your face (UK washing-up liquid). I dreamed I was Cleopatra in my Maidenform bra.

Slump: The point in the trade cycle when prices and employment are at their lowest.

Smoothing: Reducing conflict by accentuating common goals.

Social Accounting: A particular concern with the social aspects of a cost benefit analysis.

Social Audit: An examination of the extent of which the operations of an organization, public or private have contributed to social goals. Social audits can be seen as a means of giving some control to groups such as employees, consumers and the local community.

Social Control: The control that a group or culture or society exerts upon the individuals who comprise it. This control stems from the process of socialization and is established as conformity pressures towards social norms.

Social Responsibility: Another social function of business is the obligation of a firm to meet its social responsibility to its employees, the community and the public as well as its owners and customers. Social responsibility are those of corporate good citizenship in a society. Sometimes social and economic goals and the function required to perform them may be in conflict. More often in the long run enlightened self-interest and the corporate sense of social responsibility coincide.

Social Responsibility of Business: "In the real sense, the assumption of social responsibility implies recognition and understanding of the aspirations of a society and determination to contribute to its achievements." George A. Stenner. Awareness and acceptance throughout the free enterprise world, that companies, as well as public corporations, have responsibilities towards parties other than their owners. They owe a duty not merely to shareholders or to the state in case of public corporations—but to their employees, customers, suppliers and the community at large.

Social System School of Management: The social system school looks upon management as a social system, that is a system of cultural interrelationships. Sometimes, as in the case of March and Simon, the system is limited to formal organizations, using the term "organization" as equivalent to enterprise, rather than the authority-activity concept used most often in management. In other cases, the approach is not to distinguish the formal organization, but rather to encompass any kind of system of human relationships.

Social Values: In practice a manager often finds himself working with several means and chains. He is trying to choose a course of action that will contribute to several objectives and there will be a means-ends chain for each. Stable employment growth, short-term profit, low risk control are examples of internal objectives.

Socialism: An economic system characterized by state ownership of the means of production and distribution.

Social Responsibility Policies and Programmes: How can a management group that is sensitive to the changing business environment decide what socially responsible policies and programmes are feasible for their business to adopt? and, whatever policies and programmes may be adopted, how can managers assure their effective and efficient implementation? A chief executive officer who develops on his own initiative an intellectual posture favouring socially responsible performance by his company needs positive support from his board for both the general concept and specific policies and programmes. Alternatively, of course, the initiative may come from within the board.

Either way the emerging social pressure favours some kind of representation or the board that might be described as a trustship for the public interest.

Socio-Economic: The categories produced from the social stratification of a society by income and occupation. Six in number they are widely used in advertising, market research and survey research: A (upper middle class) Highest managerial, administrative or professional. B (middle class) Intermediate managerial, administrative or professional. C1 (lower middle class) Supervisory, clerical, junior managerial, administrative or professional. C2 (skilled working class) Skilled manual workers. D (working class) Semi-skilled and unskilled workers. E (lowest level of subsistence) State pensioners, widows, casual, and lowest grade workers.

Soft Sell: The use of quiet and restrained methods of Marketing a Product; for example, advertisements that rely for their effect on associations (of nostalgia, for instance), rather than on the insistent repetition of a Brand name of slogan. The opposite of Hard Sell.

Software: The maintenance manuals, training manuals, instructions for particular jobs and other material that accompanies hardware. In particular, programmes for a computer.

Sole Proprietorship: Single ownership or operation, such as in a solo professional practice. The primary advantage of sole proprietorship is simplicity in opening a business and in policy development, financial accounting, establishing personnel requirements for it, as well as the self-determination this permits. The disadvantages include sole legal and financial responsibility for the business, limited professional consultation resources, and limited opportunities for leisure time and professional development.

Solicitor: A person working within the precincts of the law, basically, he is the intermediary between the public and the dispensers of justice. His work consists for the greater part in advising clients on their legal rights, dealing personally with smaller matters from conveyancing to proceedings in magistrates' courts, and putting the client in touch with a barrister where legal action is to be taken at a higher level.

Solvency: Solvency means the capacity or ability of the business to meet its short-term and long-term obligations. The capacity to pay off the current debts of the company is represented by the liquidity ratio. The long-term solvency ratios enable shareholders, debenture-holders and other long-term creditors like financial institutions to analyse the capital structure of the company. They indicate the pattern of financing, whether long-term creditors like financial institutions to analyse the capital structure of the company. They indicate the pattern of financing, whether long-term requirements have been met out of long-term funds or not. A business (or person) is solvent if it can pay its bills or accounts as they fall due. The likely ability of a business to do this can be measured by examining its liquidity.

Source: Place where something comes from; where the tax is removed before the income is paid; image people have of a persuader which will determine his or her credibility.

Source of Funds: Where borrowers get their money from. In the case of corporations there are two sources: internal and external. Governments also have two sources: taxation and borrowing.

Span of Control: Span of control or span of management as it is often referred to is one of the more widely known organization principles. Specifically the term refers to the number of persons that report to any on supervisor or to executive. A favourite point of discussion revolves around the number of subordinates who should report to any one supervisor.

Spatial: Segmentation or division of a market according to areas or regions.

Special Drawing Right (S.D.R.s): An international reserve currency system which was created by the International Monetary Fund in October, 1969. It provides for a new type of money (known as 'paper gold') to serve by agreement of the free world nations as the first international legal tender. S.D.R.s are used alongwith gold and dollars as monetary reserves; they are not held by individuals or private businesses but used in transactions between governments and central banks.

Specialization: Part of the division of labour in which a given task is broken down as far as possible into subtasks, each of which then becomes the responsibility of a specialist worker. Specialization is therefore an important basis for mass production.

Specialization in Management: Specialization involves allocation of functions between different workers according to their qualifications, talents and aptitude. A good organization always provides for optimum use of technological improvements, it increases the all round efficiency of the worker both quantitatively and qualitatively.

Speculation: Although effectively a sophisticated form of gambling, speculation is recognized in business as a necessary constituent of a healthy free enterprise economy. The willingness of dealers of speculate on future prices can serve to maintain a fairly stable price level.

Spend: To pay money; to use time.

Sponsor: Person who pays money to help research or to pay for a business venture; company which pays to help to sport or exhibition or concert etc.; in return for advertising rights company which pays for the making of a TV programme by taking advertising time on the programme to pay money to help research or business development.

Sponsorship: The subsidising or an event, usually sporting or artistic, by a company for Advertising purposes. Events receiving wide media coverage bring the sponsoring company's name and its products to the attention of millions of viewers, and at the same time associate it with a pleasurable experience. Sports sponsorship has grown fast in recent years and now accounts for over 80% of all sponsorship; arts sponsorship has also grown, and is especially favoured by companies not normally associated with culture, for example, banks and oil refiners. Texaco sponsored Saturday afternoon broadcasts of the Metropolitan Opera for many years, and it is known for its sponsorship of the arts in the UK. For some, sponsorship is a way of getting round advertising restrictions. Cigarette manufacturers who are no longer allowed to advertise on television are enthusiastic sponsors of things like motor racing (Marlboro), tennis (Virginia Slims) and cricket (Benson & Hedges).

Spot Market: This refers to dealings at spot prices as opposed to forward dealings. In the spot market goods, options currencies, etc., are bought and sold for immediate delivery which in practice, may be two days, time in the forward market they are bought and sold for future delivery.

Spot Price: The price quoted for a transaction that is to be made on the spot; that is, the price for something when it is being paid for in cash, now. A market where things are quoted at their spot price is called a spot market.

Spot Transaction: Dealings for cash rather than for credit or in futures.

Spreadsheet: A technique, that originated in accounting, for displaying items in a wide series of columns (i.e., on a spread sheet of paper) so that calculation could be made by row or column as well as by items. The term has now largely been taken over by the computer world to refer to software packages that produce spreadsheets for visual display units from which rapid electronic calculations can be made.

Staff Management: The management of staff in an organization: Managers who have a specialist service or advisory support function and are not in the chain of command of the organization's hierarchy.

Staff: This term is most often used to describe the white collar workers usually full-time employees of an organization, as opposed to blue collar workers.

Staffing: The analysis and identification of an organization's human resources requirements, recruitment of the proper persons to meet these requirements, and initial placement of those persons to assure adequate numbers, knowledge, and skills to perform the organization's work.

Stag: A speculator on a Stock Exchange who buys newly issued securities in advance at a fixed price, presuming that there will be a shortage of such shares so that they can be rapidly sold when the price rises. (See also Bear and Bull.).

Stagflation: The terms used for the periods of recession and rising unemployment coupled with positive rates of price inflation.

Stamp Trading: Giving out stamps or vouchers to customers according to the value of their purchases the stamps being exchangeable for more goods or for cash.

Standard: Normal quality or normal conditions which other things are judged against; a person's material well being and quality of home life; quality of production; of acceptable quality; linking of the value of a currency to value of a quantity of gold normal or usual; normal printed contract form; planned costs for the period ahead planning costs for the period ahead and at the end of the period, comparing these figures with actual costs in order to make necessary adjustments in planning; way in which the results of a sample deviate from the mean or average; extent to which chance affects the accuracy of a sample; the official listing and coding of industries and products; letter which is sent without any change to various correspondents; basic rate of income tax which is paid by most taxpayers.

Standard Costing: A costing technique which uses predetermined standards. A product is costed on the basis of a budgeted output. Where the output has been fixed, the amount of material then needed is known, as is the amount of labour. The amount of overheads is taken as a constant. Each product then has a fixed material cost, a fixed direct labour cost and an overhead charge, probably stated as a fixed percentage of direct expenses. There is therefore a standard profit for the period. Actual cost will not correspond to budgeted cost, but the differences are handled through accounts known as variance accounts and the amount charged to any particular job or product is not altered until the standards are altered.

Standard Costs: Predetermined measures of what costs should be under specified conditions.

Standard Deviation: This should be distinguished from mean deviation; it is a rather more exact statistical measurement of dispersion. It is found by listing deviations from the mean, squaring these values, adding them, dividing the total by the number of items and finding the square root of the resultant value. Although similar to the mean deviation as a statistical measure of dispersion, the manner in which it is calculated given proportional significance to extreme values in the series being examined. It is also important to more complex statistical analysis, whereas the mean deviation has a very limited use.

Standard Error: A Statistical term used in production control indicating the possible degree of error that could occur in a sample taken at random.

Standard of Living: It is also referred to as the level of economic welfare, utility or real income. It refers to the level of material well-being of a individual or household. In economic analysis, the standard of living has been usually held to be determined by the quantities of goods and services (including leisure) consumed.

Standardization: There are two meanings. 1. A process of cutting down the variety of products produced, often to enable a manufacturer to make economies of scale. Some of these economies may be in a company's advertising budget, so advertising agencies have little to gain from standardization. 2. The introduction of generally accepted standards for the manufacture and/or sale of products. This may be for genuine reasons of health (as in food packaging) or safety (as in the marketing of drug doses). It may sometimes go beyond this and become standardization for its own sake: a practice that the European Commission seems particularly fond of.

Starting-Line Depreciation: A system of calculating the annual Depreciation Expense of Fixed Assets. This method charges equal annual instalments against profit over the useful life of the asset. In total, the cost of the asset any estimated residual value is depreciated. Straight-line depreciation is simple to use and thus very popular.

State Finance Corporation (SFC): State Finance Corporations have been set-up in eighteen states of India by different State Governments under the State Finance Corporation Act, 1951 to provide for long term financial needs to local, medium and small sized industries. Both proprietary firms such as sole traders and partnership firms as well as companies are authorized to borrow funds from the corporations.

State Overheads: In development: There are categories of government employment and service which are not directly involved in administration for development. Such as categories include the military, the police, the judiciary, foreign service, and legislative activity. But all these services are invariably related to the success of the development effort in some degree. The police and military services are relied upon for the preservation of the security of persons and property. The judicial service is expected to assure equity in treatment before the law. The foreign service has the responsibility for achieving friendly relations conducive to trade. And the legislative service should support effective political expression of development purpose and methodology. Indeed, there are times and places when one or more of these services has engaged directly and in a major way in a country's development programme, such as in the conduct of public works by the army or the negotiation of trade of investment agreements by the diplomats. By and large, however, the great burden of administration for development is borne by the public, civil administration of the executive branch.

Statement of Affairs: Any statement of accounts which shows the financial position of a person or organization at a particular time.

Statements And Reports: Considerable paper work is done in industry and business. A part of this work is standardized in the form of statements and reports. Another part consists of correspondence which varies considerably with the parties concerned and the subject matter. In both types of paper work improvements have been made through redesigning and standardization of forms, introduction of colour schemes, delivery and dispatch systems and improved procedures. All these contribute to ensuring relevant information being conveyed to all the concerned persons on time.

Statistics: A collection of figures arranged to illustrate a particular point.

Status: The standing of an individual in an organization. This is based on the amount of respect he is accorded by other people, whether it is because of his position in the hierarchy or because of personal qualities like charisma: The standing of a document under discussion. How formal or official is it and what is the appropriate way of responding to it?

Status Symbol: A measure of someone's status and importance (or sometimes self-importance) in an organization. Favourite status symbols are dress (e.g., 'white collar's opposed to blue) and officer and office furnishings (the size, position and furnishings of an office are often a finely calibrated guide to the occupant's status both in the hierarchy and in the importance attached to his function).

Statutory: Stated in a law or statute: concerned with a law or statute: created by or complying with a law: required by law.

Statutory Audit: An Audit required by statute of the financial statements of limited companies and other organization.

Statutory Books: The books which a company is bound by law to keep.

Statutory Law: A specific body of law created by statute, and contrasted with law created by court decision or administrative interpretation.

Steady Demand: Demand for a product which continues in a regular way.

Stewardship: The original purpose of accounting; also called accountability. King or lords who were away at war or for other purposes would leave their estimates in the hands of a steward. The steward would keep an account of the payments and receipts of the estate so that he could be discharged of responsibility when the owner returned. The steward would "render an account" to the owner, who might have been illiterate and had thus to hear it (audit derives from the Latin for 'he hears').

Stock: Supply of raw materials; quantity of goods for sale; details of stock at the beginning of an accounting period; details of stock at the end of an accounting period; number and letters which indicate an item of stock; making sure that enough stock is kept and that quantities and movements of stock are noted; reduction in the value of stock which is held in a warehouse for some time; details of how many goods are in the warehouse or store etc.; quantity of goods kept in stock; total value of stock sold in a year divided by the average value of goods in stock; estimating the value of stock at the end of an accounting period; to pay the same amount for the stock as its value as estimated by the valuer; stock held in a shop or warehouse; to pay the price fixed by a valuer for stock available or not available in the warehouse or store; to count the items in a warehouse normal or usually kept in stock; to hold goods for sale in warehouse or store; wholesaler who sells for a producer and earns a commission or when used in connection with the capital of a company, stock is similar to, but not synonymous with share capital. Shares may be converted into stock only when they are fully paid. The advantage of converting shares into stock is that transferability is made easier.

Stock Control: The system operated by a business whereby of goods and materials is kept at necessary levels.

Stock Exchange: The central market for dealing in freely transferable stocks, shares and securities.

Stock Option: Option to take or apply for shares.

Stockout Costs: Losses that a firm incurs when inventories are depleted before demand is satisfied.

Stock-in-Trade: An accounting term which appears in many balance sheets, sometimes abbreviated to 'stocks' it applies to the quantities of raw materials or finished goods in hand, and is often coupled with work in progress. Stock valuation.

Stockbroker: A member of a stock exchange who is authorized to deal in securities. Stockbrokers charge a commission, usually related to the volume of deals involved, for their services. Hence when stock markets are busy and trading volumes high, brokers do well. Most stockbrokers were once proudly independent family business. However, the great majority of them have by now either gone bust or been absorbed by large financial conglomerates.

Stockist: A marketing term for a person who agrees to hold certain minimum stocks of a specified manufactured product in return for special buying terms, entitling him perhaps to particularly favourable discount.

Stockmarket: An organized market in securities. The 1980s saw great growth in stockmarkets around the world, in both developing and developed countries (the market capitalization of Japan's stockmarkets, for example, rose from $380 billion in 1980 to $4,390 billion in 1989). As an indication of the growth in developing countries, by the end of the decade the Taiwan stockmarket was bigger than both the Canadian and the Dutch markets.

Straight Line Method: In calculating depreciation, the cost or agreed value of an asset is written off over its expected life by charging equal amounts against profit each year.

Straight Rebuy: In any organization where the same product is bought as before from the same supplier.

Strategic Planning: The basis of a corporate plan or other broad based and long-term assessment of an organization's future. Strategic planning does not predict the future but it assists in coping effectively with future contingencies: provides an early opportunity to correct inevitable mistakes: helps in making decisions about the right things at the right time: and focuses on what actions to take in order to shape the future as desired. Strategic planning begins by asking questions regarding the purpose and the operations to which an enterprise is presently devoted.

Strategy: A general method or policy for achieving specified objectives. In games theory a rule by which one player selects his choice. The rule may be 'pure strategy', i.e., a rule that he will definitely select a specified choice or a 'mixed strategy', i.e., a rule that gives the probabilities of his making each of a number of choices.

Stratification: Structure of a questionnaire which should help to ensure reliable answers and facilitate. The evaluation of results; framework for the selection of a sample that ensures that it adequately represents the population of universe.

Stratified Sampling: A technique frequently used for mass opinion polling. It involves the division of a population into subgroups or strata and then taking a random sample of each one.

Streamline: To make (something) more efficient or more simple.

Stress: Nervous tension or worry.

Strike: The ultimate form of industrial action by employees in dispute with their employers, where they withhold their labour until the dispute is settled.

Structure: Way in which something is organized; way in which a company's capital is set-up; organization of salaries in a company with different rates of pay for different types of job to arrange in a certain way; interview using preset questions and following a fixed pattern.

Structured Interview: An interview in which the interviewer asks questions exactly as they appear in the questionnaire, adding nothing and explaining nothing to the respondent. The respondent may answer only "yes", "no", or "don't know". This impersonal technique produces data that can be quickly and easily tabulated. But it places a heavy burden on the designer or the questionnaire. Inaccurate data resulting from badly constructed questions may well not be detected.

Stuff: To put papers, etc., into envelopes.

Style: Way of doing or making something; redesign of a product in order of make previous models obsolete and therefore encourage buying of the latest one; a company's own particular design used in all areas of its activities such as on packaging, stationery and office decoration.

Sub-optimisation: A manager's tendency to operate solely in the interests of his or her department rather than in the interests of the company as a whole.

Subsidiary: A company controlled by a Holding Company. A company is a subsidiary of another company if that other company is a member of it and controls the composition of its board of directors, or if the other company holds more than half the nominal value of its Equity Share Capital.

Subsidiary Company: One controlled by another, known as its holding company by virtue of that other controlling either more than half of its equity capital or being able to dictate the composition of its Board of Directors.

Subsidiary: Generally an undertaking controlled by another (the parent company).

Subsidy: A method of supporting a price. The government subsidized prices when it allows goods to be sold at a price lower than the market price by giving the seller the difference between the selling price and a viable one.

Substitute: Person or thing which takes the place of someone or something else; product which may be bought instead of another when the price of the latter changes or if it becomes unavailable; to take the place of something else.

Sunk Costs: Costs incurred in the past and unaffected by any future action and thus irrelevant to decision-making.

Superior-Subordinate Relationship: It is in the relations between a subordinate and his immediate superior that most breakdowns of co-ordination and communication between various parts of organizational structure finally show up. It is here that distortions of personal attitude and emotional disturbance become more pronounced.

Supermarket: A large, high-volume self-service store. Supermarkets are usually operated on a low-margin, high turnover basis, and now dominate the grocery trade. Now supermarkets are making inroads into other product fields as well, including pharmaceuticals and home improvements (DIY). The supermarket idea was born in the USA. John Hart Ford introduced cash-and-carry grocery retailing when he started the Great Atlantic and Pacific Tea Company (A&P) food stores in 1912. In the USA in 1916 Clarence Saunders opened his Piggly-Wiggly stores where he pioneered self-service and customer checkouts. A supermarket is distinguished from a superstore or hypermarket by its smaller size (less than 25,000 square feet) and its greater concentration on food products.

Supervisor: Anyone who supervised the work of other(s), although a supervisor, like a foreman, is usually regarded as being on the first level of line management in the hierarchy of an organization.

Supplier: Person or company which supplies or sells goods or services.

Supply: Providing something which is needed; supply which experiences quite a large percentage change in response to a change in price; amount of money which exists in a country; price at which something is provided; amount of a product which is available and the amount which is wanted by customers; general rule that the amount of a product which is available is related to the needs of potential customers; not available in large enough quantities to meet the demand; stock of something which is needed; goods needed to run an office products or services on which the business supplying them does not have charge VAT to provide something which is needed.

Surplus: Extra stock or something of which there is more than is needed; more revenue than was planned for in the budget; we do not need these items; to take a surplus into a larger amount.

Survey Research: A technique for

gathering data from large numbers of people by the use of questionnaires and using statistical sampling methods.

Survey Feedback: An organizational technique that collects and shares worker's opinions in order to solve existing problems and to help groups understand their own behaviour.

Swap: A transaction in which two parties exchange their financial assets. For example, central banks have an arrangement whereby, if they need to support their currencies, one central bank will form another central bank, denominated in its currency. The first such swap was for $50m in 1962 between the Federal Reserve Board of the USA and the Banque de France. With an interest-rate swap a borrower who has raised, say, Swiss francs, swaps the interest payments on this loan with those of another borrower who has raised, say, US dollars. This can be to the benefit of both parties.

Swaps: Swaps are of two distinct types, the interest rate swap and the currency swap. The first enables the instigating party to raise capital on more favourable terms or to exchange a fixed interest rate for a floating one. The currency swap is rather different as it involves an agreement to exchange both interest and capital payments (or repayments).

SWOT Analysis: An abbreviation for four key things to be considered in any planning process. A company's strengths; weaknesses; opportunities; and threats. Strength and weaknesses are factors internal to the company. An excellent service network or a widespread distribution system are the sort of things that might be identified as particular strengths; poor cash flow or an over-extended product mix as particular weaknesses. Opportunities and threats are factors external to the company. Careful scanning of the business environment for new technological developments might reveal opportunities. Threats might be spotted coming from changes in consumer behaviour, from government legislation, or from some major international incident.

Syndicate: A group of individuals or organizations who combine for some common goal which is to their mutual benefit.

Synectics: A more narrowly-focused form of brainstorming.

Synergy: Producing greater effects by joining forces rather than by action separately.

System: Arrangement or organization of things which work together; system of mathematics based on the number 10; way of putting documents in order for easy reference; supplies by fixing certain allowed quantities; set of programs commands, etc., which run a computer; using a computer to suggest how a company could work more efficiently by analysing the way in which it works at present; person who specializes in systems analysis; directing and controlling all the elements in an organization to achieve its basic objectives; selling products plus related services such as needs assessment and installation.

Systematic (Market) Risk: The non-diversifiable component of the risk of a security.

Systems Analysis: Activity, process or study of critically examining the ways of performing frequently occurring tasks that depend on the movement, recording or processing of information, i.e., data processing, by a number of people within an organization.

Systems Approach: The systems approach looks at the organization as a total system comprising a number of interacting variables. It studies the organization as an integrated whole encompassing many subsystems, formal organizations, individuals, social systems, environment, etc. It does not view organization as a static arrangement of jobs but acts for identifying the functions required in terms of the decision areas in achieving goal. All the variables in the system start functioning in an orderly way and preserve organizational integrity.

Systems Approach to Marketing: The marketing management philosophy is based on a system perspective of decision-making. The systems approach to marketing has substantial impact on the development of marketing thought and the management of marketing activity. This approach provides a conceptual framework for market planning, determination of the marketing mix, physical distribution and the use of operations research techniques in marketing. Systems thinking recognise the inter-relations and inter-connections among the components of a marketing system.

Systems Technique of Management: The study of management has been made more scientific and useful by the application of systems technique which the managerial scientists are increasingly using year-by-year. The term system refers to a group or complex of parts (such as people and machines) inter-related in their actions towards some goals. Typically it is the inter-relationships among these system elements, and between them and their environment, that is of most interest in systems design both for human organizations and for purely physical systems. Although these inter-relationships often are difficult to describe fully and precisely for human organization, we can anticipate that a systems approach provides a useful framework for examining organizational phenomena, and allow us to fill in whatever detail we find appropriate.

T

Tactical Planning: The purpose of tactical planning is to identify the major tasks required to achieve strategic objective. Tactical planning is thus supportive to strategic planning. For tactical planning to exist it must have the direction given by strategic planning.

Take-Over: Refers to the acquisition by one company of sufficient shares in another company to give the purchaser control of that other company.

Take over Bid: An offer made to the shareholders of a company by a person or organization to gain control of the company. Refers to an offer by one company to acquire all, or a controlling holding, of the voting shares of another company.

Tangible Assets: Assets with a physical existence, such as property, plant or equipment. Tangible assets may be contrasted with investments and with Intangible Assets, such as patents, licences, trade marks or goodwill.

Target: Thing to aim for; amount of units a factory is expected to produce; amount of sales a representative is expected to achieve; consumers at whom an advertisement is aimed; market in which a company is planning to sell its goods; to fix amounts or quantities which workers have to produce or reach; to produce the quantity of goods or sales which are expected; not to produce the amount of goods or sales which are expected; aim at or to aim to sell to; to plan to sell goods in a certain market.

Target Audience: The audience to whom a particular advertising campaign is directed, defined in demographic terms, by sex, age, income, and so on. Only when a target audience has been defined can the process of media planning begin.

Target Market: One or more segments of a market selected for special attention by a company. As consumers become more affluent and more discerning, it becomes more difficult to market products that satisfy the "masses". New products from marketing-oriented companies, therefore, are now usually aimed at specific groups of consumers.

Tariff: Literally a "list of items", more commonly, a price or tax established on items, goods, or services, an import tax.

Task Leader: The individual who may emerge in a small group as the person who tries to keep the attention of the group focused on its task and who tries to ensure that it gets done. Compare with social emotional leader.

Tax Credit: A direct reduction of tax liability for income tax purposes, authorized by law to serve some broad economic, social, or political objective. Tax credits for plant construction or energy expenditures, or for conservation improvements are examples. Tax credits permit all or some percentage of the cost of such items to be deducted from the amount of tax which would otherwise be paid.

Tax Evasion: The illegal attempt to reduce the burden of taxation on an individual or organization.

Tax Loss: Any loss which a company can transfer to another accounting period and set off against profit. The ability to carry such losses forward (and backwards against previous accounting periods profit) differs from country to country.

Tax Return: A statement to the fiscal authorities of a taxpayer's sources and totals of income and expenses during a given period.

Tax, Ad Valorem: A tax established according to the value or a portion of the value of thing that is taxed.

Taxable Income: Annual business net income, as adjusted from accounting rules to tax rules. In India there are numerous adjustments from accounting Net Profit to taxable income. For example, accounting depreciation is added back, and Capital Allowances are granted instead. Dividend income from other companies is deducted, but certain legal fees and entertainment expenses are added back.

Taxation: This includes computation of income tax as per tax laws and regulations, filling of returns and making tax payments. In recent times it also includes tax planning.

Taxi: A vehicle licensed to ply for hire, that is, to roam the streets looking for passengers wishing to be conveyed privately to destinations previously unspecified. A taxi normally has a meter showing the cost of the journey.

Taylor, F.W. (1856-1915): An American engineer who invented work study and founded the scientific management approach to the world of work (sometimes known as Taylorism) at the beginning of the twentieth century. He placed great emphasis on analysing the constituent operations of a task down to the finer details. Taylor also saw the importance of good selection and training procedures and argued for better communication between management and the shop floor and better cooperation, in general, between both sides of industry.

Team-Building: A technique that aims to help work groups by improving the quality of their members' interpersonal relations as well as their skill at solving problems and accomplishing their task. This is usually done with the aid of an external consultancy which will diagnose the way the work group functions, helping member to identify difficulties and suggest improvements.

Teamwork: The answer to better teamwork between staff and line seems to lie, first, in an understanding of their basic relationship. Company experience indicates that the following important points must be observed if effective teamwork is to exist. 1 This units that are designated as line have ultimate responsibility for the successful operation of the company. Therefore line departments must be responsible for operating decisions. 2 Staff elements contribute by providing advice and service to the line in accomplishing the objective of the enterprise. 3 Staff is responsible for providing advice and service to appropriate line elements, when requested to do so. However, staff also is responsible for offering advice and service when it is not requested, but where the staff believes it is needed. 4 The solicitation of advice and acceptance of suggestions and counsel is usually at the option of the line organization. 5 Both line and staff should have the right to appeal to higher authority in case of disagreement on staff recommendations. However, this right to appeal should not be permitted to supersede the line's responsibility for making immediate decision when required by the operating situation.

Teamwork between Staff and Line: This teamwork creates an understanding of the basic relationship that Company experience indicates.

Teaser: A short advertisement that does not reveal the name of the product being advertised to "tease" the curiosity of consumers so that they are on the lookout for the full campaign when it arrives. Teasers are not new. Used by the R.J. Reynolds Company when it launched Camel cigarettes in 1913, its teasers had slogans like "The Camels are Coming". When they came they became one of the world's best-selling cigarettes.

Technical Analysis: The sort of number-crunching relied upon by believers in chartism: the use of detailed analyses of past price movements and turnover in stock markets as a basis for predictions about the future demand of shares. Technical analysts largely ignore the underlying business of the companies whose shares they are analysing.

Technology: The branch of knowledge that deals with applied science, applied engineering, and electronics.

Technostress: The inability of individual to adjust to changing technology.

Teleconference: A discussion of conference where participants are geographically a scattered and linked by means of telecommunication such as audio conferencing or video conferencing.

Telegraphic Transfer: A swift method of transferring monies operated by a bank at the customer's request. The bank cables the relevant instructions to agent, usually another branch of the bank. The agent then effect the necessary credits or debits.

Television Rating: A measure of the popularity of television programmes based on various methods of research. In one system sophisticated equipment is attached to sets in selected homes to record which channel the set is tuned to. A diary panel is then used to determine how many people are watching the set. Television ratings (TVRS) are calculated by expressing the programme's audience as a percentage of all the households that can receive TV. TVR can also refer to the percentage of a product's target that has one opportunity to see its advertisement during a particular campaign. It is a measure of the intensity of the advertising campaign.

Tenant: A person or organization occupying or having rights to a property or real estate.

Tender: To offer money or something else of value in payment for goods or services or in payment of a debt: money or something else of value.

Tender Offer: A method of selling securities developed by the UK government, and now used all over the world. The seller sets a price (the tender price) at which it is prepared to sell the securities. Offers are invited, and applicants state what price they are prepared to pay; nothing below the tender price is acceptable. After a certain time the securities go to the highest bidder. Should not enough bids above the tender price be received the offer lapses, and the whole issue can then be with drawn.

Term Loan: A bank loan made for a fixed term of years, at a fixed rate of interest, and normally repayable by instalments spread over a period.

Test Marketing: An attempt to test a new product's performance in the marketplace by launching it in a limited area. Unlike product testing, test marketing required that the full intended national marketing strategy be simulated within the selected area. In countries with regional commercial television stations, the area chosen for test marketing is often that covered by a single television company. Full-scale test marketing is expensive and carries no guarantee that a local reaction to the product will be repeated nationally. For these reasons the practice has become less frequent in recent years, but some consumer goods do still first appear under test-marketing conditions.

The Four O's: Simple compact way of summarizing the essentials of a marketing operation which are objects, objectives, organization, and operations.

The Four P's: Simple compact way of summarizing the essentials of the marketing mix, which are product, price, promotion and place.

The Industrial Development Bank of India (IDBI): An outstanding feature in the structure of financial institution in India since independence has been the establishment of a number of development banks both at the national and state levels of which the Industrial Development Bank of India (IDBI)is the apex institution. The main function of the bank has been to regulate the issue of bank notes and keep reserves for securing monetary stability. The bank is the sole authority for the issue of currency in India other than one rupee coins/notes and subsidiary coins. As the agent of the Central Government, it undertakes the distribution of one rupee notes and coins as well as small coins issue by the Government of India. The bank acts as banker to the Government of India, state governments, commercial banks and to some of the financial institutions including state co-operative banks. It formulates and administers monetary policy in order to influence the level of aggregate demand for goods and services by varying the cost and availability of credit. The Reserve Bank also play vital role in the maintenance of the exchange value of the rupee, and acts as an agent of the government in respect of India's membership of the International Monetary Fund. The bank also undertakes a variety of developmental and promotional functions.

The Public Relations Function: While no one organizational device will assure effectiveness in discharging social responsibilities, one of the most logical internal structural changes is to build upon the present public relations function. For the most part, public relations officers are not charged simply with "telling the story". Seldom they are in a position to influence decisively the important decisions of business policy and practice. Usually their task focuses on favourable interpretation after the decision is madc.

Thematic Apperception Test (TAT): Test used to ascertain attitudes or reactions to a brand, which consists in showing pictures to the subject who then constructs a story round them. A projective technique developed in the late 1930s by the American psychologist Henry Murray. It consists of vague and ambiguous drawings (usually of one or two human figures) about each of which the subject has to make up a story. The themes that may emerge from these stories are then used to diagnose areas of emotional conflict or concern in the subject. This technique has been widely used in the selection of senior management where, for example, the incidence of achievement imagery might be of particular interest.

Theory X: In the terminology of Douglas McGregor this describes the rational economic view of human nature that people only work when they have to and, therefore, require authoritarian management. McGregor rejected this view in favour of theory.

Theory Y: In the terminology of Douglas McGregor this describes a view of human nature in which people would like to be creative in their work and take more responsibility for it. They would thus be more responsive to democratic management and its enabling function than is suggested by the proponents of theory X.

Theory Z: The term suggested by the American writer on organization theory William Ouchi for western adaptations of Japanese management parties. The theory Z organization is distinguished by several important features: lifetime employment relatively slow promotion concern for the whole person: informal control and leadership: individual responsibility: consensual decision-making: relatively less specialization. There is some evidence that theory Z organization have less absenteeism, greater productivity and better quality output than others.

Threshold Effect: The point at which advertising begins to be effective. With classified advertising the effect is immediate. With most other forms it takes time (and money) before new advertising is noticed against the background "noise" of other advertisements. All money spent on advertising is wasted until this "threshold" is reached. Any company not prepared to spend enough to pass the threshold should not spend anything.

Tight Money: Money is said to be tight when credit can only be obtained at very high interest rates.

Time Card: A card used to record hours worked by an employee who is paid on a time basis.

Time Element in Planning: One common ingredient of all planning is time and plans with respect to time can be conveniently expressed as Short Range (SR) covering a period of 1 year and less: Intermediate Range (IR) over 1 but less than 5 years and Long Range (LR) over 5 years.

Time Motion Study: This is one part of work study wherein the bodily movement in the completion of a job is studied.

Time Sharing: A situation in which two or more people or organization make use of the same piece of equipment (particularly a computer) in order to share costs and to maximize use of the resource. A term in computer jargon referring to the practice of two or more using a computer at the same time but for different purposes. This type of sharing is an additional help in maximizing the use of very expensive computer equipment and thus reducing the cost.

Time Value of Money: An expression of the fact that, if the rate of interest is positive, money in hand now is worth more than money to be received at a date in future.

Tolerance: The degree dictated either by contract or custom, by which a finished item may differ from the original specification without giving grounds for rejection.

Tolls: Charges made for using certain roads, bridges, canal blocks, etc. The monies collected are intended to pay for their building and upkeep.

Tombstone: An advertisement placed in a financial newspaper or magazine to announce the completion of a syndicated loan or a new issue of securities. It is called a tombstone because it consists of little more than a list of names and dates. The names are those of the borrower (who pays for the tombstone) and of the financial institutions which participated in the deal. They are ordered in strict seniority, the size of the type and face indicate their importance in the deal. Within the same rank participants are listed strictly alphabetically. The more the tombstones, the less dead the market.

Tools of Financial Analysis: (a) Comparative financial statements, (b) Common size statement, (c) Trend percentages or ratios, (d) Ratio analysis, (e) Fund flow analysis, (f) Cash flow analysis.

Topography: The geography, structure, or configuration of a surface, problem, plan, or other natural or human creation or artifact.

Tort: That branch of the law dealing with civil actions arising from breach of a duty imposed by common law or statute and dealing with injuries to the person or his property. It should be distinguished from the law of contract which deals with breaches of duties arising out of transactions entered into by mutual consent.

Total Assets: The total of all the assets employed in a business.

Trade: Old item given as part of the payment for a new one; amount allowed by the seller for an old item being traded in for a new one.

Trade Barrier: This is a general term to cover any government limitation on the free international exchange of merchandize. These barriers may take the form of tariffs, quotas, import deposits, restrictions on the grant of import licences or strict regulations pertaining to health and/or safety standards.

Trade: Commerce, also an occupation or job: also, to buy and sell, exchange or barter.

Trade Creditors: Suppliers of goods or services to the business who are not paid immediately at the time of purchase. At a Balance Sheet date, outstanding amounts owed to them will be shown as trade Creditors as part of Current Liabilities.

Trade Debtors: Buyers of a business's goods and services who do not pay immediately at the time of purchase. At a Balance Sheet date, outstanding amounts owed by them will be shown as trade Debtors as part of Current Assets.

Trade Discount: The means by which members of a distribution channel (the "trade" are paid for their services. Manufacturers offer wholesalers discounts on their list prices, and the wholesalers in turn discounts their prices to retailers. Such discounts, because they are given for functions performed, are also called functional discounts. Trade discounts may also be related to the speed at which goods are expected to sell. In addition to a trade discount, manufacturers frequently offer wholesalers a quantity discount. It is also normal to offer a discount for prompt payment, known as a cash discount. A cash discount might be expressed as "3/14 net 28", which means the buyer (wholesaler or retailer) will be given a 3% discount if payment is made within 14 days, and that the bill must be settled within 28 days. Trade discount is not treated separately in accounts. This is because the price which is fixed for a transaction is always after deducting the trade discount from the list price of a goods.

Trade In: To buy and sell certain items; to give in an old item as part of the payment for a new one.

Trade Mark: A particular mark or motif employed by a manufacturer to identify and to advertise his goods. Trade marks may be registered at the patent office. There is a registration fee and an annual renewal fee, but registration protects the manufacturer against wrongful use of the patent by competitors for a certain period of time.

Trade Off: Exchanging one thing for another as part of a business deal.

Trade Union: An organization of workers in a particular trade or industry which furthers the welfare of its members and acts on their behalf in collective bargaining with employers on pay and conditions of employment.

Trade-In Allowance: A price reduction given for a used product when a similar one is purchased new; an indirect form of price cutting. In car retailing, for example, prices advertised by dealers may appear to be uniform. But fierce price competition takes place between them when the trade-in allowance is being negotiated. In the case of durable house-hold goods (cookers, refrigerators, and so on) trade-in allowances are often nominal and are frequently advertised.

Trade-In Offer: In selling certain consumer durable goods vendors often offer what are referred to as trade-in terms. This means that they will make an allowance for an old model handed over as part of the contract. Most trade-in offers are a form of price cutting as the vendor cuts his profit for a quick sale, not desiring to gain much from the model taken in exchange except its diminished value.

Trading: Business of buying and selling; account of a company's gross profit; group of countries which trade with each other; series of purchases and sales from company to company which are made until the finished product is purchased by the customer; company which specializes in buying and selling goods; bad conditions for trade; selling at lower prices to increase sales volume; area of land near a town specially for factories and warehouses; situation where a company's receipts are less than its expenditure; company or country which trades with another; situation where a company's gross receipts are more than its gross expenditure; special type of stamp given away by a shop which the customer can collect and later exchange for free goods; goods held by a business for sale; selling products at higher prices to raise their prestige and achieve a higher profit margin; way of doing business which is reasonable and does not harm the customer; government department which protects consumers against unfair or illegal business; illegal buying or selling of shares by staff of a company who have secret information about the company's plans.

Trading Profit or Loss: In the annual accounts of a trading organization the first part of the profit and loss account is commonly referred to as the trading account. The balance brought down from this account to the next section of the profit and loss account is known as the trading profit or trading loss. (Popularly called gross profit or gross loss).

Trait: Any enduring characteristic of an individual's personality.

Trait Theory: Any approach to the study of leadership which emphasizes the importance of trying to identify distinguishing characteristics or traits of personality common to successful leaders.

Transaction: Piece of business buying or selling; transaction paid for in cash; purchase or sale of shares on the Stock Exchange; purchase or sale of foreign currency.

Transactional Analysis (TA): Transactional Analysis is both an approach for defining and analysing communication interaction between people and a theory of personality. The fundamental theory underlying TA holds that an individual's personality consists of three ego status—the parent, the child and the adult. These labels have nothing to do with age but rather with aspects of the ego. This technique has been propogated by Eric Berne.

Transfer Price: A price charged by one division of a firm for supplying goods or services to another division.

Transfer Pricing: The pricing of goods and services which are merely being transferred from one part to another part of the same organization.

Transit: Movement of passengers or goods on the way to a destination; goods being transported from warehouse to customer.

Transmission of Shares: Effectively, the automatic transfer of shares not by transfer deed but by what might be called operation of law.

Transnational Corporation: An expression created by Christopher Bartlett, a professor at the Harvard Business School, and Sumantra Ghoshal from Inse AD in their book of the same name. The two professors identified three types of successful international company. 1. Those (like Japan's Matsushita) that concentrated on economic efficiency through a highly centralized operation. 2. Those (like Philips and Unilever) that concentrated on responsiveness to conditions in their many local markets. 3. Those (like Sweden's L.M. Ericsson) that succeeded by developing a specific technology and marketing it assiduously all over the world. International companies of the future, argued Bartlett and Ghoshal, would not succeed with the one-dimensional approach taken by these successes from the past. They would have to be transnational corporations (TNCS), companies that combine all three dimensions. TNCS have implications for marketing, and for management in general. Of the three traditional types of successful international company, only the second really needed first-class management in all its geographic markets. The TNC will need first-class management and marketing everywhere.

Transport: Moving of goods or people; the visitors will be coming by bus or train etc., or in their own cars; system of trains used etc.; used by the general public; advertising appearing on or in forms of transportation such as buses or trains; to move goods or people from one place to another in a vehicle.

Travel: To go from one place to another showing a company's goods to buyers and taking orders from them.

Traveller's Cheques: These are issued by banks for the convenience of persons travelling at home or abroad. They are issued for various amounts, e.g., Rs. 1,000, Rs. 2,000, Rs. 10,000, etc., and can be changed into the currency of the country which the person happens to visit.

Treasure Bill: A bill of exchange issue by the government.

Trial Balance: A list of all balances contained in the ledger (or ledgers, including the cash book). It is a two-column list debit balances and credit balances being listed separately. The purpose is to check the totals of each column agree and therefore show that the rules of double entry book-keeping have been observed. It does not indicate any error arising from a total omission or an incorrect amount recorded correctly.

Trust Funds: In government, funds collected and used by the government to carry out purposes and programmes specified in a trust agreement or statute: for example, the social security, highway user and unemployment trust funds of the federal government.

Trustee: A person who is entrusted with property belonging to someone else. The purest form of trustee can be one who has absolutely no beneficial interest in the property and is, therefore, called a naked trustee.

Turn Round: To make a previously loss making company profitable; he made the company profitable in less than a year.

Turnkey Contract: A contract, usually on a large scale, where the person paying leaves the contractor, usually a specialist organization, to see to all details and settle all problems that may occur during the period of the contract.

Turnover: An Accountancy term for gross takings or total sales before any deductions.

Turnround: Value of goods sold during a year divided by the average value of goods held in stock action of emptying a ship plane etc. and getting it ready for another commercial journey making a company profitable again.

Two-Way Market: A market which is as free for buyers as it is for sellers. With securities, a two-way market is one in which brokers are as willing to sell a security at its quoted selling price as they are to buy it at its quoted buying price.

U

Ultra Vires: Beyond the powers of use mostly with reference to limited companies which are bound by the powers set out in their memorandum of association.

Unabsorbed Cost: Where overhead expenses are allocated according to a budgeted output, each unit produced has a fixed overhead charge, perhaps a percentage of its direct cost. When the output aimed at is not reached, then not all of the overheads are charged to production. The balance remaining is known as unabsorbed cost.

Unappropriated Profits: That part of the profit of a business not paid out in dividends or allocated to any particular use.

Uncertainty Avoidance: Uncertainty avoidance is the extent to which people feel threatened by ambigous situations and the degree to which they try to avoid these situations by doing such things as: 1. providing greater career stability, 2. establishing more formal rules, 3. rejecting deviant ideas and behaviour and 4. accepting the possibility of absolute truths and attainment of expertise.

Uncontrollable Costs: Costs that cannot be influenced by a given manager within a given time period. In the very long run there are few costs that cannot be controlled by someone.

Uncontrollable: Which cannot be controlled; variable or factor that cannot be controlled in marketing such as legislation or the state of the country's economy.

Undercapitalization: A company is undercapitalized when its actual capitalization (i.e., long-term resources) is lower than its requirement or as may be warranted by its earning capacity. Under capitalization, however, does not always mean insufficiency of capital.

Underdeveloped: Which has not been developed; country which is not fully industrialized; or a country not having achieved its full potential in economic development.

Underpricing: Charging a lower price than is justified by demand.

Underwriter: A person or more often a merchant bank who agrees to underwrite an issue of shares by a company. This means that in return for a commission he (or they) agree to take up a certain proportion of the shares if those shares are not subscribed by the public.

Underwriting Commission: A commission paid by a company to any person or persons (usually an Issuing House or other Financial Institution) who guarantees, for the sake of a commission, to take up any shares or debentures offered by the company to the public for which the latter do not subscribe.

Undifferentiated Marketing: The marketing of a product to the widest possible market, appealing to needs that unite consumers rather than divide them. For many years Coca-Cola very successfully marketed only one product in one kind of container. Henry Ford revolutionized automobile production when he mass produced the Model T for an undifferentiated market: one model for everybody, in any colour as long as it was black. Nowadays undifferentiated marketing has largely given way to the concept and practice of Market Segmentation. Even Coca-Cola produces a range of Cokes, plus Fanta and Sprite. It also produces them in large bottles, small bottles, plastic bottles and glass bottles. Likewise there are now cars to suit every taste, although they retain a loyalty to Henry Ford's idea of mass production by developing differentiated exteriors on a core of undifferentiated engines.

Undifferentiated: That which has no unique feature; marketing strategy which seeks to present a product to the public without stressing any unique feature of the product thus appealing to all segments of the market; product which has no unique feature to set it apart from others on the market.

Undue Influence A form of moral pressure. A contract will not be enforced by a court, if it can be shown that the defendant was in a position that prevented him forming a free and unfettered judgement.

Unearned Income: Income which does not arise from employment.

Unemployment Insurance: A form of social insurance that pays benefits to qualified people who are unemployed. Unemployment insurance is financed through a payroll tax. People qualify for benefits by accumulating covered employment as defined in state's law. Most persons receiving unemployment insurance do not continue to receive any group health insurance coverage they might have had through their most recent employer.

Unemployment: The term generally used to people who are able and willing to engage in paid employment but unable to find any.

Unfavourable: Situation where a country more than it exports; exchange rate which gives an amount of foreign currency for the home currency which is not good for trade.

Uniformity: The use of the same rules of accounting or financial statement presentation from one company to another. Improvements in uniformity are encouraged by the setting of Accounting Standards. One reason for this is to improve comparability between the financial statements of different companies. The word "Consistency" tends to be used to mean the use by any individual company of the same accounting methods year by year. This is required by Company Law.

Unilateral Contract: Strictly speaking these are not contracts at all but promises. If someone promises to do something provided something else is done, no other person being named or put under obligation he is only bound if the condition is fulfilled.

Unilateral: One-sided, a unilateral agreement is a promise to do something. The promise not being supported by any consideration.

Unissued Share Capital: The difference between the nominal amount of the Authorized Share Capital and the Issued Share Capital.

Unit Pricing: A form of pricing used by retailers to enable shoppers to make price comparisons between products. Large retailers (especially supermarkets) show the price per unit of a product in addition to its total price. For example, a grocer might carry four brands of instant coffee, each Brand available in three different sizes. Unit pricing enables the consumer to see that a 40 g jar of Brand A costs Rs. 50 per 100 gm while an 80 g jar of the same brand costs Rs. 47. But an 80 g jar of Brand B costs Rs. 46 per 100 gms while a 40g jar of Brand B costs Rs. 52.

Unit Trust of India (UTI): Established by the Government of India on 1st July, 1964 by an Act of the Parliament, the main objectives of UTI are: (i) To mobilise the small savings of the public through sale of unit schemes. (ii) To invest these small savings in a wide range of securities. (iii) To provide reasonable income with minimum risk and maximum of liquidity of investments to the unit-holders, (iv) To enable small investors to take advantages of the skill and knowledge of the experts in the field of investments, (v) To facilitate growth and diversification of the economy through capital formation.

Unity of Command: In management, this is the principle that each member of an organization should report to only one person.

Unity of Direction: There should be one head and one plan for activities having similar objectives. No organization can succeed unless it has a unity of direction. Unity of command relates to the personnel but the unity of direction relates to the whole body corporate. Unity of direction alone can produce a sense of loyalty and devotion amongst the subordinates.

Unlawful: This describes an act or contract not in itself illegal but which the law does not recognize and on which no legal action can be based. Most contracts involving wagering are unlawful.

Unlimited Company: A legal entity, in the form of a Company, whose shareholders do not have limited liability for the debts of the company. Such companies are fairly rare, but they do have the advantage that some provisions of Company Law do not apply, including the requirement to publish financial statements.

Unload: To take goods off to sell stock which is no longer needed at a lower price than usual.

Unsecured Creditors: Creditors of a company of other business whose debts are not secured.

Unsecured Loan: An accounting term for loan capital raised without security.

Unstructured Interview: Interview using no preset questions and following no fixed pattern.

Upset Price: Lowest price which the seller will accept and which is therefore the starting price at an auction.

Upward Communication: The flow of opinions, ideas, complaints, suggestions and other kinds of information from subordinates to Managers.

Usage: How something is used; degree to which those who see or hear advertisements for a product buy more of it than those who do not; dividing a market into segments according to the type of use which customers will make of the product.

User: Person who uses something; person who actually uses a product book showing someone how to use something.

Uses of Financial Statements: Different classes of people are interested in the financial statements analysis with a view to assessing the economic and financial position of any business or industrial concern in terms of profitability, liquidity or solvency.

Utility: The usefulness or satisfaction to be derived from a product by a potential buyer. Something that performs a useful service, like a public utility.

V

Vals: System of dividing people into segments according to their life styles.

Valence: The degree to which a decision maker wants a particular outcome. Valence can be either positive or negative. Bonuses, recognitions, promotions and support from significant others, for instances, would have positive valences; that is, they would be greatly desired by a rational decision maker. Reprimands, pay cuts, demotions and disapproval from significant others, on the other hand, would have negative valences.

Value: The price which an item would fetch in an open market. Distinction should be made between value in present use and value in alternative use. Value is also determined by various other factors ranging from sentiment to long-term speculation.

Value Added: Refers to the value added to a commodity at each stage of its manufacturer; for example, the value added by a flour miller to the final value of the flour, minus the cost of the wheat.

Value Added Tax (V.A.T): The underlying principle of V.A.T. is that tax is levied at each stage of the production of goods or services and on the value added at each stage; e.g., tax is paid by manufacturers on the cost of making an item, by wholesalers on the price they charge the retailer and by retailers on the price they charge the consumer. Each party in this process must account to the Customs and Excise for the tax on their output. It may deduct from this figure the amount of tax already paid by the party supplying them. A tax charged on the value added by an enterprise over a period. A multi-stage indirect tax. In principle the tax is borne by the final consumer.

Value Analysis: A technique to help a company find ways to reduce its costs without sacrificing its product's market appeal. Marketing managers and Production and Design engineers, say, get together to discuss ways that costs might be cut. Their ideas are ranked according to their cost-saving potential, and are analysed for feasibility. Any proposed changes is then checked against consumer perceptions of the product's value. Value analysis can be applied to new product ideas when they are still at the design stage, as well as to existing products.

Value For Money: A term used particularly in the public sector to denote the benefit derived from a particular expenditure for a particular purpose.

Variable Cost: An accounting term for costs that vary according to the level of output. Costs that vary in proportion to the volume of production. Normally raw materials and direct labour input will be variable costs. Some overhead costs, which cannot be directly ascribed to particular units of production or processes, may nevertheless still be variable with total production. Variable costs are sometimes called Marginal Costs by accountants. The opposite of these are Fixed Costs, which do not vary in the short term over the range of production levels being considered.

Variable Pricing: The selling of the same product or service at different prices depending on the time off location. Variable pricing is not very practical for large manufacturers of industrial goods, but it is a practice that is often found among street markets or antique sellers. For example, the prices of fruit on a market stall may be higher on Saturday mornings than they are on Thursday afternoons; the price of an antique may be higher for the well-dressed American tourist than it is for a local dealer.

Variable Rate: A rate of interest that varies in line with some benchmark (like labour). Variable rate is American for floating rate, and the opposite of fixed rate.

Variances: Differences between actual amounts of costs, revenues production levels, and so on, and the plans for these amounts set down in a budget.

Vehicle: Machine with wheels used to carry goods or passengers on a road; van or truck used for business purposes; very large lorry; specific newspaper; programme or radio programme used to carry an advertisement.

Vendor: A person selling goods.

Venture Capital: Money put up by financial institutions or wealthy individuals to back risky commercial ventures (often high-tech ones). This can either be at the beginning of the venture's life (when the money is known as start-up capital), or it can be later in its life (to rescue it, or to attempt to turn it round). For the high degree of risk involved, the investor expects a higher than average return from such ventures.

Vertical Integration: A term used with reference to the amalgamation of business organizations each of which is concerned with a different stage in the production of specific goods or services.

Vertical or Horizontal Delegation: Customarily delegation is considered as being from a higher to lower level but it can also be from a lower to a higher level or between levels on the same plane. In other words delegation can be downward, upward or between same level. Downward delegation of authority is illustrated by a sales manager to the sales staff upward delegation by state governments to the federal government and between a production manager and a marketing manager in the same level.

Video Tape: Magnetic tape for recording sound and vision used for making original recordings or taping existing television material; to record something on video tape.

Visual: Which can be seen; screen attached to a computer which shows the information stored in the computer.

Vocational Interests Tests: To measure a person's likes and dislikes concerning various occupations, hobbies and so on.

Volatility: Often used to refer to the size and frequency of fluctuation in the price of a security, or in a stockmarket index. The beta coefficient is a specific measure of a US stock's volatility vis-a-vis a base figure: the Standard & Poor's 500 Stock Index. It measures the variance of the stock's price relative to the variance of the index. The index itself has beta coefficient of one; any stock with a coefficient greater than one is more volatile than the market as a whole.

Voluntary Winding up: A winding up in which a company and its creditors are left to settle their affairs without coming to the court.

Voucher: Paper which is given in stead of money; paper which can be exchanged for cash; card bought in a store which is given as present and which must be exchanged for goods in that store; ticket given by an employer to a worker, which can be exchanged in a restaurant for good written document from an auditor to show that the accounts are correct of that money has really been paid.

W

Wage Freeze: An attempt by government to hold wages and salaries at a certain level, usually as part of a general policy aimed at stemming inflation.

Wages and Salaries: A generic term for remuneration paid to employees of a business or other organization. The distinction between a wage and a salary is fairly nebulous but, generally speaking wages are paid weekly and salaries monthly, or wages apply to manual workers and salaries to white collar job.

Waiting Time: In business parlance, time which an employee spends idle, though not through his own fault, e.g., time spent waiting for a machine to be repaired or set-up ready for use. It is obviously worthwhile to minimize this time.

Waiver: Where one person waives his rights in a contract, this is known as a waiver. Though an alteration of an existing contract, it is in effect a new agreement and requires consideration if it is to be enforceable at law.

Warehouse: Generally speaking, a place where goods are stored prior to their being sold or used.

Warehousing: Disguising the purchase of shares in company by using a nominee and others to buy stakes. These can then act in concert to make a surprise takeover bid. Many countries try to reduce the chances to this sort of surprise attack by regulating concert party behaviour and by insisting that all substantial holdings of quoted companies be declared to the public. (In the UK any stake above 3% has to be declared under normal circumstances, and any stake of over 1% during a takeover battle).

Warrant: A certificate authorising the holder to buy a specified number of shares in a company at a named price, and within a specified period of time. This is similar to a rights issue, except that the period of time in which a warrant can be exercised is much longer. Securities are often said to come with a warrants attache. A warrant is also a written instruction that makes legal a payment that would otherwise be illegal.

Warranty: A statement of fact in a contract, either express or implied; a stipulation collateral to the main purpose of the contract. If it is unfulfilled, the injured party cannot repudiate the contract but may be able to claim damages before a specified period.

Wasting Assets: Assets whose economic value decreases as they are used because they cannot particularly be renewed or replaced, e.g., coal-mines or oilfields.

Wealth: Goods and other assets in existence at any time which command a market value (i.e., price) if offered for sale.

Wealth Maximization: Refers to the assumption that the objective of a firm (company) is to maximize the wealth of its owners (shareholders).

Wealth Tax: A tax which is levied on net wealth and is normally levied at regular intervals usually one year on the net assets of individuals though in some countries such as Norway it is payable by companies as well.

Wear and Tear: Damage to a product through use over a period of time.

Weighted Average Cost: A method of determining the cost of stock (Inventories) that are on hand at the end of an accounting period. If a business buys and uses many types of raw materials it might be hard to tell which units have been used and which remain and thus difficult to calculate the exact costs. It is normal in this case to make flow assumptions such as First In First Out or Last In First Out or Average Cost. Weighted average cost values units used and units remaining at the average cost of the purchases, weighted by volume. The average may be worked out each time there is another purchase, or at predetermined intervals.

White-Collar Worker: Popular term for any member of staff who works in an office. The name deceives from the practice of (men) wearing a white shirt to work (in the days when men wore white shirts with white collar). Usually contrasted with a blue collar worker.

Wholesale: The term used for the intermediate stage in the chain of distribution. Wholesalers specialize in the process of distribution, purchasing the output of firms for resale and distribution to retailers.

Wholesaler: The middle man between manufacturer and retailer. He is able to buy in large quantities and then break these into smaller parcels for the benefit of the retailers.

Wildcat Strike: A local strike that does not have official trade union backing usually called without warning or at short notice.

Will: A legal declaration of person's wishes and intentions with reference to the disposal of his or her property after death.

Windfall Gain: Refers to a unanticipated addition to income.

Windfall Loss: Refers to unanticipated reduction in income.

Windfall Profit: A profit not anticipated. It might arise perhaps from changes in legislation. An increase in taxer duty might result in the manufacturer making additional profit on stock whereon the lower rate of duty has already been paid windfall profit, being exceptional, should be shown separately in company accounts.

Winding Up: The process of liquidation of a company. The winding up may be by the court, voluntary, or subject to the supervision of the court.

Window Dressing: Apart from its literal meaning of displaying goods in a shop window in a manner that maximizes the chances of passers by being tempted to buy them or atleast to enter the shop, this term has certain specialized meaning in the world of commerce. or The manipulation of figures in financial statements in order to make them appear better (or perhaps worse) than they otherwise would be (See also Creative Accounting).

Window Shopping: Parading up and down a shopping street, to see new products, items, more to envy than to purchase.

Win-lose method of Conflict Resolution: Win-lose methods, in which the supervisor inevitably wins and the employee inevitably loses, include the use of mental or physical power to bring about compliance. Other win-lose methods involve failing to respond to subordinates' suggestions for change.

Withholding Tax: Federal, state, or local tax withheld by employers from the paychecks of their employees and paid directly to the taxing jurisdiction.

Win-Win method of Conflict Resolution: The heart of win-win approach is using participative management techniques to gain consensus and commitment to objectives. With this method, all parties identify goals, consider obstacles to reaching them, regard alternative solutions and finally settle on the most mutually beneficial solution.

Without Recourse: These words added to a bill of exchange indicate that the holder has no recourse to the person from whom he took the bill should it not be paid.

Word Processing: The computerised creation, editing, and printing of written text: a component of office automation providing text entry through computers or terminals, and automated assistance in correcting, editing, formating, copying, deleting, storing, retrieving, and printing documents, text records, and correspondence.

Word-of-Mouth Advertising (WOM): It is marketer's dream to have a product so satisfactory to those who purchase it that they immediately tell their friends and neighbours about it. Just as immediately, those friends and neighbours go out and buy it, and they then too tell their friends and neighbours. Such word-of-mouth advertising is very powerful.

Wordprocessor: An electronic device that is fast supplanting the traditional typewriter. It consists of a computer unit which is tied in with a keyboard, display screen and printer. The keyboard is used much as that on a typewriter and the words keyed appear on a display screen where they can be amended or moved from one position to another. When the operator is satisfied with the text it can be automatically transferred to paper by means of the printer. Wordprocessors are becoming increasingly sophisticated. and the number of functions incorporated into them is being continually expanded. Some are even programmed to correct spelling errors automatically. Others are merged with stored information so that specific details, such as names and addresses are automatically added to, or incorporated within the text.

Work Design: The part of the job design process that is concerned with the actual working operations, as opposed to the personnel management aspects.

Work Experience: A period of time spent doing unpaid work in a workplace environment by young people about to leave school, as preparation for future employment.

Work Group: A group of people engaged in doing some work together who are also linked by interpersonal relations which are important to them.

Work in Progress: A term usually found alongside stock in trade in a balance sheet; i.e. stocks and work in progress. It represents the value of work commenced but not completed.

Work Measurement: An integral part of the work study process in which a variety of (subjective) methods like work sampling are used to fix a standard time for the acceptable performance of a given task by a trained worker.

Work Sampling: A technique used in work measurement and work study for obtaining information about a particular job or task by the process of sampling (usually random sampling) from the work activities at various times rather than any continuous observation.

Work Study: A study concerned with reviewing working methods and deciding how long particular jobs should take. Its aim is to reduce effort involved in various operations, to organize labour in the most economical manner and to provide data for planning, estimating and financial incentive schemes.

Working Capital: Money required by the company to meet out day-to-day expenses to finance production and stocks, to pay wages and other production expenses, etc., is called the working capital of the company. It includes stocks, loose tools, debtors, cash and other current assets. Working capital is used in operating the business. It is mostly kept in circulation by realising it back after selling the products and reinvesting it in future production. It is because of this regular cycle that sometimes the working capital is called circulating capital and its requirements are usually for short periods. It is the difference between Current

Assets and Current Liabilities. This total is also known as Net Current Assets.

Working Capital Ratio: This calculated by dividing current liabilities into current assets. It has been a measure of a firm's liquidity.

Working Capital Turnover Ratio: This ratio indicates whether or not working capital (which relates to current assets and current liabilities) has been effectively used in making sales. It is calculated as follow: Working Capital Turnover Ratio: Net Sales/Net Working Capital.

Working Control: The control over a corporation or company comprises, theoretically, ownership of at least 51 percent of the total voting shares; however, effective control can sometimes be exercised through ownership, individually or by a group acting in concert, of less than 50 percent of the shares.

Worksheet: A sheet of calculations in columnar form, used, for example, as an aid to the construction of a consolidated balance sheet or a funds statement.

Workshop: Small factory.

World Bank: The common name for the International Bank for Reconstruction and Development (IBRD), the sister organization of the International Monetary Fund. The World Bank was originally designed to help countries rebuild their economies after the Second World War. Set up in 1944 as part of the Bretton Woods agreement, it provides long-term loans (usually for 15-20 years) to governments and government organizations. To fund its lending it borrows on bond markets around the world at very fine rates. It has two specialist sibling organizations: the International Development Association (IDA), and the International Finance Corporation (IFC).

Wrapping: Special coloured paper for wrapping presents; service in a store for wrapping presents for customers; coloured paper for wrapping presents; act of covering in a tight plastic cover.

Writ: A legal document summoning a person to attend at a certain place or to perform a certain act. There are penalties for failure to comply.

Writing Down Value: The amount at which Assets are usually held in Books of Account and in financial statements. The written down value (WDV) is the historical cost less an allowance for wearing out, called Accumulated Depreciation. (Net Book Value has the same meaning). The expression may also be used for the amount of an asset that has not yet been allowed as Depreciation for tax purposes; this would be the tax written down value.

Y

Yankee Bond: A bond issued in a US capital market by a non-US borrower.

Yearbook: Reference book which is published each year with updated or new information.

Yellow Dog Contract: Illegal document signed by workers stipulating that they will not join a union.

Yellow Goods: An expression used in the USA for consumer goods that are bought infrequently, last for a number of years before needing to be replaced, and are generally expensive. They include the sort of things that come under the category of both white goods and brown goods: ovens, fridges, televisions or music sets. Yellow is thus what you get when you mix brown and white.

Yield: The return earned on an investment taking into account the annual income and its present capital value.

Z

ZAP: The practice of using a remote-control device to switch back and forth between one television channel to another. Zapping is a nightmare for advertisers and market researchers. First, it enables viewers more easily to switch away from advertisements when they are showing; second, it throws into chaos any attempt to measure rigorously which programmes an audience is watching, and for how long (see diary panel). Seasoned zappers with butterfly minds can (in all honesty) say they are watching more than two programmes at once.

Zero Base Budgeting: A system of budgeting originally developed in the USA for enterprises facing rapid changes in technology and sales. Zero base budgeting (ZBB) involves a more radical starting from scratch each year than the traditional Budget system. Managers must justify their activities as thought they were starting for the first time.

Zero Rated: Value added tax at a rate of 0%. Supplies in this category include the supply of most kinds of food (except in the course of catering), books, newspapers and power. The effect is that a taxable person who makes zero rated supplies can have his input tax refunded to him, whereas one who makes exempt supplies cannot have input tax refunded in the related 'monopolistically competitive' markets. Theoretically, its policy may be either one of price reduction to attract buyers away from the competitors or one of buttressing its monopolaid position by maintaining the thickness of the insulating wall between it and the others through the continued expenditure of sales costs.

Zero-Coupon Bond: A security bought and sold in the secondary market at a discount to its face value because it carries no coupon, that is, it pays no interest to the gradual increase in the security's market price over time, as it moves towards its face value, which is repayable on maturity. Zero-coupon bonds are also known as zeroes.

Zone: Area of a town or country area which has been given special help from the government to encourage businesses and factories to set-up there; area where there are not customs duties to divide into different areas for planning purposes; land where planning permission has been given to build small factories for light industry.

Zoning: The process by which local governments can designate the types of structures and activities that can be built and performed in a particular area. It is a complex legal process that is often affected by local politics.